Work Psychology

Understanding human behaviour in the workplace

John Arnold
Ivan T. Robertson
Cary L. Cooper

Pitman

Pitman Publishing
128 Long Acre, London WC2E 9AN

A Division of Longman Group UK Limited

First published in 1991

© Longman Group UK Ltd 1991

British Library Cataloguing in Publication Data
Arnold, Dr John
    Work psychology: Understanding human behaviour in the workplace.
    I. Title   II. Robertson, Ivan T.
    III. Cooper, Cary L.
    158.7

ISBN 0 273 03329 8

Typeset by BP Integraphics Ltd., Bath, Avon
Printed and bound in Great Britain

Contents

Figures

Case studies

Note: Case studies are provided for those chapters which focus on a single topic in work psychology. The last case study listed for each chapter can be found at the end of that chapter, and is suitable for a session of 1 hour or more. The others are positioned within the text. They are usually short vignettes which take 15–30 minutes to work on, but in Chapters 6, 7, 9 and 14 they are somewhat longer.

Preface

Work psychology is about people's behaviour, thoughts and emotions related to their work. It can be used to improve our understanding and management of people (including ourselves) at work.

All too often, work organizations have sophisticated systems for assessing the costs and benefits of everything except their management of people. Lip service is paid to the value of staff, but it is hard to avoid the conclusion that in some organizations employees are seen as necessary evils to be tolerated as good-humouredly as possible. Consequently, the thinking behind how they are managed can be rather careless or simplistic. Work psychology seeks to counter that tendency by carefully studying how people can best be assessed, motivated, led, trained and developed at work.

This book is intended for undergraduate students in business and management and psychology, as well as those studying for professional qualifications with bodies such as the Institute of Personnel Management (IPM). We have tried to make it suitable both for people encountering the subject for the first time and for those who already have some familiarity with it. We aim to give a clear and straightforward – but not simplistic – account of many key areas of contemporary work psychology. More specifically, we try to achieve several objectives in order to make this book as useful as possible to its readers.

First, we seek to blend theory and practice. Both are important. Without good theory, practice is blind. Without good practice, theory is not being properly used. We therefore describe key theories and evaluate them where appropriate. We also discuss how the concepts described can find practical application. We provide *case studies* to which material in the book can readily be applied. These can be used as classroom exercises, or as assignments for individual students. A short *Lecturers' Guide* provides additional notes on the case studies and describes how they can be used.

Secondly, we try to pitch the material at a level which the reader should find intellectually stimulating, but not *too* difficult. It is all too easy to use a slick, glossy presentation at the expense of good content. There is always the temptation to descend to over-simple "recipes for success" which insult the reader's intelligence. On the other hand, it is equally easy to lose the reader in unnecessarily complex debates. We hope we avoid both these fates.

Thirdly, we have chosen topics that we judge to be the most useful to potential readers of this book. Some usually appear in organizational behaviour texts, whereas others are generally found in books of a more specifically psychological orientation. Thus, we include chapters on: the nature of work organizations; human intellectual and personality characteristics; employee selection and appraisal; learning and behaviour modification; work motivation; decision making by individuals, groups and organizations; leadership; training; career choice and development; stress in employment and unemployment; and job redesign and new technology.

We also include some material which we think deserves greater emphasis then it usually receives in other books. Thus, in Chapter 2, we provide a brief overview of basic traditions in psychology and how they have contributed to understanding people at work. This should be especially useful for students of business and management who, we have found in our experience as teachers, need a base from which to appreciate work psychology. In Chapter 3 we examine how work psychologists obtain their data, and we devote Chapter 4 to a simple introduction to statistical techniques for dealing with those data. Explanation is provided in English, not algebra! Again, we feel that students are too often left ignorant of data-analytic techniques. This makes it hard for them to evaluate what they read, as well as depriving them of useful techniques for evaluating data of their own.

In Chapter 5, we provide some context of a quite different kind: the problems facing minority groups at work and how they might be overcome. Then, in several other chapters, we use advances in social psychology and apply them to the world of work. This is particularly true of Chapter 8 on attitudes (including job satisfaction and organizational commitment), Chapter 11 on perceiving people and Chapter 12 on decision making.

Fourthly, we provide up-to-date coverage of our material. There are currently exciting advances in many areas of work psychology, and we try to reflect these. At the same time, where the old stuff is best, we include it. There is nothing to be gained by discussing recent work *purely* because it is recent.

Fifthly, we attempt to avoid being too reliant on material from North America. Many North American texts virtually ignore work conducted in other parts of the world. No doubt we have our own blinkers, but we try to include perspectives from places other than North America, especially the UK and other European countries. Nevertheless, the USA and Canada provide much valuable material. We therefore make substantial use of research and theory originating in those countries.

The best judges of whether we meet our objectives will be those who read this book. Comments and suggestions are welcome, and should be directed to Dr John Arnold, Manchester School of Management, University of Manchester Institute of Science and Technology, PO Box 88, Manchester M60 1QD, UK.

Finally, we wish to acknowledge with gratitude the help of our colleagues in preparing this book. Sangita Patel typed drafts and redrafts of most of the book with skill, patience and efficiency. Jenny Ellison tackled the rest of it with the same qualities. Penelope Woolf at Pitman Publishing kept us going with a well-judged mixture of encouragement and pressure. Last, but not least, our academic colleagues here at the Manchester School of Management are stimulating and knowledgeable sparring partners whose perspectives contribute much to our work.

Manchester, September 1990

John Arnold
Ivan T. Robertson
Cary L. Cooper

Perspectives on work organizations

Introduction

In modern society, most people spend their working lives in an organization of some sort and, therefore, have first-hand experience of organizational life. This chapter considers some of the research findings and theoretical work that help to provide a better understanding of the nature of organizations. An examination of the structural aspects of organizations revealed by organization charts and other formal documents leads to a consideration of some of the complex interrelationships that exist between factors such as organization structure, technology and environment. The second half of the chapter discusses the use of system concepts, as a means for describing and gaining insights into organizational behaviour. In addition, contemporary, open systems approaches to organization theory are outlined. And, finally, organizations as metaphors are explored to help us in construing and understanding them.

Characteristics of organizations

An organization is "a collection of interacting and interdependent individuals who work toward common goals and whose relationships are determined according to a certain structure" (Duncan, 1981, p. 5). This definition provides a useful starting-point for an examination of organizations, although as this chapter and many other chapters throughout the book demonstrate, the nature of organizations, and the behaviour of the people who create them and work in them, are so complex that any brief definition is bound to be imperfect. The above definition does, however, make some important points, which can be elaborated upon:

1. Organizations are human creations and, fundamentally, they consist of people, rather than buildings, equipment, machinery, etc.

2. The term "organization" is general and not restricted to industrial or commercial firms. Educational and medical institutions, social clubs and a wide range of other organized human activities fall within the definition.

3. People within organizations must, to some extent, be working to common goals and co-ordinate their activities to this end. This does not, however, mean that everyone in the organization has the same set of goals and priorities, nor that all the goals are explicit and clear to everyone.

4. Although relationships between people are determined according to a certain structure, informal or unofficial groups and structures can be at least as important as the formal organization structure.

Formal organization structure

The structure of an organization is often depicted with the aid of an organization chart. A typical chart (see Fig. 1.1) provides an indication of the formal relationships between the management, supervisory and other staff in the organization. Such charts indicate the overall shape of the organization, and provide an outline of the formal decision-making structure. Usually, for instance, positions higher up the chart have more power and authority than those lower down. The lines linking the positions in the chart show the formal channels of communication used to exercise this authority, and the overall shape of the chart also shows the number of levels of authority that exist within the organization. A wide, flat chart, for example, depicts an organization with few levels of authority, where the vertical distance between the most junior and most senior position is relatively small. A narrow, tall chart shows the opposite case of an organization with many levels of authority.

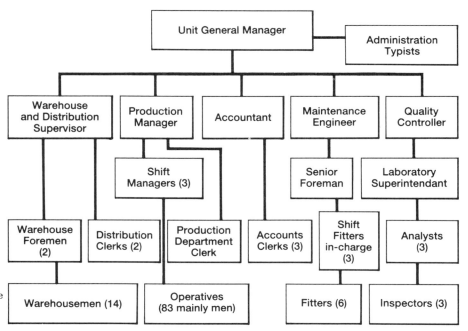

1.1 The organization chart for Savor Products Unit, a sub-unit of Ashbourne Pure Foods Ltd (reproduced with the courtesy of J.R.K. Berridge).

Roles not people

Organization charts show the relationship between specific jobs or roles within the organization. In some cases, named individuals are shown to be the holders of specific positions, but the basic function of the chart is to represent the organization structure, regardless of the particular people who fill the positions shown. This distinction between roles and people is supported in an extreme form by structural sociologists such as Perrow, who argue that in the design and analysis of organizations, it makes sense to focus on "The roles people play rather than the personalities in the roles" (Perrow, 1970, p. 2). Others (e.g. Makin *et al.*, 1989) argue that individual personalities are important considerations. The widespread use of organization charts suggests that there is at least some value in making a distinction between organizational roles and the individuals who fill them. The interrelationships between factors such as organization structure and the people who work within the organization, is a theme that will be explored at various stages in this chapter.

Specialization (division of labour)

In many organizations, it is impossible for one person to carry out all of the tasks involved, and some degree of specialization or division of labour usually takes place. Division of labour involves dividing up the activities of the organization and distributing tasks among people, so that different people do not find themselves doing the same collection of tasks. The basic division of labour used by most organizations is shown by the horizontal divisions in the organization chart (see Fig. 1.1). Often, the required specialization is achieved not only by allocating different tasks to individuals, but by dividing the organization into separate departments or sub-units either on a functional basis (e.g. sales, marketing, personnel), a product basis or perhaps into geographical regions.

Organization charts reflect not only the horizontal division of labour that is a feature of modern organizations, but also show that organizations are subdivided on a vertical basis. The organization chart reveals the chain(s) of command in the organization, and it is usually possible to trace a chain of command through from the most junior to the most senior member of the organization. In some organizations, authority and decision making may be *centralized* and be allocated to a relatively small number of people, whereas in others authority is *decentralized*.

A further characteristic of organization structure is *span of control*. At its simplest, the span of control of a manager or supervisor is indicated by the number of subordinates reporting directly to that person, and it is usually revealed on a comprehensive organization chart.

Bureaucracy and classical organization theory

Many of the aspects of organization structure considered above were first examined in work carried out by early organization theorists and management scientists, such as Taylor (1911), Fayol (1930) and Weber (1947), who developed their ideas about organizations during the early part of the twentieth century. Weber, for example, produced a series of publications concerned with the structure of organizations, and the exercise of power and authority within them. He proposed the "bureaucratic" model of organizations, where work is organized and conducted on an entirely rational basis. Some of the essential features of a bureaucracy are:

- specialization or division of labour;
- a hierarchy of authority;
- written rules and regulations; and
- rational application of rules and procedures.

Since Weber's time, bureaucracy has become a derogatory term associated with the excessive and often completely irrational use of rules and regulations. In many ways, however, Weber's work represents the beginning of modern theories of organization, and many of the issues addressed by Weber and other "classical" theorists are of lasting importance.

Dimensions of organization structure

Much of the work of the early organization theorists such as Weber was concerned with the ways in which organizations should be structured to ensure maximum efficiency, and structural aspects are still important when an attempt is made to build up a comprehensive picture of an organization.

A long-term series of studies, begun at the University of Aston in Birmingham, UK, examined various aspects of organization structure and, by extensive studies of real organizations, have attempted to identify some of the major dimensions of structure. The structural variables examined by the Aston team were:

1. *Specialization.* The extent to which specialized tasks and roles are allocated to members of the organization.
2. *Standardization.* The extent to which an organization has standard procedures.
3. *Formalization.* The degree to which rules, procedures, instructions, etc., are written down.
4. *Centralization.* The degree to which certain aspects of authority and decision making are located at the top of the organizational hierarchy.
5. *Configuration.* The shape of the organization's role structure (e.g. whether the chain of command is long or short).

After considerable data collection and analysis, the researchers were able to show that three underlying factors seemed to underpin the variations in organization structure that they observed. These underlying factors were summarized by Payne and Pugh (1976):

1. *Structuring of activites.* The extent to which employee behaviour is defined by specialized jobs, routines, procedures, etc. (factor I).

2. *Concentration of authority*. The degree to which the authority to take decisions is concentrated at the higher levels in the organization's hierarchy (factor II).

3. *Line control of work-flow*. The degree to which control is exercised through line personnel or through impersonal procedures (factor III).

Some examples of organizations with differing structural characteristics are given in Fig. 1.2. Others (e.g. James and Jones, 1976) have proposed slightly different sets of organization structure variables (see Table 1.1). Whichever structural factors are considered, it must be emphasized that factors such as specialization and standardization are concerned with the structure of the organization only, and do not provide direct evidence of how members of the organization behave in practice. As Pugh and Hickson (1976, p. 185) noted:

Table 1.1 Major dimensions of organization structure

The "Aston" studies (see Payne and Pugh, 1971)	An alternative classification (see James and Jones, 1976)
Specialization	Specialization
Centralization	Centralization
Configuration	Span of control
	Size
	Interdependence of components
Standardization	Standardization
Formalization	Pervasiveness of rules

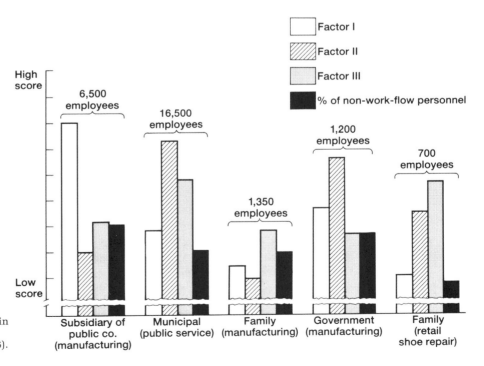

1.2 Underlying dimensions of structure in five organizations (from Pugh and Hickson, 1976).

> ... none of the variables of structure are directly related with individual behaviour in the organization. Specialization is concerned with the existence of separate functions and roles, not whether the individuals in them trespass outside their territories or not; standardization is concerned with the existence of procedures, not whether they are conformed to ...

Structure, technology and environment

The fact that organizations can be described by using certain basic concepts of structural form, raises the possibility that some structures will be more efficient than others. Woodward (1958) carried out research designed to examine the links between organization success, size and structural form. The research examined 1000 British organizations ranging in size from 250 to over 1000 employees. The commercial success of each firm was assessed and relationships between commercial success and structural form were examined. The analysis, in the first instance, established no correlations between the structural factors and successful performance. Subsequently, the researchers grouped the organizations into categories on the basis of the production methods (or technology) that they were using. The organizations were categorized into three groups:

1. *Small batch and unit production*, where products are designed and manufactured on a "custom-made" basis, involving the production of single units or small batches, often to customer specifications, e.g. prototype electronic equipment.
2. *Large batch and mass production*, where standard products are manufactured in large quantities, e.g. motor cars.
3. *Process production*, such as the continuous flow production of liquids or gases in the chemical industry.

When the organizations were regrouped on the basis of technology, various links with the structural factors became apparent (see Fig. 1.3). As Fig. 1.3 reveals, organizations in the different categories showed marked differences in span of control. The research also established links between technology and the number of levels in the management hierarchy, and the ratio of managers and supervisory staff to other personnel.

The most important point is that the successful organizations in each category had *different structures*. For example, the spans of control of successful organizations in the unit-production category were lower than those in the mass-production category. For the present purposes, the main issues of interest are the demonstration that in the sample of organizations studied:

- there was no general link between organizational success and structural form; and
- successful organizations had different structural forms, depending on the technology that they were using.

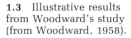

1.3 Illustrative results from Woodward's study (from Woodward, 1958).

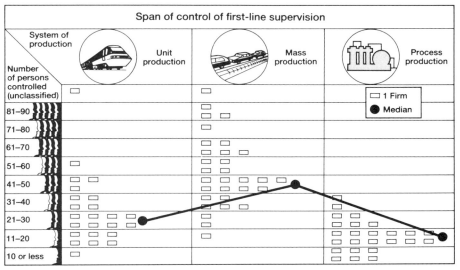

Woodward herself recognized many imperfections in the study carried out (Woodward, 1965). The specific findings and methodology of the study have also been criticized by others (e.g. Davis and Taylor, 1976). Nevertheless, the study represented a landmark in research into organizations.

A substantial amount of further research has been carried out to examine technology–structure relationships (see, e.g., Pugh and Hickson, 1976). An examination of the available work reveals that although structure and technology seem to be related, it is not clear whether structure influences technology, technology influences structure, or how much other factors have affected both (see Bedeian, 1980, for a review). Regardless of the detailed relationship between technology and structure, it is clear that there is no single ideal structural form for all organizations.

Other researchers have shown how factors other than structure can be linked with aspects of organizational design and management. Burns and Stalker (1961), for example, have shown that organizations tend to use different management practices depending on the environmental conditions (e.g. rate of technological change in the industry concerned), and Lawrence and Lorsch (1967) have examined the links between environmental factors and effective organization design.

The findings of both Lawrence and Lorsch, and Burns and Stalker, suggest that different types of organizations are likely to be successful in different environments, and few people would dispute that organizational success is dependent, to some extent, on the existence of a good match between the organization's characteristics and the surrounding environment. Some evidence does, however, suggest that the need for a good organization–environment match is not a critical determinant of an organization's success. Taken as a whole, the evidence concerning organization–environment interaction provides some rather conflicting results (Filley *et al.*, 1976). It has been suggested (e.g. Weick,

1977) that organizations do not respond to the external environment as it actually is, but to the perception of the environment built up by the members of the organization. The perceived environment may or may not correspond with "reality", and this subjective interpretation of the environment could explain some of the conflicting research results that have been obtained.

Notwithstanding the complexities of many of the issues for the moment, it is clear that there are many complex links between factors such as organization structure, technology, environment and the individuals and groups who work within the organization. Any attempt to develop a comprehensive view of organizations must take this into account.

Organizations as complex open systems

The view of an organization provided by a static organization chart and reflected in the structural dimensions of organizations, is clearly incomplete and does not provide a comprehensive picture. In an attempt to describe organizations more adequately, many writers make use of ideas derived from *systems theory* (Cummings, 1980). An open system in its simplest form involves an input, a transformation process and an output. A "closed" system, by contrast, does not involve inputs and outputs, and is independent of external forces. Organizations that are part of the social and economic fabric of the environment in which they exist, should clearly be represented as open systems. Thus, a systems view of an organization manufacturing motor cars (see Fig. 1.4) would involve an *input* of goods and materials, and the use of mass-production technology to transform the *inputs* into motor cars, the *outputs*. Other organizations have different inputs, transformation processes and outputs.

One important feature of the systems approach is that a particular system may be subdivided into smaller sub-systems. Many organizations (including car factories) could, for instance, be subdivided into a *formal system*, involving

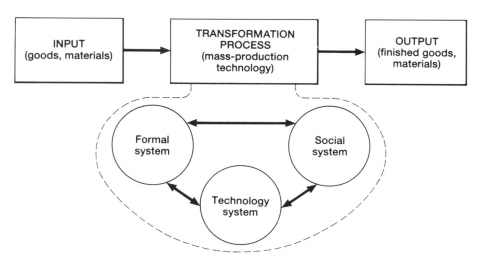

1.4 An open system view of an organization.

the formal or structural aspects of organizations discussed earlier, a *technology or production system*, and a *social system*, concerned with the individuals and groups of employees within the organization (see Fig. 1.4). Each sub-system interacts with every other sub-system, and the organization also interacts with the external environment. In turn, the sub-systems in Fig. 1.4 could be further subdivided and, of course, the organization itself is merely a sub-system of other super-systems – the economic system of the country, for example.

Describing organizations with the aid of systems concepts highlights two important issues:

1. *Interaction and interrelatedness.* Ackoff and Emery (1972) have defined a system as a "set of interrelated elements, each of which is related directly or indirectly to every other element, and no subset of which is unrelated to any other subset". Using "systems" concepts to understand organizations, helps to emphasize the point that any aspect of the organization (e.g. structure, technology, individuals, work groups, departments, etc.) cannot be considered as separate, self-contained elements or units of analysis. The elements or sub-systems in the organization system are part of a complex interconnected network.

2. *Levels of analysis.* Any system is part of a wider super-system and can be subdivided into sub-systems. For example, the social system of an organization could be considered as a whole, subdivided into systems based on groups of workers, or broken down into individual (single person) systems. Which level of analysis is most useful?

Although some writers have proposed a specific answer to this question (e.g. Katz and Kahn, 1978), it seems that the important contribution of the systems approach is that it draws attention to the existence of different levels of analysis, rather than specifying a "correct" one. In most circumstances, the level of analysis that is most useful depends on the problem being addressed and, just as there is no single ideal organization structure to adopt, there is no ideal level of analysis for all purposes. This view is confirmed to some extent by the fact that organizational psychologists and sociologists have made use of "systems" concepts to study organizations at various levels of analysis. Katz and Kahn (1978) have provided a thorough discussion of the use of systems theory to gain insights into some of the important psychological aspects of organizations. They also covered most of the more technical aspects of systems theory that have been omitted from the above discussion.

Systems theory in its strongest and most technical form makes detailed proposals about the properties of systems and the processes involved in system survival, growth and decay. Buckley (1967) and Silverman (1970) have provided some strong criticism of the use of systems theories in the study of organizations. They are critical, for instance, of the fact that some systems theorists appear to consider organizations as "natural" systems that are capable of initiating action and, for example, attempt to ensure their own survival. In other words, some theorists treat organizations as if they were living organisms capable of an independent life of their own. As Silverman (1970, p. 37) pointed out, when discussing the influences of the environment, "Organizations do not react to their environment, their members do." Silverman was also concerned that the models developed by systems theorists may represent the important features of organizations from the theorists' point of view, but fail to capture adequately the way in which the organizational factors involved are seen by members of the organization: "People act in terms of their own and not the observer's definition of the situation" (ibid.).

Many work psychologists use systems ideas in a fairly dilute form, often merely to indicate the interaction and interrelatedness of organizational factors, and to identify different variables and possible levels of analysis. They do not necessarily employ many of the more technical and often more controversial aspects of systems theory. Payne and Pugh (1971, p. 375), for instance, made some use of systems ideas to present "a framework for behaviour in organizations". Their framework incorporated a series of interlocking systems divided into four different levels of analysis:

- organization,
- department or segment within organization,
- work team or group, and
- individual.

They suggested that the main purpose of the framework is to provide an indication of the main features in organizational life, the levels of analysis and interrelationships involved. This somewhat non-technical way of using systems concepts (which is also apparent in the model proposed by Kotter, 1978, and described later in this chapter) does seem to provide a helpful way of conceptualizing organizational variables.

Socio-technical systems

A good demonstration of the interacting nature of social and technological systems is provided in some work carried out by the Tavistock Institute of Human Relations (Trist and Bamforth, 1951). The research examined the consequences of changes in methods of production in British coal mines. The traditional method of mining, known as the short-wall method, involved small groups of eight to ten men working together as a team. The teams worked fairly independently of each other and each one concentrated on removing coal from a small section of the coalface. The teams were very tightly knit systems, and close relationships often formed between team members; competition between teams, however, was often fierce. The bonds of friendship and enmity were reflected both at work and in the wider community.

Improvements in mining technology led to the installation of new mechanical coal-cutting and removing systems. To operate the new equipment, the small teams of miners were reorganized into much larger groups of 40–50, divided into specialized task groups and reporting to a single supervisor. These much larger social groups created as a consequence of the new technology were associated with many unsatisfactory changes. The new working procedures (the long-wall method) caused miners to be spread out over much larger distances, making supervision difficult. The social and psychological experiences associated with the earlier small teams were never adequately replaced under the new system.

Also, under the long-wall method, a more extensive division of labour (specialization) was introduced, and the miners became responsible for a more limited range of tasks than under the short-wall method. By and large, the miners found this reduction in the scope of their jobs distasteful. With the long-wall method, low productivity predominated. The Tavistock researchers suggested that a "composite" long-wall method would be a better means of organizing production. Under the composite method, the new technology was used, but aspects of the earlier short-wall method were also incorporated. For example, groups were allowed in order to introduce more variety into the work. The composite method, which paid attention to the interacting nature of the social and technical system, produced higher output, less absenteeism and was estimated to be working at 95% of its potential. The conventional long-wall method had lower output, higher absenteeism and worked to only 78% of its potential.

Some more recent socio-technical systems research (Trist *et al.*, 1977; Cummings, 1980) has examined the changes in quality of working life that can result from attempts to make the best possible match between social and technical systems (see also Chapter 17).

Major elements of organizational dynamics

So far, four different and interrelated elements of organizational dynamics have been mentioned: formal (structural) organizational characteristics, technology, environment and social system. Kotter (1978) has integrated these and other aspects into an overall framework for examining organizations (see Fig. 1.5). The following notes apply to Fig. 1.5:

1. *Key organizational processes.* The major information-gathering, communication, decision-making, matter/energy transporting and matter/energy converting actions of the organization's employees and machines.

2. *External environment.* An organization's *task* environment includes suppliers (of labour, information, materials, etc.), markets, competitors and other factors related to the organization's current products and services. The *wider* environment includes factors such as public attitudes, the economic and political systems, laws, etc.

3. *Employees and other tangible assets.* Employees, plant and offices, equipment, tools, etc.

4. *Formal organizational arrangements.* Formal systems explicitly designed to regulate the actions of employees (and machines).

5. *The social system.* Culture (i.e. values and norms shared by employees) and structure (i.e. relationships between employees in terms of such variables as power, affiliation and trust).

6. *Technology.* The major techniques that are used by employees while engaging in organizational processes and that are programmed into an organization's machines.

1.5 Kotter's model of organizational dynamics (from Kotter, 1978).

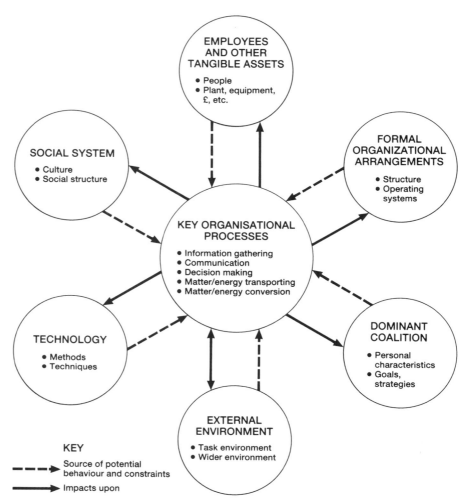

7. *The dominant coalition.* The objectives and strategies, the personal characteristics and the internal relationships of that minimum group of cooperating employees, who oversee the organization as a whole and control its basic policy making.

Schein (1980, pp. 277–278) has commented as follows on Kotter's work:

> In summary, Kotter's model provides a systematic check list of elements to analyze ... types of interactions among elements to consider. ... This type of model takes the open systems point of view to its logical conclusion in identifying the wide variety of interactions that must be analyzed if adaptability is to be maximized.

In this respect, Kotter's model is in keeping with most contemporary attempts to deal with organizations, in that it does not attempt to provide a total picture of every possible element involved, nor does it seek to understand or explain all of the possible interconnections and interrelationships, a task that is well beyond our current state of knowledge and perhaps always will be.

Organizations as metaphors

In more recent times, organizational theorists have been building on the use of metaphors to understand the nature of organizational behaviour and life. The most influential proponent of this approach has been Morgan (1986) in his book *Images of Organization*. In his framework, he sees organizations as complex entities, sometimes machine-like and at other times organic. He has identified basically eight different ways of construing organizations: as machines, as organisms, as brains, as cultures, as political systems, as psychic prisons, as flux and transformation, and as instruments of domination.

Organizations as machines

"Organizations as machines" simply means that they can be designed and operated as if they are machines, with highly visible structures, levels and routines; in other words, bureaucracies. Although these types of organizations provide continuity, form and security, they tend, according to Morgan (1986), to "limit rather than mobilize the development of human capacities, molding human beings to fit the requirements of mechanical organization rather than building the organization around their strengths and potentials". These organizations seem to function better in protected and stable industries or fields.

Organizations as organisms

When an industry is more turbulent, competitive and fast moving, it usually requires a different type of organization, an adaptable or organismic type. When we refer to an organization as being "an organism", we mean it behaves in similar ways to our own biological mechanisms. When the environment around and within us changes, our bodies adapt. Organizations that are dynamic tend to have more organismic structures and response modes. Kanter (1983), in her book *The Change Masters*, found that highly successful companies demonstrated many of the characteristics of an organismic organization.

Organizations as brains

Some organizations in some industries need to be not only resilient and flexible, but also inventive and rational. Seeing the organization as a brain is in effect thinking about the system as not only being capable of change, but also of rational or intelligent change, about "improving capacities for organizational intelligence". As Morgan (1986) has suggested, "innovative organizations must be designed as learning systems that place primary emphasis on being open to inquiry and self criticism. ... The challenge to design organizations that can innovate is thus really a challenge to design organizations that can self-organize."

Organizations as cultures

When we speak of "organizations as cultures", we are basically referring to the fact that complex systems are made up of values, principles, attitudes and ways of viewing and relating to the world that are unique to it, and different from other organizations. To quote Morgan (1986): "shared meaning, shared understanding, and shared sense making are all different ways of describing culture". It is those aspects of the organization that help us make sense of the world around us, and to guide us in our interactions and relationships.

Organizations as political systems

Organizations are not only about hierarchies and structures, or about shared cultures, but also about politics. They are about power, authority, responsibility, political activity, patronage and a host of activities and issues one might term political with a small "p". Organizational life is about wheeling and dealing, negotiating, compromising, politicking, and influencing behaviour and decisions. Each organization, in other words, has its own political system. They have their own political order, such as an autocratic management style, representative democracy or some hybrid of systems. It has its own system for the control of information, alliances and communications networks – this is basically the concept of an organization as a political system. Understanding this metaphor, and assessing an organization in these terms, is important for appreciating its current activities, as well as predicting its behaviour and future ability to survive or grow.

Organizations as psychic prisons

Perhaps the most interesting of Morgan's concepts is "organizations as psychic prisons". He draws on Plato's *Republic*, and the famous allegory of shadows in a cave, and their reality and meaning:

> The allegory pictures an underground cave with its mouth open toward the light of a blazing fire. Within the cave are people chained so that they cannot move. They can see only the cave directly in front of them. This is illuminated by the light of the fire, which throws shadows of people and objects onto the wall. The cave dwellers equate the shadows with reality, naming them, talking about them, and even linking sounds from outside the cave with the movements on the wall. Truth and reality for the prisoners rest in this shadowy world, because they have no knowledge of any other.

Many organizations are constrained by their shadows or "psychic prisons". They are confined by their own representation of themselves to the outside world, by the mythical pasts they have inherited or created, by the distortions of their own culture. By using the metaphor of the "psychic prison", we can go below the surface of organizational behaviour, and look at the collective unconscious in the system, understand what is reality and what is fantasy. In other words, we can delineate more clearly the true shape of the shadows in our organizational world.

Organizations as flux and transformation

Because the shadows or "psychic prisons" are also changing all the time, organizations can be seen to be in "flux and transformation". To truly understand an organization, therefore, we have to appreciate fully the generative processes of the system, that is, how it develops, grows and regenerates. To appreciate and understand organizations, it is necessary, as Morgan contends, to "attempt to fathom the nature and source of change, so that we can understand its logic", particularly if we are to manage these complex systems.

Organizations as vehicles for domination

Finally, organizations are also "instruments of domination", that is, they impose their will on others. We have to attempt to highlight what Morgan terms as the "dysfunctional or unintended consequence of an otherwise rational system of activity". If we don't fully understand what organizations can do to their inhabitants, how they can dominate and control their constituents, their long-term future is potentially in jeopardy.

Overview of metaphors of organization

Morgan's metaphors for organizational life are not fixed categorical systems, that is, you are either one or another, or you change from one to another. In fact, an organization can be a mix of each of the metaphors, predominantly two or three of them, and these combinations can change over time (almost by definition), as Morgan suggests:

> A machine-like organization designed to achieve specific goals can simultaneously be: a species of organization that is able to survive in certain environments but not others; an information-processing system that is skilled in certain kinds of learning but not in others; a cultural milieu characterized by distinctive values, beliefs, and social practices; a political system where people jostle to further their own ends; an arena where various subconscious or ideological struggles take place; an artifact or manifestation of a deeper process of social change; an instrument used by one group of people to exploit and dominate others; and so on.

This typology is enormously helpful in understanding, diagnosing and changing organizations. This is particularly the case for organizational change, where it is vital to understand the dynamics and nature of organization, as Machiavelli in *The Prince* suggested:

It should be borne in mind that there is nothing more difficult to arrange, more doubtful of success, and more dangerous to carry through than initiating changes. ... The innovator makes enemies of all those who prospered under the old order, and only lukewarm support is forthcoming from those who would prosper under the new.

Summary

The organizations that we live and work in are fundamental to our well-being and productivity. The structure, technology and environment of the organization influences human activity, and are interrelated in complex ways. We can best understand organizations by seeing them anthropomorphically. They are in a sense living organisms with cultures, brains, complex systems, which create their own political systems, change, barriers and roles. It is essential that we understand the dynamics of an organization, as well as its structure, if we are to have accurate communications within it. As Saul Gellerman, the American management guru, suggested:

> Nothing is more central to an organization's effectiveness than its ability to transmit accurate, relevant understandable information among its members. All the advantages of organizations – economy of scale, financial and technical sources, diverse talents, and contracts – are of no practical value if the organization's members are unaware of what other members require of them and why. Nevertheless, despite its overwhelming and acknowledged importance, the process of communication is frequently misunderstood and mismanaged.

References

Ackoff, R. L. and Emery, F. E. (1972). *On Purposeful Systems*. London: Tavistock.

Bedeian, A. G. (1980). *Organizations: Theory and Analysis*. Hinsdale, Ill.: Dryden Press.

Buckley, W. (1967). *Sociology and Modern Systems Theory*. Englewood Cliffs, N.J.: Prentice-Hall.

Burns, T. and Stalker, G. M. (1961). *The Management of Innovation*. London: Tavistock.

Cummings, T. (1980). *Systems Theory for Organizational Development*. Chichester: John Wiley.

Davis, L. E. and Taylor, J. C. (1976). Technology, organization and job structure. In R. Dubin (Ed.), *Handbook of Work, Organization and Society*. Chicago, Ill.: Rand McNally.

Duncan, W. J. (1981). *Organizational Behavior*, 2nd edn. Boston, Mass.: Houghton Mifflin.

Fayol, H. (1930). *Industrial and General Administration* (translated by J. A. Coubrough). Geneva: International Management Institute (originally published 1916).

Filley, A. C., House, R. J. and Kerr, S. (1976). *Managerial Process and Organizational Behavior*, 2nd edn. Glenview, Ill.: Scott, Foresman.

Gellerman, S. W. (1968). *Management by Motivation*. New York: AMA.

James, L. R. and Jones, A. P. (1976). Organizational structure: A review of structural dimensions and their conceptual relationships with individual attitudes and behaviour. *Organizational Behavior and Human Performance*, *16*, 74–113.

Kanter, R. M. (1983). *The Change Masters*. London: Unwin Hyman.

Katz, D. and Kahn, R. L. (1978). *The Social Psychology of Organizations*, 2nd edn. New York: John Wiley.

Kotter, J. P. (1978). *Organizational Dynamics: Diagnosis and Intervention*. Reading, Mass.: Addison-Wesley.

Lawrence, P. R. and Lorsch, J. W. (1967). Differentiation and integration in complex organizations. *Administrative Science Quarterly*, *12*, 1–47.

Makin, P. J., Cooper, C. L. and Cox, C. (1989). *Managing People at Work*. London: Routledge in association with BPS.

Morgan, G. (1986). *Images of Organization*. London: Sage.

Payne, R. L. and Pugh, D. S. (1971). Organizations as psychological environments. In P. B. Warr (Ed.), *Psychology at Work*. Harmondsworth: Penguin.

Payne, R. L. and Pugh, D. S. (1976). Organizational structure and climate. In M. D. Dunnette (Ed.), *Handbook of Industrial and Organizational Psychology*. Chicago, Ill.: Rand McNally.

Perrow, C. (1970). *Organizational Analysis*. Belmont, Calif.: Wadsworth.

Pugh, D. S. and Hickson, D. J. (1976). *Organization Structure in Its Context*. Farborough: Saxon House/D. C. Heath.

Schein, E. H. (1980). *Organizational Psychology*, 3rd edn. Englewood Cliffs, N.J.: Prentice-Hall.

Silverman, D. (1970). *The Theory of Organizations*. London: Heinemann.

Taylor, F. W. (1911). *The Principles of Scientific Management*. New York: Harper.

Trist, E. L. and Bamforth, K. W. (1951). Some social and psychological consequences of the longwall method of coal getting. *Human Relations*, *4*, 3–38.

Trist, E. L., Susman, G. I. and Brown, G. R. (1977). An experiment in autonomous working in an American underground coal mine. *Human Relations*, *30*, 201–236.

Weber, M. (1947). *The Theory of Social and Economic Organization* (edited and translated by A. M. Henderson and T. Parsons). Oxford: Oxford University Press (originally published 1922).

Weick, K. E. (1977). Enactment processes in organization. In B. M. Staw and G. R. Salancik (Eds), *New Directions in Organizational Behavior*. Chicago, Ill.: St Clair Press.

Woodward, J. (1958). *Management and Technology*. London: HMSO.

Woodward, J. (1965). *Industrial Organization: Theory and Practice*. Oxford: Oxford University Press.

Concepts of the person in work psychology

Introduction

This chapter outlines the basic sub-disciplines within psychology and briefly describes how each of them addresses some issues relevant to work psychology. Then, five fundamental theoretical traditions in psychology are described. Each tradition has made a contribution to work psychology, even though the traditions contradict each other in some respects. The nature of their contributions is briefly outlined and the portions of this book which examine those contributions in more detail are identified. The aim of this chapter is to place work psychology in the context of psychology as a whole. It is intended to act as a useful refresher for the psychology student, and perhaps more important, an orientation to fundamental psychological traditions for the non-specialist reader.

What is psychology?

Psychology has been defined in various ways. Perhaps the simplest yet most accurate definition is that provided by Miller (1966): "The science of mental life." Mental life refers to three phenomena: behaviours, thoughts and emotions. Today, most psychologists would agree that psychology involves all three.

The notion that psychology is a science is perhaps rather more controversial. A science involves the systematic collection of data under controlled conditions, so that theory and practice can be based on verifiable evidence rather than the psychologist's intuition. The aims are to describe *and* predict behaviours, thoughts and emotions. Not everyone agrees that it is appropriate to study behaviours, thoughts and emotions in a scientific manner. Some argue that human behaviour is too complex for that, and that people's behaviour changes in important ways when they are being observed or experimented upon (see also Chapter 3). Nevertheless, most psychologists do favour a scientific approach. As a result, most courses and training in psychology place considerable emphasis on practical classes and the statistical analysis of data – somewhat to the surprise of some students.

Modern psychology can be split into several sub-disciplines, each with its own distinctive focus:

1. *Physiological psychology* concerns the relationship between mind and body. For example, physiological psychologists might investigate the electrical activity in the brain associated with particular behaviours, thoughts and emotions. Or they might be interested in the bodily changes associated with feeling stressed at work.

2. *Cognitive psychology* focuses on our cognitive functioning, i.e. our thought processes. This includes topics like how well we remember information under various conditions, and how we weigh up information when making decisions.

3. *Developmental psychology* concerns the ways in which people grow and change psychologically. This includes issues like how and when children become able to understand particular concepts, and how children learn language. Also, developmental psychology is beginning to pay more attention to change and growth throughout adult life.

4. *Social psychology* concerns how our behaviours, thoughts and emotions affect, and are affected by, other people. Typical topics include how groups of people make decisions, and the extent to which a person's attitudes towards particular groups of people influence his or her behaviour towards them.

5. *Personality psychology* focuses on people's characteristic tendency to behave, think and feel in certain ways. It is concerned with issues like exactly how people differ from each other psychologically, and how those differences can be measured. It also increasingly recognizes that situations as well as personality influence a person's behaviour, thoughts and emotions. Hence some attention is also paid to defining how *situations* differ from each other psychologically.

Work psychology is defined in terms of its context of application. It is not in itself one of the sub-disciplines of psychology defined above. Instead, work psychologists use concepts, theories and techniques derived from all of those sub-disciplines. The same is true of psychologists working in other applied contexts such as education and health.

It would be dishonest to pretend that psychology is a well-integrated discipline with generally accepted principles. Underlying each sub-discipline are several competing and quite different concepts of the person. These are most apparent in personality psychology – not surprisingly, because personality psychology is concerned with the essence of human individuality. These competing conceptions of humanity will now briefly be examined because, of course, they underlie work psychology. The interested reader can find much fuller coverage of each in texts such as Mischel (1986) and Pervin (1984).

The psychoanalytic approach

Sigmund Freud (1856–1939) is probably the best-known psychologist who ever lived. He developed a completely new approach to human nature, which has had a great influence on many areas of pure and applied social science, literature and the arts. Perhaps in reaction to the stilted Viennese society in which he spent much of his life, Freud proposed that our psychological functioning is governed by instinctive forces, many of which exert their effect outside our consciousness. He developed his ideas in a series of famous published works (e.g. Freud, 1960).

Freud identified three facets of the psyche:

1. The *id*. This is the source of instinctual energy. Prominent among those instincts are sex and aggression. The id operates on the *pleasure principle*: it wants gratification and it wants it now. It has no inhibitions, and cannot distinguish between reality and fantasy.

2. The *ego*. This seeks to channel the id impulses so that they are expressed in socially acceptable ways at socially acceptable times. It operates on the *reality principle*: it can tolerate delay, and it can distinguish between reality and fantasy. But it cannot eliminate or block the id impulses – only steer them in certain directions.

3. The *superego*. This is the conscience – the source of morality. It develops during childhood and represents the internalized standards of the child's parents. It defines ideal standards and operates on the principle of *perfection*.

According to Freud, these parts of the psyche are in inevitable and perpetual conflict. Much of the conflict is unconscious. Indeed, Freud's concept of the psyche has often been likened to an iceberg – two-thirds underwater (unconscious) and one-third above water (conscious). When conflicts get out of hand we experience anxiety, though often we cannot say *why* we feel anxious. Anxiety can arise from:

- fear that our id impulses will be uncontrollable;
- feelings of guilt about our behaviour or desires; and
- realistic fear about what is going to happen to us.

Because anxiety is unpleasant, people try to avoid it. One way to do this is to distort reality and push unwelcome facts out of consciousness. Freud proposed a number of *defence mechanisms* which accomplish this. They include:

1. *Projection*. We see in other people what we don't like in ourselves. It is easier to cope with righteous indignation about somebody else's faults than to come to terms with our own.

2. *Denial*. We pretend things aren't as they really are.

3. *Reaction formation*. We deal with an unacceptable impulse by expressing its opposite. Thus, for example, anti-pornography campaigners may be expressing indirectly their own sexual impulses!

Defence mechanisms require energy, and therefore detract from a person's capacity to live a full life. When asked what a psychologically healthy person should be able to do, Freud replied "love and work" (not necessarily at the same time, presumably!). Even many people who have little time for his general approach regard this as a valid point.

For Freud, the key to understanding a person is to uncover unconscious conflicts, most of which have their origins in childhood and are very difficult to change. They are revealed most clearly when the person's guard is down, e.g. in dreams or in apparently accidental slips of the tongue ("Freudian slips") where the person expresses what they *really* feel. Freud believed that virtually no behaviour is truly accidental, but that people can rarely account for it accurately. If correct, this would make a mockery of current work psychology, much of which is based on self-reports (e.g. questionnaires), which are taken more or less at face value by the psychologist.

Some psychologists who initially followed Freud subsequently broke away, though they remained within the psychoanalytic school of thought. The work of one, Erik Erikson, is covered in Chapter 15. Their biggest quarrels with Freud were that the drives he proposed were too few and too simple and that the ego was more powerful than he gave it credit for. They tended to place greater emphasis than Freud on social behaviour, and believed that strivings for ideals reflect something more noble than rationalization of instincts. Adler (1927), for example, focused on self-respect, and Fromm (1947) concentrated on a person's tendency to grow and develop.

Within psychology as a whole, the psychoanalytic school of thought lost its earlier domination around the 1950s, and has never regained it. Critics complain that it is highly interpretive, incapable of being proved or disproved, and therefore unscientific. They argue that Freud was a product of his time (but aren't we all?), and was over-influenced by its hang-ups about sex. Many also claim that he does not account for women's psychological functioning nearly as well as men's.

Nevertheless, the psychoanalytic approach is far from dead. Freudian terms and concepts (e.g. defence mechanisms) have found their way into common parlance. Kline (1988) has argued that some Freudian concepts can be demonstrated satisfactorily and ought to be used more in investigating people's everyday functioning. Although most people in work organizations do not have the time (or the inclination) for the detailed, somewhat mystical and time-consuming procedures required by the psychoanalytic approach, some psychologists have nevertheless used psychoanalytic concepts in the world of work. For example, in their book *The Neurotic Organization*, Kets de Vries and Miller (1984) examined the individual and collective functioning of managers in work organizations from a psychoanalytic perspective. They identified five neurotic styles:

1. *Paranoid*: suspicion of others and hypervigilance for hidden threats.
2. *Compulsive*: perfectionism and concern for the "proper" way of doing things.
3. *Dramatic*: frequent drawing of attention to self, and a desire for activity and excitement.

4. *Depressive*: feelings of guilt, inadequacy and hopelessness.

5. *Schizoid*: withdrawal, lack of involvement and lack of excitement or enthusiasm.

Kets de Vries and Miller argued that "sick" organizations need to resolve these neuroses, which are usually reflected by its most senior managers. They examined the defence mechanisms resulting from such psychological conflict. They also discussed methods of dealing with the defence mechanisms and the underlying conflict. Despite its drawbacks, many psychologists would argue that psychoanalytic work deserves a more prominent place in contemporary work psychology. Books like *The Neurotic Organization* offer some hope of achieving this.

The trait approach

This approach is essentially concerned with measuring a person's psychological characteristics. These characteristics, which include intellectual functioning, are generally assumed to be quite stable, and probably biologically based. Some theorists have developed personality types, or "pigeon-holes", into which any individual can be placed. One good example dates back to ancient Greek times when Hippocrates wrote of four types: phlegmatic (calm), choleric (quick-tempered), sanguine (cheerful, optimistic) and melancholic (sad, depressed).

These days, psychologists more often think in terms of traits than types. A trait (pronounced "tray") is an underlying dimension along which people differ one from another. Hence rather than putting people into a pigeon-hole, trait theorists place them on a continuum, or, more accurately, a number of continua. Trait psychologists such as Eysenck (1967) and Cattell (1965) have identified specific traits through much careful experimental and statistical investigation. Some of this work is covered in more detail in Chapter 6. The favoured assessment devices of trait psychology are personality questionnaires, which ask a person a number of questions about their behaviour, thoughts and feelings. The better questionnaires are painstakingly developed to ensure that the questions are clear and responses to them are stable over short time periods (see also Chapter 6).

Most trait psychologists argue that the same traits are relevant to everyone, though for any individual some traits (usually those on which they have extreme scores) will be more evident than others in their behaviour. However, some trait psychologists have taken a rather more flexible approach. Allport (1937) argued that for any given person, certain traits may be *cardinal* (i.e. pervasive across all situations), *primary* (i.e. pervasive across many situations) or *secondary* (i.e. evident only in certain quite restricted situations).

Trait theory carries the danger of circularity. How do we know somebody scores high on a particular personality trait? – because they behave in a certain way. Why does the person behave in that way? – because they score high on that personality trait. Behaviour is therefore taken as a sign of certain traits, which is all very well so long as the underlying traits not only exist but also determine behaviour. There has been considerable debate in psychology on this latter point. Increasing attention is now being paid to identifying how traits and situations interact to determine behaviour (Mischel, 1984). For example, in situations where social rules are strict and widely understood (e.g. funerals), personality differences are unlikely to affect behaviour as much as in unstructured situations which lack clearly defined do's and don'ts.

Despite such caveats, the trait approach has had a great influence in work psychology. This is particularly evident in selection and vocational guidance, where the aim is to establish whether one or more persons will be good at, and/or enjoy, certain kinds of work. The notion that people have stable characteristics which strongly influence their behaviour is central to those endeavours (see Chapters 6 and 7 and Chapter 15, pp. 266–9). The possibility that experience changes personality is less often considered, even though there is some evidence for it (see Chapter 15, pp. 274–5).

Also, it is probably fair to say that managers find trait psychology quite attractive. After all, it brings an aura of stability and predictability to the behaviour of their staff, which all too often seems changeable and confusing. Underlying this is perhaps our tendency to see people, not situations, as the cause of behaviour (see Chapter 11, pp. 200–3).

Large sums of money are spent on the development and use of personality tests such as the 16PF (Institute for Personality and Ability Testing, 1986) and the Occupational Personality Questionnaires (Saville and Holdsworth Ltd, 1984). The latter were developed by the British consultancy firm Saville and Holdsworth with the backing of many large organizations. Such ventures testify to the continuing prominence of the trait approach in work psychology.

The behaviourist approach

In its more extreme forms, behaviourism makes no inferences whatever about what is going on inside the organism. It is concerned only with observable behaviour and the conditions (situations) which elicit particular behaviours. A leading advocate of this position is B. F. Skinner (see, e.g., Skinner, 1971). He and other learning theorists have argued that our behaviour is environmentally controlled. He invoked the concept of *reinforcer* to refer to any favourable outcome of behaviour. Such an outcome reinforces that behaviour, i.e. makes it more likely to occur again in a similar situation (a more detailed description of this and other related concepts can be found in Chapter 9).

Of course, when we ask *why* a particular outcome reinforces a particular behaviour, it becomes difficult to avoid reference to a person's internal states. We might say a person liked or wanted that outcome, and then we would probably enter a debate about *why* they liked or wanted it. Some behavioural psychologists have acknowledged the necessity of taking internal states into account, and have suggested that biologically based drives or needs are the bases for reinforcement (Hull, 1952). Skinner's reliance solely on observable behaviour may perhaps have been viable for the rats and pigeons with which he performed his experiments, but most psychologists now agree that it is inappropriate for human beings.

A more recent offshoot of learning theory is *social learning* (e.g. Bandura, 1977). This differs from traditional learning theory in a number of ways, and is examined in more detail in Chapter 9. Briefly, advocates of social learning theory stress our capacity to learn from the experiences of others, to delay gratification, and to administer our own reinforcement. In short, they paint a picture of people as much more thoughtful and self-controlled than traditional learning theory would suggest.

Concepts from learning and social learning have been used quite a lot in work psychology. In training (see Chapter 14), rewards can be used to reinforce the desired behaviours when trainees perform them. Trainees can also learn appropriate behaviours if they are performed (modelled) for them by a competent performer. More generally, in *organizational behaviour modification*, rewards are used to reinforce behaviours such as turning up for work on time or taking appropriate safety precautions (see Chapter 9). Some organizations make extensive use of *mentoring* in their career development (see Chapter 15), based partly on the assumption that the experienced mentor will model desirable behaviours that the less experienced young employee will learn.

Phenomenological approaches

Phenomenology concentrates on how people experience the world around them. It emphasizes our capacity to construct our own meaning from our experiences (Spinelli, 1989). With roots in philosophy as well as psychology, phenomenologists assert that our experience of the world is made up of an interaction between its "raw matter" (i.e. objects) and our mental faculties. Thus, for example, a piece of music exists in the sense that it consists of a series of sounds, but it only has meaning when we place our own interpretation on it.

Phenomenologists argue that what appears to be objectively defined reality is in fact merely a widely agreed *interpretation* of an event. They also assert that many interpretations of events are highly individual and not widely agreed. Thus phenomenology places a high value on the integrity and sense-making of individuals. That general sentiment underlies many somewhat different perspectives that can loosely be called phenomenological – hence the title of this section refers to "approach*es*", not "approach". Several of these perspectives also portray the person as striving for personal growth or *self-actualization*, that is, fulfilment of their potential. This variant of phenomenological theory is often referred to as *humanism*.

A good example of humanism has been provided by Carl Rogers (e.g. Rogers, 1970). He has argued that if we are to fulfil our potential, we must be *open to our experience*. That is, we must recognize our true thoughts and feelings, even if they are unpalatable. Unfortunately, we are often not sufficiently open to our experience. We may suppress experiences which are inconsistent with our self-concept, or which we feel are in some sense wrong. Rogers has argued that we often readily experience only those aspects of self which our parents approved of. Parents define *conditions of worth* – in effect, they signal to the child that they will be valued and loved only if they are a certain sort of person.

For Rogers, the antidote to conditions of worth is *unconditional positive regard* (UPR). In order to become a fully functioning person, we need others to accept us, "warts and all". This does not mean that anything goes. Rogers argues for a separation of person and behaviour, so that it is all right (indeed desirable) to say to somebody "that was not a sensible thing to do", but *not* all right to say "you are not a sensible person". Only when a person realizes that their inherent worth will be accepted whatever their actions, can they feel psychologically safe enough to become open to their experience. Further, because Rogers believes that people are fundamentally trustworthy, he has argued that they will not take advantage of UPR to get away with murder. Instead, UPR encourages more responsible behaviour.

Humanism has been criticized for being naive. Certainly in the authors' experience most business/management students find it hard to swallow. However, social workers and others in the caring professions are much more sympathetic. So are psychology students. As far as work psychology is concerned, the basic point that people's *interpretations* of events are crucial has been heeded to some extent. Many questionnaire-based measures of people's experiences at work have been developed (see Cook *et al.*, 1981). On the other hand, contrary to phenomenological tradition, people's responses on such questionnaires are often taken as approximations of an objective reality rather than as a product of the individual's interpretive faculties.

Phenomenological approaches find expression in some theories of work motivation (see Chapter 10). They also have relevance to career development (Chapter 15) and to the design of jobs (Chapter 17). Some counsellors make extensive use of Rogers' ideas when working with clients on career decisions and other work-related issues. By and large, though, phenomenological approaches are not currently dominant in work psychology.

The social cognitive approach

Since about the mid-1970s, psychology has become increasingly influenced by a fusion of ideas chiefly from social psychology and cognitive psychology but also from behaviourism and phenomenology. *Social cognition* focuses on how our thought processes are used to interpret social interaction and other social-psychological phenomena such as the self. There is also a recognition that our thought processes reflect the reality of the social world in which we live, as well as formal logic. There is little role here for emotions, despite some arguments that feelings take precedence over thoughts (Zajonc, 1980).

Advocates of social cognition see the person as motivated to understand both self and the social world in order to establish a sense of order and predictability. The existence of other people (whether or not they are actually physically present) affects the nature of thought processes. Also, conceptions of self act as a filter through which information is processed. For example, we tend to take in information about ourselves that is consistent with our self-concept more readily than inconsistent information. We also remember it better.

To some extent, social learning (see Chapter 9) has fused with social cognition. After all, learning from the experiences of others requires thought, including the relatively complex cognitive operation of imagining ourself in the position of somebody else. Another important concept here is *self-efficacy* (Bandura, 1982), which concerns the extent to which a person believes they can perform the behaviour required in any given situation. Self-efficacy is frequently a good predictor of behaviour.

The *schema* is another key concept in social cognition. It is a knowledge structure that a person uses to make sense of situations. For example, a stereotype is a schema (see Chapter 11). Schemata are in effect ready-made frameworks into which one's experiences can be fitted. Schemata that involve sequences of actions are termed *scripts* (Abelson, 1981). Scripts guide our own behaviour and also enable us to develop expectations about the behaviour of others in any given type of situation. Events which cannot be accommodated within our schemata and scripts are experienced as puzzling, and may lead us to revise them. This is analogous to scientists changing their theories in the light of new evidence (Kelly, 1955).

The impact of social cognition on work psychology has not yet been very great. As a general rule, work psychology is slow to incorporate new theoretical perspectives (Webster and Starbuck, 1988). This is partly because it usually takes a while to determine how new theories can be applied. In the case of social cognition, however, there is also the "problem" that its relative complexity limits its capacity to generate straightforward "off the shelf" techniques that can be applied across a range of situations.

Nevertheless, ideas from social cognition are certainly highly relevant to the world of work. In Chapter 11, this can be seen in the context of person perception. In Chapters 9 and 14, the importance of social cognition in learning and training is apparent. Other work has shown how social cognitive phenomena can enhance our understanding of work behaviour. For example, Gioia and Manz (1985) have argued that scripts play a key part in learning behaviour from others (vicarious learning) at work. Social cognition is likely to become more prominent in work psychology, especially when coupled with social learning.

Summary

Modern psychology can be divided into several sub-disciplines that reflect different facets of human psychological functioning. Cutting across these divisions are competing theoretical traditions in psychology. These are the psychoanalytic, trait, behaviourist, phenomenological and social cognitive

Table 2.1 Key characteristics of five theoretical traditions in psychology

	Thinking/ reasoning	Self-actualization	The unconscious	Biologically based needs/drives	Personal change	Self-determination
Psychoanalytic (Freud)	✗	✗	✓	✓	✗	✗
Trait	✓	✗	✗	✓	✗	o
Behaviourist (Skinner)	✗	✗	✗	✗	✓	✗
Phenomenological (Rogers)	o	✓	o	✓	✓	✓
Social cognitive	✓	o	o	✗	o	✓

Key: ✓ = Emphasized; o = acknowledged but not emphasized; ✗ = de-emphasized or considered rare.

traditions. They make some contradictory assumptions about the fundamental nature of the person. Their differences and similarities are summarized in Table 2.1. Each tradition finds some expression in work psychology. The differences between them emphasize that any apparent coherence of work psychology is due to the fact that it always takes place in the work setting. It does not possess a generally agreed view of human nature.

References

Abelson, R. P. (1981). Psychological status of the script concept. *American Psychologist*, *36*, 715–729.

Adler, A. (1927). *Practice and Theory of Individual Psychology*. New York: Harcourt Brace World.

Allport, G. W. (1937). *Personality: A Psychological Interpretation*. New York: Holt, Rinehart and Winston.

Bandura, A. (1977). *Social Learning Theory*. Englewood Cliffs, N.J.: Prentice-Hall.

Bandura, A. (1982). Self-efficacy mechanism in human agency. *American Psychologist*, *37*, 122–147.

Cattell, R. B. (1965). *The Scientific Analysis of Personality*. Harmondsworth: Penguin.

Cook, J. D., Hepworth, S. J., Wall, T. D. and Warr, P. B. (1981). *The Experience of Work*. London: Academic Press.

Eysenck, H. J. (1967). *The Biological Basis of Personality*. Springfield, Ill.: Thomas.

Freud, S. (1960). *The Psychopathology of Everyday Life*. London: Hogarth (first published 1901).

Fromm, E. (1947). *Man for Himself*. New York: Holt, Rinehart and Winston.

Gioia, D. A. and Manz, C. C. (1985). Linking cognition and behavior: A script processing interpretation of vicarious learning. *Academy of Management Review*, *10*, 527–539.

Hull, C. L. (1952). *A Behavior System*. New Haven, Conn.: Yale University Press.

Institute for Personality and Ability Testing (1986). *Administrator's Manual For The Sixteen Personality Factor Questionnaire*. Champaign, Ill.: IPAT.

Kelly, G. A. (1955). *The Psychology of Personal Constructs*, Vols. 1 and 2. New York: Norton.

Kets de Vries, M. F. R. and Miller, D. (1984). *The Neurotic Organization*. London: Jossey-Bass.

Kline, P. (1988). *Psychology Exposed*. London: Routledge.

Miller, G. A. (1966). *Psychology: The Science of Mental Life*. Harmondsworth: Penguin.

Mischel, W. (1984). Convergences and challenges in the search for consistency. *American Psychologist*, *39*, 351–364.

Mischel, W. (1986). *Introduction to Personality*, 4th edn. New York: CBS College Publishing.

Pervin, L. A. (1984). *Personality*, 4th edn. Chichester: John Wiley.

Rogers, C. R. (1970). *On Becoming a Person*. Boston, Mass.: Houghton Mifflin

Saville and Holdsworth Ltd (1984). *The Occupational Personality Questionnaires*. Available to qualified users from Saville and Holdsworth Ltd, Thames Ditton, Surrey, KT7 05R, UK.

Skinner, B. F. (1971). *Beyond Freedom and Dignity*. New York: Knopf.

Spinelli, E. (1989). *The Interpreted World*. London: Sage.

Webster, J. and Starbuck, W. H. (1988). Theory building in industrial and organizational psychology. In C. L. Cooper and I. T. Robertson (Eds), *International Review of Industrial and Organizational Psychology 1988*. Chichester: John Wiley.

Zajonc, R. B. (1980). Feeling and thinking: Preferences need no inferences. *American Psychologist*, *35*, 151–175.

Work psychology: Its origins, subject matter and methods

Introduction

This chapter kicks off with a brief look at the roots and history of work psychology, including the Hawthorne studies and other milestones. Attention then turns to modern work psychology: the areas it covers, the relationship between theory and practice, professional affairs and key academic journals. The issue of whether work psychology is more useful than so-called common sense is examined. If it is to be useful, work psychology must be based on sound information. This chapter therefore concludes with an analysis of how work psychologists go about obtaining information using various research methods (survey, observation and experiment). The strengths and weaknesses of each are illustrated with examples. By the end of the chapter, the reader should know the topics that work psychology covers, and be able to describe and evaluate the research methods used by work psychologists.

The origins of work psychology

Work psychology has at least two distinct roots. One resides in a pair of traditions that have often been termed "fitting the man [*sic*] to the job" (FMJ) and "fitting the job to the man [*sic*]" (FJM). The FMJ tradition manifests itself in employee selection, training and vocational guidance. These endeavours have in common an attempt to achieve an effective match between job and person by concentrating on the latter. The FJM tradition focuses instead on the job, and in particular the design of tasks, equipment and working conditions which suit a person's physical and psychological characteristics.

Much early work in these traditions was undertaken in response to the demands of two world wars. In the UK, for example, there was concern about the adverse consequences of the very long hours worked in munitions factories during the First World War and again in the Second World War (Vernon, 1948). The extensive use of aircraft in the Second World War led to attempts to design cockpits that optimally fitted pilots' capacities. In both the UK and the USA, the First World War highlighted the need to develop methods of screening people so that only those suitable for a post were selected for it. This was mainly achieved through the development of tests of ability and personality. One major source of such work in the UK was the National Institute of Industrial Psychology, which was established by the influential psychologist C. S. Myers between the two wars, and survived in various forms until 1971. The UK Civil Service began to employ psychologists in earnest after the Second World War. Their brief was, and largely still is, to improve Civil Service procedures, particularly in selection. Especially from the 1960s onwards, some other large organizations have also employed psychologists, and many independent consultants also work in these areas (see Stewart, 1982, for examples of what such consultants do).

The FMJ and FJM traditions essentially concern the relationship between individuals and their work. The other root of work psychology can be loosely labelled *human relations*. It is concerned with the complex interplay between individuals, groups, organizations and work. It therefore emphasizes social factors at work much more than FMJ and FJM.

The importance of human relations was highlighted in some famous research now known as the "Hawthorne Studies". These were conducted in the 1920s at a large factory of the Western Electric Company at Hawthorne, near Chicago, USA. The studies were reported most fully in Roethlisberger and Dickson (1939). Originally, they were designed to assess the effect of the level of illumination on productivity. One group of workers (the experimental group) was subjected to changes in illumination, whereas another (the control group) was not. The productivity of both groups increased slowly during this investigation; only when illumination was at a mere fraction of its orginal level did the productivity of the experimental group begin to decline. These strange results suggested that other factors apart from illumination were determining productivity.

This work was followed up with what came to be known as the Relay Assembly Test Room Study. A small group of female assembly workers was taken from their large department, and stationed in a separate room so that their working conditions could be controlled effectively. Over a period of more than a year, changes were made in the length of the working day and working week, the length and timing of rest pauses and other aspects of the work context. Productivity increased after every change, and the gains were maintained even after all conditions returned to their original levels.

Why did these results occur? Clearly, factors other than those deliberately manipulated by the researchers were responsible. The researchers had allowed the workers certain privileges at work, and had obviously taken a close interest in the group. Hence some factor probably to do with feeling special, or guessing what the researchers were up to, seemed to be influencing the workers' behaviour. The problem of a person's behaviour being affected simply by knowing they are in an experiment has come to be called the "Hawthorne Effect". The more general lessons here are: (1) it is difficult to experiment with people without altering some conditions other than those intended, and (2) people's behaviour is substantially affected by *their interpretation* of what is going on around them (Adair, 1984).

These conclusions were extended by a study of a group of male workers who wired up equipment in the Bank Wiring Room. A researcher sat in the corner and observed what went on. At first this generated considerable suspicion, but apparently after a time the men more or less forgot about the researcher's presence. Once this happened, certain phenomena became apparent. First, there were social *norms*, i.e. shared ideas about how things should be. Most importantly, there was a norm about what constituted an appropriate level of production. This norm was high enough to keep management off the men's backs, but less than they were capable of. Workers who consistently exceeded the norm or fell short of it were subjected to social pressure to conform. Another norm concerned supervisors' behaviour. Supervisors were expected to be friendly and informal with the men: one who was more formal and officious was strongly disapproved of. Finally, there were two informal groups in the room, with some rivalry between them. The Bank Wiring Room showed clearly how social relationships between workers were important determinants of work behaviour. These relationships were often more influential than either official company policy or monetary rewards.

There has been much criticism of the experimental methods used by the Hawthorne researchers and considerable debate about the exact reasons for their findings. However, subsequent research by other social scientists confirmed and extended the general message that human relations matter. For example, Trist and Bamforth (1951), working in British coal mines, showed that if technology is introduced which disrupts existing social groups, rules and relationships, then there are serious consequences for productivity, industrial relations and employee psychological well-being. Their work gave birth to the *sociotechnical systems* approach to work design (see also Chapters 1 and 17).

Work psychology today

One source of confusion is that work psychology has a lot of different names. In the UK and the USA, the old-established term (still sometimes used) is *industrial psychology*. The newer label in the USA is *industrial/organizational psychology* (I/O psychology for short). In the UK, it is often called *occupational psychology*, but this term is uncommon in most other countries. Throughout Europe, increasing use is made of *the psychology of work and organization* and *work and organizational psychology* to describe the area. Just to confuse things further, some specific parts of the field are given labels like *vocational psychology, managerial psychology* and *personnel psychology*. Meanwhile, there are also some bigger areas of study to which psychology contributes greatly. These include *organizational behaviour* and *human resources management*.

Our advice for the confused reader is: don't panic! The differences between these labels do mean something to those who work in the field, but should not unduly bother most of us. The main distinction mirrors that made in the earlier section between individually orientated and group or organization-orientated topics. The label "occupational psychology" is most commonly applied to the first, and "organizational psychology" to the second (Blackler, 1982). But many psychologists in the workplace regularly cross this rather artificial boundary. We use the term *work psychology* because of its simplicity, and because to us it encompasses both the individual and organizational levels of analysis.

A reading of the previous two chapters and this one so far should have given the reader a reasonable idea of what work psychology is. To put flesh on the bones, we now list 12 areas in which work psychologists operate as teachers, researchers and consultants. This list is adapted from the British Psychological Society (1986) Register of Members of the Division of Occupational Psychology.

1. *Selection and assessment*: for all types of job by a variety of methods, including tests and interviews.
2. *Training*: identification of training needs; design, delivery and evaluation of training.
3. *Performance appraisal*: identification of key aspects of job performance, design of systems for accurate performance assessment, training in appraisal techniques.
4. *Organizational change*: analysis of systems and relationships with a view to possible change; implementation of any such change (e.g. new technology).
5. *Ergonomics*: analysis and design of work equipment and environments to fit human physical and cognitive capabilities.
6. *Vocational choice and counselling*: analysis of a person's abilities, interests and values, and their translation into occupational terms.
7. *Interpersonal skills*: identification and development of skills such as leadership, assertiveness, negotiation, group working and relationships with other individuals.
8. *Equal opportunities*: monitoring, and if necessary enhancement, of opportunities for minority groups at work.
9. *Occupational safety and health*: examination of causes of accidents and the introduction of measures to reduce their frequency of occurrence.
10. *Work design*: allocation of tasks so that jobs are as satisfying and motivating as possible.
11. *Attitude surveys*: design, conduct and analysis of surveys (e.g. by questionnaire or interview) of employee opinions and experiences at work.
12. *Well-being and work*: investigation of factors which lead to stress in work and unemployment, and identification of ways to prevent and manage stress.

How can one tell whether somebody who claims to be a work psychologist is in fact appropriately qualified? In the UK, the British Psychological Society (BPS) oversees the professional practice of psychologists. To become a chartered psychologist (C. Psychol.) a person must possess not only an approved degree of psychology (or the equivalent), but also several years of appropriate specialist postgraduate training and/or work experience. It is also possible to be a chartered *occupational* psychologist, though some people who could become one prefer to stick with the generic C. Psychol. To be a chartered occupational psychologist, a person must be eligible for membership of the Division of Occupational Psychology of the BPS. In turn, this requires demonstrable *practical expertise and experience* in several of the areas listed above – *knowledge* is not enough.

Chartered psychologists and chartered occupational psychologists are bound by BPS ethical guidelines and disciplinary procedures. Information on all these matters, including lists of chartered psychologists, can be obtained from the British Psychological Society, St Andrews House, 48 Princess Road East, Leicester LE1 7DR, UK.

As already indicated, work psychologists can be teachers, researchers and consultants. Many are found in institutions of higher education, where they tend to undertake some of these activities, especially the first two. Others work as independent consultants, advising organizations and individuals who seek their services on a fee-paying basis. Still others are employed by larger organizations to give specialist advice, in effect acting as internal consultants. In the UK, the Civil Service, the armed forces, the Post Office and British Telecom have been prominent in this regard.

Work psychology is predominantly problem-centred. There is no single dominant theoretical perspective, and work psychology has sometimes been somewhat isolated from theoretical developments in mainstream psychology (see Chapter 2). Herriot (1984), for example, has taken work psychologists to task for ignoring developments in social psychology in their study of employee selection.

A theory in psychology can be defined as an organized collection of ideas which serves to predict what a person will do, think or feel. To be successful, it needs to specify:

1. The particular behaviours, thoughts or emotions in question. These should have significance for human affairs.

2. Any differences between people in how they characteristically exhibit the behaviours, thoughts or emotions in question.

3. Any situational factors which might influence whether the behaviours, thoughts or emotions in question occur.

4. Any consequences of the interaction between 2 and 3 for the behaviours, thoughts or emotions.

5. Any ways in which the occurrence of particular behaviours, thoughts or emotions might feed back to produce change in 2 and 3.

Some might argue that theory, in any case, has little to offer practice. But the present authors firmly believe that *good* theory is essential to good practice. It is nonsense to say, as people sometimes do, that an idea is good in theory but not in practice. A good theory does a good job of describing, explaining and predicting behaviour, thoughts or emotions which have important outcomes. Basing practice on it must be better than basing it on nothing, or on an inferior theory. As the distinguished social psychologist Kurt Lewin (1945) long ago argued, there is nothing so practical as a good theory.

Unfortunately, Miner (1984) found that organizational science theories which had been generally supported by research were no more likely than less supported theories to have been developed into practical techniques. Perhaps more optimistically, he found that most of the theories which had both a high level of validity and usefulness of application had been produced by people whose initial training had been in psychology (as opposed to, for example, political science, organizational behaviour or sociology). And most of those theories concerned motivation (see Chapter 10). Miner's analysis is dependent on his own judgements of scientific validity and usefulness of application. It must therefore be treated cautiously. On the other hand, he claimed he had no wish to see psychology do so well, so undue favouritism can probably be ruled out!

Where can one find out about advances in work psychology? Some can be found in books. General texts like this one give a necessarily brief account of major developments. Other specialist books are devoted to particular topics and sometimes even particular theories. For example, Warr (1987) has brought together much evidence from diverse sources to explain psychological well-being in employment and unemployment. He has also developed an analogy with the impact of vitamins on *physical* health in order to improve our understanding of environmental influences on *mental* health.

Many new theoretical developments, and also tests of established theories, can be found in certain academic journals. Leading journals of work psychology include *Journal of Occupational Psychology* (published in the UK), *Journal of Applied Psychology* (USA), *Journal of Organizational Behavior* (USA/UK), *Applied Psychology: An International Review* (The International Association of Applied Psychology – mainly European), *Organizational Behavior and Human Decision Processes* (USA), *Personnel Psychology* (USA), *Human Relations* (UK/USA) and *Journal of Vocational Behavior* (USA). There are also other prestigious journals which include work psychology along with other disciplines applied to work behaviour. These include *Academy of Management Journal* (USA), *Academy of Management Review* (USA), *Administrative Science Quarterly* (USA) and *Personnel Review* (UK).

This is of course a formidable list, and plenty more could be added to it. But there are subtle differences between journals in content and approach which soon become evident to the observant reader. This makes an information search easier if one has carefully defined the topic one wishes to explore. Also, computerized literature searches can be accomplished by most academic libraries, and take much of the drudgery out of the quest for knowledge. Most of the journals listed above concentrate on carefully designed evaluations of theories or psychological techniques. They also carry review articles summarizing the current position and perhaps proposing new directions. Some of the material in the remainder of this chapter and the next should help the reader evaluate journal articles.

Work psychology and common sense

One of the better jokes about psychologists is that they tell you what you already know in words that you do not understand. Like all good jokes, it has a grain of truth – but only a grain. To see why, let us look more closely first at the notion of common sense, and then at its relationship with work psychology.

Common sense is sometimes expressed in proverbs such as "look before you leap". Yes, one says, that's common sense – after all, it would be stupid to proceed with something without checking first to see if it was wise. But the reader may already have called to mind another proverb: "He who hesitates is lost." Well, yes, that's common sense too. After all, in this life we must take our chances when they come, otherwise they will pass us by.

This example illustrates an important feature of common sense. It can be contradictory. Interestingly, one research study found that students sometimes endorsed pairs of contradictory proverbs of this kind as both having high "truth value" (Halvor Teigen, 1986). And so they should. Both *are* true – sometimes, and in some circumstances. Psychology is in the business of working out when, and in what circumstances.

Another feature of common sense is that people often disagree about what it is (Schwieso, 1984). Quite often, in debates, both (or all) parties claim that common sense is on their side. Usually they do not get to grips with the assumptions they are making about what common sense is.

But perhaps the most pervasive feature of common sense is that often it comes *after the event*. We observe what happens, think about the event, and construct an explanation for it. We forget that we could equally well have explained the event differently, and that we could have explained it just as readily if it had happened to turn out quite differently. Indeed, this capacity to generate explanations is an important part of being human. We have a variety of "theories" in our heads for explaining what goes on around us (see also Chapter 11). But we are too much inclined to suppose that the one we choose is the one everyone else would choose, and call it common sense.

Also, we tend to fall into the trap of assuming that things we ourselves experience are also experienced by most other people, and that things we do not experience never happen to anyone. Psychologists generally seek to establish what is "true on the whole", while acknowledging that there are some exceptions, and in the long term trying to develop theory which accommodates such exceptions. This puts psychologists in a potential no-win situation. People may refuse to accept psychological findings which do not match their particular experience and, conversely, they may deride findings which *do* match their experience as "just common sense".

One good example of so-called common sense in the work setting concerns the maxim "a happy worker is a productive worker". This is often taken to mean that if we increase a person's job satisfaction (though note that this is only one aspect of happiness) they will then work better. The logical leap from statement to inference is problematic in itself, because it assumes that the relationship x (happiness) is *associated* with y (productivity) and can be translated to x *causes* y – not at all the same thing (see Chapter 4).

Most people, including those who subscribe to the notion that job satisfaction leads to work performance, can soon see possible reasons why this might not in fact be so. Some of us might derive our job satisfaction from social relationships at work and invest energy in those rather than work performance. Limitations of a person's ability or the machines they work with may be the key determinants of performance. Even if satisfaction and performance are linked, doing a good job may cause satisfaction rather than satisfaction leading to doing a good job. In fact, according to Iaffaldano and Muchinsky (1985), the correlation (see Chapter 4) between job satisfaction and work performance is 0.17. This means, in effect, that "a happy worker is a productive worker about 3% more than we would expect just by chance". Somehow this statement does not carry the comforting certainty of the original!

All this is not to claim that only psychologists can see beyond the ends of their noses. As is made clear above, people readily abandon simplistic versions of common sense. We can argue that even without psychologists, our understanding of how the world works generally seems to be good enough to live a reasonably contended life (Furnham, 1983). In fact, psychologists are increasingly interested in how we make sense of our day-to-day lives (see Chapter 11), and how we use language to construct a coherent account of our reality (Potter and Wetherell, 1987).

It is now time to ask how work psychologists collect their information and what they do with it. After all, if psychologists want people to believe them, they need to show that their conclusions are based on sound data and analysis. The remainder of this chapter, and the next, examine these issues.

Research methods in work psychology

Let us suppose that a psychologist wants to examine whether working in an environment where the pace of work is not under one's own control (e.g. on an assembly line) makes a person feel negative about their work (see Cox, 1978, ch. 7). How might the psychologist investigate this issue? We now discuss three methods of investigation.

The survey method

One distinguishing feature of a survey is that it does not seek to intervene in naturally occurring events, nor to control them. It simply takes a snapshot of what is happening, usually by asking people about it. Thus, a psychologist might devise a questionnaire which asks people whether the pace of their work is under their control, and about their job satisfaction (see Chapter 8 for more on how attitudes can be assessed using questionnaires).

The first point to make is that even this requires some care. Questionnaires cannot be just thrown together (as they are in some popular magazines) if they are to do a proper job. They must be carefully devised so that they unambiguously measure what they are supposed to measure, i.e. so that they are *valid* (see Chapter 6). Secondly, it is important to ask the right people to fill in the questionnaire. Ideally, the respondents should be a random sample of all those people to whom the survey is relevant. That means that everyone to whom the survey was relevant would have an equal chance of participating in it. In practice, of course, this is rarely the case. We also need to consider whom the questionnaire applies to. If we ask only those people who are working at a controlled pace, there would be no basis for comparison with anybody else.

One way around this might be to include some questions that ask the respondents what effect they think the paced nature of their work has on them. For some psychologists, how people make sense of such things is important in its own right. But for most, this would be unacceptable. They would insist that comparison was necessary with people whose work was *not* paced. The trouble is, these people may differ from those whose work *is* paced in all sorts of ways, any one (or more) of which could explain the differences in work attitudes between the groups.

This leads to a third point: exactly what questions should be asked in the survey. The psychologist might ask about any number of things: age, sex, work experience, educational attainment, abilities required by work, job status, supervision, friendships at work, wage levels and working conditions are just a few. If the paced and non-paced groups differed on one or more of these, it would be difficult to tell what was responsible for any difference between the groups in job satisfaction. We could not be certain whether paced work led to (low) job satisfaction, or low job satisfaction led to paced work. The latter might occur if managers gave the least interesting jobs to those employees who expressed dissatisfaction. Another possible interpretation would be that some third factor, for example a person's prior work experience, determined *both* a person's job satisfaction *and* the kind of work they do. Unless we knew about their prior experience, we would not be able to tell.

Thus the survey method has both advantages and disadvantages (see Fowler, 1984). It can be used with people directly involved in the issues to be investigated. It can investigate their experiences in their day-to-day setting. It is relatively easy to conduct, and makes relatively low demands on people's time. These are advantages. On the other hand, the lack of control makes it very difficult to establish cause and effect. The survey takes the world as it is. The world is complicated, and unless the survey takes all relevant factors into account, it is in danger of arriving at erroneous conclusions. Various sophisticated statistical techniques can reduce this danger, but not eliminate it.

Longitudinal surveys can help to clarify what causes what. In a longitudinal survey, data are gathered on more than one occasion. This can help to tease out possible causal connections. Conditions pertaining at time 1 may cause those at time 2 but not presumably vice versa! Again, though, there remains the danger of key information not being collected.

Sometimes, survey research collects information from sources other than the people concerned (e.g. from the personnel records of a company). But often *all* the data consists of people's *self-reports* of their behaviour, thoughts and/or emotions. These may not be accurate or complete. It can also lead to a problem called *common method variance*, which is where the relationship between variables is artificially high simply because all the data are obtained by the same method.

Finally, survey information can be collected using an interview (see Brenner, 1981). Market researchers and social researchers often conduct them. The interview is in effect often used as a talking questionnaire. However, it can also be employed to explore issues with respondents in more depth than a questionnaire allows. Conducting research interviews is a skilled business. Care must be taken to gain the trust of the respondent, explore issues to the extent required, and avoid accidentally influencing the respondent's answers. Some would say this last goal cannot be achieved.

The observational method

Another way of gathering information is by *observation*. Like a survey, observational research does not seek to influence or control what is happening: it studies the real world as it is. Unlike a survey, it does not normally involve asking people questions. The observer usually simply records what goes on, especially things relevant to the research question(s) being investigated. The Bank Wiring Room study at the Hawthorne plant is one example (see pp. 30–1).

Clearly, observational research is better than survey research at recording people's actual behaviour, but it is probably less good at identifying their thoughts and emotions. For this reason, observation would not be a particularly appropriate way of investigating whether machine-paced work affected job satisfaction. Nevertheless, an observer might note the frequency with which people in paced and non-paced work make comments to their workmates indicating boredom or alienation, or let their attention wander.

In some observational research, the observer actually takes part in the events he or she is investigating. This is called *participant observation*. For example, Becker *et al.* (1961) reported a participant observation study of how student doctors are socialized into the role of medic. One or more of the researchers accompanied the students in their activities and participated in some (though not operations!).

Observation is normally done with the knowledge of those being observed, though in some circumstances participant observation allows the possibility of covert observation if the researcher conceals his or her true purpose. This was not the case in Becker *et al.*'s (1961) study. Covert observation raises ethical issues. Deception of the people being researched should be attempted only when there is no alternative, and when the issue is sufficiently important to justify it. Overt observation, on the other hand, has its practical problems. The people being observed may not behave as they normally do because they know they are being watched. Furthermore, it is difficult to know exactly *how* their behaviour would change, or the guesses they would make about *why* they were being observed. The purpose of the observation should normally be explained as far as possible, but naturally those being observed may still draw their own conclusions.

The experimental method

The claim of psychology to be a science rests partly on its extensive use of experiments. One key advantage of an experiment is that it allows the psychologist *control* over what happens. This in turn permits much more precision about causes and effects. On the other hand, there are some disadvantages too. These are discussed below, but first let us examine a concrete example.

The most controlled environment is the psychologist's laboratory. To return to our earlier example, the psychologist might set up a conveyor belt in the laboratory. He or she would probably choose a task typical of conveyor-belt work, perhaps checking that boxes of chocolates have been properly packed. The boxes come along the conveyor belt at a set speed, and the worker has to remove any faulty ones. People might be asked to work on this task for a period of several weeks, and to indicate their job satisfaction at various points during that period.

All this would cost a lot of money. A large research grant would be required. The psychologist would probably also take the opportunity to record other things apart from job satisfaction, such as work performance (proportion of incorrectly packed boxes spotted) and even some physiological measures of stress (e.g. heart rate, blood cholesterol levels).

But this would not be enough on its own. It would also be necessary to include a *control group* as well as the *experimental group* already described. The control group should as far as possible do the same job as the experimental group, except that their task would not be machine-paced. Hence, the control group would perhaps be given piles of boxes of chocolates, and instructed to check them. Data on job satisfaction, etc., would be collected from members of the control group in the same way and at the same times as from the experimental group. By careful planning, the psychologist can come close to ensuring that the conditions experienced by the experimental and control groups differ *only* in whether or not their task is machine-paced: they have the same task, they perform it in the same laboratory (though the groups may not see each other or even be aware of each other's existence); they can be paid the same amount with the same pay rules; they can perhaps be supervised in the same way, though the difference between paced and non-paced work may make this difficult to achieve; and the groups can be given the same opportunities (or lack of them) for interaction with other workers. It would not be easy to ensure that the two groups got through the same *amount* of work. The control group could be told that they had to check the same number of boxes per day or week as the experimental group. However, this would introduce some degree of pacing, though not nearly as rigid as a conveyor belt.

Two key terms in experimental jargon are as follows: the *independent variable* is what the psychologist manipulates in order to examine its effect on the *dependent variable*. In this example, therefore, the independent variable is whether or not the work is machine-paced, and the dependent variable is job satisfaction. More complex experiments often have more than one independent variable, and more than one dependent variable.

Another important point concerns the people who undertake the work for the sake of the experiment (often called the *subjects*). Ideally, they would be typical of people who do that kind of work. If so, this would increase the confidence with which experimental results could be applied to the "real world". An attempt to recruit such people to the experiment could be made by advertising in local newspapers. This might not be successful, however. Because most researchers work in higher education, they would be tempted to recruit students because they are easy to find – and they usually need the money that is normally paid to those who participate in experiments! But because students are unlikely to work at conveyor belts for much of their career, their reactions in the experiment might not be typical of those who do. Whoever participates in the experiment, individuals would normally be assigned at random to either the experimental group or the control group. This helps to ensure that the people in the two groups do not differ in systematic ways.

It should now be clear that the laboratory experiment allows the psychologist enough control to make unambiguous inferences about the effects on job satisfaction of machine-paced work. Or does it? The psychologist's control necessarily makes it an artificial situation because the real world is rarely so neat and tidy. Unless the psychologist indulges in a huge (and unethical) deception, the experimental subjects will know that they are not in a real job, and that the experiment will last only a few weeks. This could crucially affect their reactions to the work, as could the guesses they make about what the psychologist is up to. These guesses will be partly inspired by unintentional cues from the experimenter via, for example, tone of voice and body posture. Such cues are termed *demand characteristics*. Every experiment has them.

The artificiality of the laboratory experiment is seen by some as a fatal flaw. Sometimes it is possible to conduct a *field experiment* instead. For a work psychologist, this would take place in a real work setting, probably with the people who worked there. It would gain over the laboratory experiment in realism, but almost certainly lose in control. Even if managers and union officials at a chocolate factory were prepared to allow the psychologist to create experimental and control groups on the factory floor, they would probably not allow the random assignment of subjects to groups. Also, they probably could not arrange things like identical supervision and opportunities to interact with co-workers for the two groups even if they wanted to.

Occasionally, it is possible for psychologists to conduct a field experiment using events that are occurring anyway. This is sometimes called a *natural experiment*. For example, a chocolate factory may be changing some, but not all, of its chocolate inspection from self-paced work to conveyor belts (see Kemp *et al.*, 1983, for a rather similar naturally occurring field experiment). The psychologist could use this profitably, especially if he or she was able to obtain data on job satisfaction, etc., both before and after the change was made. Here again, though, the gain in realism is balanced by a loss of control and the consequent presence of confounding factors. For example, the people working at the factory might have some choice of which form of work they undertook, which immediately violates random allocation to groups. On the other hand, one might argue that if this is the way the world works, there is nothing to be gained by trying to arrange conditions which do not reflect it.

Finally, it should be noted that questionnaires and observations may be used to collect data in experiments as well as in other forms of research. This highlights the distinction between research *methods* and data-gathering *techniques*. The three methods described here (survey, observation and experiment) differ in their settings and procedures and ultimately in their assumptions about psychological research.

Summary

Work psychology encompasses both the interaction between an individual and their work, and the relationships between people in the work setting. This includes staff selection, training, vocational guidance, management development, ergonomics, organizational development, equal opportunities and job redesign among other things. Work psychologists act as researchers, teachers and consultants in these areas. In the UK, the British Psychological Society oversees the professional qualifications of work psychologists. Psychology can sometimes seem like common sense, but the latter is a slippery concept. It is often contradictory, and people do not always agree about what it is. Common sense is invoked after the event, whereas theory aims to *predict* events. Work psychologists conduct research using surveys, observation and experiments. The latter allow the psychologist more control than the others over the variables of interest. This permits greater confidence about cause and effect, but often at the cost of rather artificial situations in which people may behave differently from usual.

References

Adair, J. G. (1984). The Hawthorne effect: A reconsideration of the methodological artifact. *Journal of Applied Psychology, 69*, 334–345.

Becker, H. S., Geer, B., Hughes, E. C. and Strauss, A. (1961). *Boys in White: Student Culture in Medicial School*. Chicago, Ill.: University of Chicago Press.

Blackler, F. H. M. (1982). Organizational psychology. In S. Canter and D. Canter (Eds), *Psychology in Practice*. Chichester: John Wiley.

Brenner, M. (1981). Skills in the research interview. In M. Argyle (Ed.), *Social Skills and Work*. London: Methuen.

British Psychological Society (1986). *Register of Members of the Division of Occupational Psychology*. Leicester: BPS.

Cox, T. (1978). *Stress*. London: Macmillan.

Fowler, F. J. (1984). *Survey Research Methods*. London: Sage.

Furnham, A. (1983). Social psychology as common sense. *Bulletin of The British Psychological Society, 36*, 105–109.

Halvor Teigen, K. (1986). Old truths or fresh insights? A study of students' evaluations of proverbs. *British Journal of Social Psychology, 25*, 43–49.

Herriot, P. (1984). *Down from the Ivory Tower: Graduates and Their Jobs*. Chichester: John Wiley.

Iaffaldano, M. T. and Muchinsky, P. M. (1985). Job satisfaction and job performance: A meta-analysis. *Psychological Bulletin, 97*, 251–273.

Kemp, N. J., Wall, T. D., Clegg, C. W. and Cordery, J. L. (1983). Autonomous work groups in a greenfield site: A comparative study. *Journal of Occupational Psychology, 56*, 271–288.

Lewin, K. (1945). The research center for group dynamics at Massachusetts Institute of Technology. *Sociometry, 8*, 126–136.

Miner, J. B. (1984). The validity and usefulness of theories in an emerging organizational science. *Academy of Management Review, 9*, 296–306.

Potter, J. and Wetherell, M. (1987). *Discourse and Social Psychology: Beyond Attitudes and Behaviour*. London: Sage.

Roethlisberger, F. J. and Dickson, W. J. (1939). *Management and the Worker*. New York: John Wiley.

Schwieso, J. (1984). What is common to common sense? *Bulletin of the British Psychology Society*, *37*, 43–45.

Stewart, A. M. (1982). The occupational psychologist. In S. Canter and D. Canter (Eds), *Psychology in Practice*. Chichester: John Wiley.

Trist, E. L. and Bamforth, K. W. (1951). Some social and psychological consequences of the long-wall method of coal getting. *Human Relations*, *4*, 1–38.

Vernon, H. M. (1948). An autobiography. *Occupational Psychology*, *23*, 73–82.

Warr, P. (1987). *Work, Unemployment and Mental Health*. Oxford: Clarendon Press.

Basic statistics and data analysis in work psychology

Introduction

In this chapter, we examine a topic which is given too little coverage in most texts of this kind, but highly detailed and daunting treatment in specialist books on behavioural science statistics. We attempt to explain key concepts concerning how data can be examined and how conclusions can (or cannot) be drawn from them. We do this in English as opposed to Statistese. This should enable the reader unfamiliar with statistics and/or uncertain of his or her ability in that area to grasp the basics without feeling much pain. We also provide some worked examples which put the principles into practice. The concepts and techniques described here are important. They are applicable to data of many kinds. The interested reader will find more detailed information in texts such as Rosenthal and Rosnow (1984) and Ferguson and Takane (1989).

Key principles in hypothesis testing

Much research in work psychology examines one or both of the following questions:

- Do two or more groups of people *differ* from each other?
- Do two or more variables *correlate* (i.e. go together) within a particular group of people?

Work psychologists ask these questions because the answers to them enhance our understanding of human behaviour in the workplace. For example, the first question is central to the issue described in the previous chapter concerning the effect of machine-paced work on job satisfaction. If a psychologist conducted an experiment something like that described on pp. 38–40, he or she would obtain job satisfaction data from each individual within the experimental group (which experienced machine-paced work) and the control group (which experienced self-paced work). Clearly, to establish the effect of machine-pacing on job satisfaction, it is necessary to compare the job satisfaction scores of the two groups. This could be done using a statistical technique called a *t*-test, which is described later in this chapter.

To move on to the second question above, a psychologist might conduct a survey (see pp. 36–8) in order to establish whether or not people's age is associated with the amount of job satisfaction they experience. It would be possible to divide people into age groups (e.g. 20–29, 30–39, etc.) and compare pairs of groups using a *t*-test. But this would lose information about people's ages, e.g. 29-year-olds would be lumped together with 20-year-olds. Also, the age-grouping would be arbitrarily chosen. It would be better to see whether age and job satisfaction go together by means of a *correlation*. This essentially plots each person's age against their job satisfaction on a graph, and assesses the extent to which as age increases, job satisfaction either increases or alternatively decreases. Correlation is discussed further below.

Psychologists test *hypotheses* in their research. An important concept here is the *null hypothesis* (H_0). Essentially, this hypothesis states that there is "nothing going on". Thus, if a psychologist was investigating whether two or more groups differed in their job satisfaction, the null hypothesis would be that they did not. If the psychologist was investigating whether age and job satisfaction are associated, the null hypothesis would be that they are not. That is, knowing someone's age would tell you nothing about their level of job satisfaction and vice versa.

In each case, we can also make an *alternative* or *experimental* hypothesis (H_1). This can either be directional or non-directional. For example, directional alternative hypotheses would specify whether people undertaking machine-paced work would experience higher or lower job satisfaction than those undertaking self-paced work, or whether job satisfaction increases or decreases as age increases. Non-directional hypotheses would be less specific. They would simply state that there was a difference between groups in levels of job satisfaction (but not which group was higher) or that age and job satisfaction do go together (but not whether older people are more satisfied or less satisfied).

Hypotheses refer to the *population(s)* from which the sample(s) of people who participate in research are drawn. They do *not* refer to those samples alone. In essence, then, when doing research, a psychologist is asking: "Given the data I have obtained from my research sample, is the null hypothesis or the alternative hypothesis more likely to be true for the population as a whole?" Note that "population" does not mean everyone in the whole world, or even a particular country. It should refer to those people to whom the psychologist wishes to generalize the results. This might be "production line workers in the UK" or "people currently employed in France".

Interestingly, researchers are sometimes less than specific concerning what population they wish to draw conclusions about. Also, they sometimes use "samples of convenience", i.e. people they can get hold of most easily. Ideally, those who participate in the research should be a *random sample* of the population of interest, i.e. everyone in the population should stand an equal chance of participating in the research. This is rarely, if ever, achieved. Surveys often involve questionnaires being sent to a random sample of people from a given population, but of course not everybody replies and one inevitably wonders whether responders differ in important ways from non-responders. It is therefore more common for researchers to try to show that their inevitably non-random sample is reasonably *representative* (e.g. as regards age, sex, type of employment, location) of the population as a whole. Put another way, the proportions of people of each age, sex, etc., among those participating in the research should not differ much from those in the wider population. But it is still possible that participants differ from non-participants in other respects, including those of interest in the research.

The statistical analysis of data in work psychology most often involves an assessment of *the probability of accepting the alternative hypothesis when the null hypothesis is in fact true for the population.* The lower this probability, the more confident the psychologist is that the alternative hypothesis can be accepted, and the null hypothesis can be rejected. This probability is also called *statistical significance*, a crucial concept in psychology.

Typically, psychologists are prepared to accept the alternative hypothesis (thus rejecting the null hypothesis) only if there is a probability of 0.05 or less that the null hypothesis is true given the data the psychologist has collected. Erroneously rejecting the null hypothesis is sometimes called *type I error*. The psychologist is therefore saying: "I must be at least 95% sure that I can reject the null hypothesis before I am prepared actually to do so." This might be considered rather conservative – perhaps *too* conservative. After all, how many of us wait until we are 95% certain of something before we act on the basis of it in our day-to-day lives? There is also the other side of the coin, less often considered by psychologists: the probability of accepting the null hypothesis when the alternative hypothesis is in fact true. Erroneously accepting the null hypothesis is sometimes called *type II error*.

If the psychologist finds that, on the basis of his or her data, there is less than a 0.05 (i.e. 1 in 20) chance of mistakenly rejecting the null hypothesis, he or she will usually declare that the result is *statistically significant at the 0.05 level*. If the probability is less than 0.01 (i.e. 1 in 100), the result is *statistically significant at the 0.01 level*. A similar rule applies for a probability of 0.001 (1 in 1000). These are of course arbitrary cut-off points. Basically, the lower the probability, the more confident the psychologist is in rejecting the null hypothesis. Notice that the lower the probability, the more "highly statistically significant" the result is said to be.

But how does the psychologist calculate statistical significance given his or her research data? He or she uses one or more techniques referred to collectively as *statistical tests* of the data. We now examine this in general terms. There are some worked examples later in the chapter, each of which demonstrates a particular statistical test procedure.

Some common statistical tests

The *t*-test

Suppose for a moment that a psychologist is interested in seeing whether production managers are more or less numerate than accountants. He or she administers a test of numeracy to (say) 20 of each and obtains a mean score of 25 for the production managers and 30 for the accountants. Clearly, the accountants score higher on average, but what other information is required before deciding whether to accept or reject the null hypothesis that the populations of production managers and accountants do not differ in their numeracy?

First, we need to consider whether the difference between sample means is large relative to the overall range of scores. After all, if scores in the sample ranged from 10 to 50, a difference of 5 between the two means might not imply very much. But, if scores ranged only from (say), 20 to 35, a difference of 5 might seem quite large in comparison.

The most commonly used measure of the spread of scores is the *standard deviation*. The formula for calculating it appears later in this chapter. Here, we can note that the standard deviation is a function of the differences between each individual score and the overall mean score, and of the sample size. Hence, if all scores were exactly the same, the standard deviation would be zero, because there would be no differences between individual scores and the mean. Apart from this exceptional case, we can normally expect about 68% of all individual scores to be within one standard deviation either side of the mean. About 96% of scores are within two standard deviations of the mean.

Sample size is also important in evaluating the significance of a difference between two means. Suppose for a moment that the null hypothesis was in fact true. If a psychologist repeatedly took samples of 20 production managers and 20 accountants, he or she would *on average* expect their mean scores to be equal. But of course in small samples, it only takes one or two exceptional scores to make quite a big difference between the two group means. Thus although on average the mean scores for the samples should be equal, in some samples there are quite big differences. If the psychologist repeatedly took bigger samples (say 100 production managers and 100 accountants), then the influence of a few "rogue" scores would be more diluted. If the null hypothesis was in fact true, we would again expect the difference between the two group means to be zero, but this time there would be less variation from that figure between samples.

So, to evaluate the statistical significance of a difference between two mean scores in a research study, we need to consider not only the magnitude of difference between means, but also the *standard deviation* and the *sample size*. For any given difference between means, the smaller the standard deviation, and the larger the sample size, the more likely it is that the psychologist could reject the null hypothesis.

Typically, in order to assess whether two mean scores show a statistically significant difference, psychologists use a *t-test*. This statistical procedure takes into account the factors noted above. A worked example appears later in this chapter. A t score of more than about 2 or less than about -2 generally indicates a statistically significant difference between means, but the exact value required for significance depends on sample size. Most statistical textbooks include tables which show the minimum values (sometimes called *critical values*) of t required to achieve statistical significance at the 0.05, 0.01 and 0.001 levels for any given sample size.

The *t*-test requires that the data are *quantitative*. That is, the data should reflect scores on a dimension along which people vary, not different types, or

4.1 The normal distribution.

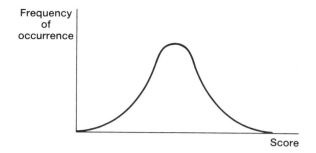

pigeon-holes, into which they fall. Strictly, the data should also be such that a difference of a given number of units between two scores should reflect the same amount of difference no matter what the absolute level of the scores. Therefore, a score of 100 should be the same amount more than 90 as 20 is more than 10. This may seem straightforward, but with many self-report measures (e.g. job satisfaction) we cannot strictly be sure whether it is the case. Further, scores should approximate to a *normal distribution* (see Fig. 4.1). This is a technical term for a bell-shaped distribution of scores which peaks at the mean, and drops off at equal rates on either side of it, with that rate being linked to the standard deviation. In fact, unless departures from normal distributions are dramatic, the *t*-test is *not* usually invalidated. In the jargon, it is a *robust* test.

A somewhat different version of the *t*-test can be employed if we wish to see whether the means of two sets of scores from the *same* people differ significantly. So, for example, we might be interested in assessing people's performance at a task before and after training. The formula is somewhat different but most of the principles for this *t*-test for non-independent samples are the same as those for the independent samples *t*-test described above.

Analysis of variance

What happens when the scores of more than two groups are to be compared? In this situation, another very common statistical test is performed, i.e. *analysis of variance*. Essentially, it is a generalization of the *t*-test procedure. The resulting statistic is called *F*, and the principles concerning statistical significance are applied to *F* in the same way as to *t* (see above). The same limitations to the use of *t* also apply to *F*. *F* can also be used instead of *t* to compare just two means. Indeed, $F = t^2$ in this instance.

F reflects the ratio of variation in scores between groups to variation in scores within groups. The greater the former relative to the latter, the higher the *F* value, and the more likely it is that the population means differ (i.e. there is a low probability of obtaining our results if the null hypothesis is in fact true for the population). If a statistically significant *F* value is obtained, we can reject the null hypothesis that the population means are identical. If we wish, we can then use a modified form of the *t*-test to identify which particular pair or pairs of groups differ significantly from each other.

Data from more complex research designs can be analysed using analysis of variance. Suppose, for example, the psychologist is interested in the effects of both machine-paced work *and* style of supervision on job satisfaction. He or she runs an experiment with four groups of people. One group does machine-paced work under close supervision, another does the same work under distant supervision, the third does self-paced work under close supervision, and the fourth performs self-paced work under distant supervision. Analysis of variance can be used to examine the statistical significance of the separate effects of each factor (pacing of work and style of supervision) on job satisfaction. It can also identify *interaction effects*. For example, the impact of close *vs* distant supervision might be greater (or even opposite) when work is self-paced than when it is machine-paced.

Chi-square

As indicated earlier, data are not always expressed as a point on a continuous dimension. Suppose, for example, a psychologist wishes to examine whether production managers and marketing managers differ in their views of "human nature" at work. The psychologist devises a way of assessing whether each of 50 production managers and 50 marketing managers believes in "theory X" (people have to be controlled and forced to work), "theory Y" (people are essentially responsible and trustworthy) and "social" (people are most concerned with social relationships at work) (see Chapter 10). Each manager is classed as believing in one of these three views of human nature.

The psychologist cannot use *t* or *F* because the data are *categorical*, not continuous. Believing in one view of human nature is not "more" or "less" than believing in another, it's simply different. Hence, although the psychologist might arbitrarily give a manager a score of 1 if they believe in theory X, 2 for theory Y and 3 for social, the numbers are not part of a scale. Believing in theory Y is not "more" or "less" than believing in theory X. The psychologist is therefore interested in determining whether there is a statistically significant difference between the two groups of managers in the frequency with which they endorse each view of human nature. The statistical test employed in this instance is known as chi-square. The more the groups differ, the higher the chi-square figure for the data, and the less likely it is that the null hypothesis is true. As with *t* and *F*, critical values of chi-square at various levels of statistical significance can be checked in tables in most statistics texts. Unlike *t* and *F*, these critical values do not depend directly on sample size. Instead, they depend on the number of rows and columns in the data when tabulated. In the above example, the table would contain six cells altogether: 2 (types of manager) $\times$ 3 (views of human nature). The figure in each cell would be the number of managers falling into that category. The chi-square procedure compares the observed numbers with those that would be expected if the proportion subscribing to each view of human nature was the same for each type of manager. A worked example of chi-square appears later in this chapter.

Correlation

The second question posed at the start of this chapter concerned whether two or more variables tend to go together. Correlation is most commonly used in survey research (see pp. 36–8). Thus, for example, a psychologist might wish to find out whether job satisfaction and intention to leave one's job are connected. Alternatively, he or she might be interested in seeing whether self-esteem and salary are connected. In these cases, the variables are on continuous scales, as for *t*-tests, but unlike *t*-tests the psychologist is not looking to compare mean scores. Instead, he or she wishes to find out whether the two variables correlate (co-relate).

There are several different but similar statistical tests of correlation, each of which produces a *correlation coefficient*. The most common of these is the Pearson's product–moment correlation coefficient, or *r* for short. Correlation coefficients cannot exceed a value of 1, and cannot be lower than -1. A Pearson's *r* of 1 would mean that when scores on the two variables of interest were plotted on a graph, a straight line could be drawn through all the plotted points (see Fig. 4.2a). This line would rise from left to right, indicating that as variable *A* increased, so did variable *B*. This line would not need to be at any particular angle, nor would it necessarily go through the origin.

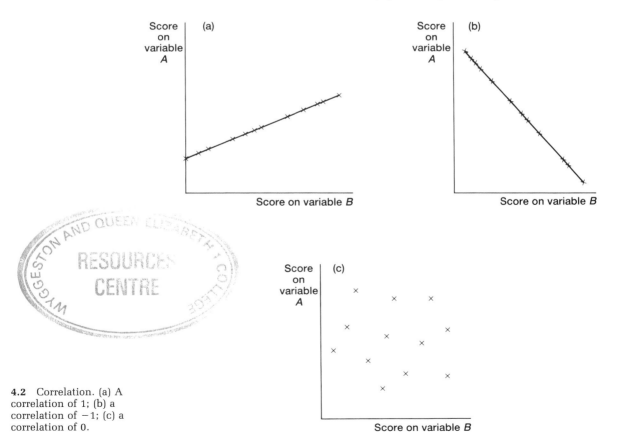

4.2 Correlation. (a) A correlation of 1; (b) a correlation of -1; (c) a correlation of 0.

An *r* of −1 would also mean that a straight line could be drawn through all the plotted points, but this time it would slope the other way, so that as *A* increased, *B* decreased (Fig. 4.2b). An *r* of zero would mean not only that it was impossible to draw a straight line through all the data points, but also that there was no tendency whatever for scores on either of the two variables to rise of fall with scores on the other one (see Fig. 4.2c).

The reader may already have grasped that an *r* of zero is a statistical representation of the null hypothesis that there is no linear relationship between the variables. The psychologist, therefore, typically asks "does the correlation coefficient I have obtained with my sample differ sufficiently from zero for me to reject the null hypothesis?" Just as with other statistics, for any given sample size, we can look up the critical value of *r* required to achieve particular levels of statistical significance. Thus, for example, with a sample size of 20, the critical value of *r* for significance at the 0.05 level is ±0.444. The corresponding values at the 0.01 and 0.001 levels are ±0.590 and ±0.708.

A worked example of Pearson's *r* appears later in this chapter. At this point, however, it is worth saying a little about how it can be calculated. One method (see later in this chapter for another) is as follows. First, each score on each variable is converted to a *z-score*. That is, it is transformed to reflect the number of standard deviations it is above or below the sample mean. Those *z*-scores greater than zero (i.e. positive) are above the mean and those less than zero (i.e. negative) are below it. Then for each person in the sample, the *z*-score on variable *A* is multiplied by that on variable *B*. These *cross-products* for each person are added together and divided by the total sample size. With a little imagination, the reader can perhaps see how an *r* of zero is obtained when variables *A* and *B* are unrelated. In this situation, the following four occurrences are about equally frequent (see Fig. 4.3a):

- positive *z*-scores on both variables;
- positive *z*-score on variable *A*, and a negative one on *B*;
- negative *z*-score on variable *A*, and a positive one on *B*; and
- negative *z*-scores on both variables.

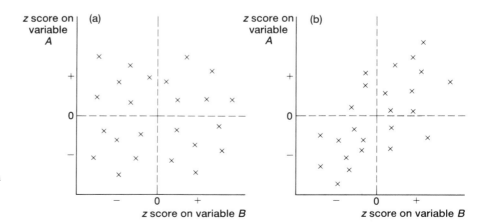

4.3 Cross-products in correlation. (a) A correlation of 0; (b) a positive correlation.

In the first and last cases above, the cross-product will be a positive number (i.e. greater than zero), whereas in the second and third it will be negative. When the cross-products for each person in Fig. 4.3a are added, the positive and negative ones will cancel each other out, thus giving an *r* of zero. But when there is a positive correlation between the variables (see Fig. 4.3b), most of the cross-products are positive (remember, a negative number multiplied by another negative number produces a positive number).

A special case of *r* occurs when one of the variables has only two values. This is analogous to a non-independent samples *t*-test, because in effect the two levels of one variable are being examined to see if they are associated with significantly different mean scores on the other variable. The values of *r* and *t* are not identical, but their associated levels of statistical significance are.

Another form of correlation is the *Spearman rank correlation (rho or ρ)*. This is employed when the data do not reflect absolute scores, but only a rank order so that we know, for example, score *x* is greater than score *y*, but not by how much. The formula for calculating *ρ* looks different from that for *r*, but in fact boils down to the same thing. *ρ* can also be useful when the data are highly *skewed* (see Fig. 4.4) and when there are a few scores hugely different from the others. In both cases, *r* can be distorted, but because the highest score gets a rank of 1 whether it is 2 or 100 units greater than the next highest score, *ρ* "irons out" such difficulties.

Whatever the exact correlation technique, it is important to remember the old maxim "correlation does not imply causality". Often, a psychologist would like to infer that the reason two variables are correlated is that one causes the other. This may seem plausible, but it is hard to be sure. Suppose that a psychologist finds a highly significant positive correlation between self-esteem and salary. If both are measured at the same time, there is no basis on which to decide whether self-esteem causes salary or salary causes self-esteem. It is fairly easy to think of possible explanations for either causal direction. It is also possible that some other variable(s) (e.g. social status, educational attainment) cause *both*, but unless we have measured them, we can only speculate.

Obtaining data over time (a *longitudinal study*) can help, in so far as it may help uncover whether scores on one variable at time 1 predict scores on the other at time 2. But even then, prior occurrence is only necessary – not sufficient – for causality. We could also enter an interesting philosophical debate about the notion of causality – but now is not the time!

4.4 Skewed distributions. (a) A positively skewed distribution; (b) a negatively skewed distribution.

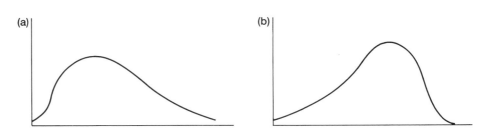

(a)

(b)

Multiple regression

Just as analysis of variance is a generalization of the *t*-test for more than two groups, so multiple regression is an extension of correlation for more than two variables. Suppose a psychologist wishes to assess the correlation with self-esteem of salary, educational attainment and social status. He or she might well find that the latter three variables are all correlated with each other, and also with self-esteem. In this case, the psychologist might wonder which one(s) really matter in predicting self-esteem.

Multiple regression is a statistical technique that would allow the social scientist to assess the *relative* importance of salary, educational attainment and social status as predictors of self-esteem. It involves estimation of the correlation of each of the three variables with self-esteem *independent of the other two* (the technique can of course be extended to larger numbers of variables). In this way, the researcher can end up with an equation that specifies the weighting to be given to each predictor variable in predicting self-esteem, as well as an overall indication of just how predictable self-esteem is using all the predictor variables. But note: just because variables are designated "predictors" in multiple regression analyses, it does not mean they are necessarily actual "causes" of the variable to be predicted.

Multiple regression is a much-used technique in work psychology. It is quite complex. Its intricacies are beyond the scope of this book but the interested reader can find out more by consulting Berry and Feldman (1985) or Cohen and Cohen (1983).

Other phenomena in statistical testing

Effect size

The reader may have wondered whether statistical significance is necessarily the same as significance for practical purposes. At least one behavioural science statistics text (Rosenthal and Rosnow, 1984) repeatedly reminds its readers that statistical significance depends on the size of the effect (e.g. the difference in means between two groups relative to the standard deviation; or the value of *r* for two variables) *multiplied by* the size of the study. Thus, when research uses large samples, quite small effect sizes can lead us to reject the null hypothesis – probably correctly, of course, *but* if the effect is so small, albeit detectable, are we going to worry about it? For example, a psychologist might find that, in a large sample, marketing managers score on average two points higher on a numeracy test than production managers, and that this difference is highly statistically significant. So what? Should anybody be concerned?

Ultimately, that particular question may be answered by assessing the relationship between numeracy and work performance, focusing particularly on the extra work performance one could expect given a specified increase in numeracy, and then translating this into practical benefits (see Chapter 7 concerning utility analysis).

However, it is also useful to consider effect size in more abstract terms. We can think of it as *the degree to which the null hypothesis is false*. For t, we can consider the difference between group means as a proportion of the standard deviation of scores (d) to be a measure of effect size. For r, we can use the proportion of variance in scores common to both variables. This is r^2. Thus, a correlation of 0.60 indicates that $0.60 \times 0.60 = 0.36$ or 36% of the variance in one variable is "accounted for" by scores in the other. With large samples, it is often possible for a correlation of only 0.20 or less to be statistically significant. In this case, the variables share just 4% of variance. This sounds small, but Rosenthal and Rosnow (1984, pp. 207–211) have demonstrated that it can nevertheless reflect practical outcomes of real importance.

For F, one often-used indicator of effect size is called *eta* (η). It reflects the proportion of the variation in scores that is accounted for by group membership. Like r^2, η^2 can be considered an indicator of the proportion of total variance accounted for.

There is nothing mysterious about indices of effect size. They are often quite simply derived, and are sometimes even routinely calculated on the way to a test of statistical significance.

Statistical power

Statistical power refers to the probability of rejecting the null hypothesis when it is indeed false and therefore should be rejected. It is, in other words, the probability of avoiding making a type II error. Like all probability estimates, it can vary from zero to one.

The level of power operating in any particular research study depends on the level of statistical significance the psychologist wishes to work at, the size of the sample, and the size of the effect under examination. The chief practical lesson to be learned is that small sample sizes have very low power, i.e. a high probability of missing a relationship that does exist.

Cohen (1977) has produced tables which specify the sample sizes required to achieve certain levels of power for particular statistical tests at specified significance levels and effect sizes. One example will illustrate the point about sample size. Suppose that there *is* a difference in numeracy between production managers and marketing managers, such that the difference in means is half a standard deviation (i.e. $d = 0.5$). If a psychologist had a sample of 20 of each type of manager, the chance of detecting the difference in means at the 0.05 significance level would be only 0.3, or 30%. So there would be a 70% chance of obtaining a non-significant result, even though there was a difference between population means. It would require 85 in each group to achieve a power level of 0.90, which would mean that there was only a 10% chance of failing to find a difference significant at the 0.05 level when the difference between population means was half a standard deviation.

These observations about statistical power are very important. Often in research, one investigator reports a statistically significant finding with a moderate to large sample size. Then another researcher attempts to replicate the result with a smaller sample, fails to find a statistically significant effect, and declares that the original finding must have been a fluke. But close examination shows that the *effect size* in the second study is as large as in the first – only the smaller sample size prevents statistical significance being achieved.

Garbage in, garbage out

One final point should be noted before we turn to some worked examples. No statistical wizardry can rescue poor sampling, or poor measures. If the psychologist's measure of numeracy is a poor one (for example, it only assesses one aspect of numeracy, or people's scores are unreliable: see Chapter 7), then he or she is not likely to draw any accurate conclusions.

Statistical examples

This section of the chapter provides examples of the main statistical techniques discussed earlier. In keeping with our objective of imparting statistical knowledge in the most straightforward way possible, we have provided only the necessary minimum when it comes to formulae and the examples are as direct and uncluttered as possible. The whole section is preceded by an introduction of statistical terms and formulae that are of use in most of the examples. Terms and formulae peculiar to each example are introduced in the preamble to the relevant example. Readers are advised to familiarize themselves with the general terms and formulae before tackling the examples. In the interests of clarity, we have used a simplified version of statistical notation (e.g. subscripts have been omitted where possible). We hope that this will benefit the reader and not offend the statistical purist.

Relevant statistical terms and formulae of general use

Σ = the sum of

Example: for four scores $x_1 = 2$, $x_2 = 3$, $x_3 = 2$, $x_4 = 5$,

$\Sigma x = 2 + 3 + 2 + 5 = 12$

mean = sum of scores divided by the number of scores = $\bar{x}$

Example: for five scores $(x_1 \ldots x_5) = 4, 3, 6, 3, 4$

$$\bar{x} = \frac{x_1 + x_2 + x_3 + x_4 + x_5}{5} = \frac{4 + 3 + 6 + 3 + 4}{5} = \frac{20}{5} = 4$$

$$\bar{x} = \frac{\Sigma x}{n}$$

deviation = distance from the mean = $x_i - \bar{x}$
(where x_i = any of i different scores)

Example: for five scores

x_i	$- \bar{x}$	$= x_i - \bar{x}$
(sum)	(mean)	(deviation)

$$x_1(=4) - \bar{x}(=4) = \quad 0$$
$$x_2(=3) - \bar{x}(=4) = -1$$
$$x_3(=6) - \bar{x}(=4) = \quad 2$$
$$x_4(=3) - \bar{x}(=4) = -1$$
$$x_5(=4) - \bar{x}(=4) = \quad 0$$

sum of squares = sum of squared deviation scores = SS

Example: for five scores

$$\begin{aligned} SS &= (x_1 - \bar{x})^2 + (x_2 - \bar{x})^2 + (x_3 - \bar{x})^2 + (x_4 - \bar{x})^2 + (x_5 - \bar{x})^2 \\ &= 0^2 + (-1)^2 + 2^2 + (-1)^2 + 0^2 \\ &= 0 + 1 + 4 + 1 + 0 = 6 \end{aligned}$$

computational formula for $SS = \Sigma x^2 - \dfrac{(\Sigma x)^2}{n}$

i.e. (1) square each score and add them;
    (2) add up all of the scores, square the total and divide by the number of scores;
    (3) subtract (2) from (1).

population variance = average squared deviation =
sum of squared deviations divided by number of scores in the population

$$= \frac{SS}{n} = \sigma^2$$

sample variance (i.e. the variance of the scores in the sample)

$$= \frac{SS}{n}$$

sample variance (as an estimate of population variance) =
sum of squared deviations divided by 1 less than the number of scores in sample

$$= \frac{SS}{n - 1*} = S^2$$

* N.B.: Because we are using a sample to estimate the variance of the population, $n - 1$, rather than n should be used.

Standard deviation = square root of average squared deviation

$$= \text{square root of variance} = \sqrt{S^2} = S; \text{ or } \sqrt{\sigma^2} = \sigma$$

level of statistical significance = probability of committing a type I error
$= \alpha$

degrees of freedom = the number of scores that are free to vary = d.f.

Example: in a sample of five scores with a mean of 4, once four scores (4, 3, 6, 3) are known, the fifth score *must* be 4; hence d.f. = 5 − 1 = 4.

standard score = scores expressed in "deviation from the mean" units

$$= \frac{x_i - \bar{x}}{S} = z$$

Example:

	Score	Mean	S	z
x_1	4	4	1.22	0.00
x_2	3	4	1.22	−0.82
x_3	6	4	1.22	1.64
x_4	3	4	1.22	0.82
x_5	4	4	1.22	−0.00

Statistical test: Student's *t*-test

"Student" was a pseudonym of the statistician who invented the test. In this example, the investigator is interested in assessing whether or not there is a statistically significant difference in mean scores on a particular variable (V_1) for two specific groups of people (*A*, *B*). This may be, for example, because the groups have been exposed to different treatments (e.g. different training procedures) or because the groups differ in some way (e.g. male *vs* female, employed *vs* unemployed, over 35 years old *vs* under 35 years old), which is expected to be associated with differences on the dependent variable. The formula used in the example below is appropriate if the variances in the two groups are similar (homogeneous). (Note that a pooled variance estimate is calculated and used.) If the variances in the groups are not homogeneous, a different formula is needed. Another different formula is needed if the two groups involved are not independent samples, e.g. if the study had involved the same group on two occasions.

Relevant formulae

(i) $t = \dfrac{\bar{x}_A - \bar{x}_B}{S_{\bar{x}_A - \bar{x}_B}}$

S^2 = pooled variance for both groups

$S^2 = \dfrac{(n_A - 1)S_A^2 + (n_B - 1)S_B^2}{(n_A - 1) + (n_B - 1)}$

$S_{\bar{x}_A - \bar{x}_B} = \sqrt{\dfrac{S^2}{n_A} + \dfrac{S^2}{n_B}}$

Substituting $\sqrt{\dfrac{S^2}{n_A} + \dfrac{S^2}{n_B}}$ for $S_{\bar{x}_A - \bar{x}_B}$ in formula (i):

(ii) $t \qquad = \dfrac{\bar{x}_A - \bar{x}_B}{S} \times \dfrac{1}{\sqrt{1/n_A + 1/n_B}}$

$\qquad\qquad \uparrow \qquad\qquad \uparrow \qquad\qquad \uparrow$

(significance test)   (effect size)   (size of study)

Data

Group *A*	Group *B*
12.5	19
14.5	21
8	14.5
10	17
13	20
$\bar{x}_A = 11.6$	$\bar{x}_B = 18.3$
$S_A^2 = 6.68$	$S_B^2 = 6.70$

$S^2 = \dfrac{4 \times 6.68 + 4 \times 6.70}{8}$

$\quad = \dfrac{26.72 + 26.80}{8} = 6.69$

Using formula (i) for t:

$t = \dfrac{\bar{x}_A - \bar{x}_B}{S} \times \dfrac{1}{\sqrt{1/n_A + 1/n_B}}$

$t = \dfrac{11.6 - 18.3}{\sqrt{6.69}} \times \dfrac{1}{\sqrt{0.2 + 0.2}}$

$\quad = \dfrac{-6.7}{2.59} \times \dfrac{1}{0.63}$

$\quad = -2.59 \times 1.58$

$\quad = \underline{-4.10}$

Interpretation

At the 95% level (i.e. $\alpha = 0.05$; setting the possibility of type I error to 5%), the critical value of t [for $(n_A - 1) + (n_B - 1) = 8$ degrees of freedom] $= 2.31$. The observed value of 4.10 exceeds (in magnitude terms) this value; therefore, there *is* a statistically significant difference between the means of the two groups and the null hypothesis of no difference between the groups is rejected. Note that the sign ($+$ or $-$) of t is merely a function of which mean is used as the first term in the calculation of t. It has no effect on the interpretation of significance, when a two-tailed test is being used. The test is said to be two-tailed when the investigator is interested in whether one (either) group is different from another. If he or she is investigating a more specific hypothesis – that one (specific) group has the larger mean – then a one-tailed test is needed. Put simply, a two-tailed test allows either of the two means to be larger; in a *one*-tailed test, *one* (specific) mean must be larger if statistical significance is to be attained. The value of t needed to show statistical significance in a one-tailed test is smaller than that needed for a two-tailed test.

Statistical test: Analysis of variance

This example is similar to the previous one in that the investigator is interested in differences between groups. In this case, however, a third group (C) has been utilized in addition to groups A and B. Of course it would be possible to do several different t-tests to check for statistically significant differences (i.e. *A vs B*, *A vs C*, *B vs C*). With only three groups, this would probably be acceptable. The problem with multiple t-tests, or the multiple use of any test on the same samples, is that as more tests are done, the overall probability of committing a type I error is increased.

$1 - \alpha =$ the probability of commiting no error; i.e. for each test at the 95% ($\alpha = 0.05$) level $= 1 - 0.05 = 0.95$

the probability of no error on a second test $= (1 - \alpha)(1 - \alpha) = 0.95 \times 0.95 = 0.90$

The general formula $= (1 - \alpha)^T$, where T equals the number of tests done: Hence with $\alpha = 0.05$, when there are three groups and three t-tests, the experiment-wise probability of no error is reduced to $0.95^3 = 0.86$, i.e. an 86% chance of avoiding an error. With five separate tests, the chance of avoiding error falls to 77%. The procedures involved in the analysis of variance ensure that the selected α level applies to the total risk of type I error for the study. In effect, the analysis procedures perform all of the relevant comparisons simultaneously.

The analysis of variance procedure literally divides up the variance in a set of data into different components. Initially, the total variance is divided up into variance within the groups and variance between the groups. By comparing these variances, it is possible to assess differences between the groups. If all groups were similar, the mean value for each group would be similar and so would the variance about this mean. The variation between groups would be much the same as the variation within groups and, in this case, the *F* ratio, obtained by dividing between-group variance by within-group variance, would be close to 1. If the *F* ratio is large, implying more variation between groups than within them, this would indicate that the groups' scores differ from each other.

Relevant formulae

$$SS_{total} = \Sigma x^2 - \frac{(\Sigma x)^2}{nk}$$

where k = number of groups.

$$SS_{within} = \Sigma SS \text{ within each group}$$

$SS_{between}$ = the number of observations in each group multiplied by the SS of the group means

Note that SS total = $SS_{between}$ + SS_{within}

Variance (usually called mean square in analysis of variance) =

$$\frac{SS}{\text{degrees of freedom}} = MS$$

$$F = \frac{MS_{between}}{MS_{within}}$$

Data

Group A	Group B	Group C	$k = 3$
12	14	16	
14	11	15	
11	12	14	
13	14	17	
10	11	14	
$\bar{x}_A = 12$	$\bar{x}_B = 12.4$	$\bar{x}_C = 15.2$; $\bar{x} = 13.2$	
$\Sigma x_A = 60$	$\Sigma x_B = 62$	$\Sigma x_C = 76$	
$\Sigma x_A^2 = 730$	$\Sigma x_B^2 = 778$	$\Sigma x_C^2 = 1162$	

$n = 5$; $\Sigma x = 198$; $\Sigma x^2 = 2670$; $(\Sigma x)^2 = 39\,204$

$$SS_{total} = \Sigma x^2 - \frac{(\Sigma x)^2}{nk}$$

$$= 2670 - \frac{39\,204}{15} = \underline{56.4}$$

$$SS_{within} = SS_A + SS_B + SS_C$$

$$= 10 + 9.2 + 6.8$$

$$= \underline{26}$$

$$SS_{between} = 5[(12 - 13.2)^2 + (12.4 - 13.2)^2 + (15.2 - 13.2)^2]$$

$$= \underline{30.4}$$

Analysis of variance (ANOVA) table

Source of variation	d.f.	SS	MS	F
Between groups	$(k - 1) = 3 - 1 = 2$	30.4	$\dfrac{SS}{d.f.} = 15.2$	F = 7.00
Within groups	$(n - k) = 15 - 3 = 12$	26	$\dfrac{SS}{d.f.} = 2.17$	
Total	$(n - 1) = 15 - 1 = 14$	56.4		

Interpretation

At $\alpha = 0.05$, the critical value for F with d.f. (2, 12) is 3.59.

The observed value of 7.00 exceeds this and we conclude that there are statistically significant differences between groups and the null hypothesis of no differences between the groups is rejected.

Statistical test: χ^2 (chi-square)

As noted in the earlier part of this chapter, researchers may sometimes have access to important data that are in categorical form, rather than continuous scores. For example, a researcher might be interested in organizational roles (e.g. x, y) and preferred management style (e.g. A, B or C). In such a situation, a t-test or analysis of variance cannot be used, because the variables in the study are not measured on a continuous scale and the calculation of various statistics needed to compute t or F (e.g. means) for the groups would be meaningless.

Chi-square provides a useful procedure for examining statistical significance in categorical data. The basis of the chi-square test involves casting the data into a contingency table. In the case of this example, this will be a 2 (*X, Y*) × 3 (*A, B, C*) table. If there was an even distribution of styles across the organizational roles, then the number of cases in each cell of the table would reflect this. In other words, the null hypothesis of no relationship between organizational role and management style would lead us to *expect* a certain number of cases in each cell.

By comparing the expected values with the *observed* values, chi-square provides a test of the extent to which the variables involved are associated.

Relevant formulae

The expected frequency in a cell, $E = \dfrac{TR \times TC}{n}$

where TR = total number of cases in the row in which the cell belongs
     TC = total number of cases in the column in which the cell belongs
      n = total number of cases

chi-square $= \chi^2 = \Sigma \dfrac{(O-E)^2}{E}$

where   O = observed number of cases in each cell
      E = expected number in each cell

Data

Person	Organizational role	Preferred management style
1	*x*	*A*
2	*x*	*B*
3	*x*	*A*
4	*x*	*B*
5	*x*	*C*
6	*x*	*A*
7	*x*	*B*
8	*x*	*A*
9	*x*	*B*
10	*x*	*A*
11	*x*	*B*
12	*x*	*A*
13	*x*	*A*
14	*x*	*B*
15	*x*	*A*
16	*y*	*B*
17	*y*	*C*
18	*y*	*C*
19	*y*	*C*

(*contd*)

20	y	B
21	y	C
22	y	C
23	y	A
24	y	C
25	y	B
26	y	C
27	y	C
28	y	B
29	y	C
30	y	A
31	y	C
32	y	C

| | | Preferred management style | | | |
		A	B	C	Row totals
Organizational role	x	8	6	1	15
	y	2	4	11	17
Column totals		10	10	12	32

Calculation of χ^2

Example: the calculation of expected frequencies for the top left-hand cell:

$$E = \frac{15 \times 10}{32} = 4.6875$$

$$\chi^2 = \frac{(8 - 4.6875)^2}{4.6875} + \frac{(6 - 4.6875)^2}{4.6875} + \frac{(1 - 5.625)^2}{5.625}$$

$$+ \frac{(2 - 5.3125)^2}{5.3125} + \frac{(4 - 5.3125)^2}{5.3125} + \frac{(11 - 6.375)^2}{6.375}$$

$$\chi^2 = 2.3408 + 0.3675 + 3.8028 + 2.0654 + 0.3243 + 3.3553$$

$$= 12.26$$

$$\text{d.f.} = (3 - 1)(2 - 1) = 2$$

Interpretation

The critical value of χ^2 for $\alpha = 0.05$ is 5.99. Therefore, because the observed χ^2 is larger than this value, we conclude that the null hypothesis of no relationship is rejected.

Statistical test: Pearson product–moment correlation coefficient

The Pearson product–moment correlation coefficient is one of the most widely used procedures in work psychology. In many studies, investigators wish to know whether two variables are associated with each other. Variables are said to be associated if they vary together, i.e. large (or small) values on one variable are consistently associated with large (or small) values on the other.

The Pearson product–moment correlation coefficient provides a single statistic (usually referred to as "*r*"), which indicates the precise magnitude of the linear association between two variables. The values of *r* vary from $+1$ through 0 to -1 (see p. 49). The square of the correlation coefficient r^2 represents the proportion of variability in one variable that is associated with the other.

If two sets of scores are positively correlated (i.e. values on one variable increase as values on the other increase) the standard (z) scores (see p. 49) will also vary together. This is obvious if you recognize that, *for a correlation to be large and positive*, an extreme high score on one variable (and hence a high z-score) must be coupled with a similarly high score on the other variable.

The formula

$$r = \frac{\Sigma z_x z_y}{n}$$

makes sense when considered in this light. For example, if high scores on one variable (i.e. positive z values) are consistently linked with low scores (i.e. negative z values) on the other, the product of the two scores $z_x z_y$ will be negative (because a negative multiplied by a positive = negative) and the value for *r* will be between 0 and -1. If there is no consistent link between the variables, the size and direction of the product term $z_x z_y$ will vary, and when the values for each pair of scores are added together (summed), they will cancel each other out, giving an *r* of zero. Notice that in the formula the sum of the product terms $z_x z_y$ is divided by *N*, which will be the same as the number of product terms added together (see Fig. 4.5). In other words, *r* is the mean of the

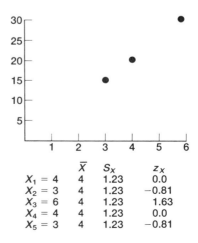

	$\overline{Y}$	S_Y	z_Y
$Y_1 = 20$	20	6.12	0.0
$Y_2 = 15$	20	6.12	−0.81
$Y_3 = 30$	20	6.12	1.63
$Y_4 = 20$	20	6.12	0.0
$Y_5 = 15$	20	6.12	−0.81

	$\overline{X}$	S_X	z_X
$X_1 = 4$	4	1.23	0.0
$X_2 = 3$	4	1.23	−0.81
$X_3 = 6$	4	1.23	1.63
$X_4 = 4$	4	1.23	0.0
$X_5 = 3$	4	1.23	−0.81

4.5 Correlation and standard scores.

sum of the products of the z-scores. Remembering that z-scores represent distances from the mean (sometimes referred to as *moments*) makes the use of the term "product moment correlation" obvious.

The formula for the correlation coefficient provides a basis for estimating values on one variable from values on the other. For example, if the correlation between two variables is known (i.e. the value of r is known), then if we know someone's z-score on one variable (X), the best estimate of their score on the other (Y) is given by:

$$z_y = rz_x$$

Of course, unless the correlation is perfect (i.e. $r = 1$), our estimate will not be entirely accurate.

It is possible to translate the estimated z-score, in this case z_y, to a raw score $\hat{y}$. As noted above, however, this score will not necessarily correspond to the observed score y_i (unless $r = 1$).

Notice that if $r = 0$, the best estimate of z_y will be $z_y = 0$. In other words, when there is no correlation and hence no basis for predicting any specific value of y, the best guess is the mean score. Indeed (until $r = 1$), the estimated scores tend to be closer to the mean than the real scores. The deviation scores for these estimated values and the sum of squares for these deviation scores (see pp. 56–8) is given by:

$$\text{deviation scores for estimates} = \hat{y}_i - \bar{y}$$

$$\text{sum of squares for estimates} = \Sigma(\hat{y}_i - \bar{y})^2$$

Similarly, the deviation scores and sum of squares for the actual values (which will always be larger than those for the estimated values) can be calculated:

$$\text{deviation scores for actuals} = y_i - \bar{y}$$

$$\text{sum of squares for actuals} = \Sigma(y_i - \bar{y})^2$$

$\Sigma(\hat{y}_i - \bar{y})^2$ represents the part of the total variation in Y that is associated with X. This is made clear by considering what would happen to this value if none of the variation in Y was associated with X. In this case, r would be zero, all estimates of $\hat{y}$ would be $\bar{y}$ (i.e. the mean) and the value in question, $\Sigma(\hat{y}_i - \bar{y})^2$, would also be zero. As the degree of association between X and Y increases, r will increase and the value of $\Sigma(\hat{y}_i - \bar{y})$ will increase relative to the actual sum of squares, $\Sigma(y_i - \bar{y})^2$.

The ratio of these terms:

$$\frac{\Sigma(\hat{y}_i - \bar{y})^2}{\Sigma(y_i - \bar{y})^2}$$

represents the proportion of variability in Y that is associated with X.

As noted on pp. 49–51, the square of the correlation coefficient (r^2) can also be interpreted to represent the proportion of variability in Y that is associated with X. Indeed,

$$r^2 = \frac{\Sigma(\hat{y}_i - \bar{y})^2}{\Sigma(y_i - \bar{y})^2} = \text{proportion of variability in } Y \text{ associated with } X$$

Computation of r

As is often the case, the definitional formulae for a statistic, in this case r, are not convenient for computation. The following formula, which produces identical results to those given earlier, is much more convenient for calculation:

$$r_{xy} = \frac{n\Sigma x_i y_i - (\Sigma x_i)(\Sigma y_i)}{\sqrt{[n\Sigma x_i^2 - (\Sigma x_i)^2][n\Sigma y_i^2 - (\Sigma y_i)^2]}}$$

where each value for XY is obtained by multiplying the value obtained for X by the value obtained for Y on the same person.

Data

Person	X	Y	XY
1	5	3.0	15.0
2	9	2.1	18.9
3	15	1.7	25.5
4	13	1.5	19.5
5	7	2.9	20.3
6	10	3.4	34.0
7	11	4.2	46.2
8	4	1.0	4.0
9	16	3.2	51.2
10	8	1.5	12.0
	$\Sigma x = 98$	$\Sigma y = 24.5$	$\Sigma xy = 246.6$
	$(\Sigma x)^2 = 9604$	$(\Sigma y)^2 = 600.25$	
	$\Sigma x^2 = 1106$	$\Sigma y^2 = 69.65$	
		$(n = 10)$	

$$r_{xy} = \frac{n\Sigma xy - (\Sigma x)(\Sigma y)}{\sqrt{[n\Sigma x^2 - (\Sigma x)^2][n\Sigma y^2 - (\Sigma y)^2]}}$$

$$r_{xy} = \frac{2466 - (98)(24.5)}{\sqrt{[11\,060 - 9604][696.5 - 600.25]}}$$

$$r_{xy} = \frac{2466 - 2401}{\sqrt{[1456][96.25]}}$$

$$r_{xy} = \frac{65}{374.353}$$

$$r_{xy} = \underline{0.17}$$

For $\alpha = 0.05$ with $(n - 2)$ 8 degrees of freedom, the critical value for $r = 0.63$. Therefore (because the observed value for r is less than this), we accept the null hypothesis that there is no correlation between the variables X and Y.

Summary

In this chapter, we have introduced the reader to some key concepts in the analysis and interpretation of psychological data. Most often, the data concern possible psychological differences between groups of people, or whether two or more psychological variables are related to each other within one group of people. Statistical significance is perhaps the most important general concept but others, particularly effect size, are also noteworthy. We have described several specific statistical tests: specifically the t-test, correlation, analysis of variance and chi-square. We have also shown how "portable" concepts like statistical significance are applied to these tests. Finally, we have provided worked examples which illustrate how to use the statistical tests described in the first part of the chapter. We hope we have demonstrated that it is not too difficult to understand the fundamentals of statistical analysis. The concepts and tests should help the reader to analyse his or her own data (not necessarily confined to psychology) and to evaluate analyses done by other people.

References

Berry, W. D. and Feldman, S. (1985). *Multiple Regression in Practice*. London: Sage.

Cohen, J. (1977). *Statistical Power Analysis for the Behavioral Sciences*. London: Academic Press.

Cohen, J. and Cohen, P. (1983). *Applied Multiple Regression/Correlation Analysis for the Behavioral Sciences*. Hillsdale, N.J.: Lawrence Erlbaum Associates.

Ferguson, G. A. and Takane, Y. (1989). *Statistical Analysis in Psychology and Education*, 6th edn. New York: McGraw-Hill.

Rosenthal, R. and Rosnow, R. L. (1984). *Essentials of Behavioral Research, Methods and Data Analysis*. New York: McGraw-Hill.

Minority groups at work

Introduction

Increasingly, women, ethnic minorities, the disabled and other minority groups are entering the workforce in ever larger numbers. If we are to overcome the obvious entry obstacles, work-related and career blockage problems of these minority groups, we must know something about the extent and nature of their difficulties at work. This chapter will explore three minority groups in the workplace – women, ethnic minorities and the disabled – helping to identify the sources of their stress, as well as suggesting ways of remedying them.

Women at work

The role of women in society is radically changing in most Western countries (Lewis and Cooper, 1989). Vast numbers of women are beginning to work full-time and to aspire to climb the same "organizational ladders" as their male counterparts (Davidson and Cooper, 1984). In the UK, for instance, the male labour force has grown at a much slower rate than the female one. In addition, in the early 1950s, there were 2.7 million married women in jobs, but by the early 1980s that figure had risen by 143% to over 6.7 million. And, most interesting of all, at the start of the 1950s, only one-quarter of working women were married, whereas today over two-thirds of all women who are working are married.

But what does this trend mean for the health and well-being of women? Will they join the growing number of men who suffer from stress-related illnesses as a result of work? Cooper *et al.* (1988) reviewed the literature in the field to answer these types of questions. What follows is a summary of their work.

More and more research work is being conducted in this area, and although there are medics who feel that working women are less at risk than men (*Lancet*, 1979), the early studies in this field have been disturbing. One of the most interesting and comprehensive investigations was carried out by Haynes and Feinleib (1980). Their sample was drawn from the Framingham Heart Study, which is the most comprehensive investigation of heart disease yet conducted.

Many of the inhabitants of Framingham, Massachusetts, USA, had been undergoing regular medical screening for the past 20 years. The main purpose of the study was to identify the precursors to heart disease in that population. Interested to identify the impact of employment on working women, Haynes and Feinleib collected data on the employment status and behaviour of 350 housewives, 387 working women (employed outside the home for over one-half of their adult years) and 580 men (between the ages of 45 and 64) in the Framingham study. All 1317 subjects in the investigation were followed for the development of coronary heart disease over an 8-year period.

Their main finding was that working women did not have a significantly higher incidence of coronary heart disease than housewives, and their rates were lower than for working men. They then analysed the data in terms of married (including divorced, widowed and separated) *vs* single working women, and found a substantial increase in incidence of heart disease in married working women. But the most revealing of all their results appeared when married working women with children were compared with those without children. In this case, they found that "among working women, the incidence of coronary heart disease rose as the number of children increased". This was not the case, however, for women who were housewives; indeed, that group showed a slight decrease with increasing number of children.

In addition to these results, Haynes and Feinleib found that working women as a whole "experienced more daily stress, marital dissatisfaction, and aging worries and were less likely to show overt anger than either housewives or men". Indeed, in a review of the research literature on marital adjustment in dual-career marriages, Staines *et al.* (1978) found that of the 13 major studies in this area, using either an American national or regional sample, at least 11 of them showed that marital adjustment was worse for dual-career wives than for non-working wives.

On the other hand, Newberry *et al.* (1979) examined the psychiatric status and social adjustment of a matched group of working married women and housewives drawn from a community sample. They used the Social Adjustment Scale, Gurin's Symptom Check List and the Schedule for Affective Disorders and Schizophrenia. They found that although there was no difference between the two groups on overall psychiatric symptoms, depressive symptoms, diagnosable psychiatric disorders or treatment for an emotional problem in the past year, married working women did differ from housewives in their attitudes towards work and the home. Indeed, they found that housewives suffered from greater "work impairment", feelings of inadequacy, disinterest and overall work maladjustment than working wives. On the other hand, working wives were found to be more impaired, disinterested and inadequate in respect of their housework as compared to their work.

Although there is some scattered evidence, as above, that working women may not be "at risk" of stress-related illness or other negative social consequences, the data are beginning to mount to the contrary, particularly for working women who are married with a family. In a study of psychiatric disorders among professional women, Welner *et al.* (1979) found, for example, that women GPs had a significantly higher rate of psychiatric depression than a control group, and that women with children were found to have significantly more career disruption than those without children. In addition, Davidson and Cooper (1980a) found that married female executives with children were under greater stress than single or divorced working women. Indeed, Hall and Hall (1980) suggest that the main source of stress among dual-career couples stems from the fact that the number of demands on the partners exceeds the time and energy to deal with them. Families, in this context, add a further series of potential problems, particularly when work organizations are doing very little, if anything, to help the dual-career family, and specifically the wife who is expected to be both mother and worker.

Aside from these findings, some startling results have emerged from the total Framingham sample in regard to type A coronary-prone behaviour and women. Two distinguished cardiologists, Friedman and Rosenman (1974), found a significant relationship between the behavioural patterns of people and their prevalence of stress-related illness, particularly coronary heart disease. Type A behaviour is characterized by "extremes of competitiveness, striving for achievement, aggressiveness, haste, impatience, restlessness, hyperalertness, explosiveness of speech, tenseness of facial muscles, feelings of being under pressure of time and under the challenge of responsibility". Type B behaviour, on the other hand, is characterized by the relative absence of the behaviour associated with type A individuals. On the basis of large-scale prospective research work, Rosenman *et al.* (1966) found that this type A behaviour pattern in all groups of people is a significant precursor to coronary heart disease and other stress-related illness: type A men aged 39–49 and 50–59 years had 6.5 and 1.9 times the incidence of coronary heart disease as type B men, respectively.

In this context, one interesting finding of the Framingham study is that working women who score high on type A are *twice* as likely to develop coronary heart disease as male type As. Indeed, in a study in the UK carried out by one of the authors (Davidson and Cooper, 1980b), it was found that senior female executives had significantly higher type A behaviour scores than male executives, which in terms of these Framingham results may mean that female professional women may be at greater risk of actual coronaries than the mythical "high-flying" male executive.

Sources of stress for women at work

As we can see, women at work can suffer, but what are some of the determinants of this stress? A number of causes of stress can arise from "within the woman" herself. Many women, taking on management positions in particular, may discover conflicts within themselves. A great deal of learning about sex-roles takes place among women during the early phases of their lives, and this can translate itself into an attitude that creates difficulties later in working life or life generally. Larwood and Wood (1979), in their book *Women in Management*, described internal blocks that women experience which derive from early sex stereotyping and socialization. First, many women are caught in a "low expectation trap", particularly when performing a job usually done by men. Women can feel that their performance is unequal to the task. This feeling is often a self-fulfilling prophecy. Secondly, some theorists believe certain women fear success, and many avoid success in order to "behave in a socially approved manner" (Horner, 1970). This feeling can inhibit further effort and achievement. Thirdly, most women are not socialized to be assertive or aggressive or to seek power and control. As McClelland (1975) has pointed out, the most successful male managers are the most assertive and have considerable desire for power. Women would, therefore, seem, disadvantaged from their "pink" cradle of birth. It can be countered, however, that there is a different management style that is compatible with the more traditional, less aggressive female role. Fourthly, many women have been expected and encouraged to be dependent upon men, a fact that some researchers believe makes women less self-reliant and more amenable to influence.

This "culture trap" creates difficulties for working women because most organizations are dominated by male values and behaviours, while women are still encouraged to pay a less achievement-orientated, less aggressive, more dependent role. Perhaps, as women gain hold of more significant and powerful positions in industry, the more aggressive values of contemporary business will change, to be replaced by an amalgam of female and male values. In the meantime, however, women are at a disadvantage and are forced to use the behavioural armoury of their male associates to succeed. Some common stress factors faced by female managers and the resulting symptoms of strain are pointed out in Fig. 5.1

Role expectations

A major source of stress for career women derives from the concept of the professional woman held by themselves and others. While a man can suffer

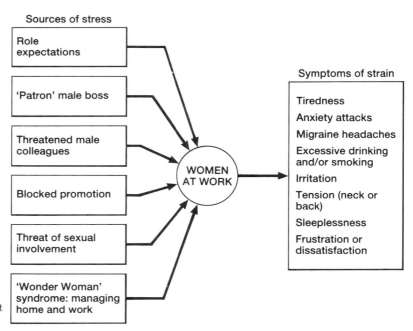

5.1 Stress and women at work.

from lack of role clarity and role conflict, he does so because of his individual situation, not because he is a man. The same cannot be said of a woman attempting to fill a role previously held only by men. Self-doubt and concern about meeting other people's expectations must continually hover over the thoughts and actions of women at work.

"Patron" male boss

While some male bosses may feel threatened by a young career woman who works doubly hard to prove herself, most research indicates that most men are supportive of their female subordinates. This especially holds true for a highly competent female subordinate who does not threaten her boss's relationship with male colleagues. The supportive male boss plays a "patron" role, which holds potential strains of its own for the woman. The patron protects and advances his protégé, but at the same time uses her competence for his own advancement. Although this shielding and advancement has definite advantages, it also holds built-in pressures. First, the woman may feel she must always perform at her best to meet her patron's expectations. Secondly, she can identify with him and suffer the professional "trials and tribulations" that he experiences. Thirdly, significant people within the organization may not recognize her talents, which are always seen as fused with his. Fourthly, the career woman in this case is still playing a dependent role by not "making a mark" based on her own resources. All these factors intertwine to create layers of expectations, which can place significant stress on the career woman.

Threat of sexual involvement

Sexuality at work is a double-edged sword for the working woman. On the one hand, she may experience the pressures of sexual harassment from men who hold the keys to her future success. On the other hand, a woman may utilize her sexual role to achieve career objectives, often resulting in unforeseen complications. Although there is little evidence that this manipulative sexual role is often played by career women, it is certain that both males and females can potentially use sexuality at work. More often than not, the main stress factor a woman experiences as a result of an explicit sexual advance from a colleague involves the many issues surrounding the advance. Is he attracted to her physical attributes or her intellect and work capabilities? If he is interested in her as a woman, what does this mean to her about her skill, and about his professional attitude towards her? This conflict can present an enormous source of stress for women, especially perhaps at the beginning of their careers, when they may lack self-confidence.

Threatened male colleagues

Although many women claim they are helped by their male bosses, they often report that male colleagues of similar rank are excessively competitive, create stress for them and seem to feel threatened by them. Some men at the junior and middle levels, for example, feel particularly threatened because they see their organizations promoting women as "tokens" of equality. Male colleagues who are threatened by their female counterparts, for whatever reason, can and do create strains for women. This reaction can be as subtle as failing to provide complete information needed to make an important decision or by maintaining a distant and cool working relationship. It can be argued that this occurs commonly enough among men working together, and therefore why should women be shielded?

Blocked promotion

Women struggling up the career ladder face obstacles at all levels, some of which involve the conflict between work and home. Many companies expect an employee to be willing to move for a job promotion or to take on short-term assignments away from home. Female managers with a family, for example, are unlikely to be able to do either, often appearing less of a "company man" than their male counterparts.

The "wonder woman" syndrome

Most working women also have the responsibility for a home and family as well. Juggling a job and a family is often done at the expense of a woman's physical and psychological health. The dual-career family is becoming the norm, a fact that involves considerable strain for the women and men involved. Evidence that women are paying a price for the "wonder woman" role appears in coronary heart disease figures, as previously mentioned.

What organizations can do

Cooper *et al.* (1988) and Lewis and Cooper (1989) have highlighted the kinds of strategies that might help to minimize the problems of working women and dual-career couples in general. Such strategies should provide a firm foundation by means of which the alleviation of home/work interface stresses and strains can be accomplished.

Flexible working arrangements

There is a wide range of flexible working arrangements that organizations can provide their male and female employees, which can help them to accommodate to changing family patterns. *Flexitime* is obviously one good example. In order that a dual-career wife and husband can meet the psychological responsibilities associated with their children's education or, indeed, free themselves of guilt, many parents feel that they must take their children to school and/or pick them up. This is very difficult to accomplish under the current 9 to 5 (or later) arrangements, and would be made much easier under flexitime conditions – as long as it was applicable for both husband and wife. Although flexitime is useful during the working week, it could also be extended to cover the school holidays.

Many dual-career parents are concerned about arrangements for their children during the summer months when they are at home. There are several ways of coping with this problem: allowing the dual-career wife or husband to have a lighter workload during these months; allowing them to build up a backlog of working time during the rest of the year to relieve them during the summer months; providing facilities on site during the summer months for young children (perhaps by the use of students training in the field of primary education); or some combination of all of these.

Another more flexible working arrangement could be achieved by introducing more *part-time* work in a variety of different forms: limiting the number of days a week by allowing individuals to work 3- or 4-day, 40-hour weeks. This last suggestion is growing in popularity, and if the dual-career husband and wife were able to work on this basis they could, by careful planning, easily manage their domestic work arrangements between them. In 1972, an American Management Association survey estimated that between 700 and 1000 firms of over 100,000 employees *in toto* were on a 4-day, 40-hour week in the USA. By the 1980s, the number of firms grew to 3000, covering over 1 million workers. Indeed, many firms are moving to a 3-day, 38-hour week without either a decline in productivity or job satisfaction (Foster *et al.*, 1979).

Allied to many of these suggestions is the notion that organizations should provide a crèche or nursery facilities in the workplace. These are growing in number in many of the "advanced thinking" organizations. Many educationalists and psychologists have thought this to be a good idea, as it provides the mother or father with the opportunity of seeing their children some time during the working day. A less satisfactory solution would be community-based nurseries, but these may be necessary for those who work for small companies, or who are self-employed. The benefits that organizations could derive from the introduction of the *industrial kibbutzim* seem so obvious that it is surprising that more companies have not followed suit.

Working at home

With the advent of the microprocessor revolution, it should become easier for dual-career husbands and wives in certain types of jobs to work at home. The need for a central workplace should decrease quite dramatically over the next decade or two. Already, employees can take home a computer terminal or indeed a minicomputer itself to carry out many of the tasks that they were once able to do only in a centralized work environment. In order to allow such a working practice, organizations will have to rid themselves of their deep-rooted, nefarious suspicion of their fellow workers, namely, that the latter will take every opportunity to exploit their employers and work as little as possible, and that only by overseeing them will the work get done! Indeed, it is this very control that has made the process of work unsatisfying and has encouraged the compartmentalization of work and home life to the detriment of the former. As C. Wright Mills (1959) suggested: "Each day men sell little pieces of themselves in order to try and buy them back each night and weekend with little pieces of fun."

Some organizations may one day realize that they may not need a centralized workplace at all. For the time being, however, work organizations ought to explore the variety of jobs that could easily be done at home and provide their employees with the necessary degree of flexibility to enable them to work there. At the very least, it is worth an experiment.

Smoothing the way for women

Many women who have played the traditional family "caring" role need particular help if they are to change the pattern of their marriage and fulfil a more dual role. One problem these women may face, after many years away from work, is a lack of confidence and the feeling that they are out of date (or, in fact, actually are out of date). It is in the interest of employers and the wider community to provide opportunities for these women to be brought up to date with current developments. This might best be done by professional associations or, indeed, by work organizations providing courses for updating ex-employees who have temporarily left employment to raise a family. As Fogarty *et al.* (1971) have suggested: "The important thing in the interests of both employers and of young mothers themselves is to minimize the interruption to a highly qualified woman's career and to keep her as closely in touch as possible with her particular world of work." Any help the industrial organization can give its former employees in maintaining their skills may pay off greatly in the future, not only in terms of "goodwill" but in reducing costs of retraining or initial training of replacement staff. As far as the question of confidence is concerned, this can be achieved during the updating activity or by specialized courses prior to retraining or updating, depending on the length of time between the termination of full employment and the return to work.

Maternity and paternity leave

What many women at work need, if they are preparing to have a family, is some sense of security about their job. In this respect, it seems only sensible to have some reasonable maternity leave with a guaranteed right to return to work after it, and with some financial security during the leave period. Most countries in the European Community have guarantees against dismissal during pregnancy, a guarantee of paid maternity leave (usually between 8 and 12 weeks, and up to 6 months in many Eastern European countries), and guarantees of the right to return to work either immediately following the period of paid maternity leave or unpaid leave after some prearranged return period (in some cases up to 2–3 years later). Different countries have different arrangements in this respect (see Davidson and Cooper, 1984).

Paternity leave is also particularly important in the changing circumstances of the family. Few organizations provide this contemporary innovation, but many will have to consider it in the near future if they want to deal more systematically with what may end up, if ignored, as an uncontrolled absenteeism problem in the years ahead. Dual-career families will increasingly need the flexibility of short-leave periods, and the provision of leave for both men and women should help to ease the problem.

Ethnic minorities at work

The UK is a multiracial and multicultural society. As in many multicultural societies, we find incidences of discrimination, inequality and certain injustices (Alderfer and Thomas, 1988). The workplace is no exception to this rule, with many ethnic minorities suffering at all stages of the employment process, in recruitment, selection, career development, type of job, etc. We will focus in this section on the problems of the ethnic minorities, which in the UK context refers to people of Asian, African and Caribbean descent. In this regard, we will be drawing on the excellent work of Iles and Auluck (1991) for this review of the experience of ethnic workers in Britain.

Ethnic minorities in the workforce

Much of the information we can glean on ethnic workers comes from the Labour Force Survey, published by the Department of Employment (1988), which was based on a survey of 60,000 households between 1985 and 1987. In this survey, it was discovered that nearly 5% of the working population is from the ethnic minorities (African, Afro-Caribbean or Asian origin). It was also found that significantly more individuals from these groups, as opposed to the indigenous white population, are unemployed and less economically active. If we take male employment, for example, 61% of ethnic males are economically active, while the figure for white males is 84%. In addition, for nearly all age groups, nearly twice as many of these minorities are unemployed than their white counterparts. However, more recent figures suggest that unemployment rates among minority groups are declining at a faster rate than for whites. This increase in employment, however, is in the secondary labour market, casual employment and lower paid jobs.

Although the unemployment and activity rates of ethnic women are comparable to their male counterparts, in contrast to white females, they tend to be more economically active later in life, particularly Afro-Caribbean women (Department of Employment, 1988). Nevertheless, ethnic women have been found to earn significantly less than white women, and ethnic women graduates earn only 71% of their white counterparts (Breugel, 1989). Also, those women from minority groups who work are more likely to be found in manual jobs, in full-time employment, and in jobs below their qualification level (Breugel, 1989).

Discrimination against ethnic minorities at work

In the UK, there seems to be substantial evidence of racial discrimination in the workplace against ethnic minorities (Smith, 1976). In a study by the Commission for Racial Equality (1985) in Leicester, it was found that significantly more white applicants for jobs at a shopping centre were successful than applicants from other ethnic groups, even when their qualifications and experience were similar. Another study by Brown and Gay (1985) found that ethnic applicants matched to whites in terms of gender, experience and qualifications were less successful in being called for interview in three major UK cities. Much of these studies suggest that it is the acceptability of the applicants in terms of white standards, such as attitudes, appearance, etc., that decide their fate (Jenkins, 1986). This particularly adversely affects ethnic applicants during the recruitment and selection process.

This not only applies to blue-collar workers, but also to graduates. In a study of non-university graduates (Brennan and McGeevor, 1988), it was found that less than 50% of ethnic graduates were employed 12 months after graduation, whereas over 70% of whites were in full-time employment. In addition, it has been found that ethnic university graduates (Johnes and Taylor, 1989) were significantly less likely to find employment after graduation, and a significant number were still unemployed 6 months after obtaining their qualifications.

It will not be surprising to many that the major professions contain few people from the ethnic minorities. It was found, for instance, by the Commission for Racial Equality (1987), that in the accounting profession white applicants were significantly more successful than their equally qualified ethnic counterparts, that all partners in these firms were white and that 95% of the professional staff were white. This also applies to some extent in education, the police service, nursing (in terms of senior nursing jobs), etc. (Commission for Racial Equality, 1988a,b; Oakley, 1987). In the USA, it has also been found that progress toward middle and senior management positions for ethnic minorities is slow or in some industries non-existent (Fernandez, 1975). This is also the case in the UK, with very few attending appropriate management courses in higher education and few employed in the larger organizations.

Problems faced by ethnic minorities at work

There is a range of problems faced by minorities in the workplace. First, the selection and recruitment process is biased against them in one form or another. Secondly, they have very few role models in the work environment who could mentor them and socialize them towards organizational life. Thirdly, they don't get the feedback they need in terms of performance appraisal to guide them in climbing of career ladders. Fourthly, employing organizations don't know how to deal with subtle discrimination at work from bosses and colleagues alike. This is not helped by differentiation in pay, conditions and training and development for ethnic minorities found in some companies in some industries, and at all levels.

What can be done to help ethnic minorities at work?

Iles and Auluck (1991) make a number of very useful suggestions about what can be done to help the ethnic minorities at work. First, organizations should have recruitment initiatives to employ more members of the ethnic minorities. This is a likely scenario in any case given the demographic downturn of the 1990s in the UK. Secondly, they suggest that more systematic or formalized selection procedures should be introduced to minimize selection bias and match the skills, qualifications and personal characteristics of the applicants to the job itself. In this regard, it is particularly important to train selection interviewers to be aware of their implicit biases and possible discriminatory practices (Toplis, 1983). Assessment centres may also prove useful to minimize the impact of the interview, using multiple activities and approaches to selection. This kind of training could also be extended to "equality training" for work groups, where work teams could explore the ways in which they subtly utilize discriminatory practices and behaviours in the course of their productive activity. Thirdly, it is also vital to encourage more accurate and less biased performance appraisal at work. It has been found time and time again (Schmitt and Lappin, 1980) that assessors are biased or have more confidence in appraising people similar to themselves. Unfortunately, white and ethnic workers are frequently assessed against different performance criteria, which will ultimately affect their development and advancement. And, finally, one ought to consider the issue of "positive action" in recruiting ethnic minorities in the workplace. This is a controversial area, which has been the policy of the US for decades, but has only been recently discussed in the UK. Positive action at least can provide the first steps in equality of opportunities for minority groups in our society, and should be given a fair hearing, examining in detail the US experience.

The disabled worker

There has always been a confusion in people's minds about the differences between disability and handicap. Haggard (1985) has provided a useful differentiation: "disability refers to a reduced repertoire of generally valuable biological, physical and social skills ... handicap refers to the reduced personal, social, educational, economic and cultural opportunities available as a consequence". With the introduction of new technology, which now makes a disability less of a handicap, more and more is being done to encourage and develop the disabled in the workplace.

McHugh (1991) provides a very thorough and useful summary of the problems and opportunities for the disabled, including those suffering from epilepsy, deafness, blindness, heart disease, motor deficits, severe learning difficulties, neurological disorders and many others. He outlines how the disabled are stigmatized in society and in the workplace, but how efforts are being made to "normalize" them by providing vocational training, career opportunities, etc. However, we still have the problem in people's minds about the cost and benefits associated with providing these opportunities, particularly among senior managers, to whom the costs loom large. Nevertheless, the demographic changes taking place in the 1990s will mean that we will increasingly need man/womanpower from many sources not considered in the past. In addition, as Hurley (1989) has suggested, the movement towards computer-aided design, office technology, computer-aided learning and the wide range of computer-assisted production systems will mean "a shift from manual bodily-dependent work, towards more mental ideas-dependent work". As McHugh (1991) highlights, this will mean "more and more work will be done from home through a link to a central computer, and there will be considerable flexibility of working hours and days". This may mean that the "homebound" disabled will have more contact with people outside their previously bounded world, although not as much as they would if they were able to operate in a centralized work environment (Flack, 1981).

The future will also hold more opportunities for the disabled in terms of learning networks through computers, or equipment that will enable the otherwise severely handicapped to use equipment or, from a work point of view, be more mobile, by the touch of a computer key. But to provide the opportunities, equipment, facilities and infrastructure, we will need the willing participation and involvement of senior management to invest in the future of the disabled. Up until now, this process has been very slow and difficult to progress, because of management's concern about the "bottom line", the investment in equipment in terms of its payoff. The changes in demography and society's attitude towards the disabled are rapidly developing, together with the improved cost–benefit ratio, which should mean that the 1990s will be the start of the decade to create a role in the workplace for the disabled: not a marginal role, in "disabled-type" jobs, but in all walks of work life. As Lord Snowdon once remarked, "just because someone is disabled doesn't mean he or she doesn't have a range of other talents. If you mention the names of Milton, Beethoven and Nelson, probably the last thing you would think they had in common was that they were disabled" (McHugh, 1991).

Summary

There are a number of groups of workers who are obviously less advantaged than others. These include women, the ethnic minorities and the disabled. By any measures we can see that members of these groups have relatively poor access, opportunities and career prospects. We need to ensure that these groups are provided with the opportunities, facilities and resources necessary for them to enter and develop in the workforce. This might be helped by the so-called "demographic timebomb" of the 1990s. This will be greatly helped by more systematic and valid personnel selection techniques, which minimize inherent bias (see Chapter 7) by flexible working arrangements to accommodate the disabled and working mothers, by "flexi-place" as well as flexitime, and by new technology which meets the needs of people working from home or is more "user friendly". The UK workforce will, in the short and medium term, need to utilize all its human resources if it is to survive as a competitive economy. In the longer term, it must begin truly to grapple with the problems of discrimination of minorities at work, if we are to survive as a society.

References

Alderfer, C. and Thomas, D. A. (1988). The significance of race and ethnicity for understanding organisation behaviour. In C. L. Cooper and I. T. Robertson (Eds), *International Review of I/O Psychology, 1988*, pp. 1–41. Chichester: John Wiley.

Brennan, J. and McGeevor, P. (1988). *Graduates at Work: Degree Courses and the Labour Market*. London: Jessica Kingsley.

Breugel, I. (1989). Sex and race in the labour market. *Feminist Review, 32* (Summer), 49–68.

Brown, C. and Gay, P. (1985). *Racial Discrimination 17 Years after the Act*. London: Policy Studies Institute.

Commission for Racial Equality (1985). *Positive Action and Equal Opportunity in Employment*. London: CRE.

Commission for Racial Equality (1987). *Chartered Accountancy Training Contracts: Report of a Formal Investigation*. London: CRE.

Commission for Racial Equality (1988a). *Medical School Admissions: Report of a Formal Investigation*. London: CRE.

Commission for Racial Equality (1988b). *Ethnic Minority School Teachers: A Survey in Eight Local Education Authorities*. London: CRE.

Cooper, C. L., Cooper, R. D. and Eaker, L. H. (1988). *Living with Stress*. Harmondsworth: Penguin.

Davidson, M. J. and Cooper, C. L. (1980a). The extra pressure of women executives. *Personnel Management*, June, 48–51.

Davidson, M. J. and Cooper, C. L. (1980b). Type A coronary prone behaviour and stress in senior female managers and administrators. *Journal of Occupational Medicine, 22*, 801–806.

Davidson, M. J. and Cooper C. L. (1984). *Working Women: An International Survey*. New York: John Wiley.

Department of Employment (1988). *Labour Force Survey*. London: HMSO.

Fernandez, J. P. (1975). *Black Managers in White Corporations*. New York: John Wiley.

Flack, J. (1981). Minicomputers and the disabled user. *Bulletin of The British Psychological Society, 34*, 209.

Fogarty, M. P., Rapoport, R. and Rapoport, R. N. (1971). *Sex, Career and Family*. Beverly Hills, Calif.: Sage.

Foster, L. W., Latack, J. C. and Riendl, L. J. (1979). The effects and promises of the shortened work week. *Proceedings of the Academy of Management Annual Conference*, New Orleans, USA, August.

Friedman, M. and Rosenman, R. H. (1974). *Type A Behaviour and Your Heart*. London, Wildwood House.

Haggard, M. P. (1985). Concepts of impairment, disability and handicap. *Bulletin of The British Psychological Society, 38*, 83.

Hall, D. T. and Hall, F. (1980). Stress and the two career couple. In C. L. Cooper and R. L. Payne (Eds), *Current Concerns in Occupational Stress*. Chichester: John Wiley.

Haynes, S. G. and Feinleib, M. (1980). Women, work and coronary heart disease: Prospective findings from the Framingham Heart Study. *American Journal of Public Health, 70*, 133–141.

Horner, K. (1970). *Femininity and Successful Achievement: A Basic Inconsistency. Feminine Personality and Conflict*. San Francisco, Calif.: Brooks/Cole.

Hurley, J. (1989). The new technologies and the changing nature and organization of work. *The Irish Journal of Psychology, 10* (3), 368–380.

Iles, P. and Auluck, R. (1991). The experience of black workers. In M. J. Davidson and J. Earnshaw (Eds), *Vulnerable Workers* Chichester: John Wiley.

Jenkins, R. (1986). *Racism and Recruitment: Managers, Organisations and Equal Opportunities in the Labour Market*. Cambridge: Cambridge University Press.

Johnes, G. and Taylor, J. (1989). Ethnic minorities in the graduate labour market. *New Community*, *15* (4), 527–536.

Lancet (1979). Women, work and coronary heart disease (editorial), 12 July 1979, pp. 76–77.

Larwood, L. and Wood, M. (1979). *Women in Management*. London: Lexington Books.

Lewis, S. and Cooper, C. L. (1989). *Career Couples*. London: Unwin Hyman.

McClelland, D. C. (1975). *The Inner Experience*. New York: Irvington.

McHugh, M. F. (1991). Disabled workers – psychosocial issues. In M. J. Davidson and J. Earnshaw (Eds), *Vulnerable Workers*. Chichester: John Wiley.

Mills, C. (1959). *The Power Elite*. New York: Oxford University Press.

Newberry, P., Weissman, M. and Myers, J. (1979). Working wives and housewives: Do they differ in mental status and social adjustment? *American Journal of Orthopsychiatry*, *49*, 282–291.

Oakley, R. (1987). *Employment in Police Forces: A Survey of Equal Opportunities*. London: Commission for Racial Equality.

Rosenman, R. H., Friedman, M. and Strauss, R. (1966). CHD in the Western Collaborative Group Study. *Journal of the American Medical Association*, *195*, 86–92.

Schmitt, N. and Lappin, I. (1980). Race and sex as determinants of the mean and variance of performance ratings. *Journal of Applied Psychology*, *65*, 428–435.

Smith, D. (1976). *The Facts of Racial Disadvantage*. London: Political and Economic Planning.

Staines, G. L., Pleck, J. H., Shepard, L. and O'Connor, P. (1978). *Wives' Employment Status and Marital Adjustment*. University of Michigan: Institute of Social Research Working Paper.

Toplis, J. W. C. (1983). Training interviewers to avoid unfair discrimination. Paper presented to the British Psychological Society, London, December.

Welner, A., Marten, S., Wochnick, E., Davis, M., Fishman, R. and Clayton, J. (1979). Psychiatric disorders among professional women. *Archives of General Psychiatry*, *36*, 169–173.

CHAPTER 6

The contents and context of assessment

Introduction

Two main principles underlie the roles that personnel selection and assessment procedures play in organizational settings. The first principle is that there are individual differences between people (e.g. differences in aptitudes, skills and other personal qualities). This simple principle leads to the very important conclusion that people are not equally suited to all jobs and suggests that procedures for matching people and jobs could have important organizational benefits. The second principle is that future behaviour is, at least partly, predictable. The goal of selection and assessment activities is to match people to jobs and ensure the best possible levels of future job performance; the belief that *future job performance* can be estimated is an important facet of the second principle mentioned above. The essential function of personnel selection and assessment procedures (e.g. interviews, psychometric tests) is to provide means of estimating the likely future job performance of candidates.

Since the early part of this century, a great deal of research within work psychology has concentrated on the development and evaluation of personnel selection procedures. Much of this work will be considered in the next chapter. This chapter is not concerned with personnel selection methods as such, but focuses on those aspects of psychological theory and practice that underlie the successful application of personnel selection procedures. The major topics covered in this chapter are related to the two principles given above. First, the topic of individual differences, particularly in ability and personality, is dealt with. Next, because personnel selection involves the matching of people to the requirements of jobs, job analysis is covered. The final part of the chapter concentrates on topics concerned with the development of procedures for predicting future job performance, specifically validation processes and the measurement of job performance.

Individual differences

Although there are many approaches to conceptualizing and understanding human individual differences, only one kind of approach (which represents individual differences as measurable, structural concepts) has been widely influential in personnel selection and assessment research and practice. This approach, which has been applied to both cognitive abilities and personality, is the trait-factor analytic approach. The basis of trait theory is that there are cross-situational generalities in behaviour. In other words, personality traits explain why people behave in similar ways in different circumstances. This emphasis on the person as the source of individual differences contrasts most sharply with the emphasis in behaviour theory on the situation as the source of individual differences in behaviour (see Chapter 2).

In their attempts to explain personality, psychologists have tended to emphasize the role of either internal (person) factors or external (situational) factors. This does not necessarily mean that such theorists do not accept the importance of both situation and person factors, merely that their focus of attention has been on one or the other.

Recent theoretical and research work has developed an important, more sophisticated concept than the idea that both people and situations are important. This is the idea that people and situations interact with each other to determine behaviour. An influential current theory which adopts an interactionist perspective is Bandura's (1977, 1986) social cognitive (previously referred to as social learning) theory. The impact of this theory can be seen in various fields of work psychology, including behaviour analysis and modification (Chapter 9) and training and learning (Chapter 14).

Intelligence

In the early years of the twentieth century, two French psychologists, Alfred Binet and Theodore Simon, developed what is generally accepted as the first satisfactory test of human intelligence. At the turn of the nineteenth century, France, in common with other industrialized nations, had introduced compulsory education. Most of the children entering school seemed well able to benefit from the regular schools. Some were perhaps in need of special help, but could be dealt with by the regular system. A third group, however, were retarded to the point of being unable to benefit from the regular system. It was not always easy to identify the children in need of special treatment, and the test developed by Binet and Simon was intended to help in identifying these children by assessing their intellectual capabilities.

The approach adopted by Binet and Simon is still the basis for contemporary intelligence tests. In essence, Binet and Simon considered that intelligence could be measured by assessing a person's ability to answer a carefully selected collection of questions. Although the questions in modern tests (see Table 6.1) sometimes differ from those used by Binet and Simon, the principle of sampling behaviour on a carefully selected set of tasks is still at the basis of most tests. Clearly, by sampling behaviour one runs the risk of drawing false conclusions about a person – perhaps because of the particular questions asked, the circumstances in which the test is taken, or for various other reasons.

Table 6.1 Some items from an intelligence test

Q 7 Mountain is to molehill as valley is to . . . .
       1   2   3   4   5
      hollow chasm hill plain mound

Q 8 The third member of this
     series is omitted. What is it? 0.1, 0.7, . . ., 34.3, 240.1

Q 9 Which one of the five words on the right bears a similar relation to each of the
     two words on the left?

                          1   2   3   4   5
        Class; shape   Rank Grade Analyse Size Form

Q10 Here are five classes. Write down the number of the class which contain two,
     and two only, of the other four classes:

        1   2   3   4   5
        Terriers Mammals "Scotties" Dogs Canines

Q11 Sniff is to handkerchief as shiver is to . . .

        1   2 3   4   5
        blow fire catarhh burn sneeze

Q12 How many members of the following series are missing?

        1, 2, 5, 6, 7, 11, 12, . . ., 20, 21, 22, 23

Q13 Which one of the five words on the right bears a similar relation to each of the
     two words on the left?

                         1   2   3   4   5
        Stream; tolerate   Brook Contribute Bear Support Pour

Q14 Working from the left, divide the fourth whole number by the fifth fraction:

        8, 6, 5/7, 3, 9, 2/9, 3/8, 1, 17/32, 4/9

Source: The AH5 Test.

Binet and Simon certainly recognized that test scores alone were not enough and they proposed that, before any decision about a child was taken, other types of assessment should also be made.

Since the pioneering work of Binet and Simon, psychologists have carried out a considerable amount of work in their attempts to measure intelligence and to understand its structure. Much of this work makes use of statistical methods, developed to aid research into human intelligence. These statistical methods (the principal ones are correlation and factor analysis) are now used in many disciplines. An elementary understanding of these methods is essential to the comprehension of the psychology of human mental abilities. Correlation is dealt with in Chapter 4 and the reader who is unfamiliar with correlation and the calculation and interpretation of correlation coefficients should consult that chapter before going further. Factor analysis, because of its important influence on theoretical work in intelligence, will be outlined at the appropriate point in this chapter.

Structure of intelligence

Human beings are capable of showing considerable ability in a wide range of pursuits. For some (e.g. a bookmaker's clerk), considerable numerical skill is required; for others (e.g. a journalist), the ability to use words correctly and fluently is important; while yet others (e.g. an architect) need the ability to visualize objects in three dimensions. It would be possible to suggest many further occupational areas and associated abilities. The important point, however, is that it may be superficial to consider intelligence as a single or unitary attribute that can be represented by an overall measure.

Table 6.2 shows a typical correlation matrix derived by intercorrelating the results of a group of people in a collection of tests. Notice that although some of the correlations are smaller than others, none of them is negative. In other words, people who do well in one test, do well (or at least not very badly) in the others. The results in Table 6.2 are typical of those obtained when people are tested on a wide range of intellectual tasks. Results such as this led Spearman (1927) to propose the so-called two-factor theory of the structure of intelligence. This suggested that an underlying factor of general intelligence ("g") was helpful in performance in all areas of human ability. The existence of such a factor would explain why there is a persistent positive correlation between such a wide range of tests of human intellectual ability. Spearman explained the fact that performance in different types of test varied by proposing that, as well as "g", there was a series of test specific factors ("s").

Other researchers, notably Thurstone (1938), opposed Spearman's view. Thurstone's view was that intelligence is made up of a loosely related set of "primary abilities" and that the relationships between the various aspects of human performance could be explained more effectively by these underlying primary abilities than by a general factor or "g". Thurstone proposed 12 or so "primary mental abilities", including:

1. *Verbal comprehension* (v): important in reading, comprehension and verbal reasoning.

2. *Space or visualization* (s): concerned with the perception and visualization of objects in space.

3. *Number* (n): the speed and accuracy of straightforward arithmetic calculation.

Table 6.2   Correlations between some intellectual tests

	Maths	English	Geography	IQ
Maths test				
English test	+0.51			
Geography test	+0.52	+0.34		
IQ test	+0.55	+0.50	+0.48	

Source: Adapted from Satterly (1979).

Table 6.3   Sizes of correlations in a correlation matrix

	A			B		
	1	2	3	4	5	6
1 Verbal reasoning	X					
2 Vocabulary		X				
3 Spelling	High		X			
4 Spatial reasoning	░	░	░	X		
5 Drawing accuracy	░	░	░		X	
6 Geometry	░	░	░	High		X

Factor analysis

Investigations of the structure of human abilities usually involved the use of a statistical technique known as factor analysis. Factor analysis is a mathematical technique that can be used to analyse a correlation matrix. It will show how each of the tests used to produce the original correlation matrix can be divided up and allocated to a smaller collection of underlying factors. Table 6.3 shows a correlation matrix. To simplify things, the actual correlation coefficients have not been given, but merely an indication of where the correlations have high values.

The correlations between the tests in group A (1–3) are high, as are the correlations between the tests in group B (4–6). The correlations of tests from group A with tests from group B are only moderate. What this pattern of correlations suggests is:

1.   The tests in group A all have something in common (probably a "verbal" factor).
2.   The tests in group B also have something in common (probably a "spatial" factor).

Notice also that all of the tests are correlated positively with each other (the correlations in the hatched areas although lower are still positive). These positive correlations between all of the tests suggest:

3.   The existence of some factor common to all tests (presumably "g").

Table 6.4 shows how a factor analysis for this matrix might appear. The factor analysis provides a numerical statement of the factors underlying the correlation matrix, and the loading of each test on each factor indicates the extent to which the test involves this factor. The first test (verbal reasoning), for example, loads heavily on factor I ("g"), less heavily on factor II (verbal) and not at all on factor III (spatial).

A hierarchy of abilities

The factor analysis in Table 6.4 produces both a general intelligence factor (which would offer support for Spearman) and some specific factors (supporting

Table 6.4 The results of a factor analysis

	Factors		
	I (g)	II (verbal)	III (spatial)
Verbal reasoning	0.6	0.5	
Vocabulary	0.7	0.4	
Spelling	0.8	0.3	
Spatial reasoning	0.4		0.6
Drawing accuracy	0.5		0.5
Geometry	0.5		0.7

Thurstone). Some of the differences between the theories of Spearman and his followers and Thurstone and his were due to the use of different techniques of factor analysis, the use of different samples for investigation, and so on. In fact, a reconciliation of the two theories is not as difficult as it might at first seem.

The "compromise" theory was proposed by Burt (1940) and elaborated by Vernon (1961, 1969). The hierarchical organization of mental abilities that they proposed (see Fig. 6.1) incorporates both general and specific factors. At the top of the hierarchy is "g", the broad general ability factor that is involved in all intellectual performance. But intellectual performance is not explained by "g" alone. Differences of intermediate generality are also important, between verbal–numerical–education (v:ed), for example, and practical–mechanical–spatial–physical (k:m) factors. In turn, the major group factors may be subdivided into increasingly less general minor and specific factors. In general, psychologists in the UK have adopted this hierarchical view of mental abilities. American psychologists have been inclined to adopt a view more in line with Thurstone's original ideas and have continued to search for related specific abilities. Guilford (1967), for instance, developed a "structure of the intellect" model that classifies abilities by operation, product and content (see Fig. 6.2). Guilford argued and attempted to demonstrate that it should be possible to produce tests that are independent (i.e. not intercorrelated) for each cell in the cube shown in Fig. 6.2, i.e. 120 separate abilities in all.

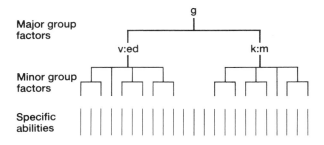

6.1 The hierarchical structure of human abilities.

6.2 Guilford's structure of the intellect model (from Guilford, 1967).

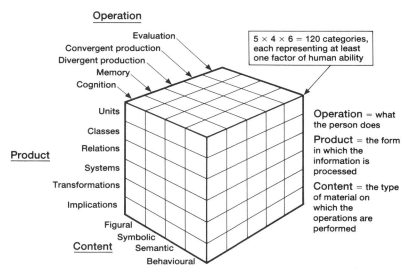

Operation

Evaluation
Convergent production
Divergent production
Memory
Cognition

5 × 4 × 6 = 120 categories, each representing at least one factor of human ability

Units
Classes
Relations
Systems
Transformations
Implications

Product

Operation = what the person does

Product = the form in which the information is processed

Content = the type of material on which the operations are performed

Figural
Symbolic
Content   Semantic
Behavioural

Intelligence tests

So far, we have managed to discuss the underlying structure of intelligence without directly confronting the problem of what intelligence actually is! The defining of intelligence presents problems for psychologists, and to this day there is no universally accepted definition. Many psychologists will settle for the definition first proposed by Boring (1923, p. 35): "Intelligence is what intelligence tests measure." In fact, this definition is not as meaningless as it seems at first sight. Tests of general intelligence are designed to examine the ability of people to carry out certain mental operations. The various tests of general intelligence ("g") are all interrelated and people obtain similar scores in different tests. Thus "g" is a quality that can be measured reliably and with some precision; but as Eysenck and Kamin (1981, p. 25) have pointed out, "... we cannot at this stage say that 'g' is the same as the term is understood by the man in the street". Eysenck, however, clearly considers that what intelligence tests measure is pretty close to what most people think of as intelligence. Others such as Kamin (Eysenck and Kamin, 1981) hold a different view, and argue that IQ tests do not provide a good measure of what most people regard as intelligence.

Both of these authors are eminent psychologists but hold quite different views about our current ability to measure intelligence. They do not disagree that the available tests measure something with reasonable accuracy – they disagree fundamentally about what such tests do measure.

Regardless of whether the available tests measure what we think of as intelligence or some other qualities, tests of intelligence and specific abilities have been used with some success in personnel selection (see Chapter 7). Many tests of specific abilities (mechanical, verbal, numerical, etc.) and of "g" can be used to provide quite good predictions of people's competence in certain jobs.

Tests have been criticized on various grounds. One criticism is based on the argument that intelligence tests do not measure pure underlying intelligence but a mixture of it and of taught or acquired knowledge.

Vernon (1956, p. 157) distinguished between intelligence and attainments in the following way:

> ... the former refers to the more general qualities of thinking –
> comprehension, level of concept developing, reasoning and grasping
> relations – qualities which seem to be acquired largely in the course of
> normal development without specific tuition; whereas the latter refers
> more to knowledge and skills which are directly trained.

Unfortunately, it is one thing to make such a distinction in writing but quite another to put it into practice by developing tests that are "pure" tests of one or other factor. Proponents of intelligence tests believe that this can be done; others consider that it has not been done properly and is probably impossible.

In the personnel selection context, tests are also criticized because they are biased in favour of certain ethnic or cultural groups. Consider Vernon's description of intelligence given above – as qualities which seem to be acquired largely in the course of normal development. What is the "normal environment" in which this "normal development" takes place? White middle-class family groups, some critics would say! The argument of cultural bias asserts that the intellectual development that takes place naturally is dependent on the specific environmental and cultural background in which a person develops; so that perfectly intelligent people from certain socio-economic or ethnic backgrounds will fail to develop the normal qualities assessed in the tests. The consequence will be that, despite their underlying intelligence, the tests will label them as unintelligent.

A rational and unbiased examination of the advantages and disadvantages of psychological tests in the light of criticisms such as the ones raised above is of value to both the science of psychology and to society. The criticism that intelligence tests are biased against certain ethnic groups is, at least in part, based on the frequently replicated finding that ethnic minority groups (mostly black Americans) produce lower scores on cognitive tests than whites (see Schmitt and Noe, 1986, for a review of evidence). Despite these sub-group differences, the prevailing view of the scientific community is that it is not unfair to use such tests for selection decision making. In essence, this conclusion is based on the finding that although there are consistent differences between sub-groups in mean scores, the accuracy of prediction of the tests (i.e. the prediction of future levels of work performance) is the same for different ethnic groups. Most of the evidence on the fairness or otherwise of cognitive testing in selection is from studies in the USA, and such data may need to be interpreted differently in the European context.

There is a wide range of different tests available to measure general intelligence (i.e. Spearman's "g" factor) and various specific abilities (mechanical, spatial, numerical, etc.), and several publishers of psychological tests are operating in the UK. Evidence concerning the value of cognitive tests and the fairness of such tests is discussed in Chapter 7.

Trait views of personality

Psychoanalytic theories of human personality such as Freud's are often criticized by other psychologists for their lack of scientific rigour, lack of satisfactory definition of key concepts and the fact that the theories either do not generate testable predictions about human behaviour or, when predictions are made, that they do not work out in practice. One of the strongest critics of these theories is Eysenck (e.g. Eysenck and Wilson, 1973), who has developed an alternative approach to personality based on the rigorous application of scientific methods and statistical analysis. Eysenck, working in the UK, and the British-born psychologist Cattell, working in the USA, pursue an approach that attempts to uncover the underlying personality traits which they believe can be used to explain human behaviour in a variety of different situations.

Trait theories perhaps come closest to describing the structure of personality in a way that matches our everyday use of the term. Trait theories use words such as shy, outgoing, tense and extroverted to describe the basic factors of human personality. These basic elements – traits – represent predispositions to behave in certain ways, in a variety of different situations. In the UK, the main exponent of the approach is Hans Eysenck (1970, 1981; Eysenck and Eysenck, 1985).

Trait theorists such as Eysenck (1970) and Cattell (1965) use the technique of factor analysis in attempts to identify the underlying structure of human personality. Eysenck argues that personality is best understood in terms of a hierarchical organization (see Fig. 6.3). The underlying building blocks for personality can be represented by a small number of basic dimensions (types) that have been identified from the factor analysis of large numbers of personality questionnaires asking people how they behave and feel in various situations. Two major dimensions emerging consistently from factor analytic studies conducted by Eysenck and others are *extroversion* and *neuroticism*. Extroverts are lively, sociable, excitable people and neurotics are characterized by high levels of anxiety and tension. Two important points should be borne in mind in relation to these dimensions. The first is that they are continuous dimensions and most people are not extreme in either extroversion or neuroticism. The second point is that the dimensions are independent; in other words, someone's position on one dimension bears no relationship to his or her position on the other.

As well as providing empirical evidence concerning basic human personality factors, Eysenck's work provides a theory concerning the origins and development of personality. This involves the impact of both inherited, neurological differences and environmental influences due to the processes of conditioning and socialization. The main measuring instruments associated with Eysenck's theory are the Eysenck Personality Inventory (EPI: Eysenck and Eysenck, 1964), a self-report questionnaire that measures the factors extroversion and neuroticism, and the Eysenck Personality Questionnaire (EPQ: Eysenck and Eysenck, 1975) which measures extroversion and introversion, together with a third factor – psychoticism.

Working in the USA, Cattell, using similar statistical techniques to those of Eysenck, also pursues a trait approach to personality. One notable difference between the two theorists is the number of stable factors that they feel need to be

6.3 The hierarchical organization of personality (from Le François, 1980; adapted from Eysenck, H. J., 1967, *The Biological Basis of Personality*, Charles C. Thomas).

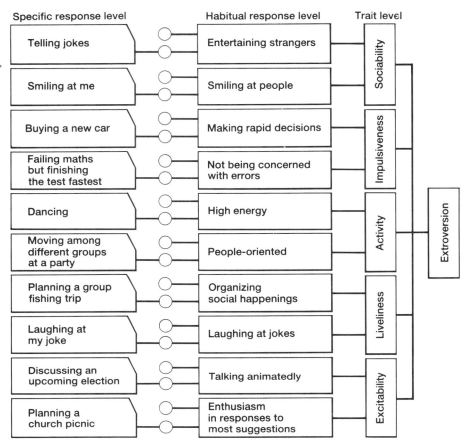

used to describe and measure personality structure. Although neither Cattell nor Eysenck base theories entirely on data from self-report questionnaires, some of the differences between them become apparent when the questionnaires used by each of them are compared. The EPI uses two dimensions (extroversion–introversion and neuroticism), and Eysenck recognizes the existence of a third important factor – psychoticism. Cattell's main personality questionnaire (the 16PF) includes 16 personality factors. To some extent, the differences are due to the different statistical procedures that the researchers employ.

Research exploring the similarities and differences between the models of Eysenck, Cattell and other trait-orientated theorists has produced some fairly consistent evidence of the existence of five (the so-called big five) major personality factors. This suggests that perhaps the EPI/EPQ focuses on a more limited set of factors than is useful, whereas the 16PF uses too many. It is certainly true that several attempts to replicate Cattell's 16 factors have not been very successful (see, e.g., Howarth and Browne, 1971; Kline and Barrett, 1983) and have generally suggested that a smaller number of factors fit the data more efficiently.

Although the big five factors appear consistently in factor analytic studies of personality, there is reluctance among some researchers to be too specific about defining and specifying the nature of the factors. They may, however, be represented crudely by the following:

- introversion–extroversion (surgency);
- consideration, agreeableness;
- conscientiousness, carefulness;
- emotional stability, anxiety, neuroticism; and
- intelligence, inquiry, openness to experience.

The articles by Digman and Takemoto-Chock (1981) and McCrae and Costa (1985) provide more information on this line of research and further details on the five factors.

Personality tests

Although several studies have shown that the factors measured by many personality tests can be related to the big five, the tests themselves provide scores on a variety of personality dimensions. For example, as already mentioned, the EPQ assesses three personality factors (extroversion, neuroticism and psychoticism). Table 6.5 gives some information on the better known personality questionnaires available in the UK.

As with all kinds of psychological measures, personality tests need to satisfy various well-established psychometric criteria before they can be considered to be acceptable measuring instruments. These criteria are concerned with assessing the extent to which the test measures what it is intended to

Table 6.5 Personality questionnaires

Instrument	Personality characteristics measured
Eysenck Personality Questionnaire (EPQ: Eysenck and Eysenck, 1964)	Extroversion, Neuroticism (or emotional stability) Psychoticism
The Sixteen PF (16 PF: Cattell *et al.*, 1970). Several versions of short/long forms are available and measure second-order personality factors, etc., in addition to the 16 factors mentioned here	16 personality factors, e.g. submissiveness (mild, humble, easily led, docile, accommodating); self-assurance (placid, serene, secure, complacent); tender-mindedness (sensitive, clinging, over-protected)
The Occupational Preference Questionnaire (OPQ: Saville and Holdsworth Ltd, 1984)	30 personality dimensions are measured in the most detailed version of the OPQ (the Concept Model). Other versions/models of the questionnaires are available. Illustrative personality dimensions are: Caring (considerate to others, helps those in need, sympathetic, tolerant) Emotional control (restrained in showing emotions, keeps feelings back, avoids outbursts) Forward planning (prepares well in advance, enjoys target-setting, forecasts trends, plans projects)

measure (the issue of validity) and the precision or consistency of measurement that the test achieves (reliability). These concepts are discussed in relation to personnel selection and psychometric testing later in this chapter.

Job analysis

Job analysis procedures are designed to produce systematic information about jobs, including the nature of the work performed, the equipment used, the working conditions and the position of the job within the organization. It is worth noting that satisfactory job analyses are prerequisites for many decisions and activities that have a crucial influence on the lives of personnel within the organization, including the design and validation of personnel selection procedures, training and career development schemes, job design or redesign, job evaluation and safety. There is a wide range of techniques and procedures available, and Algera and Greuter (1989), Greuter and Algera (1989) and Spector *et al.* (1989) provide overviews and critical examinations of the major techniques.

Although not always clear-cut, there is an important distinction between job-orientated and worker-orientated job analysis procedures. As the term suggests, job-orientated procedures focus on the work itself, producing a description in terms of the equipment used, the end results or purposes of the jobs, resources and materials utilized, etc. By contrast, worker-orientated analyses concentrate on describing the psychological or behavioural requirements of the job, such as communicating, decision making and reasoning.

The sources of job analysis data may be divided into four categories:

- written material;
- job-holders' reports;
- colleagues' reports; and
- direct observation.

Written material

In many organizations, written job descriptions are available (except for newly created jobs) and can provide the analyst with useful information. It is worth checking by observation and other methods that available descriptions are up to date and provide comprehensive information about the job. If so, a great deal of time and effort may be saved. Unfortunately, in many organizations, existing job descriptions are rarely up to date, comprehensive or detailed enough. Published analyses of jobs may provide useful leads but are of limited value, because jobs analysed elsewhere are likely to be similar but not identical to the one under consideration. An accountant's, secretary's or production manager's job will vary considerably from one organization to another, perhaps in ways that are crucial. Other written material such as production data, organization charts, training manuals, job aids, etc., may also provide useful, additional information.

Job-holders' reports

Interviews in which job-holders are asked, through careful questioning, to give a description of their main tasks and how they carry them out provide extremely useful information, and such interviews are usually an essential element in any job analysis. On the other hand, it is difficult to be sure that all of the important aspects of the job have been covered by the interview and that the information provided by the job-holder is not too subjective, biased (owing to faulty memory perhaps) or even deliberately untrue.

Workers' reports may also be obtained by asking them to complete a diary or activity record. As this is done on a regular basis as the job is being carried out, it avoids problems associated with faulty memory, etc. It is, however, a difficult and time-consuming procedure. Stewart (1967) has provided an example of the use of this method to analyse the jobs of British managers.

Flanagan (1954) developed a procedure known as the critical incident technique. In brief, using this technique involves asking the interviewee to recall specific incidents of job behaviour that are characteristic of either very good or very poor performance on the job. This can provide the analyst with a clear grasp of the job behaviour(s) that are important and enable him or her to differentiate between good and poor job-holders – extremely useful information in the context of personnel selection!

McCormick *et al.* (1972) have produced the Position Analysis Questionnaire (PAQ), which is an example of a structured questionnaire approach to job analysis. The elements in the questionnaire are worker-orientated in that they focus on generalized aspects of human behaviour and are less tied to the technology of specific jobs. The PAQ consists of nearly 200 items organized into six major divisions:

- information input;
- mediation processes (i.e. the mental processes of reasoning, decision making, etc.);
- work output;
- interpersonal activities (i.e. relationships with others);
- work situation and job context; and
- miscellaneous aspects.

One problem with the PAQ is that it requires a fairly high level of reading ability on the part of respondents (Ash and Edgell, 1975). Nevertheless, the PAQ is an extremely well-researched and valuable means of analysing jobs.

The development work for the PAQ was carried out in the USA by McCormick and others, and the development of a British job analysis questionnaire has been a particularly welcome development. Banks and colleagues (Banks *et al.*, 1983; Banks, 1988) have developed the Job Components Inventory (JCI). This inventory focuses on both job and worker facets and the outputs from the analysis include quantified profiles of the absolute and relative skills required for the job under investigation. The JCI was developed within an education and training context and as yet it has not been used extensively with personnel selection.

A self-contained technique for analysis, which is job- rather than worker-orientated, has been described by Fine and Wiley (1974). Known as Functional Job Analysis (FJA), this approach makes use of a standardized language to describe what job-holders do and provides a means of examining the complexity and the orientation of the job. Orientation here is described as the extent to which the job is directed towards "data", "people" or "things" and, as a result of analysis, can be expressed in percentage terms. The basic unit of analysis in FJA is the task, i.e. an action or action sequence organized over time and designed to contribute to a specific end result or objective. Using a very similar definition of the task, Annett and others (Annett *et al.*, 1971; Shepherd, 1976) have developed a means of analysis known as Hierarchical Task Analysis (HTA). Because HTA is particularly useful in the development of training, this procedure is discussed in more detail in Chapter 14.

A popular procedure for collecting job analysis information in the UK involves the use of Kelly's (1955) repertory grid technique (e.g. Smith, 1980). This approach provides systematic worker-orientated data. It has an advantage over other means of obtaining worker-orientated data such as PAQ, in that it does not limit the responses of the job-holder by providing a prestructured set of categories.

Another more recent addition to the set of worker-orientated job analysis approaches is the Threshold Traits Analysis System (TTAS) developed by Lopez (Lopez *et al.*, 1981; Lopez, 1988). This approach groups 33 worker attributes into five major categories: physical, mental, learned, motivational and societal. The TTAS also provides a procedure for linking particular job functions with particular traits. This linking of required traits or worker attributes and job functions is clearly of great importance in the personnel selection context (see below).

Colleagues' reports

In addition to gleaning information directly from job-holders, it is useful to obtain data from subordinates, peers and superiors. For example, when collecting critical incident data the views of a job-holder, a subordinate and a superior on the nature of such critical incidents might provide for interesting comparisons.

For structured job analysis questionnaires, a comparison of the responses of job-holders and their supervisors provides a basis for assessing the (convergent) validity of the questionnaire. Although some studies have looked at other instruments (e.g. Banks and Miller, 1984, with the JCI), most of this work has used the PAQ. These studies have revealed reasonably good agreement between job incumbents and supervisors. A more puzzling and troublesome finding, however, has been the reasonably high correlations found between the PAQ results of job experts and naive raters, often students working from job titles, or written descriptions of the job (see, e.g., Friedman and Harvey, 1986). The concern raised by these findings is that even trained analysts' responses on the PAQ are influenced at least partly by commonly held stereotypes (hence the correlation with untrained raters working only from a job title) rather than entirely by valid and substantive job factors.

It is often useful to conduct a job analysis using a variety of methods rather than just one. On this basis, as well as being useful for personnel selection, the resulting information may be useful in other areas of the organization, such as training and development or job evaluation. One procedure that explicitly uses more than one method is Levine's (1983) Combination Job Analysis Method (C-JAM).

Direct observation

In any job analysis exercise, some direct observation of the job being carried out is invariably helpful. It is, of course, possible that the presence of the analyst may alter the job-holder's behaviour, and as with the approaches described earlier, the data obtained cannot be perfect. Yet data derived from observation, perhaps even from participant-observation, where the analyst does all or some of the job, can provide insights that no other method can.

Job analyses are usually best developed by using as many different approaches and means of data collection as possible and pooling the results.

Using job analysis information

The job analysis is used in a number of ways. A job description can be prepared from the job analysis data. It can be useful in the selection procedure to give candidates some understanding of the job and can also be used within the organization to provide information for training, job evaluation and other purposes. Bottomly (1983) has provided practical guidance on the development and use of job evaluation procedures. The job analysis also provides information that might be used when recruitment advertisements, etc., are prepared to attract candidates for the job. (Detailed advice on this topic is beyond the scope of the present book but further information may be found in Fordham, 1975.)

A personnel specification represents the demands of the job translated into human terms. It involves listing the essential criteria that candidates must satisfy and also those criteria that would exclude candidates from consideration. Moving from a job analysis to a clear specification of the psychological qualities thought to be required by a successful job-holder is a difficult process. Various procedures have been suggested and used to make this step, but it is important to remember that none of them is entirely objective and that some *inferences* are required. It is also worth noting that the inferential steps needed and the nature of these inferences are different depending on whether one is designing a sign- or sample-based selection procedure (a fuller explanation of the differences between sign- and sample-based procedures is given in Chapter 7). Essentially, sample-based selection procedures incorporate some of the actual tasks of the job into the selection procedures (e.g. a test of typing speed). Sign-based procedures involve selection techniques that look for the psychological qualities (e.g. intelligence) thought to be signals (signs) of likely job success. For sample-based procedures the steps involved are probably more straightforward. The starting point is, of course, a job-orientated analysis of the tasks involved. Once the tasks have been specified clearly, the major problem becomes one of adequately sampling the tasks and deciding which ones to include in the (sample-based) selection procedure (for further discussion of the issues see Smith and Robertson, 1986; Greuter and Algera, 1989).

With sign-type predictors, the problems of inference become more difficult and profound. Broadly, the problems involved here may be tackled in one of two ways. The first involves a direct approach, which involves studying the job content and specifying the traits (cognitive or personality) required for successful job performance. This approach is exemplified in Fleishman's Task Abilities Scales (TAS: Fleishman and Quantance, 1984). Using a fixed set of ability factors (e.g. verbal comprehension, reaction time, limb co-ordination), the analyst is required to use behaviourally anchored scales to rate the extent to which each ability is involved in doing the job in question. The indirect approach is exemplified by the PAQ, in which each element identified in the job analysis may be related (using "weights" derived from experts) to human characteristics. Thus the various elements involved in the job are translated into human requirements such as mechanical ability, near visual acuity, verbal comprehension, etc. (see Sparrow *et al.*, 1982, for an example).

Whether a sign or sample approach is adopted, the final stage in the development of a personnel selection procedure involves choosing which selection procedure(s) will provide the best information about the candidates who are to be assessed. This may involve developing a work sample test that is representative of the tasks involved in the job, using a pencil and paper test to assess numerical ability or a variety of other possibilities. What is crucially important is, that by this stage in the process, the candidate qualities on which the selection procedure needs to focus should be clearly specified. The many different selection procedures available and the research concerning their use in personnel selection are considered in Chapter 7.

Case study 6.1   Using job analysis procedures

Royal Tobacco Industries (RTI) had been diversifying for several years to minimize their dependence on tobacco products. One of their most recent acquisitions was the Bridge Engineering Company. Bridge Engineering was a specialist engineering company in the West Midlands of England which specialized in precision engineering for the motor-car, light goods vehicles and aeroplane industries. RTI felt that Bridge Engineering had a strong customer base and a highly skilled and experienced workforce. This provided the potential for Bridge to become the market leader in the supply of certain precision parts on a European and eventually worldwide basis. Karl-Heinz Tissen was installed by RTI as managing director. Although the potential of Bridge Engineering was substantial, their current performance was based mainly on a small number of experienced personnel in various key roles throughout the company. Their skill and expertise were crucial to the company's success, but it was also important to recruit highly competent people into the company to fill the roles that would emerge if RTI's plan was successful. Karl-Heinz Tissen's first project on the personnel front was to arrange for a systematic job analysis of the key functions in the existing company structure.

Suggested exercise

Explain why it was so important for Tissen to conduct the job analysis project and consider how he might have used the resulting information.

Validation processes

The key stage in the personnel selection process occurs when the selection decision is taken and a candidate is either offered a position within the company or turned away. At this point, various pieces of evidence concerning the current or past performance of candidates (e.g. behaviour at an interview, psychological test scores or references), usually referred to as predictors, are used to decide whether or not a candidate is suitable for the job in question. Although the selection decision is the key stage in the selection process, there are many other important elements in the selection process leading up to and following the selection decision itself.

Figure 6.4 provides an outline of the main elements involved in designing a personnel selection procedure. The process begins with a job analysis, followed by the choice of selection instruments. Information on the work performance of job-holders is then used to examine the validity of the selection instruments (i.e. whether high and low scores on the selection instruments are associated with good and poor work performance).

A thorough job analysis provides a basis for suggesting that candidates who satisfy particular selection criteria are likely to be suitable for the job in question. The analysis may suggest, for example, that certain personality and dispositional characteristics are desirable together with specific previous experience, technical qualifications and levels of intelligence and specific abilities. The next stage in the process is to identify selection instruments (e.g. intelligence tests, group discussion exercises, interviews, application forms) that can be used to examine whether candidates meet the required criteria or not. The advantages and disadvantages of various selection instruments as predictors will be examined in the next chapter, but first another issue must be addressed. Job analysis may suggest that certain selection criteria are appropriate but does not (and cannot) provide any definite evidence that candidates who meet the criteria actually turn out to be better employees than candidates who do not. Such evidence is obtained by examining the validity and reliability of the proposed predictors.

Criterion-related validity

Criterion-related validity refers to the strength of the relationship between the predictor (e.g. psychological test scores or interview ratings) and the criterion (e.g. subsequent work behaviour, indicated by measures such as output figures or supervisor's ratings). Criterion-related validity is high if candidates who

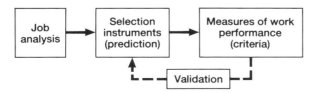

6.4 The personnel selection system.

6.5 Some hypothetical predictor and criterion scores. (a) Job knowledge test; (b) intelligence test.

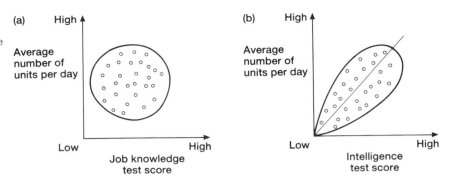

obtain high predictor scores obtain high criterion scores *and* candidates who obtain low scores on a predictor also obtain low criterion scores. Figure 6.5 shows a scatterplot of some hypothetical data obtained by using two predictors – a job knowledge test score and an intelligence test score – and one criterion (work performance) measure: average number of units produced per day.

An inspection of the scatterplot in Fig. 6.5 shows that the criterion-related validity of the intelligence test appears to be quite good. The participant's scores in this test correspond closely to the number of units produced. Although the predictor and criterion scores are obviously closely related, it is worth noting that the correspondence is not perfect. For perfect correspondence, all of the points would lie exactly on the diagonal line in Fig. 6.5. For the job knowledge test there is no correspondence at all and, as Fig. 6.5 clearly shows, the points are distributed more or less in a circle and high scores on one variable can be associated with either high or low scores on the other variable.

The strength of the relationship between predictor scores and criterion scores is usually expressed as a correlation coefficient (referred to as a validity coefficient). Perfect correlation between two variables will produce a correlation of 1. No correlation at all will produce a coefficient of zero (see also Chapter 4).

Correlation and prediction

When the correlation between variables is high, it is possible to predict the score of one when supplied with someone's score on the other. Consider for example Fig. 6.6, where the predictor–criterion relationship is perfect, i.e. a validity (correlation) coefficient of +1. In the case of a future candidate, it would be possible to obtain his or her score on predictor A and thus predict a score on the criterion.

If the organization wished to select staff who would produce an average of at least 50 units per day, what should be done? As Fig. 6.6 shows, if only people who obtained a score of above 105 on predictor A were offered jobs by the organization, all future employees would be likely to produce 50 units (or

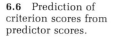

6.6 Prediction of criterion scores from predictor scores.

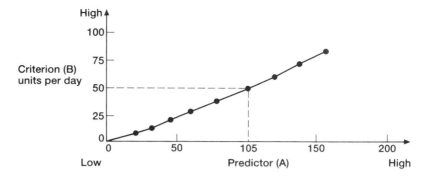

more) per day. Unfortunately, in practice, selection can rarely be conducted in such an idealized and clear-cut fashion and there are a number of practical problems that must be considered.

Less than perfect predictor–criterion relationships

Research (e.g. Muchinsky, 1986; Robertson and Smith, 1989; Ghiselli, 1973) has shown that it is most unusual in practical situations to obtain validity coefficients much in excess of +0.5 – let alone the coefficient of +1.0 that will allow perfect prediction. Nevertheless, validity coefficients of considerably less than +1.0 can provide a basis for improved personnel selection.

Theoretically, the ideal way to collect criterion-related validity data is to use a predictive (or follow-up) design. This design involves collecting predictor information (e.g. interview ratings, test scores) for candidates and then following up the candidates (e.g. during their first year of employment) to gather criterion data on their work performance. One important feature emerging from data collected in this way, is that the work performance of people with both high and low predictor scores needs to be examined. The true relationship between predictor and criterion scores can be established only by allowing candidates with the full range of predictor scores to be given an opportunity to conduct the job. Candidates with poor scores on the predictor may be capable of satisfactory job performance. What this means in practice is that the predictor scores should not be used to take selection decisions until after a validity study has been conducted. In other words, until the relationship between predictor and criterion is firmly established, candidates should be offered employment regardless of their performance on the predictors. Often this is a difficult step for an organization to take. If job analysis and other information (in the absence of validity data) suggest that the use of certain predictors should improve their selection decisions, many organizations would not be happy to allow candidates with low scores on these predictors to enter employment. Sometimes it is possible to convince an organization not to use the results of potential predictors and to continue to use their existing methods while a validation study is carried out. Often, however, organizations cannot accept the constraints of a complete predictive validity (follow-up) design and some compromise is needed.

Another practical problem with the predictive validity design is that of ensuring that the predictor results obtained by new employees are not revealed to other members of the organization before a validity study has been conducted. Obviously, a supervisor who is given a new employee with either a high or low predictor score could be affected by these results. The supervisor's behaviour towards the new employee might be influenced and/or estimates of the new employee's work performance could be biased.

An alternative for conducting criterion-related validity studies is the concurrent design. In the concurrent design, predictor data are obtained from existing employees on whom criterion data are already available. One advantage of the concurrent design is that the organization is not required to collect predictor data from candidates (for employment) without making use of the data for selection decisions. Predictor data are collected from existing employees only. A second advantage of the concurrent design is that there is no time delay between the collection of predictor and criterion data. Existing employees' predictor scores are correlated with their criterion performance. The criterion data are likely to be already available, or at least they can be collected quickly. There is certainly no need to wait for the lengthy follow-up period involved with the predictive design. Figure 6.7 compares the two designs in a hypothetical situation and indicates the considerable differences in time scales and data collection effort that can occur.

Because of these advantages, the concurrent design is attractive to many organizations. However, there are disadvantages. The workers presently employed by an organization provide a population that may be very different from the population of job applicants. Current job-holders have already survived existing company selection procedures and represent a preselected group of people who have been with the organization for some time. No data are available on people who were not hired by the company, nor on those who were hired but have subsequently left it. Thus the concurrent sample is incomplete and not representative of the potential workforce. If, as a result of a concurrent validity study, a link between, say, scores in an arithmetic test and job performance is established, it is difficult to be sure if the people tested come to the job with such skills or whether arithmetic skills are acquired as a result of training and job experience. Such problems make it hard to be certain about the actual predictive value of results derived from a concurrent validity study.

One important point to make about any validity study, regardless of whether predictive or concurrent procedures are used, concerns the fact that the initial validity study should always be followed by a "cross-validation" study on a second sample of people – to cross-check the results obtained. For studies that involve relatively few predictors, this requirement is perhaps not essential and represents a "counsel of perfection". However, when a study has investigated many possible predictors and those with the strongest predictor–criterion relationship are to be used for selection purposes, cross-validation is more important. The more potential predictors are used, the more likely it becomes that random or chance variations will produce apparent relationships between some of these predictors and the criterion measure(s). Relationships due to chance would be unlikely to occur again in the cross-validation sample – only "real" relationships would produce the same results in both samples.

6.7 A comparison of predictive and concurrent designs.

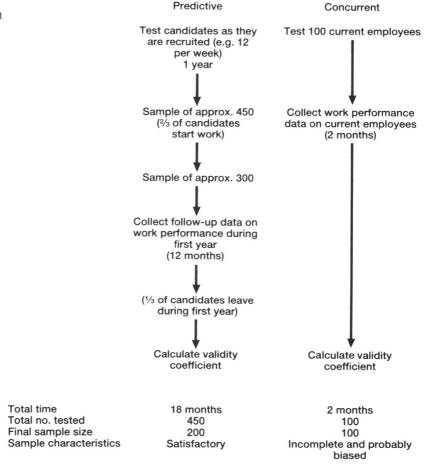

	Predictive	Concurrent
Total time	18 months	2 months
Total no. tested	450	100
Final sample size	200	100
Sample characteristics	Satisfactory	Incomplete and probably biased

Other types of validity

Criterion-related validity is the most important type of validity as far as selection is concerned, but there are also other important types of validity.

Face validity

A selection test or procedure displays face validity if it "looks right" as common sense. Requiring an applicant for a carpenter's job to make a "T-joint" from two pieces of wood would show face validity. On the other hand, asking the applicant to carry out a test of general intelligence would probably have much less face validity for the candidate, because the link between that test and job performance would probably be less clear to the candidate.

Content validity

Like face validity, content validity is established on a logical basis rather than by calculating validity coefficients or following other technical, statistical procedures. A predictor shows content validity when it covers a representative sample of the behaviour domain being measured. For example, a content valid test of car-driving ability would be expected to cover all of the essential activities that a competent driver should be able to carry out. A test that did not include an emergency stop and a reversing exercise would be lacking in content validity.

Construct validity

This involves identifying the psychological characteristics (or constructs), such as intelligence, emotional stability or manual dexterity, which underlie successful performance on the task in question (job, selection test, etc.). Because construct validity involves relationships between predictors and characteristics that are not directly observable, it can be assessed only by indirect means. Exploring the construct validity of any psychological instrument is an important facet of understanding what the instrument actually measures. As material in Chapter 7 shows, the construct validity of several frequently used personnel selection methods is not well understood.

Reliability

Validity, in its various forms, deals with the extent to which a test or other measuring technique measures what it sets out to measure. Another extremely important characteristic of any measurement technique is reliability. Reliability refers to the consistency with which a test (or other technique) provides results. In essence, a predictor (or criterion) is reliable if it produces consistent conclusions. Equally, if the same candidate produces very different scores when she takes a test on two different occasions, the reliability of the test must be questioned. Any measuring instrument (whether predictor or criterion) used in a selection procedure must be both valid and reliable. In technical (psychometric) terms, reliability refers to the extent to which a measuring instrument is free from random variation. Various well-established procedures and formulae are available for assessing the reliability of a measure and further details may be found in more advanced texts (e.g. Smith and Robertson, 1986; Anastasi, 1988).

Measuring work performance

The discussion of the process of personnel selection has shown how satisfactory selection decisions are based on strong relationships between predictors and criteria. The only specific criterion measure mentioned has been "average output per day". The average output per day produced by an employee is clearly an important measure of success, but what about other factors such as absenteeism? An average output figure that did not take absences into account would all too easily give a false impression of an employee's value to the organization. What about less clear-cut factors such as attitude to co-workers, willingness to do overtime, potential for promotion to a supervisory position? The point being made is that the identification of employees who will produce high daily outputs (or any other single factor) may not be the sole requirement of an organization's selection system. Thus, in any organization, there is a wide range of criteria that could be used to assess an employee's value to the company. Some possible measures include:

- production records (including quality and quantity of output, wastage, attainment of targets);
- absenteeism, lateness, disciplinary record; and
- ratings made by managers, supervisors, co-workers, subordinates.

The use of ratings and other methods to provide information on an employee's job performance is an established procedure within most organizations. Performance appraisal information is used for a variety of purposes, including promotion, salary, career development, counselling and training, as well as in the validation of personnel selection procedures. Of the available methods of obtaining appraisal data, rating scales are by far the most widely used (see Landy and Rastegary, 1989).

Rating scales

As Fig. 6.8 shows, a variety of different graphical rating scales can be used to elicit performance appraisal data. Such scales vary in the extent to which they provide a satisfactory basis for performance appraisal. Like many forms of psychological measurement, the key issues revolve around the problems of reliability and validity. Such scales should provide a clear indication of the meaning that can be assigned to each point on the scale (validity), so that both the rater and anyone else who needs to interpret the rating on the scale can make a valid inference. Clearly, with a scale such as (a) in Fig. 6.8, clear and unambiguous interpretation is impossible, because the scale provides so little information. It is also important that the scale can be used consistently, either by different raters or by the same rater on different occasions. Again a scale such as (a) presents problems here, because so much subjective judgement is needed that the judgements may well change from rater to rater or from trial to trial. Although a scale such as (c) probably provides a better basis for validity and reliability, such graphical rating scales contain many possible sources of error.

Leniency

This relates to a characteristic of the person doing the rating. Some people appear to be "easy" raters and tend to provide a greater proportion of high

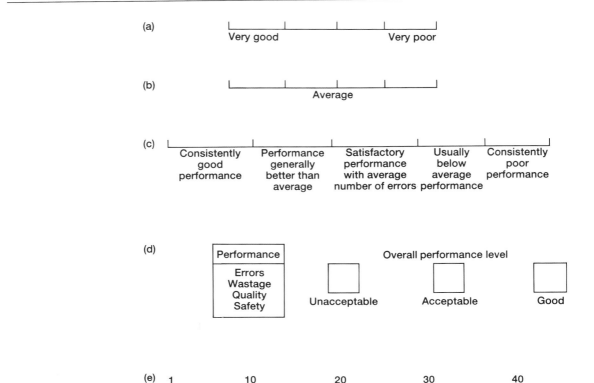

6.8 Graphical performance rating scales of various kinds.

scores (positive leniency). At the other extreme are the harsh or severe raters (negative leniency). Leniency can often be observed when the results of two or more judges are compared.

Halo

The halo error involves a tendency to let our assessment of an individual on one trait influence our evaluation of that person on other specific traits. In other words, if we believe that someone is outstandingly good in one important area of performance, we might rate them high in all areas, regardless of their true performance.

Central tendency error

Many raters are very reluctant to provide ratings at the extremes of the scale that they are using and may tend to produce ratings that group around the midpoint of the scale. This may not necessarily be because the "true" distribution of ratings should be like this, but because the rater is inhibited about assigning very high or low ratings.

Behaviourally anchored scales

One problem with many unsatisfactory rating scales is that the "anchors" which define the points on the scale are such broad, generalized descriptions, such as "average", "good" or "excellent", that it is impossible to be sure that the terms are interpreted in the same way by everyone who uses the scales. One promising means of providing unambiguous anchor points on a scale is to use Behaviourally Anchored Rating Scales (BARS). BARS use anchors that describe specific behaviour which is critical in determining levels of job performance (Smith and Kendall, 1963). BARS are developed using a four-step procedure:

1. With the aid of a group of "experts" (employees/supervisors/managers), define the aspects of performance needed for successful job performance.

2. Use a second group of "experts" to provide examples of specific behaviour associated with high, average or low performance.

3. A third group takes the examples from step 2 and independently matches them with the aspects from step 1. This "retranslation" acts as a cross-check on the two previous steps. Examples that are not assigned correctly to the aspect for which they were written do not provide unambiguous behavioural anchors for that aspect of job performance and should not be used.

4. The final step involves using more "experts" to assign scale values to the surviving items, which then serve as the behavioural anchors for the scale. The research evidence concerning BARS (e.g. Schwab *et al.*, 1975) suggests that they produce results which are slightly better than well-constructed graphic rating scales. These results lead some people to question whether the effort involved is worth the trouble. Two points are worth bearing in mind here. First, a well-constructed graphic scale may require an amount of effort equal to that involved in constructing a BARS. Secondly, if the correct procedure is followed, a BARS is highly likely to be worthwhile and have good psychometric properties. Other more recent scale development procedures include Behaviour Observation Scales (BOS). BOS development procedures will also ensure the development of reasonably sound scales. Somewhat disappointingly, however, no procedures have been able to produce scales immune to rating errors. Research concerning the appropriateness and benefits of different procedures has been reviewed by Latham and Fry (1986).

Other criteria

Although rating scales have always been the dominant criteria within personnel selection validity studies, a variety of other criteria can, and should, be used. The relevance and quality of criteria that can be predicted by any personnel selection method are of overriding importance. Logical evaluation of any method makes it obvious that it is only as useful as the criteria that it can predict. For example, a method that predicts supervisors' ratings of job performance quite well may not predict job tenure at all. Thus, an organization wishing to select future employees who will stay with them for a long time (e.g. because training is long and costly) would get little benefit from such a selection procedure. Alternative criteria, used in personnel selection research, include: absenteeism, turnover/tenure, accidents/safe working behaviour, promotion, salary/grade progression, job performance tests.

Multiple *vs* single criteria

When utilizing data on someone's performance within an organization, one important issue to consider is whether to use a single overall measure or multiple criteria (i.e. many measures of job success). In a much-quoted and important article, Dunnette (1963, pp. 251–252) made the following points:

> Over the years our concept of the criterion has suggested the
> evidence of some single all encompassing measure of job success
> against which other measures (predictors) might be compared ...
> much selection and validation research has gone astray because of an
> overzealous worshipping of the criterion. ... Thus, I say: junk the
> criterion! Let us cease searching for single or composite measures of
> job success and proceed to undertake research which accepts the world
> of success dimensionality as it really exists.

This issue still arouses controversy and not all personnel psychologists share Dunnette's desire always to use multiple criteria.

It is important to point out that the use of a single criterion does not necessarily mean utilizing only one measure of success; normally it involves combining the data from several measures to form a composite single criterion. By and large, in the specific context of personnel selection, most psychologists would agree with Dunnette that it is more efficient to use multiple criteria rather than a single composite. One predictor, for instance, may predict the ability of a manager to influence colleagues and subordinates, while another might predict his or her technical problem-solving skills. The use of a single composite criterion would not allow such detailed (and surely useful) validity data to be obtained. Despite the desirability of multiple criteria, practical considerations, including the difficulties involved in communicating with non-specialists, usually mean that only a small number of criteria are used in any validation study. For other purposes, such as job evaluation or the development of incentive payment systems, composite criteria may be more or less essential.

Case study 6.2   Personality and job performance

Karl Wessenberg had been managing director of Linguafrank, a company producing language training material, since he began the company 10 years ago. Browsing through a trade magazine, Paul noticed and was impressed by an advert for JIC Associates. JIC Associates were a small but dynamic human resources company who specialized in the assessment of senior personnel in organizations. At this time, Karl had a difficult decision to make concerning the selection of a new editor for Linguafrank's highly successful but now rather out of date series of Travellers' Aid audio-cassette tapes. The previous editor was about to move on to a job with a TV company.

The JIC consultant who visited Paul in his office showed him some very attractively produced psychological testing material. After a brief discussion of the kind of person needed to fill the editor's role and an extremely impressive demonstration of the computer-produced reports by the JIC testing system, Paul was very enthusiastic about enlisting JIC's help to solve his selection problem. In due course, JIC prepared advertisements, tested a small group of the large number of applicants and made a recommendation to Paul on the two best candidates. Paul chose Charles Smith as his new editor.

Charles was a disaster almost from day one. Although he was clearly highly intelligent, his personality and attitudes were completely unsuited to Linguafrank. Charles Smith's outgoing, rather laid-back style was seen as much too casual by the Linguafrank personnel. He found that the job was not what he expected in a variety of ways and was desperately unhappy in the job.

Suggested exercises

1. Consider what went wrong and why?
2. Prepare some briefing notes explaining what Paul Wessenberg should have done and the kinds of questions he should have asked in his initial contacts with JIC.

Summary

Assessment in organizational settings is a common activity which can have a useful impact on individual and organizational success and well-being. This chapter has provided an overview of the conceptual basis and measurement procedures involved in assessing individual differences. Job analysis provides the basis for many human resource activities in organizations and it is particularly important in personnel selection. A range of structured approaches to job analysis is available, though the most thorough and reliable information may be obtained using structured questionnaires. Job analysis information may be used to develop sign- or sample-based selection procedures. Because the reliability and validity of such procedures determine the quality of personnel entering the organization, it is crucial that selection procedures provide valid assessments of future work behaviour. Several different (e.g. predictive or concurrent) validation processes are available for assessing validity.

References

Algera, J. and Greuter, M. (1989). Job analysis for personnel selection. In M. Smith and I. T. Robertson (Eds), *Advances in Selection and Assessment*. Chichester: John Wiley.

Anastasi, A. (1988). *Psychological Testing*. New York: Macmillan.

Annett, J., Duncan, K. D., Stammers, R. B. and Gray, M. J. (1971). *Task Analysis*. Training Information Paper No. 6. London: HMSO.

Bandura, A. (1977). *Social Learning Theory*. Englewood Cliffs, N.J.: Prentice-Hall.

Bandura, A. (1986). *Social Foundations of Thought and Action: A Social Cognitive Theory*. Englewood Cliffs, N.J.: Prentice-Hall.

Banks, M. H. (1988). Job Components Inventory. In S. Gael (Ed.), *Job Analysis Handbook*. New York: John Wiley.

Banks, M. H. and Miller, R. L. (1984). Reliability and convergent validity of the Job Components Inventory. *Journal of Occupational Psychology*, *57*, 181–184.

Banks, M. H., Jackson, P. R., Stafford, E. M. and Warr, P. B. (1983). The Job Components Inventory and the analysis of jobs requiring limited skill. *Personnel Psychology*, *36*, 57–66.

Boring, E. G. (1923). Intelligence as the tests test it. *New Republic*, *35*, 35–37.

Bottomly, M. (1983). *Personnel Management*. Plymouth: Macdonald & Evans.

Burt, C. (1940). *The Factors of Mind*. London: University of London Press.

Cattell, R. B. (1965). *The Scientific Analysis of Personality*. Baltimore, Md.: Penguin.

Cattell, R. B., Eber, H. W. and Tatsuoka, M. M. (1970). *Handbook for the Sixteen Personality Factor Questionnaire (16PF)*. Windsor: National Foundation for Educational Research.

Digman, J. M. and Takemoto-Chock, N. K. (1981). Factors in the natural language of personality: Re-analysis and comparison of six major studies. *Multivariate Behavioral Research*, *16*, 149–170.

Dunnette, M. D. (1963). A note on the criterion. *Journal of Applied Psychology*, *47*, 251–254.

Eysenck, H. J. (1970). *The Structure of Human Personality*. London: Methuen.

Eysenck, H. J. (1981). General features of the model. In H. J. Eysenck (Ed.), *A Model for Personality*. New York: Springer-Verlag.

Eysenck, H. J. and Eysenck, M. J. (1985). *Personality and Individual Differences: A Natural Science Approach*. New York: Plenum Press.

Eysenck, H. J. and Eysenck, S. B. G. (1964). *Manual of the Eysenck Personality Inventory*. London: University of London Press.

Eysenck, H. J. and Eysenck, S. B. G. (1975). *Manual of the Eysenck Personality Questionnaire*. London: Hodder and Stoughton.

Eysenck, H. J. and Kamin, L. (1981). *Intelligence: The Battle for the Mind*. London: Pan.

Eysenck, H. J. and Wilson, G. D. (1973). *The Experimental Study of Freudian Theories*. London: Methuen.

Fine, S. A. and Wiley, W. W. (1974). An introduction to functional job analysis. In E. A. Fleishman and A. R. Bass (Eds), *Studies in Personnel and Industrial Psychology*. Homewood, Ill.: Dorsey Press.

Flanagan, J. C. (1954). The critical incident technique. *Psychological Bulletin*, *51*, 327–358.

Fleishman, E. A. and Quantance, M. K. (1984). *Taxonomies of Human Performance*. London: Academic Press.

Fordham, K. G. (1975). Job advertising. In B. Ungerson (Ed.), *Recruitment Handbook*, 2nd edn. Guildford: Gower Press.

Friedman, L. and Harvey, R. J. (1986). Can raters with reduced job descriptive information provide accurate Position Analysis Questionnaire (PAQ) ratings? *Personnel Psychology*, *39*, 779–789

Ghiselli, E. E. (1973). The validity of aptitude tests in personnel selection. *Personnel Psychology*, *26*, 461–477.

Greuter, M. and Algera, J. (1989). Criterion development and job analysis. In P. Herriot (Ed.), *Assessment and Selection in Organizations*. Chichester: John Wiley.

Guilford, J. P. (1967). *The Nature of Human Intelligence*. New York: McGraw-Hill.

Guion, R. M. (1965). *Personnel Testing*. New York: McGraw-Hill.

Howarth, E. and Browne, J. A. (1971). An item factor analysis of the 16 PF. *Personality*, *2*, 117–139.

Kelly, G. A. (1955). *The Psychology of Personal Constructs*. New York: Norton.

Kline, P. and Barrett, P. (1983). The factors in personality questionnaires among normal subjects. *Advances in Behavioral Research and Therapy*, *5*, 141–202.

Landy, F. J. and Rastegary, H. (1989). Criteria for selection. In M. Smith and I. T. Robertson (Eds), *Advances in Selection and Assessment*. Chichester: John Wiley.

Latham, G. P. and Fry, L. W. (1986). Measuring and appraising employee performance. In S. Gael (Ed.), *Job Analysis Handbook*. New York: John Wiley.

Le Francois, G. R. (1980). *Psychology*. Belmont, Calif.: Wadsworth.

Levine, E. L. (1983). *Everything You Always Wanted to Know About Job Analysis*. Tampa, Fl.: Mariner Publishing.

Lopez, F. (1988). Threshold traits analysis system. In S. Gael (Ed.), *The Job Analysis Handbook*. New York: John Wiley.

Lopez, F. M., Kesselman, G. A. and Lopez, F. F. (1981). An empirical test of a trait-oriented job analysis technique. *Personnel Psychology*, *34*, 479–502.

McCormick, E. J., Jeanneret, P. and Meacham, R. C. (1972). A study of job characteristics and job dimensions as based on the position analysis questionnaires. *Journal of Applied Psychology*, *36*, 347–368.

McCrae, R. R. and Costa, P. T. (1985). Updating Norman's "Adequate Taxonomy": Intelligence and personality dimensions in natural language and in questionnaires. *Journal of Personality and Social Psychology*, *49*, 710–721.

Muchinsky, P. M. (1986). Personnel selection methods. In C. L. Cooper and I. T. Robertson (Eds), *International Review of Industrial and Organizational Psychology, 1986*. Chichester: John Wiley.

Robertson, I. T. and Smith, M. (1989). Personnel selection methods. In M. Smith and I. T. Robertson (Eds), *Advances in Selection and Assessment*. Chichester: John Wiley.

Satterly, D. J. (1979). Covariation of cognitive styles, intelligence and achievement. *British Journal of Educational Psychology*, *49*, 179–181.

Saville and Holdsworth Ltd. (1984). *The Occupational Personality Questionnaires*. Available to qualified users from Saville and Holdsworth Ltd., Thames Ditton, Surrey KT7 0SR, UK.

Schmitt, N. and Noe, R. A. (1986). Personnel selection and equal employment opportunity. In C. L. Cooper and I. T. Robertson (Eds), *International Review of Industrial and Organizational Psychology, 1986*. Chichester: John Wiley.

Schwab, D. P. and Heneman, H. G. III. (1969). Relationship between interview structure and interview reliability in an employment situation. *Journal of Applied Psychology*, *53*, 214–217.

Schwab, D. P., Heneman, H. G. III and DeCotis, T. (1975). Behaviorally anchored rating scales: A review of the literature. *Personnel Psychology*, *28*, 549–562.

Shepherd, A. (1976). An improved tabular format for task analysis. *Journal of Occupational Psychology*, *47*, 93–104.

Smith, M. (1980). An analysis of three managerial jobs using repertory grids. *Journal of Management Studies*, *17*, 205–213.

Smith, M. and Robertson, I. T. (1986). *The Theory and Practice of Systematic Staff Selection*. London: Macmillan.

Smith, P. C. and Kendall, L. M. (1963). Retranslation of expectations: An approach to the construction of unambiguous anchors for rating scales. *Journal of Applied Psychology*, *47*, 149–155.

Smith, P. C., Kendall, L. M. and Hulin, C. L. (1969). *The Measurement of Satisfaction in Work and Retirement*. Chicago, Ill.: Rand McNally.

Sparrow, J., Patrick, J., Spurgeon, P. and Barwell, F. (1982). The use of job component analysis related aptitudes in personnel selection. *Journal of Occupational Psychology*, *55* (3), 157–164.

Spearman, C. (1927). *The Abilities of Man*. London: Macmillan.

Spector, P. E., Brannick, M. T. and Coovert, M. D. (1989). Job analysis. In C. L. Cooper and I. T. Robertson (Eds), *International Review of Industrial and Organizational Psychology, 1989*. Chichester: John Wiley.

Stewart, R. (1967). *Managers and their Jobs*. London: Macmillan.

Thurstone, L. L. (1938). Primary mental abilities. *Psychometric Monographs*, No. 1.

Vernon, P. E. (1956). *The Measurement of Abilities*, 2nd edn. London: University of London Press.

Vernon, P. E. (1961). *The Structure of Human Abilities*, 2nd. edn. London: Methuen.

Vernon, P. E. (1969). *Intelligence and Cultural Environment*. London: Methuen.

Personnel selection and assessment

Introduction

Although a large variety of personnel selection procedures has been developed and used in organizational settings, the relevant research shows rather clearly that not all of the methods are equally useful. This chapter examines the main personnel selection procedures that are available for use. As well as understanding the methods available for personnel selection and assessment procedures, it is also useful to have a clear grasp of the research evidence concerning each method. After examining the evidence concerning the validity of each of the major methods, this chapter also explores the extent to which the various methods are used and shows how the costs and benefits derived from selection procedures may be expressed in financial terms.

Personnel selection procedures

Table 7.1 shows the major personnel selection procedures that are available for use and also gives a brief explanation of what the methods involve. Most of the methods are well known; many readers will have first-hand experience of some of them and detailed explanations of what is involved are superfluous. One or two methods do, however, require a little explanation. Brief explanations are therefore given below for work-sample tests, biodata and assessment centres.

Work-sample tests, as their name suggests, require candidates to conduct a sample of the kind of work that is involved in the job for which they are being considered. The most widely used work-sample test is the typing test, i.e. a test given to applicants for jobs that require typing skills. A well-known work-sample test used for executive positions is the in-tray or in-basket test. This requires candidates to work through the contents of a typical in-tray (containing memos, notes, letters, production data, sales information, etc.) and decide what action they will take.

When using predictors such as interviews, psychological tests or work-sample tests, the specific areas to be investigated in the interview or the particular tests to be used are normally derived from job analysis data (see Chapter 6).

Table 7.1   Personnel selection methods

1. **Interviews**

   Many involve more than one interviewer. When several interviewers are involved, the term *panel* interview is used. The most important features of an interview are the extent to which a pre-planned structure is followed and the proportion of questions that are directly related to the job (see pp. 117–19).

2. **Psychometric Tests**

   This category includes tests of cognitive ability (such as general intelligence, verbal ability, numerical ability) and self-report measures of personality (see Chapter 6).

3. **References**

   Usually obtained from current or previous employers, often in the final stages of the selection process. The information requested may be specific or general and open-ended.

4. **Biodata**

   Specifications of biographical information about a candidate's life history. Some biodata inventories may contain many (e.g. 150+) questions and ask objective questions such as professional qualifications held and more subjective ones such as preferences for different job features.

5. **Work Sample Tests**

   Such tests literally use samples of the job in question (e.g. the contents of an in-tray for an executive position or specific kinds of typing for a secretarial post). The applicant is given instructions and then a specific amount of time to complete the tasks.

6. **Handwriting Analysis**

   Inferences are made about candidates' characteristics by examining specific features of their handwriting (e.g. slant, letter shapes). Obviously, a reasonably lengthy sample of the candidate's normal writing is required.

7. **Assessment Centres**

   This procedure involves a combination of several of the previously mentioned techniques (e.g. psychometric tests, interviews, work-samples). Candidates are usually dealt with in groups and some of the techniques used require the candidates to interact (e.g. simulated group decision-making exercises).

The information from the job analysis provides a basis for deciding which factors (e.g. numerical ability, good personal relationships) might be important for job success. Biographical data are often developed in a different way. When a candidate applies for a job with an organization, it is likely that he or she will complete an application form and other documents in which he or she is expected to provide certain biographical information concerning his or her age, previous employment, personal history and education. The basic procedure for using biographical data is to collect information on a number of candidates and correlate it with subsequent performance. Items of information that predict subsequent performance can then be identified. Items of information chosen on this basis do not necessarily have any obvious link with the job; it has merely been demonstrated, on a statistical basis, that they predict future performance.

In most practical situations, it is not sensible to base selection decisions on the use of one predictor only (such as the results of one test) or even on one type of predictor. When several different predictors are used together, the basic aim should be to ensure that the various predictors complement rather than duplicate each other. One successful method of selection that makes use of many different predictors is the "assessment centre" approach. Assessment centres make use of many different predictors, including interviews, psychological tests, in-basket exercises and group discussions. They extend for a period of, say, 2–3 days, although they may be as short as 1 day or as long as 1 week. Candidates are usually assessed by trained assessors who are often senior managers in the organization. A typical assessment centre would involve groups of six candidates being assessed by three to six assessors. Assessment centres are used frequently to evaluate people who already work within an organization. The information gained from the assessment centre is then used to help take decisions concerning promotion and career development in general.

Signs and samples

Before examining how good the various personnel selection procedures are at predicting candidates' subsequent work performance, it will be useful to clarify one of the main ways in which personnel selection methods differ from each other. Wernimont and Campbell (1968) made an important distinction between what they described as *signs* and *samples* of behaviour; the distinction is relatively straightforward, though rather important. Consider, for example, how a candidate for a sales position may react to being asked to complete a personality questionnaire, containing questions like "Do you often wish that your life was more exciting?" Consider also how the same candidate may react to being required to conduct a role play exercise and expected to persuade a client to make a purchase. The relevance of the role play exercise and its obvious potential to provide the selection decision makers with a realistic *sample* of the candidate's behaviour is obvious. Although it may not be so obvious to the candidate, the results of the personality test may also provide important *signs* relating to certain job-relevant psychological characteristics. The previous chapter showed how job analyses may be conducted and explained, in general terms, and that job analysis data are used to design selection procedures. It is important to realize, however, that job analysis data may be used in two broadly different ways in the design of selection procedures depending on whether the selection procedure will be used to assess samples or signs of behaviour. Figure 7.1 illustrates these two approaches. The more traditional use of job analysis involves moving from the analysis to make inferences about the kind of psychological characteristics (signs) needed for successful job performance. By contrast, the sample approach involves focusing on the job tasks and designing selection procedures that provide representative samples of the actual behaviour needed for successful job performance. The strengths and weaknesses of selection procedures based on these alternative approaches will be described later in this chapter.

7.1   Using job analysis information.

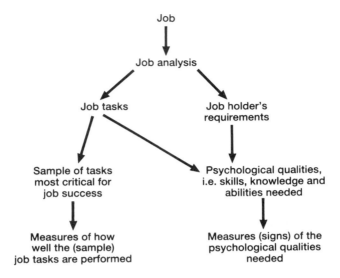

How well do selection methods work?

Before it is feasible to consider how well selection methods work, it is necessary to be clear about what it means for a selection method to work. The previous chapter introduced the concept of criterion-related validity and demonstrated how this could be evaluated by means of validation procedures. Obviously, criterion-related validity is an essential requirement for a selection method but other criteria are also important. Table 7.2 lists a number of other features of

Table 7.2   Major evaluative standards for personnel selection procedures

1. **Discrimination**

    The measurement procedures involved should provide for clear discrimination between candidates. If candidates all obtain similar assessments (i.e. scores, if a numerical system is used) selection decisions cannot be made.

2. **Validity and Reliability**

    The technical qualities of the measurement procedures (see Chapter 6) must be adequate.

3. **Fairness/Adverse Impact**

    The measures must not discriminate unfairly against members of any specific sub-groups of the population (e.g. ethnic minorities).

4. **Administrative Convenience**

    The procedures should be acceptable within the organization and capable of being implemented effectively within the organization's administrative structure.

5. **Cost and Development Time**

    Given the selection decisions (e.g. number of jobs, number of candidates, type of jobs) involved, the costs involved and the time taken to develop adequate procedures need to be balanced with the potential benefits. This is essentially a question of utility (see pp. 127–9).

personnel selection methods that are also important. A comprehensive evaluation of any selection method would require a thorough examination of the method in relation to each of the features given in Table 7.2. In the interests of clarity and simplicity, the evaluation of selection methods that follows is concentrated almost exclusively on criterion-related validity.

Estimating the validity of personnel selection procedures

As the previous chapter explained, predictive or concurrent validation processes may be used to estimate the criterion-related validity of a selection procedure. Most of the selection procedures mentioned so far in this chapter have been examined in this way and investigators have conducted validation studies on many selection procedures in many industries. Any single validation study is unlikely to provide a definitive answer on the validity of a selection method. This is because any particular study can be conducted on only a *sample* of relevant people and of course has to be conducted in a specific organization, at a particular time, using particular measures. There may be specific factors, to do with the sample of people used, the measures, the timing of the study, etc., which influence the study results and bias the results in some way. It is obvious, then, that to estimate the validity of a particular selection procedure, more than one study is needed, so that any bias due to the particular features of any particular study will not have an unduly large influence. But how many studies are required and how can we summarize and aggregate the results of several studies in order to draw conclusions? This problem of cumulating the results of many studies is not unique to personnel selection research and has exercised the minds of psychologists in many fields in recent years. Various statistical techniques have been developed to resolve the problem and an outline of the techniques is given below. The techniques described below are discussed within the context of personnel selection but have applications in many areas of work psychology (see Hunter and Hirsh, 1987, for a review).

An example will help to illustrate the way in which the results of validation studies may be cumulated and summarized. A researcher may, for example, be interested in the extent to which a particular individual difference characteristic, such as intelligence, achievement motivation or verbal ability (call this factor X) is predictive of managerial performance. As already noted, any individual study, using a particular sample of managers, will not give a definitive result for the validity of factor X. Consider for a moment why this is so. In other words, consider what things might cause the results of any specific study to be less than perfectly accurate. Table 7.3 provides a list of these features with a brief explanation of how they may influence the accuracy of the results obtained from any study. As Table 7.3 makes clear, some of the major problems are caused by sampling error and imperfect reliability in the selection method, imperfect reliability in the criterion measure, and range restriction in the selection method scores. Consider these sources of error in relation to our example of the predictive validity of factor X. The sources of error are usually referred to as artefacts, because they are not part of the natural relationship under investigation – but are a consequence of the particular investigative

Table 7.3   Major sources of distortion in validation studies

1. **Sampling Error**

    The small samples (e.g. 50–150) used in many validation studies mean that the results obtained may be unduly influenced by the effects of small numbers of people within the sample whose results are unusual. As sample size increases, these irregularities usually balance each other out and a more reliable result is obtained.

2. **Poor Measurement Precision**

    The measurement of psychological qualities at both the predictor (i.e. selection method) and criterion (i.e. job performance) stage of the validation process is subject to unsystematic error. This error (unreliability) in the scores obtained will reduce the ceiling for the observed correlation between predictor and criterion: the error is unsystematic and random and thus this element of the predictor or criterion score will not correlate systematically with anything. This means that as reliability decreases, the maximum possible correlation between predictor and criterion will decrease.

3. **Restricted Range of Scores**

    The sample of people used in a validation study may not provide the full theoretically possible range of scores on the predictor and/or criterion measures. A restricted range of scores has a straightforward statistical effect on limiting the size of the linear correlation between two variables. So, like unreliability, range restriction in a sample serves to reduce the magnitude of the observed correlation coefficient.

procedures used in the study. If the researcher in our example was able to identify 10 studies of the predictive validity of factor X, each study would be inaccurate due to the artefact. Sampling error would be present because in each study the sample involved would not be perfectly representative of the population. Studies with larger samples would of course be less prone to sampling error. As far as unreliability and range restriction are concerned, these artefacts will adversely affect observed validity coefficients. Test reliability (see Chapter 6) may be calculated and expressed in a numerical form: zero indicating total unreliability (i.e. in a totally unreliable test, someone's score on a second administration could not be predicted from their scores on the first).

To illustrate the impact of even modest deviations from reliability (0.8 is taken as the ideal, acceptable lower limit), Table 7.4 shows how the confidence interval for estimating an individual's true score on the test gets wider and wider as test reliability decreases. Even with good reliability (0.8), two apparently quite different observed scores such as 94 and 112 could, due to lack of measurement precision, have identical true scores. When data from unreliable tests are used to calculate correlation coefficients, the effect is clear. An unreliable test

Table 7.4   The impact of different reliabilities on estimated true score

	Reliability		
	0.9	0.8	0.6
Observed score	100	100	100
Probable (95% confident) range within which candidate's true score falls	91–109	87–113	81–119

(or any set of scores) contains a large amount of random error. Obviously, these random factors will not vary systematically (i.e. correlate) with any other factors; hence, as the reliability of a measure decreases, the opportunity for the measure to correlate with any other variable also decreases. Indeed, in technical terms, the reliability of a measure sets a precise limit on the possible magnitude of its correlation with any other variable: the square root of the reliability is the maximum possible level of correlation (see Moser and Schuler, 1989). Similarly, the availability of only a restricted range of scores will set an artificially low ceiling on the magnitude of any observed correlation. Consider what may happen, for example, in a predictive validity study when the candidates who score badly on the selection tests are not offered employment. If these low-scoring candidates were offered jobs they would be expected to perform badly. This link between people with low selection test scores producing low job performance scores is an important element in producing high validity coefficients. When these low scorers are excluded from the sample, the resulting validity coefficient can be based only on high and average scorers, where differences in job performance will be much less extreme. The resulting validity coefficient will thus be limited in magnitude. If the degree of range restriction in a study is known, then it is a simple matter to make a statistical correction for this range restriction (see Smith and Robertson, 1986, for the relevant formula).

The statistical procedures of meta-analysis (see Hunter *et al.*, 1982) involve methods for estimating the amount of sampling error in a set of studies and hence calculating a more accurate estimate of the validity coefficient in question. More complex meta-analysis formulae also allow the estimation of validity coefficients corrected for unreliability and range restriction (see Hunter *et al.*, 1982). Notice that removing the effect of sampling error does not change the magnitude of the validity coefficient; it changes the estimated variance in observed coefficients and hence narrows the confidence interval around the mean coefficient. As expected from the discussion of these artefacts, correcting for unreliability and range restriction *will* increase the magnitude of the mean validity coefficients. The development and use of meta-analytic procedures has had a major impact on personnel selection research and has enabled investigators to get a much clearer picture of the validity of personnel selection methods. Meta-analysis techniques have been applied to the available research evidence on the validity of all major personnel selection procedures, and Table 7.5 provides a simplified summary of the results of meta-analytic investigations of the validity of selection procedures. The major research evidence on each of the techniques listed in Table 7.5 is discussed below.

The validity of personnel selection procedures

Interviews

Interviews have always been the most popular form of personnel selection. In their survey of selection practices in the UK, Robertson and Makin (1986)

Table 7.5 A summary of meta-analytic studies of the validity of selection
procedures

Selection method	Evidence concerning overall criterion-related validity
Work samples	
Trainability tests	
Assessment centres	Good
Cognitive tests	
Biodata	
Interviews	Poor to good, depending on the type of interview
Personality assessment	Poor to moderate
References	Poor
Handwriting	Nil

found that over 80% of companies always used interviews. Similar results have
been obtained in more recent surveys (Bevan and Fryatt, 1988). The interview is
not a uniform selection procedure and the available research shows that structured interviews, utilizing job-related questions, are much better predictors of a
candidate's subsequent performance than more open procedures. Several meta-
analytic studies of interview validities (e.g. Wiesner and Cronshaw, 1988) have
revealed the superiority of structured, job-related interviews. Although there is
no clear proof of this, one of the benefits of getting interviewers to follow a
predetermined structure and to ask only job-related questions is probably that
of minimizing the opportunity for irrelevant information, prejudice and bias to
have an effect on the decision. When constrained by a structure and question
strategy, interviewers are probably forced to pay more attention to job-related
items of information.

The situational interviewing approach developed by Latham and colleagues (e.g. Latham and Saari, 1984) provides a good example of the structured, job-related interview approach. Like all good selection procedures, this
approach begins with a thorough analysis of the job. With the aid of job experts,
critical situations involving examples of particularly good or poor performance in the job are identified. The critical incidents approach (Flanagan, 1954)
is sometimes useful at this stage. Job experts are also used to provide realistic
behavioural examples of good and poor performance for each key situation;
these examples are then used to provide benchmarks for interviewers to use
when scoring the responses of interviewees. The overall format of situational
interview development and use involves the following stages:

1. Job analysis is used to identify key situations.

2. Job experts produce benchmark behaviours.

3. Using information gathered in the first two stages, situational questions are
    developed and a behaviourally based scoring key for each question is also
    developed.

4. Interviewers are trained in observation, interpersonal and judgemental
    skills and given practice with the interview questions.

5. Interviews are conducted by presenting interview questions one at a time (either orally or on cards) to candidates. Twelve or so questions may be used in a typical interview. Often these may be selected by interviewers from a larger bank of questions developed earlier in the process.

Table 7.6 gives an example of a question and scoring key taken from a study reported by Robertson *et al.* (1990). In recent years, situational interviews have probably been the most popular form of structured job-related interviews and in general they have produced good validity data (see also Weekley and Gier, 1987). Other structured interview formats have also produced good results (e.g. Janz, 1982; Orpen, 1985).

Psychometric tests

For personnel selection purposes, psychometric tests may be divided into two categories: cognitive tests (e.g. general intelligence, spatial ability, numerical ability) and personality tests such as the 16PF (Cattell *et al.*, 1970) or the Occupational Personality Questionnaire (OPQ: Saville and Holdsworth Ltd, 1984). The personality tests used in selection and assessment activities are usually based on some kind of trait-factor analytic model of personality as discussed in Chapter 6. For more than two decades, the status of personality

Table 7.6 An example of a situational interview

Example situation and high-, medium- and low-response anchors to assess adaptability (flexibility)

Two young people in their early 20s have approached the organization for finance to set up a new venture making and selling equipment to enable home computer users to translate games easily between different models of computers. They are enthusiastic and talented, but freely confess that they have no business, manufacturing or selling experience. What advice will you give them?

Scale points

Low	Contact someone else (e.g. accountant) for information on cash flows
	Tell them not to go ahead, too risky, no market
Medium	Recommend information to them
	Tell them to recruit business person
	Tell them accountant will prepare cost report
	Arrange for them to see organization's experts
	Ask them to talk more once they have thought some more about their business proposition
High	Say the organization is enthusiastic about them as customers
	Ask them about legal side of game translation
	Do they have a prototype?
	Contact Patent Office
	Seems a big area of growth at the moment
	Obtain information and recommend: Board of Trade, new businesses, offer organization's own information, accountants

tests as predictors of performance has been low (see, e.g., Guion and Gottier, 1965). This is reflected in the low mean validity for personality testing given in Table 7.5. There have been recent signs that personality testing may be about to take what many see as its rightful place as a useful selection method. Some authors (e.g. Adler and Weiss, 1988) have argued persuasively that personality is an important determinant of behaviour at work. Studies are also beginning to emerge which show that personality constructs can provide useful predictions of work performance (e.g. Day and Silverman, 1989; Hough *et al.*, in press). At the time of writing, however, not enough studies have made their way into the scientific, refereed journals for the rather unflattering results concerning personality testing in Table 7.5 to need amendment.

Personality tests may have several unique characteristics, making them rather different from other predictors and perhaps providing some explanation of their strong appeal to many practitioners coupled with a somewhat elusive validity. It may well be, for example, that for many jobs, quite different personality profiles (e.g. different 16PF or OPQ score patterns) may be equally effective; furthermore, scores in the middle range on some personality traits may be preferable to scores at either extreme. Traditional validation procedures with their strong emphasis on bivariate, linear correlational methods of analysis, may not be appropriate for personality testing.

Unlike personality testing, cognitive ability testing has produced extremely good validity data across a wide range of occupational areas. Although the results have varied a little from study to study (partly due to the different statistical corrections made by different authors), meta-analyses of the validity of cognitive tests (e.g. Hunter and Hunter, 1984) have consistently shown good validity for what most investigators now refer to as general mental ability, which seems analagous with general intelligence or "g" (see Chapter 6). Perhaps even more remarkable is an argument, first advocated, together with supporting data, in a very important and influential article by Schmidt *et al.* (1981) and since replicated by Burke *et al.* (1986). These investigators obtained validity data from five different job families and showed that the validity of apparently different classes of ability tests (e.g. verbal, perceptual, quantitative) did not vary substantially across jobs or job families. Schmidt *et al.* (1981) used these data to suggest that cognitive selection tests are equally valid across different jobs. Although the proponents of the use of cognitive tests have refrained from arguing to this extreme (see Schmidt *et al.*, 1985), the extreme form of this argument suggests that all cognitive tests are equally valid in all jobs and more simply that general mental ability tests are valid for *all* jobs!

In the 1970s, particularly in the USA, cognitive ability testing was increasingly unpopular and it was common for people to argue that such tests had no useful role in personnel selection. The recent meta-analytic work and the evidence for validity generalization (i.e. the generalization of validity across job families) have caused personnel psychologists to revise these views. The scientific community may not support the view that cognitive tests are equally valid across all jobs, but equally no one doubts that such tests provide useful predictions of job performance across a wide range of occupational areas. Given their relatively low cost and good criterion-related validity, cognitive tests (general mental ability tests in particular) are likely to be used in selection procedures for some time to come.

This concentration by selection researchers on the use of general mental ability testing is something of a paradox in at least two ways. The first paradox is that while selection research is focusing on a unitary trait of general mental ability, research into intelligence itself is moving away from this simple conceptualization of intelligence (Sternberg and Wagner, 1986; Wolman, 1985) and developing multifaceted models of intelligence. The second paradox is that despite the improved status of cognitive testing as a personnel selection procedure, there has been relatively little development of new testing strategies or procedures. For example, advances in the computerization of tests and testing theory have had relatively little impact on cognitive testing procedures (see Robertson, 1988). Although the use of computers to generate narrative reports based on conventional testing sessions is widespread, computerization has had no real impact on the use or development of more advanced applications of testing theory. Several computerized versions of existing tests have been developed and although a potentially useful step, this represents no more than a change in administration procedure. Within the UK, recently developed cognitive tests have improved face validity but are based on traditional psychometric testing theory (Gulliksen, 1950) and models of the intellect (see Chapter 6).

In the USA in the 1970s, arguments against the use of cognitive tests in personnel selection were often based on the belief that such tests were unfair to ethnic minorities. The evidence on this issue will be reviewed briefly in a separate section on fairness later in this chapter.

Work-sample tests

As noted earlier in this chapter, work-sample tests provide an example of an alternative to the "sign-based" approach to personnel selection exemplified by psychometric testing. Two fundamental forms of work sample testing may be identified. First, there is the work-sample test administered to the experienced candidate. Examples include the typing tests and in-tray tests mentioned earlier in this chapter. These kinds of tests have consistently produced good validity data (see Robertson and Kandola, 1982; Hunter and Hunter, 1984; Muchinsky, 1986). Trainability work-sample tests were originally developed in the UK by Sylvia Downs and are suitable for candidates who are not trained in the relevant job. Indeed, the main purpose of trainability work-sample tests is to assess whether an applicant is suitable for training or not. Trainability tests have been developed for several occupational areas and have also produced consistently good validity data (Robertson and Downs, 1989).

One problem which may apply to work-sample tests in general was identified by Robertson and Downs (1989) in their meta-analytic study of trainability testing. They showed that the validity of trainability tests attenuated over time. In other words, the longer the follow-up period involved in the validation study, the smaller the validity coefficient. This attenuation in validity may be because trainability tests, like all work-sample tests, are closely tied to the specific tasks of the job. As time passes, these job-specific facets of performance may become less important.

Another issue of practical concern with respect to trainability tests is the extent to which these tests, which are costly and time-consuming, measure something unique that cannot be assessed more cost-effectively by cognitive testing (see Robertson and Downs, 1989). Further research is needed to investigate the overlap between trainability tests and cognitive ability.

Assessment centres

Assessment centres seem to be an increasingly popular method of selection and assessment in organizational settings. As well as being used to choose between external candidates, assessment centres are often also used in internal promotion/assessment schemes. Assessment centres have already been described briefly earlier in this chapter. As far as criterion-related validity is concerned, assessment centres perform well (Gaugler *et al.*, 1987). There are, however, some problems with the construct validity of assessment centres. Beginning with the seminal study of Sackett and Dreher (1982), several other investigators (e.g. Robertson *et al.*, 1987; Reilly *et al.*, 1990) have shown that the convergent and discriminant validity of assessment centres is poor. Table 7.7 shows part of a typical dimension (i.e. individual psychological characteristic or construct by exercise matrix). Convergent validity would be apparent if ratings of a particular dimension (e.g. problem-solving ability) were strongly intercorrelated across different exercises.

Similarly, discriminant validity would be shown if correlations of different dimensions within the same exercises were small. Examinations of the psychometric properties of assessment centres have consistently shown low convergent and discriminant validity. If the ratings of the same dimension across different exercises do not correlate (i.e. poor convergent validity), this suggests that the dimensions (constructs) being measured are not stable from one situation to another – or that the measurement procedure is inadequate. Either way, these are troubling results and show that although assessment centres clearly measure something of importance (because their criterion-related validity is good), there is considerable uncertainty about what they do measure.

Table 7.7 Part of an assessment centre dimension by exercise matrix

Dimension	Exercise			
	In-tray	Group discussion	Role play	Presentation exercise and report
Problem-solving skills	✓	✓	✓	✓
Interpersonal ability	—	✓	✓	—
Written skills	✓	—	—	✓

Other methods

The use of biographical data as a selection procedure is an interesting and sometimes controversial topic. Like several of the other personnel selection procedures discussed in this chapter, biodata have several unique features that distinguish them from other approaches. The fundamentals of the biodata approach involve identifying correlations between items of biographical information and criterion measures (e.g. work performance, absenteeism). These correlations are established empirically by conducting a predictive or (more often) concurrent validation study.

Biodata items that predict the criterion are then combined into a questionnaire which may be administered to applicants. Information from the prior validation stage can then be used to provide a scoring procedure. For example, items may be assigned weights based on their ability to predict the relevant criterion (Guion, 1965). Weights may also be assigned by other procedures (see Drakeley, 1989). It should be stressed at this point that the correlations observed between biodata items and the criterion will be influenced by chance factors and, before using the results of a biodata validation study for selection purposes, cross-validation, preferably using a second sample, is needed. It is also clear from empirical research that the validity of biodata items is not always stable over time and it is advisable to revalidate periodically. Both Muchinsky (1986) and Drakeley (1989) have recommended revalidation every 3–5 years. Meta-analytic studies have revealed that biodata provide reasonably good criterion-related validity.

Most of the problems with the use of biodata arise from the uncritical use of empirically derived items. In other words, many biodata studies have involved the identification of items that predict the criterion, with no attempt to consider *why* the items are predictive. For example, why should it be that living in a particular area of town or having had a newspaper delivery round as a child be associated with job success? Two problems may be associated with this kind of empiricism. One problem is that the observed biodata item may be a surrogate for some other variable, e.g. what if the area of town in question is predominantly inhabited by a particular social or ethnic group? The other, more general problem is that while they may provide predictive value, such items provide no help in *understanding* the determinants of job success.

With these problems in mind, the rational approach to the development of biodata has been utilized. This approach is in line with attempts by some authors (e.g. Owens and Schoenfeldt, 1979) to develop a theoretical rationale for the predictive validity of biodata. Using the rational approach involves clear hypotheses about specific job-relevant constructs, such as ability to work in a team, which may be tapped by specific biodata items (e.g. membership of clubs and societies). Only items with a potential rational connection with the criterion will then be tried out, even in the pre-validation version of the biodata questionnaire. This approach is clearly much more appealing from the explanatory point of view, although evidence to date (Mitchell and Klimoski, 1982) suggests that it has slightly poorer validity than the empirical approach. Gains in fairness and understanding may, however, outweigh this loss of validity.

Reference reports are widely used methods for obtaining information on candidates (Robertson and Makin, 1986), although it seems likely that in many situations potential employers take up references only when they are about to make a job offer. This high level of usage is not, however, matched by a comparable amount of research on references. In general, the validity evidence for reference reports is not particularly good (Reilly and Chao, 1982; Hunter and Hunter, 1984), although some studies (e.g. Carroll and Nash, 1972; Williams and Dobson, 1987) have found useful criterion-related validity. One reason for the poor validity of references may be that they are not reliable and referees do not give consistent views on candidates (see Dobson, 1989). Given their high level of usage, further research into references would seem to be important. For example, although a study by Kryger and Shikiar (1978) touched on the issues, there are no studies that directly address the issue of fairness (i.e. unfair discrimination against specific sub-groups of the population) of references. From the practical point of view, Dobson (1989) has provided examples of reference formats and suggestions on how to maximize the validity of references.

Self-assessment and peer assessment both have the potential to be used for selection decision making. Self-assessment is rarely used in practical selection settings and there are obvious problems with leniency, etc. (see Ash, 1980). Studies of the validity of self-assessment in personnel selection have rarely found encouraging results (see Reilly and Chao, 1982; Schmitt and Robertson, 1990). One possible promising line of research involves using ideas and measurement procedures from self-efficacy theory (Bandura, 1986). Recent research has shown that correlations between self-efficacy ratings and measures of job performance are reasonably good (e.g. Earley, 1986; Lee and Gillen, 1989). Whether or not this can be made to pay off in practical selection contexts remains to be seen.

Compared to self-assessment, peer assessments have been found to have consistently good validity (Reilly and Chao, 1982; Hunter and Hunter, 1984; Schmitt *et al.*, 1984). Their use is obviously limited to circumstances where peers are in a position to make an assessment of a candidate (e.g. internal promotion). Although peer assessment systems are used extensively in some settings (e.g. promotion in the university system), the use of such systems is likely to be limited by the lack of enthusiasm shown for such systems by participants (see Cederblom and Lounsbury, 1980; Love, 1981). Although in some circumstances (such as career counselling rather than assessment) peer assessment may be popular (Roadman, 1964), its use seems likely to be limited to specific kinds of organizations and circumstances.

Other potential selection methods not mentioned so far in this chapter include graphology (handwriting analysis), astrology and polygraphy (the use of the so-called lie detector test). In brief, none of these procedures is used to any great extent in the UK, although some continental European companies make extensive use of graphology (Shackleton and Newell, 1991). As far as validity is concerned, there is relatively little research available on the use of these methods for personnel selection, but the clear balance of available evidence is that none of the methods show any useful criterion-related validity. Summaries of the evidence on graphology and polygraphy may be found in Ben-Shakhar (1989). Smith and Robertson (1986) provide a review of the relevant research on astrology and graphology.

Case study 7.1   Organization expansion and selection procedures

Although Dr Lyn Evans enjoyed computer science and her work in the research and development (R&D) division of GenFive Computers, she had realized that her future career progression was limited by the small number of senior technical posts in the company. With this in mind, she took a Masters degree in Management which broadened her grasp of managerial concepts and practices. Shortly after obtaining her MSc, Lyn made a crucial career move and left the R&D division to join the sales and marketing division of GenFive.

In the next few years, Lyn and GenFive were very successful and Lyn became marketing director. Shortly after her appointment as marketing director, GenFive was poised to make a rapid expansion of their sales and marketing force and began to sell their products direct to retail stores and to approach small businesses direct (something they had never done before).

An enormous expansion of the field sales force was needed, together with a restructuring of the current sales and marketing into seven geographical regions, each with a semi-autonomous regional manager. Lyn had little over a year to achieve the necessary organizational changes, and 3–4 years to expand the sales force (from 20 to over 200). Her most important problem was the selection of her future regional managers (either from the existing team of 25 sales personnel or from outside recruitment). Next, and no less important, was the recruitment and selection of over 200 new sales personnel.

Suggested exercise

Use your knowledge of the material covered in Chapters 6 and 7 to prepare a plan for Lyn Evans to achieve her goals over the next 5 years.

Social and economic factors

The impact of personnel selection procedures on candidates

Iles and Robertson (1989) have recently pointed out that there has been relatively little work in personnel selection which has looked at the issues involved from the perspective of candidates. The only candidate-centred area of work which features extensively in the personnel selection research literature concerns the extent to which selection procedures are fair to different sub-groups (usually ethnic minorities or women) of the population. A large amount of research material focusing on this issue has been produced. A variety of terms such as bias, adverse impact, fairness and differential validity are used in the literature on this issue and a clear grasp of the meanings and definitions of some of these terms is crucial to an understanding of the research results.

First, it needs to be made clear that a test is not unfair or biased simply because members of different sub-groups obtain different scores on the tests. Men and women have different mean scores for height; this does not mean the rulers are unfair measuring instruments. However, it would be unfair to use height as a selection criterion for a job, if the job could be done by people of any height, because it is important for selection criteria to be job-related. Normally, of course, the extent to which a selection method is related to job

performance can be estimated by validation research; and it is clear, therefore, that fairness and validity are closely related.

Unfortunately, it is possible for tests to appear to be valid and yet be biased against some sub-groups. This may happen if the relationship between the test score and job performance is not the same for the two sub-groups. For example, it is possible to imagine that the link between job performance and certain personality or ability factors could be different for two sub-groups of the population. A validity study, based on a mixed sample of people, would produce results that were somewhat incorrect for both sub-groups; if the results were used to develop a selection procedure, the predictions of candidates' work performance would be in error. Of course, the situation would be even worse if the validity study was based on only one sub-group but then used to select members of another. In this case, the errors for the selected group would be much greater than for the validation group, resulting in obvious unfairness. This description of possible unfairness leads to the definition of test bias (fairness), which is accepted by most work psychologists:

> A test is biased for members of a sub-group of the population if, in the prediction of a criterion for which the test was designed, consistent non zero errors of prediction are made for members of the sub-group (Cleary, 1968, p. 115).

When, triggered by civil rights movements in the USA, fairness first became an issue in personnel selection research, it was felt that many selection procedures including tests were unfair. This was because of consistent differences in mean scores between different sub-groups of the population (see Schmitt and Noe, 1986). As the discussion above makes clear, sub-group differences in mean scores are not the same as fairness. A procedure is biased or unfair when, in line with Cleary's (1968) definition, it shows differential validity for different groups.

In general, research on personnel selection has shown that, although there are examples of sub-group differences on selection instruments (e.g. black–white differences on aptitude tests or male–female differences on strength tests), there is little evidence for significant differences in sub-group validity coefficients (see Schmitt and Noe, 1986; Schmitt, 1989).

The fact that scientific research provides little evidence of differential validity for well-established selection procedures does not imply that all selection methods are unbiased, nor does it imply that unfair discrimination does not take place. It is clear, for example, that despite the 1976 Race Relations Act, unfair discrimination still takes place in the UK. Brown and Gay (1985), for example, showed that a disproportionate number of black applicants compared with similarly qualified white applicants were not invited for interview after applying for various jobs.

It is also clear that some personnel selection procedures provide more opportunity for unfairness than others and in some cases there is clear evidence of unfairness (see Reilly and Chao, 1982). In particular, unstructured procedures with poor reliability and validity provide recruiters with the opportunity to exercise their prejudices and biases. Well-researched selection procedures such as assessment centres, work-sample tests and structured interviews minimize the opportunity for bias and, as research has clearly shown, there is little, if any, evidence of unfairness with these methods. Such methods are a weapon against unfairness, rather than, as some ill-informed commentators have asserted, a cause of unfairness.

Financial utility

Like many organizational practices, personnel selection procedures cost money to implement. Using selection procedures with good predictive validity is always important, but unfortunately procedures with good predictive validity alone do not guarantee that a selection procedure will be cost-effective. Other important factors determining cost effectiveness (usually referred to as utility) include:

- selection ratio, i.e. $\dfrac{\text{no. of jobs}}{\text{no. of candidates}}$;
- the variation in selected applicants' job performance;
- the number of people selected;
- the expected average length of stay in the job of selected applicants; and
- the cost of the selection procedures(s).

Let us now examine in a little more detail the role that validity, selection ratio and the other factors play in determining utility. Figure 7.2a shows the situation for a validity coefficient of 0.1. The shaded areas (B and C) identify people who will be hired by the organization. Notice, however, that although all of these people achieve the minimum score on the predictor, only a proportion of them (B) also show satisfactory work performance. Similarly, although all the people in the unshaded areas (A and D) fail to achieve the cut-off score on the predictor, some of them are capable of satisfactory work performance (those in area A). Areas B and D represent correct selection decisions and contain people who have been justifiably rejected, known as true negatives (area D). Area C contains the false positives, i.e. people who would be hired but

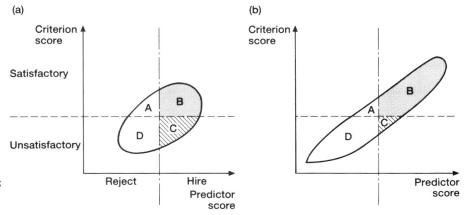

7.2 The effect of different validity coefficients on proportions hired. (a) Validity coefficient = 0.1; (b) validity coefficient =0.5.

produce unsatisfactory work performance. Area A contains the false negatives, i.e. people who would not be hired but are capable of satisfactory work
performance. Areas A and C represent errors in the selection process. Note that
unless the validity coefficient is 1.0, there will *always* be errors of selection.

Validity

As Fig. 7.2b shows, when validity increases (0.5), the proportions in areas A and
C decrease and the proportion of correct decisions (areas B and D) increases.
Thus, as validity increases, the quality of selection decisions also increases.

Selection ratio

Clearly, when the selection ratio is greater than 1.0 (i.e. there are more available jobs than applicants), the use of any selection procedure is likely to be of
relatively little benefit. In this situation, the organization may be forced to
accept anyone who applies for a job. In practice, even with a selection ratio of
more than 1.0, it may still be sensible for an organization to make use of
selection criteria and leave jobs empty rather than hire totally unsuitable
employees. When the selection ratio is less than 1.0 (i.e. more applicants than
jobs), the organization can gain obvious benefits from using selection. Consider
the situation for two different selection ratios. If the selection ratio is 0.7 (i.e.
seven jobs for every ten applicants), the organization can afford to refuse jobs to
the people with the lowest 30% of scores on the predictor. If, however, the
selection ratio is 0.4, the bottom 60% of applicants can be rejected.

Other factors

A moment of reflection will make it clear that for a job where there is a great
deal of difference between the best and the worst job holder, good selection can
be of more value than when the differences are small. In the latter situation,
even a major error in selection will only produce someone who is a little worse
than the best employee; the most accurate selection decision produces only a
small increase in performance.

The benefits or losses from any selection procedure are obviously in proportion to the number of people who are finally selected and these new
employees will have their effect for as long as they stay with the company. In
other words, 10 bad selection decisions on people who stay with the organization for 10 years are much more financially damaging to the organization than
one poor decision on someone who leaves after a year. Finally, the cost of any
selection procedure needs to be subtracted from the gain produced.

The concepts outlined above may be combined to produce an equation
which enables personnel decision makers to calculate the financial consequences of various selection strategies. Once this can be done, it is then feasible
to estimate the financial benefits of selection. Studies where selection utility has

been estimated have shown very clearly that, even with modest validity coefficients, striking financial gains may be made. Schmidt *et al.* (1984), for example, showed that gains of over US$1 million per annum could be expected if cognitive ability tests were used to select the 80 or so US Park Rangers recruited each year. Schmidt *et al.* (1979) showed even more dramatic gains could be obtained if the Computer Programmer Aptitude Test (Hughes and McNamara, 1959) was used to select computer programmers in the USA. With a selection ratio of 0.5 (i.e. two applicants per job), gains of between US$13 and 37 million could be expected!

Summary

A variety of personnel selection procedures is available for use in organizational settings. Research over the last 10–15 years has provided a much clearer picture of the criterion-related validity of these procedures. Some of the methods, such as cognitive ability tests, seem to have broad applicability across a range of situations. As well as examining the validity of personnel selection procedures, research has also concentrated on the impact of the procedures on candidates. One area that has been reasonably well researched involves an examination of the fairness (to different sub-groups) of the various techniques. Developments in utility theory have enabled the estimation of the financial benefit that may be gained through improved personnel selection.

Case study 7.2   An opportunity for work psychology

Nicole Schneider was the first professionally qualified work psychologist that Milligans had ever employed. Milligans had a chain of family-fun theme parks throughout Europe, several bistro-type restaurants and three hotels. Almost all of their sites were in holiday resorts and the majority of sites were only full during the summer months. Several theme parks ran with only a skeleton staff during the winter and some closed completely. The hotels and restaurants, with varying success, remained open throughout the year, but were much busier during the summer.

Milligans' staffing needs, particularly at more junior levels, were seasonal and they recruited large numbers of temporary employees to work during the peak summer months. Managers at almost all of the sites were constantly complaining about the quality of their temporary staff. In turn, the staff themselves often resigned before their expected date of departure and complained about the behaviour of Milligans' customers.

Nicole made three interventions which, in the course of 3 years, brought about a dramatic improvement in the situation. First, after thorough job analyses of the relevant temporary jobs, she introduced a performance assessment system which included behaviourally anchored rating scales. The managers were trained in the usage of the system and it was implemented during Nicole's first summer with Milligans. The results of the assessment scheme, together with the prior job analysis data, gave her a much more precise grasp of the problems and why the managers complained about the quality of temporary staff.

During the next year, Nicole and her two

personnel assistants developed a set of structured, situational interview questions and scoring procedures. Several of the articles from the work psychology literature provided models of how to develop the questions and associated scoring procedures. In addition to the situational interviews, Nicole and her colleagues developed trainability work-sample tests for the main temporary jobs involved.

During Nicole's second summer, the tests and interviews were used at a selected set of Milligans' sites. They were administered by Nicole's assistants and a specially trained small group of Milligans' junior managers. The interview and test results were not used to take selection decisions – unless the site managers felt very strongly that they wanted to use the results immediately. The data collected at this stage, together with the end of season performance ratings, gave Nicole the basis for a predictive validity study. Some simple utility calculations showed that despite the extra time needed to conduct the selection procedures, the new interviews and trainability tests would provide significant financial gain for Milligans.

Although not all of the site managers were convinced by Nicole's results, some were persuaded sufficiently to try the new procedures. From the next summer onwards there was a steady improvement in the quality of seasonal staff recruited and more and more site managers began to use the selection procedures.

Suggested exercises

1. Explain why the circumstances in this case study made it possible for Nicole Schneider to have such a quick and effective impact.
2. Consider other tactics and selection procedures that Nicole Schneider might have used. Explain whether or not you feel that these would have been equally successful.

References

Adler, S. and Weiss, H. M. (1988). Recent developments in the study of personality and organizational behaviour. In C. L. Cooper and I. T. Robertson (Eds), *International Review of Industrial and Organizational Psychology, 1988*. Chichester: John Wiley.

Ash, R. A. (1980). Self assessments of five types of typing ability. *Personnel Psychology*, *33*, 273–282.

Bandura, A. (1986). *Social Foundations of Thought and Action: A Social Cognitive Theory*. Englewood Cliffs, N.J.: Prentice-Hall.

Ben-Shakhar, G. (1989). Non-conventional methods in personnel selection. In P. Herriot (Ed.), *Assessment and Selection in Organizations*. Chichester: John Wiley.

Bevan, S. and Fryatt, J. (1988). *Employee Selection in the UK*. Sussex: Institute of Manpower Studies.

Brown, E. and Gay, P. (1985). *Racial Discrimination 17 Years After the Act*. Policy Studies Institute No. 646. London: Policy Studies Institute.

Burke, M. J., Raju, N. S. and Pearlman, K. (1986). An empirical comparison of the results of five validity generalization procedures. *Journal of Applied Psychology*, *71*, 349–353

Carroll, S. J. and Nash, A. N. (1972). Effectiveness of a forced reference check. *Personnel Administration*, March–April, 42–46.

Cattell, R. B., Eber, H. W. and Tatsuoka, M. M. (1970). *Handbook for the Sixteen Personality Factor Questionnaire (16PF)*. Windsor: National Foundation for Educational Research.

Cederblom, D. and Lounsbury, J. W. (1980). An investigation of user acceptance of peer evaluation. *Personnel Psychology*, *33*, 567–579.

Cleary, T. A. (1968). Test bias: Prediction of grades of negro and white students in integrated colleges. *Journal of Educational Measurement, 5*, 115–124.

Day, D. V. and Silverman, S. B. (1989). Personality and job performance: Evidence of incremental validity. *Personnel Psychology, 42*, 25–36.

Dobson, P. (1989). Reference reports. In P. Herriot (Ed.), *Assessment and Selection in Organizations*. Chichester: John Wiley.

Drakeley, R. J. (1989). Biographical data. In P. Herriot (Ed.), *Assessment and Selection in Organizations*. Chichester: John Wiley.

Earley, P. C. (1986). Supervisors and shop stewards as sources of contextual information in goal-setting: A comparison of the United States with England. *Journal of Applied Psychology, 71*, 111–117.

Flanagan, J. C. (1954). The critical incident technique. *Psychological Bulletin, 51*, 327–358.

Gaugler, B., Rosenthal, D. B., Thornton, G. C. and Bentson, C. (1987). Meta-analysis of assessment center validity. *Journal of Applied Psychology, 72*, 493–511.

Guion, R. M. (1965). *Personnel Testing*. New York: McGraw-Hill.

Guion, R. M. and Gottier, R. F. (1965). Validity of personality measures in personnel selection. *Personnel Psychology, 18*, 135–164.

Gulliksen, H. (1950). *Theory of Mental Tests*. New York: John Wiley.

Hough, L. M., Eaton, N. K., Dunnett, M. D., Kamp, J. D. and McCloy, R. A. (1990). Criterion-related validities of personality constructs and the effect of response distortion on those validities. *Journal of Applied Psychology*, vol 75, 467–760.

Hughes, J. L. and McNamara, W. J. (1959). *Manual for the Revised Programmer Aptitude Test*. New York: Psychological Corporation.

Hunter, J. E. and Hirsh, H. R. (1987). Applications of meta-analysis. In C. L. Cooper and I. T. Robertson (Eds), *International Review of Industrial and Organizational Psychology, 1987*. Chichester: John Wiley.

Hunter, J. E. and Hunter, R. F. (1984). Validity and utility of alternative predictors of job performance. *Psychological Bulletin, 96*, 72–98

Hunter, J. E., Schmidt, F. L. and Jackson, G. B. (1982). *Meta-analysis: Cumulating Research Findings Across Studies*. Beverly Hills, Calif.: Sage.

Iles, P. A. and Robertson, I. T. (1989). The impact of personnel selection procedures on candidates. In Herriot, P. (Ed.), *Assessment and Selection in Organizations*. Chichester: John Wiley.

Janz, T. (1982). Initial comparisons of patterned behavior description interviews versus unstructured interviews. *Journal of Applied Psychology, 67*, 577–580.

Kryger, B. R. and Shikiar, R. (1978). Sexual discrimination in the use of letters of recommendation. *Journal of Applied Psychology, 63*, 309–314.

Latham, G. P. and Saari, L. M. (1984). Do people do what they say? Further studies on the situational interview. *Journal of Applied Psychology, 69*, 569–573.

Lee, C. and Gillen, D. J. (1989). Relationship of type A behaviour pattern, self-efficacy and perceptions on sales performance. *Journal of Organizational Behaviour, 10*, 75–81.

Love, K. G. (1981). Comparison of peer assessment methods: Reliability, validity, friendship bias and user reactions. *Journal of Applied Psychology, 65*, 451–457.

Mitchell, T. W. and Klimoski, P. M. (1982). Is it rational to be empirical? A test of methods of scoring biographical data. *Journal of Applied Psychology, 71*, 311–317.

Moser, K. and Schuler, H. (1989). The nature of psychological measurement. In P. Herriot (Ed.), *Assessment and Selection in Organizations*. Chichester: John Wiley.

Muchinsky, P. M. (1986). Personnel selection methods. In C. L. Cooper and I. T. Robertson (Eds), *International Review of Industrial and Organizational Psychology, 1986*. Chichester: John Wiley.

Orpen, C. (1985). Patterned behavior description interviews versus unstructured interviews: A comparative validity study. *Journal of Applied Psychology, 70*, 774–776.

Owens, W. A. and Schoenfeldt (1979). Towards a classification of persons. *Journal of Applied Psychology, 64*, 569–607.

Reilly, R. R. and Chao, G. T. (1982). Validity and fairness of some alternative employee selection procedures. *Personnel Psychology, 35*, 1–62.

Reilly, R. R., Henry, S. and Smither, J. W. (1990). An examination of the effects of using behavior checklists on the construct validity of assessment center dimensions. *Personnel Psychology, 43*, 71–84.

Roadman, H. E. (1964). An industrial use of peer ratings. *Journal of Applied Psychology, 48*, 211–214.

Robertson, I. T. (1988). Computer-assisted testing and assessment. *Guidance and Assessment Review, 4*, 1–3.

Robertson, I. T. and Downs, S. (1989). Work sample tests of trainability: A meta-analysis. *Journal of Applied Psychology, 74*, 402–410.

Robertson, I. T. and Kandola, R. S. (1982). Work sample tests: Validity, adverse impact and applicant reaction. *Journal of Occupational Psychology, 55*, 171–183.

Robertson, I. T. and Makin, P. J. (1986). Management selection in Britain: A survey and critique. *Journal of Occupational Psychology, 59*, 45–57.

Robertson, I. T. Gratton, L. and Sharpley, D. (1987). The psychometric properties and design of managerial assessment centres: Dimensions into exercises won't go. *Journal of Occupational Psychology, 60*, 187–195.

Robertson, I. T., Gratton, L. and Rout, U. (1990). The validity of situational interviews for administrative jobs. *Journal of Organizational Behaviour, 11*, 69–76.

Sackett, P. R. and Dreher, G. F. (1982). Constructs and assessment center dimensions: Some troubling empirical findings. *Journal of Applied Psychology, 67*, 401–410.

Sackett, P. R., Schmitt, N., Tenopyr, M. L., Kehoe, J. and Zedeck, S. (1985). Commentary on forty questions about validity generalization and meta-analysis. *Personnel Psychology, 38*, 697–798.

Saville and Holdsworth Ltd (1984). *The Occupational Personality Questionnaires.* Available to qualified users from Saville and Holdsworth Ltd, Thames Ditton, Surrey KT7 0SR, UK.

Schmidt, F. L., Hunter, J. E., Pearlman, K. and Hirsh, H. R. (1985). Forty questions about validity generalization and meta-analysis. *Personnel Psychology, 38*

Schmidt, F. L., Hunter, J. E., McKenzie, R. C. and Muldrow, T. W. (1979). Impact of valid selection procedures on work-force productivity. *Journal of Applied Psychology, 64*, 609–626.

Schmidt, F. L., Hunter, J. E. and Pearlman, K. (1981). Task differences as moderators of aptitude test validity in selection: A red herring. *Journal of Applied Psychology, 66*, 166–185.

Schmidt, F. L., Mack, M. J. and Hunter, J. E. (1984). Selection utility in the occupation of U.S. Park Ranger for three modes of test use. *Journal of Applied Psychology, 69*, 490–497.

Schmitt, N. (1989). Fairness in employment selection. In M. Smith and I. T. Robertson (Eds), *Advances in Selection and Assessment.* Chichester: John Wiley.

Schmitt, N., Gooding, R. Z., Noe, R. D. and Kirsch, M. (1984). Meta-analysis of validity studies published between 1964 and 1982 and the investigation of study characteristics. *Personnel Psychology, 37*, 407–422.

Schmitt, N. and Noe, R. A. (1986). Personnel selection and equal employment opportunity. In C. L. Cooper and I. T. Robertson (Eds), *International Review of Industrial and Organizational Psychology, 1986.* Chichester: John Wiley.

Schmitt, N. and Robertson, I. T. (1990). Personnel selection. *Annual Review of Psychology*, *41*, 289–319.

Shackleton, V. J. and Newell, S. (1991). Management selection: A comparative survey of methods used in top British and French companies. *Journal of Occupational Psychology*, *64*, pp. 23–36.

Smith, M. and Robertson, I. T. (1986). *The Theory and Practice of Systematic Staff Selection*. London: Macmillan.

Sternberg, R. J. and Wagner, R. K. (1986). *Practical Intelligence*. Cambridge: Cambridge University Press.

Weekley, J. A. and Gier, J. A. (1987). Reliability and validity of the situational interview for a sales position. *Journal of Applied Psychology*, *72*, 484–487.

Wiesner, W. H. and Cronshaw, S. F. (1988). A meta-analytic investigation of the impact of interview format and degree of structure on the validity of the employment interview. *Journal of Occupational Psychology*, *61*, 275–290.

Wernimont, P. F. and Campbell, J. P. (1968). Signs, samples and criteria. *Journal of Applied Psychology*, *52*, 372–376.

Williams, A. P. O. and Dobson P. (1987). *The Validation of the Regular Commissions Board*. Army Personnel Research Establishment.

Wolman, B. (1985). *Handbook of Intelligence*. New York: John Wiley.

Attitudes at work

Introduction

This chapter examines attitudes and attitude change. In the first place, it provides a comprehensive definition of an attitude. Secondly, it briefly describes the ways in which attitudes can be measured. Then attention turns to attitude change: what features of the communicator, the message and the recipient of the message determine whether attempts at persuasion will be successful? Attitude change might not be very important if it was not reflected in behaviour change, so the connection between attitudes and behaviour is then examined. Finally, we look at two important work attitudes: job satisfaction and organizational commitment. In each case, we describe their nature, measurement, causes and consequences.

What is an attitude?

The concept of attitude refers, as Secord and Backman (1969) defined it, to "certain regularities of an individual's feelings, thoughts and predispositions to act toward some aspect of his environment". Feelings represent the *affective*, thoughts the *cognitive*, and predispositions to act the *behavioural* component of an attitude. Attitudes are evaluative, i.e. they reflect a person's tendency to feel, think or behave in a *positive* or *negative* manner towards the object of the attitude. Attitudes can be held about the physical world around us (e.g. British architecture), about hypothetical constructs (e.g. worker participation, flexible rostering, etc.) and about other people (e.g. the boss, mother-in-law, the Prime Minister, etc.).

The affective component of an attitude is reflected in a person's physiological responses (e.g. blood pressure) and/or in what the person says about how they feel about the object of the attitude. The *cognitive* component refers to a person's perception of the object of the attitude and/or what the person says he or she believes about that object. The *behavioural* component is reflected by a person's observable behaviour towards the object of the attitude and/or what they say about their behaviour towards it. In practice, the term "attitude" is usually taken to mean the cognitive and/or affective components. Behaviour is most often construed as an *outcome* of attitudes (see pp. 142–3).

Is it worth making distinctions between the three components of attitude? This is disputed (see Cacioppo *et al.*, 1989), but the answer seems to be yes. Breckler (1984) has shown that although our feelings, beliefs and behaviours towards an object do tend to be consistent with each other, they are not so highly consistent that they can be thought of as the same thing. Hence, for example, it is possible for a person to *feel* positive about their job (affective attitude) but *believe* their job has few attractive elements (cognitive attitude). Thus they can hold two different attitudes to their job simultaneously. Which attitude is expressed, and which one will influence behaviour on any given occasion, may therefore depend on whether the person is concentrating on their emotions or on their beliefs at that time (Millar and Tesser, 1989).

How are attitudes measured?

Attitudes are almost always assessed using self-report questionnaires. In other words, attitude measurement depends upon what people *say* about their feelings, beliefs and/or behaviour towards the particular object in question. Attitude questionnaires are not just thrown together any old how. There are several fairly sophisticated techniques for ensuring they measure the attitude in question properly. Two of these are *Thurstone scaling* and *Likert scaling*.

In the Thurstone approach, or the *equal interval scale*, the psychologist generates a number of potential questionnaire items, ranging from highly favourable about the topic in question to highly unfavourable, e.g. in terms of one's attitude towards war, from "war is glorious" to "there is no conceivable justification for war". After collecting, say, about 100 such statements, the psychologist asks a sample group of those ultimately to be assessed to rate each statement on an 11-point scale on the degree of favourableness of the attitude statement. The psychologist then includes in the final attitude questionnaire only those statements where (a) there is a high degree of agreement between evaluators on its degree of favourableness, and (b) the average scale value of the item ranges up the 11-point scale at equal intervals from 1 to 11. Perhaps 20–22 statements are included in the final questionnaire, each of which is separated from the previous one by a scale value of, say, roughly half a point. A person's attitude score is the mean or median scale value of all the statements with which they express agreement.

The second approach is the Likert technique, which is sometimes known as the *summated scale*. This is generally much easier and quicker than Thurstone scaling. In this approach, the psychologist selects a large number of statements that relate to the attitude object concerned. They should either be clearly pro the object, or clearly anti it. Unlike Thurstone scaling, there is no requirement to establish all points between the extremes. Respondents indicate their agreement or disagreement with each item. Only those items which (a) tend to be responded to in the same way and (b) elicit the same responses on two occasions are chosen for inclusion. Whereas in the Thurstone method the respondents might reply with either a yes or no or not applicable, in the Likert method a 5-, 7- or 10-point response scale is utilized for each item, usually in terms of strongly agree to strongly disagree. Scores are reversed on anti-items but not on pro-items, and the person's overall attitude score is the sum or mean of their item responses. Because the anti-item scores have been reversed, a high score indicates a favourable attitude.

One difficulty with both these techniques is that they are subject to the "social desirability effect", i.e. to respondents giving the socially desirable answer, as, for instance, "Of course I don't think war is glorious" when, in fact, they think just the opposite. There are techniques available to minimize this effect. For example, in the questionnaire shown in Fig. 8.1, one of the authors wanted to find out what people thought about male and female managers. Instead of asking them directly, he devised two questionnaires which were exactly alike, except that in each version a single line was different – "male" and "female". The two versions of the questionnaire were distributed among a random sample of the general public and the differences between the two forms were assessed, without the issue of male *vs* female stereotypes ever being raised on the questionnaire.

8.1   Stereotyped attitudes towards male *vs* female managers.

Description of a character you may know

Is 20 years old
Graduate
Trainee manager
Woman/man*
Unmarried
Enjoys films

*A single version only given on each form

Whereabouts on these scales would you place this character?
Please put a tick in the appropriate box according to where you think she/he would most probably be best described on the scale.

Will be a "high flyer"		Will not necessarily be a "high flyer"
Is inclined to be "bossy"		Is inclined to be meek
Is a good mixer socially		Is rather shy socially
Is very studious		Is not very studious
Would assume leadership in groups		Would not assume leadership in groups
Contains emotions		Expresses emotions freely
Is self-confident		Is not self-confident
Is ambitious		Is not particularly ambitious
Is assertive		Is not particularly assertive

How much do you think he or she will be earning   (a) when he/she is 30?   £............/p.a.
(b) when he/she is 60?   £............/p.a.

Attitude change

Changing attitudes is an important part of many people's work. Sales staff try to persuade potential customers to hold a positive attitude to whatever they are selling. Politicians and others interested in social or economic change try to influence public attitudes concerning those issues (see, e.g., Eiser and van der Pligt, 1988, ch. 7). Managers often seek to change the attitudes of colleagues and subordinates on issues such as marketing strategy or work practices. It should be noted that such attempts are ultimately aimed at changing behaviour, and/or the behavioural component of attitudes. The connection between attitudes and behaviour is examined further on pp. 142–3. Now, however, let us examine some of the factors which determine the success or otherwise of attempts to change a person's attitudes.

Communicator credibility

The credibility of a communicator rests on his or her *expertness* and *trustworthiness* as perceived by the person on the receiving end of the communication (Hovland and Weiss, 1951). Expertness concerns how much the communicator knows about the subject of the communication. Trustworthiness usually depends mainly on whether the communicator has a record of honesty, and on whether he or she appears to be arguing against his or her own interests (Eagly *et al.*, 1978). For example, although the British American Tobacco Company would be low in credibility if it argued that there was no relationship between smoking and lung cancer, it would have great credibility if it argued that smoking definitely leads to lung cancer. This highlights the fact that credibility depends not only on the communication source, but also on the particular issue and arguments presented.

However, the picture is not quite so simple. Sometimes a low-credibility communicator has as much persuasive effect as a high-credibility one – *but* not immediately, not until a few weeks later. This has been termed the *sleeper effect*, and is thought to be due to the person remembering the message but forgetting the source (Cook *et al.*, 1979). So there is hope even for unpopular politicians and propagandists!

Communicator attractiveness

Tannenbaum (1956) and others (e.g. Rogers, 1978) have found that the amount of attitude change is directly related to the degree of attractiveness of the change agent. In Tannenbaum's work, the attractiveness of the communicator was measured through the use of the semantic-differential technique. The ratings of the subjects on the following six evaluation scales were obtained: fair–unfair, dirty–clean, tasty–distasteful, good–bad, pleasant–unpleasant, worthless–valuable. The power of attractiveness may well rest on the desire of the receiver of the message to be like the communicator. There is also some evidence that attractiveness is especially useful when the message is likely to be unpopular (Eagly and Chaiken, 1975), though its power can be undone if the communicator is perceived to be deliberately exploiting his or her attractiveness.

Extremity of message

Which is more effective – extremely stated or moderately stated information? Many of the early findings by Hovland and his associates indicated significantly greater opinion or attitude change the larger the change advocated (Hovland and Prizker, 1957), and many of these aspects are still operative today. This relation was found to be much the same for individuals initially holding extreme opinions and for those holding less extreme ones. But as Hovland pointed out, the generality of these findings may be limited. If the issue is one in which the individual is deeply involved, results opposite to the above may occur. The change agent who attacks an attitude towards an issue in which a person is deeply involved is attacking an attitude which is part of the individual's self-concept. "The advocate of extreme change will therefore be resisted and the target of the information, in defining his self-esteem, may be driven still further away from the position advocated by the communicator" (Krech *et al.*, 1962).

One-sided *vs* two-sided arguments

Is it better to give both sides of an argument (though portraying the favoured one more convincingly), or is a one-sided message more persuasive? This issue was first examined by Yale University researchers (Hovland *et al.*, 1949) in their studies of training and indoctrination films used by the American armed forces during the Second World War. One-sided and two-sided communications were used to evaluate empirically the effectiveness of messages in convincing the soldiers that a long hard war was likely with Japan. They found that:

1. The two-sided presentation was more effective for men who initially held the opposed opinion that the war with Japan would be a short one (less than 2 years). For men who initially favoured the position of the communication (that war would last longer than 2 years), the one-sided presentation was more effective. This finding was subsequently replicated in a study by McGinnies (1966).

2. Better educated men were influenced less by the one-sided than by the two-sided presentation. Thus, persons who value their own independence of judgement and their own intellectual competence may view the acceptance of a one-sided communication as incompatible with maintaining self-esteem.

More recent research has suggested some reasons why one-sided or two-sided arguments might be more effective in different situations. For example, a number of studies have indicated that one-sided arguments may allow the individual more time to contemplate the arguments they receive (Chattopadhyay and Alba, 1988). This may be necessary to persuade people with limited cognitive ability and/or low familiarity with the issues. Also, as Tesser and Shaffer (1990) have contended: "perhaps the need to decide the relative merits of two sides of an unfamiliar issue leads people to concentrate on receiving the message at the expense of thinking about its implications in detail".

Use of fear

Is the use of threat effective in changing attitudes? Janis and Feshbach (1953) studied the effects of different intensities of fear-arousing messages in an illustrated lecture on dental hygiene. They found that change in attitude and behaviour was *inversely* related to the intensity of fear arousal. Of subjects exposed to the mild fear appeal, 36% followed the recommendations (e.g. tooth-brushing) of the lecture. But only 8% of those who heard the high fear lecture did so. Some other research has produced similar findings (e.g. Dembroski *et al.*, 1978).

However, fear arousal can in some circumstances be effective in changing attitudes and behaviour. For example, Dabbs and Leventhal (1966) used it successfully in persuading students to get themselves inoculated against tetanus. Some psychologists have argued that what matters is giving people an effective method of avoiding the fate they are afraid of. Without this, fear arousal makes people "switch off" – it is too horrible for them to contemplate (Rogers and Mewborn, 1976). But offering sure-fire strategies to avoid the feared fate is often difficult. Many insurance companies present fear-arousing messages (e.g. about having a disabling accident), and then suggest that buying one of their insurance policies is an effective strategy. They forget that, for most people, monetary reward neither avoids such an occurrence nor fully compensates for it.

The situation in which attitude change takes place

There are three significant aspects of such situations:

- group *vs* individual;
- commitment in public or private; and
- the effect of the group.

For a long time there have been conflicting views as to whether one should attempt to change attitudes in groups or on a one-to-one basis with the isolated individual. Research has shown that it depends on the nature and composition of the group. If the group is divided on the attitude concerned, it is probably best to attempt to change the person on his or her own. But if not, as Krech *et al.* (1962) suggested, "a situation in which a communication is addressed to a group largely composed of persons favourable to the communicator's position will greatly increase the effectiveness of his communication upon the dissident minority". This may, however, depend on who these people are. Kelley and Woodruff (1956) found among a group of university students that when they thought that "other students" on campus approved of a particular speech (by applauding), their own attitudes towards the speech changed. This was not the case with students who were told that the applause came from a group of people from the town whom they did not know.

Requiring people to commit themselves publicly to a change in attitude has long been used by change agents (Kiesler, 1971). One might term this requirement "the Billy Graham effect". If a person makes their stand public, they will be less likely to change their position as a result of persuasion in the opposite direction. This is demonstrated by various religious revivalist groups that encourage public commitments in the hope of preventing public reconversion or a lapse in faith. As Krech *et al.* (1962) noted: "Public commitment has been found to be an effective procedure; private commitment has been found to be ineffective."

Considerable research has been carried out into the impact of groups on attitudes and action. Lewin's (1953) study, the first of its kind, assessed the impact of group decision making on the attitudes of women towards certain foodstuffs. In this early investigation, Lewin divided a group of housewives into a lecture group and discussion group, the object of which was to change their attitudes towards offal – beef hearts, sweetbreads and kidneys, which normally they did not eat. The first group was lectured about the various nutritionally beneficial qualities of these meats and how they could be made attractive. The second group was asked to discuss the subject as a group with a nutrition expert. Each group was then asked how many of its number planned to try these meats. In addition, a follow-up study was carried out on the subsequent buying behaviour of the housewives. It was found that 3% of those in the lecture group had served the meats, while 32% of those involved in the discussion did so.

Events before the persuasive message

If the recipient of a persuasive message has been *forewarned* about that message, they are more likely to resist it *if* they feel threatened or demeaned by that attempt. Generally, people tense up (both physically and psychologically) if they are led to expect a challenge (Cacioppo and Petty, 1979). But if the recipient is already amenable to being persuaded, forewarning can soften them up, and perhaps produce some attitude change even before they have heard the arguments (Hass, 1975).

Another relevant factor concerns what has sometimes been called *inoculation*. Some attitudes are widely held in our society, e.g. it is commonly believed that fresh fruit is good for you. Such beliefs are never challenged or questioned, or only very rarely. In some classic research, McGuire and Papageorgis (1961) found that it was *easier* to change attitudes that had not earlier been challenged, than those that had. Challenge leads the recipient to think of reasons why they were correct all along. These reasons act as antibodies against subsequent attempts at persuasion.

Characteristics of the recipient of the message

The recipient's level of education and familiarity with the issues have already been identified as significant factors in determining the effectiveness of attempts at persuasion. It should also be noted that any persuader has an uphill task if the recipient of the message has already thought about the issues, because there is considerable evidence that most people process information consistent with their point of view more fully than inconsistent information. Beyond this, it is not possible to talk in terms of persuasibility as a personality characteristic. Some research has shown that people with low-self-esteem are more persuasible than others, but this does not necessarily hold true. Low self-esteem *may* lead to dependence on the views of other people, but it may also lead to a defensive, unchanging reaction where the recipient of the message *projects* their own inadequacies onto the persuader (see p. 20).

Overview of attitude change: Central *vs* peripheral routes to persuasion

Petty and Cacioppo (1985) have made a distinction between the *central route* to persuasion, which involves careful thought and weighing up of arguments, and the *peripheral route*, which relies more on emotional responses but relatively little thought. They argue that attitude change through the central route is longer-lasting and more closely associated with behaviour than that through the peripheral route. Chaiken (1987) has come up with a similar distinction between the *systematic* and *heuristic* processing of information.

Persuasive messages processed through the central route need to contain strong arguments that stand up to scrutiny. People who enjoy thinking, are able to concentrate, feel involvement in the issues in question and feel personally responsible for evaluating the message are most likely to process persuasive messages by the central route. For them, the fate of the persuasive message depends more on their weighing up of the arguments than simply remembering those arguments (Cacioppo and Petty, 1989), though the latter is also important when evaluating two-sided messages (Chattopadhyay and Alba, 1988).

Peripheral processing of information occurs when the recipient of the persuasive message is unwilling or unable to pay it very much attention. When this is the case, the strength of the argument matters less, and peripheral cues matter more, in determining the success or otherwise of the attempt at attitude change. These peripheral cues include communicator attractiveness and expertise, sheer length of the message (irrespective of the quality of its content) and reactions of other recipients of the message (see, e.g., Wood and Kallgren, 1988).

Clearly, this distinction is important for those who wish to change the attitudes of others. It gives some guidance about which aspects of the message, its content and its context are important to different audiences in different situations. The relevant research is currently at the stage of theory development rather than theory application (see Tesser and Shaffer, 1990, pp. 503–512 for a summary) and still has significant gaps (Eiser, 1986, pp. 47–49). But it promises much for future practice.

Attitudes and behaviour

It could be argued that attitudes only matter if they affect actual behaviour. For example, racial prejudice in the workplace is damaging to the extent that it finds expression in discrimination or other negative behaviour towards minority groups. To what extent do attitudes predict behaviour? The answer based on an early review of the research evidence seemed to be "not very much" (Wicker, 1969). People's avowed feelings and beliefs about someone or something seemed only loosely related to how they behaved towards it.

A number of possible reasons were suggested for this lack of correspondence. One was social pressures of various kinds: laws, societal norms and the views of specific people can all prevent a person behaving consistently with their attitudes. So can other attitudes, limitations on a person's abilities, and indeed their general activity levels. There was also some suggestion that the research on this issue was badly designed, and therefore failed to find correspondence between attitudes and behaviour that did in fact exist. In particular, it was argued that measures of attitude were often general (e.g. attitudes about law-breaking), whereas measures of behaviour were specific (e.g. committing motoring offences). Also, behaviour was assessed on only one occasion or over a short time period. Longer-term assessments of multiple instances of the behaviour would be a fairer test of whether attitudes predict behaviour.

Ajzen and Fishbein (1980) have developed a model of the relationship between attitudes and behaviour designed to overcome these difficulties. This model is called the "theory of reasoned action" and is outlined in Fig. 8.2. It assumes that actions are best predicted by intentions, and that intentions are in turn determined by a person's attitude *and* their perception of social pressure.

Note that in the theory of reasoned action, "attitude" is defined in quite precise terms – it concerns *beliefs* about the *consequences* of *behaviour*, and not general beliefs or feelings about the object of the attitude. This is similar to expectancy theories of motivation (see Chapter 10). Note also that "subjective norm" takes into account both the opinions of other people and the person's wish (or lack of it) to comply with those opinions. The theory of reasoned action also acknowledges that people vary in the relative importance of attitude and subjective norm in determining their intentions. The theory of reasoned action has proved successful in predicting behaviour in a wide range of settings.

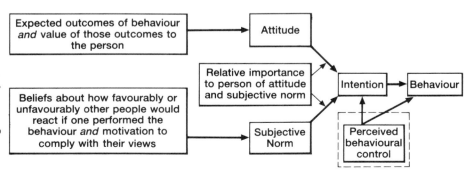

8.2 The theory of reasoned action (adapted from Ajzen and Fishbein, 1980). *Note:* The section surrounded by broken lines indicates the extension of the model to the "theory of planned behaviour" (Ajzen and Madden, 1986).

However, relatively few of these directly concern work behaviour (though many concern consumer behaviour). This is perhaps an example of how work psychology sometimes neglects theoretical advances in social psychology. Sheppard *et al.* (1988) reported that research studies have typically found that the theory of reasoned action explains about half the variance in behaviour. This is quite an impressive performance.

The theory of reasoned action has been adapted by Ajzen and Madden (1986), and its name has been changed to the "theory of planned behaviour". It now includes the notion of *perceived behavioural control*. This reflects the extent to which the person believes they can perform the necessary behaviours in any given situation, and is therefore similar to the concept of self-efficacy (see Chapter 9). Perceived behavioural control is thought to influence behaviour directly, and also indirectly through intentions. Some research (e.g. McCaul *et al.*, 1988) has indicated that the addition of concepts reflecting control does indeed further improve the extent to which behaviour can be predicted.

Clearly, Ajzen and Fishbein's work is a crucial contribution to understanding the relationship between attitudes and behaviour. It could perhaps be applied more than it has been to work attitudes in order to check their connection with work behaviour.

Case study 8.1   A lunchtime drink

Jerry Lander felt that there was nothing wrong with drinking a glass or two of beer during his lunchbreak. He could afford it easily enough. He claimed that he had never seen any evidence that a lunchtime drink harmed his work performance during the afternoon. He found that it helped him feel that much more relaxed and happy at work. Nevertheless, he could do without a drink without much difficulty if he had to. Jerry liked the friendship and approval of other people, and at lunchtime the nearby bar was full of acquaintances he could chat to. Work was an important part of Jerry's life and he was keen to gain promotion. Unfortunately, his boss did not approve of alcoholic drink at lunchtime – or indeed at any other time. Nor did most of his colleagues, with whom he had to work closely. They seemed to view it as a sign of personal inadequacy.

Suggested exercise

Use the theory of reasoned action/planned behaviour to decide whether Jerry Lander is likely to drink a glass of beer during his lunchbreak on most working days.

So far in this chapter we have deliberately avoided discussing specific attitudes, in order to ensure that we cover the important general points. Now it is time to be more specific. We therefore conclude this chapter by looking at two concepts central to work psychology: job satisfaction and organizational commitment.

Job satisfaction

What is job satisfaction?

Locke (1976) defined job satisfaction as a "pleasurable or positive emotional state resulting from the appraisal of one's job or job experiences". The concept generally refers to a variety of aspects of the job that influence a person's levels of satisfaction with it. These usually include attitudes towards pay, working conditions, colleagues and boss, career prospects, and the intrinsic aspects of the job itself. Caldur and Schurr (1981) suggested that in the field of job satisfaction there are three different approaches. First, that work attitudes such as job satisfaction are dispositional in nature, i.e. that they are "stable positive or negative dispositions learned through experience" (Staw *et al.*, 1986; Griffin and Bateman, 1986). The second approach is the "social information processing" model, which suggests that job satisfaction and other workplace attitudes are developed or constructed out of experiences and information provided by others at work (Salancik and Pfeffer, 1978; O'Reilly and Caldwell, 1985). The third is the information processing model, which is based on the accumulation of cognitive information about the workplace and one's job. In a sense, this is the most obvious approach – it argues that a person's job satisfaction is influenced directly by the characteristics of their job (Hackman and Oldham, 1976).

Measuring job satisfaction

There have been many measures of job satisfaction in the workplace from the Job Description Index (JDI: Smith *et al.*, 1969) to Warr *et al.*'s (1979) Job Satisfaction Scales to the more recent job satisfaction scale of the Occupational Stress Indicator (OSI: Cooper *et al.*, 1987). They all tend to involve scales which explore pay, work activities, working conditions, career prospects, relationships with superiors and relationships with colleagues. Table 8.1 provides an example of a measure of job satisfaction from the OSI, which contains all of the elements that usually make up a job satisfaction measure.

Sources of job satisfaction

The major determinants of job satisfaction seem to derive from all three of the theoretical approaches identified above. Thus, regarding the job itself, the major determinants of job satisfaction derive from Hackman and Oldham's (1976) core constructs of skill variety, task identity, task significance, autonomy and feedback (see also Chapter 17). Hackman and Oldham (1976) defined their constructs as:

1. *Skill variety*. The extent to which the job requires a range of skills.
2. *Task identity*. The extent to which the worker can complete a "whole" piece of work, as opposed to a small part of it.

Table 8.1   An example of a measure of job satisfaction from the OSI

How You Feel About Your Job

Very much satisfaction	6
Much satisfaction	5
Some satisfaction	4
Some dissatisfaction	3
Much dissatisfaction	2
Very much dissatisfaction	1

1.	Communication and the way information flows around your organization	6 5 4 3 2 1
2.	The relationships you have with other people at work	6 5 4 3 2 1
3.	The feeling you have about the way you and your efforts are valued	6 5 4 3 2 1
4	The actual job itself	6 5 4 3 2 1
5.	The degree to which you feel "motivated" by your job	6 5 4 3 2 1
6.	Current career opportunities	6 5 4 3 2 1
7.	The level of job security in your present job	6 5 4 3 2 1
8.	The extent to which you may identify with the public image or goals of your organization	6 5 4 3 2 1
9.	The style of supervision that your superiors use	6 5 4 3 2 1
10.	The way changes and innovations are implemented	6 5 4 3 2 1
11.	The kind of work or tasks that you are required to perform	6 5 4 3 2 1
12.	The degree to which you feel that you can personally develop or grow in your job	6 5 4 3 2 1
13.	The way in which conflicts are resolved in your company	6 5 4 3 2 1
14.	The scope your job provides to help you achieve your aspirations and ambitions	6 5 4 3 2 1
15.	The amount of participation which you are given in important decision making	6 5 4 3 2 1
16.	The degree to which your job taps the range of skills which you feel you possess	6 5 4 3 2 1
17.	The amount of flexibility and freedom you feel you have in your job	6 5 4 3 2 1
18.	The psychological "feel" or climate that dominates your organization	6 5 4 3 2 1
19.	Your level of salary relative to your experience	6 5 4 3 2 1
20.	The design or shape of your organization's structure	6 5 4 3 2 1
21.	The amount of work you are given to do whether too much or too little	6 5 4 3 2 1
22.	The degree to which you feel extended in your job	6 5 4 3 2 1

Source: Cooper *et al.* (1987).

3.   *Task significance.* The extent to which the job has an impact on the lives of other people, either inside or outside the organization.

4.   *Autonomy.* The extent to which the job allows the job holder to exercise choice and discretion in their work.

5.   *Feedback.* The extent to which the job itself provides information on how well the job-holder is performing.

Other research has found that goal-setting is also very important (Latham and Yukl, 1976). Obviously, the way a person perceives their job will influence their level of job satisfaction, and therefore job design takes on a significant role in this context (see also Chapter 17). In addition, as Griffin and Bateman (1986) have observed: "in general, most studies find significant and positive correlations between leader behaviours such as initiating structure and consideration, and satisfaction". So leader behaviour is also important in satisfaction at work. Other social factors have more subtle influences, as predicted by the social information processing approach. O'Reilly and Caldwell (1985) demonstrated that both workers' task perceptions and their job satisfaction were influenced by the opinions of others in their work groups. The dispositional approach to job satisfaction has received some support from Staw *et al*, (1986), who found considerable continuity in job satisfaction over many years. Strictly, though, this research did not rule out the possibility that more satisfied people tended to have, or obtain, objectively better jobs.

Organizational commitment

What is organizational commitment?

Organizational commitment has been defined by Mowday *et al*. (1979) as "the relative strength of an individual's identification with and involvement in an organization". This concept is generally thought to have three components (Griffin and Bateman, 1986): (1) a desire to maintain membership in the organization, (2) belief in and acceptance of the values and goals of the organization and (3) a willingness to exert effort on behalf of the organization. If a person is committed to an organization, therefore, he or she has a strong identification with it, values membership, agrees with its objectives and value systems and, finally, is prepared to work on its behalf.

The concept of commitment has received a lot of attention in recent years. Some researchers have broken it down slightly differently from the way described above. For example, Allen and Meyer (1990) have distinguished between:

1. *Affective commitment*: this essentially concerns the person's emotional attachment to their organization.

2. *Continuance commitment*: a person's perception of the costs and risks associated with leaving their current organization.

3. *Normative commitment*: a moral dimension, based on a person's felt obligation and responsibility to their employing organization.

Interestingly, these three components approximate respectively to the affective, behavioural and cognitive components of attitudes identified at the start of this chapter. Other observers have pointed out that people feel multiple commitments at work – not only to their organization, but also perhaps to their location, department, work group or trade union (Reichers, 1985; Barling *et al*., 1990).

Measuring organizational commitment

A number of questionnaires have been developed to measure the various aspects or theories of commitment discussed above. For example, the most widely used scale is the Organizational Commitment Questionnaire (OCQ), which was developed by Mowday *et al.* (1979). It is a 15-item questionnaire that has been used as a total commitment scale, but has also been broken down into sub-scales by various researchers (Bateman and Strasser, 1984). The OCQ is comprised of items like "I feel very little loyalty to this organization", "I am willing to put in a great deal of effort beyond that normally expected in order to help this organization be successful" and "I really care about the fate of this organization." There are other similar scales in use as well. For example, Warr *et al.* (1979) developed a 9-item scale. An example item is "I feel myself to be part of the organization." These measures tend to concentrate on what Allen and Meyer (1990) have termed affective commitment (see above). There are also plenty of other questionnaire measures designed to measure other components and concepts of commitment.

Causes and consequences of organizational commitment

As with job satisfaction, there are several distinct theoretical approaches to organizational commitment. One of these, the behavioural approach, sees commitment as being created when a person does things publicly, of their own free will, and which would be difficult to undo (Kiesler, 1971). Rather like Bem's (1972) self-perception approach, it is suggested that the person examines their own behaviour and concludes that because they did something with significant consequences in full view of others, when they could have chosen not to do so, they really must be committed to it. Therefore, if a person freely chooses to join an organization, and subsequently performs other committing behaviours (e.g. voluntarily working long hours), they will feel more committed to it. This is a neat theory. There is a certain amount of evidence in favour of it (Mabey, 1986; see also Chapter 15).

More commonly, however, it has been suggested that people's commitment can be fostered by giving them positive experiences. This reflects a kind of social exchange approach. The person is essentially saying "if this work organization is nice to me, I will be loyal and hardworking". Many researchers have tried to identify exactly *which* pleasant experiences matter most for organizational commitment. On the whole, it seems that factors intrinsic to the job (e.g. challenge, autonomy) are more important in fostering commitment than extrinsic factors such as pay and working conditions (Mottaz, 1988). This seems especially true for the affective component of commitment (i.e. commitment based on emotional attachment). On the other hand, continuance commitment (i.e. the extent to which leaving would be costly for the person) is more influenced by the person's perception of their past contributions to their organization and their present likely attractiveness (or lack of it) to other employers (Meyer *et al.*, 1989). But there is also some suggestion that commitment is partly a function of the person rather than what happens to them at work (Bateman and Strasser, 1984), i.e. some people are perhaps more prone to feel committed than others.

The distinction between affective and continuance commitment is also significant for work performance. Meyer *et al.* (1989) found that workers high on affective commitment to their organization tended to be better performers than those low on affective commitment. But the opposite pattern of results was observed for continuance commitment. This makes sense: high continuance commitment is based partly on a perceived lack of employment options, and one reason for a person lacking options may be that they are not much good at their work! Other research has suggested that low organizational commitment is linked to employee turnover (i.e. voluntary leaving), which is not surprising given the definition of organizational commitment.

Summary

In this chapter, we have taken a close look at attitudes. In particular, we have focused on what they are, how they can be measured, how they can be changed and their links with behaviour. Like most social psychological phenomena, attitudes are more complicated than they seem at first sight. They have several different components which may or may not fit together nicely. Changing attitudes is difficult. But it is not impossible, especially if the persuader is aware of research findings on attitude change. A person's attitudes predict their behaviour quite well *if* the right attitude is assessed, and if the person's perceptions of social pressures and their own capabilities are also taken into account. Two key work attitudes are job satisfaction and organizational commitment. They can both be measured satisfactorily, and both are influenced by the nature of the person's job. Organizational commitment in particular has some important consequences for work behaviour.

Case study 8.2 Attitudes to job search

Imagine that you are a careers adviser at a university or polytechnic. You have become concerned at the number of students who do not seem to start thinking about what they will do after graduation until well into their final year of study. You know that it usually takes at least 6 months to obtain a job, and sometimes a lot longer. You also know that while some graduates seem happy enough to be unemployed or doing casual work for some months after graduation, many others are not. They regret not having begun to plan for their future early enough.

You decide that you should try to change students' approach to planning for their future career. You decide to compose a handout of not more than 200 words which will be distributed to students during their penultimate year of study.

Suggested exercise

Using the information in this chapter, compose a handout of not more than 200 words designed to persuade students to start their career planning earlier. Let someone else read your handout. Ask them to tell you whether or not they find it persuasive, and why. Justify your wording of the handout to that person.

References

Ajzen, I. and Fishbein, M. (1980). *Understanding Attitudes and Predicting Social Behavior*. Englewood Cliffs, N.J.: Prentice-Hall.

Ajzen, I. and Madden, J. T. (1986). Prediction of goal-directed behavior: Attitudes, intentions, and perceived behavioral control. *Journal of Experimental Social Psychology*, *22*, 453–474.

Allen, N. J. and Meyer, J. P. (1990). The measurement and antecedents of affective, continuance and normative commitment to the organization. *Journal of Occupational Psychology*, *63*, 1–8.

Barling, J., Wade, B. and Fullagar, C. (1990). Predicting employee commitment to company and union: divergent models. *Journal of Occupational Psychology*, *63*, 49–61.

Bateman, T. and Strasser, S. (1984). A longitudinal analysis of the antecedents of organizational commitment. *Academy of Management Journal*, *27*, 95–112.

Bem, D. J. (1972). Self-perception theory. *Advances in Experimental Social Psychology*, *6*, 1–62.

Breckler, S. J. (1984). Empirical validation of affect, behavior and cognition as distinct attitude components. *Journal of Personality and Social Psychology*, *47*, 1191–1205.

Cacioppo, J. T. and Petty, R. E. (1979). Effects of message repetition and position on cognitive responses, recall, and persuasion. *Journal of Personality and Social Psychology*, *37*, 97–109.

Cacioppo, J. T. and Petty, R. E. (1989). Effects of message repetition on argument processing, recall, and persuasion. *Basic Applied Social Psychology*, *10*, 3–12.

Cacioppo, J. T., Petty, R. E. and Green, T. R. (1989). From the tripartite to the homeostasis model of attitudes. In A. R. Pratkanis, S. J. Breckler and A. G. Greenwald (Eds), *Attitude Structure and Functions*. Hillsdale, N.J.: Lawrence Erlbaum Associates.

Caldur, B. J. and Schurr, P. H. (1981). Attitudinal processes in organizations. In L. Cummings and B. Staw (Eds), *Research in Organizational Behavior*, Vol. 3, pp. 283–302. Greenwich, Conn.: JAI Press.

Chaiken, S. (1987). The heuristic model of persuasion. In M. P. Zanna, J. M. Olson and C. P. Herman (Eds), *Social Influence: The Ontario Symposium*. Hillsdale, N.J.: Lawrence Erlbaum Associates.

Chattopadhyay, A. and Alba, J. W. (1988). The situational importance of recall and inference in consumer decision making. *Journal of Consumer Research*, *15*, 1–12.

Cook, T. D., Gruder, C. L., Hennigan, K. M. and Flay, B. R. (1979). History of the sleeper effect: Some logical pitfalls in accepting the null hypothesis. *Psychological Bulletin*, *86*, 662–679.

Cooper, C. L., Sloan, S. and Williams, S. (1987). *Occupational Stress Indicator*. Windsor: NFER/Nelson.

Dabbs, J. and Leventhal, H. (1966). Effects of varying the recommendations in fear-arousing communication. *Journal of Personality and Social Psychology*, *4*, 525–531.

Dembroski, T. M., Lasater, T. M. and Ramirez, A. (1978). Communicator similarity, fear-arousing communications, and compliance with health care recommendations. *Journal of Applied Social Psychology*, *8*, 254–269.

Eagly, A. H. and Chaiken, S. (1975). An attribution analysis of the effect of communicator characteristics on opinion change: The case of communicator attractiveness. *Journal of Personality and Social Psychology*, *33*, 136–144.

Eagly, A. H., Wood, W. and Chaiken, S. (1978). Causal inferences about communicators and their effect on opinion change. *Journal of Personality and Social Psychology, 36*, 424–435.

Eiser, J. R. (1986). *Social Psychology: Attitudes, Cognition and Social Behaviour.* Cambridge: Cambridge University Press.

Eiser, J. R. and van der Pligt, J. (1988). *Attitudes and Decisions.* London: Routledge.

Griffin, R. W. and Bateman, T. S. (1986). Job satisfaction and organizational commitment. In C. L. Cooper and I. T. Robertson (Eds), *International Review of Industrial and Organizational Psychology, 1986*, pp. 157–188. Chichester: John Wiley.

Hackman, J. R. and Oldham, G. R. (1976). Motivation through the design of work: Test of a theory. *Organizational Behavior and Human Performance, 16*, 250–279.

Hass, R. G. (1975). Persuasion or moderation? Two experiments on anticipatory belief change. *Journal of Personality and Social Psychology, 31*, 1155–1162.

Hovland, C. and Prizker, H. (1957). Extent of opinion change as a function of amount of change advocated. *Journal of Abnormal and Social Psychology, 54*, 257–261.

Hovland, C. and Weiss, W. (1951). The influence of source credibility on communication effectiveness. *Public Opinion Quarterly, 15*, 635–650.

Hovland, C., Lumsdaine, A. and Sheffield, F. (1949). *Experiments on Mass Communication.* Princeton, N.J.: Princeton University Press.

Janis, I. and Feshbach, S. (1953). Effects of fear arousing communications. *Journal of Abnormal and Social Psychology, 48*, 78–92.

Kelley, H. H. and Woodruff, C. L. (1956). Members' reactions to apparent group approval of counter-norm communication. *Journal of Abnormal and Social Psychology, 52*, pp. 67–74.

Kiesler, C. A. (1971). *The Psychology of Commitment.* London: Academic Press.

Krech, D., Crutchfield, R. S. and Ballachey, E. L. (1962). *Individual in Society.* New York: McGraw-Hill.

Latham, G. P. and Yukl, G. A. (1976). Effects of assigned and participative goal setting on performance and job satisfaction. *Journal of Applied Psychology, 61*, 166–171.

Lewin, K. (1953). Studies in group decision. In D. Cartwright and A. Zander (Eds), *Group Dynamics.* Evanston, Ill.: Row and Peterson.

Locke, E. A. (1976). The nature and causes of job satisfaction. In M. D. Dunnette (Ed.), *Handbook of Industrial and Organizational Psychology*, pp. 1297–1349. Chicago, Ill.: Rand McNally.

Mabey, C. (1986). *Graduates into Industry.* Aldershot: Gower.

McCaul, K. D., O'Neill, H. K. and Glasgow, R. E. (1988). Predicting the performance of dental hygiene behaviors: An examination of the Fishbein and Ajzen model and self-efficacy expectations. *Journal of Applied Social Psychology, 18*, 114–128.

McGinnies, E. (1966). Studies in persuasion: Reactions of Japanese students to one sided and two sided communications. *Journal of Social Psychology, 70*, pp. 62–74.

McGuire, W. J. and Papageorgis, D. (1961). The relative efficacy of various types of prior belief – defense in producing immunity against persuasion. *Journal of Abnormal and Social Psychology, 62*, 327–337.

Meyer, J. P., Paunonen, S. V., Gellatly, I. R., Goffin, R. D. and Jackson, D. N. (1989). Organizational commitment and job performance: It's the nature of the commitment that counts. *Journal of Applied Psychology, 74*, 152–156.

Millar, M. G. and Tesser, A. (1989). The effects of affective-cognitive consistency and thought on attitude–behavior relations. *Journal of Experimental Social Psychology, 25*, 189–202.

Mottaz, C. J. (1988). Determinants of organizational commitment. *Human Relations*, *41*, 467–482.

Mowday, R., Steers, R. and Porter, L. (1979). The measurement of organizational commitment. *Journal of Vocational Behavior, 14*, 224–247.

O'Reilly, C. A. and Caldwell, D. F. (1985). The impact of normative social influence and cohesiveness on task perceptions and attitudes: A social information-processing approach. *Journal of Occupational Psychology, 58*, 193–206.

Petty, R. E. and Cacioppo, J. T. (1985). The elaboration likelihood model of persuasion. In L. Berkowitz (Ed.), *Advances in Experimental Social Psychology*, Vol. 19. London: Academic Press.

Reichers, A. E. (1985). A review and re-conceptualization of organizational commitments. *Academy of Management Review, 10*, 465–476.

Rogers, C. R. (1978). *Personal Power*. London: Constable.

Rogers, R. W. and Mewborn, C. R. (1976). Fear appeals and attitude change: Effects of a threat's noxiousness, probability of occurrence, and the efficacy of coping responses. *Journal of Personality and Social Psychology, 34*, 56–61.

Salancik, G. R. and Pfeffer, J. C. (1978). A social information processing approach to job attitudes and task design. *Administrative Science Quarterly, 23*, 224–253.

Secord, P. F. and Backman, C. W. (1969). *Social Psychology*. New York: McGraw-Hill.

Sheppard, B. H., Hartwick, J. and Warshaw, P. R. (1988). A theory of reasoned actions: A meta-analysis of past research with recommendations for modifications and future research. *Journal of Consumer Research, 15*, 325–343.

Smith, P. C., Kendall, L. M. and Hulin, C. L. (1969). *The Measurement of Satisfaction in Work and Retirement*. Chicago Ill.: Rand-McNally.

Staw, B. M., Bell, N. E. and Clausen, J. A. (1986). The dispositional approach to job attitudes: A lifetime longitudinal test. *Administrative Science Quarterly, 31*, 56–77.

Tannenbaum, P. (1956). Initial attitude toward source and concept as factors in attitude change through communication. *Public Opinion Quarterly, 20*, 413–426.

Tesser, A. and Shaffer, D. (1990). Attitudes and attitude change. In M. R. Rosenzweig and L. W. Porter (Eds), *Annual Review of Psychology*, Vol. 41. Palo Alto, Calif.: Annual Reviews Inc.

Warr, P., Cook, J. and Wall, T. (1979). Scales for the measurement of some work attitudes and aspects of psychological well-being. *Journal of Occupational Psychology, 52*, 129–148.

Wicker, A. W. (1969). Attitudes versus actions: The relationship of overt and behavioral responses to attitude objects. *Journal of Social Issues, 25*, 41–78.

Wood, W. and Kallgren, C. A. (1988). Communicator attributes and persuasion: Recipients' access to attitude-relevant information in memory. *Personality and Social Psychology Bulletin, 14*, 172–182.

The analysis and modification of work behaviour

Introduction

For many psychologists, psychology primarily involves the scientific study of human *behaviour*. The italics in the previous sentence stress the point that for many people the focus of attention in psychology is on what people actually do, rather than what they may be thinking or feeling. Indeed, it is obviously extremely difficult to form an impression of what someone thinks or feels without attending to their behaviour, whether the behaviour involved is their speech, speed of movement, facial expression or whatever. This focus on behaviour as the crucial unit of analysis is particularly important in work psychology. What people actually do at work is critical to organizational success and it is no accident that the field of organizational *behaviour* has become an important area of research and study with business and management schools.

In 1980, Davis and Luthans made the following comment:

There is today a jungle of theories that attempt to explain human behaviour in organizations. Unfortunately, many of the theoretical explanations have seemed to stray from behaviour as the unit of analysis in organizational behaviour. There is a widespread tendency for both scholars and practitioners to treat such hypothetical constructs as motivation, satisfaction and leadership as ends in themselves. We think it is time to re-emphasize the point that behaviours are the empirical reality, not the labels attached to the attempted explanation of the behaviours (p. 281).

The viewpoint that Davis and Luthans proposed is derived from the ideas of behaviourist psychology (e.g. Skinner, 1974). Behaviourist ideas have a long and influential history within fundamental psychology (see Chapter 2) and in many areas of applied psychological research and practice. In rudimentary terms, the behaviourist view argues that a satisfactory and useful science of psychology must be based on the observation and analysis of external, observable behaviour. Behaviourists argue that to focus attention on internal psychological processes which cannot be directly observed is both unscientific and unlikely to provide a coherent and systematic understanding of human behaviour. Thus, internal psychological states, processes, emotions, feelings and many other aspects of human subjective experience are rejected as topics for study in favour of an examination of behaviour, the external conditions in which the behaviour is exhibited and the observable consequences of behaviour. For some, this represents a limited and restricting view of human psychology, but for behaviourists it represents a philosophically clear and practical view from which to develop an understanding of behaviour. As this chapter demonstrates, the research of the behaviourists has produced a variety of interesting ideas, many of which have been applied with enthusiasm and some success in organizational settings. In some areas of applied research, the pure form of behaviourism (which rejects any form of internal mental process as unscientific) has been diluted with the acceptance of ideas and techniques from other theoretical perspectives.

This chapter provides several examples of the use of behaviourist ideas in practice and also shows how behaviourist concepts may be incorporated into more general theories such as social cognitive theory (Bandura, 1977, 1986) to produce useful organizational applications.

Conditioning and behaviour

The application of behaviourist ideas within organizations is explored later in this chapter, but first an outline of the major research findings and key concepts of behaviourism will be provided. Two main types of conditioning provide the basis of the behaviourist approach: classical (respondent) conditioning and instrumental (operant) conditioning.

Classical conditioning

Classical conditioning is a simple but important form of learning first identified by the Russian physiologist Pavlov who was studying the digestive and nervous system of dogs. He did in fact win a Nobel Prize in 1904 for this work, but it was a chance discovery resulting from this original research that earned him lasting fame. Like all dogs, the ones in Pavlov's laboratory would salivate when food was placed in their mouths. Pavlov noticed, however, that once the dogs had been in the laboratory for some time, the sight of their food dish arriving, or even the approaching footsteps of the attendant who fed them, would be enought to cause salivation. Pavlov recognized that the salivation which occurred in response to the dish or attendant's footsteps involved some form of very basic learning on the part of the animals. After his initial observations, Pavlov went on to investigate the phenomenon in a controlled, experimental setting. He arranged for the amount of saliva produced by the dogs to be measured. Then he sounded a tone slightly before food was placed in the animals' mouths. After several trials it was found that the tone by itself would produce salivation and therefore the dogs had been conditioned to respond to the tone.

The general form of classical conditioning involves an unconditioned stimulus (UCS), such as food, which produces an automatic unconditioned response

(UCR), such as salivation. Conditioning occurs when the unconditioned stimulus becomes associated with a conditioned stimulus (CS), such as a bell. In fact, classical conditioning is an extremely widespread phenomenon and it is clear that Pavlov had discovered something of considerable importance and generality. Although we can only guess at the scope and variety of phenomena that can be explained in terms of classical conditioning, such conditioning is often closely involved in our emotional or gut reaction to the various experiences. Many people experience strong emotional reactions to certain situations, often because in the past these have been paired with particularly vivid, painful or pleasant experiences.

In his original work, Pavlov went on to pair other conditioned stimuli (e.g. a shape) with the tone. After several trials, the dogs salivated to the shape alone. This procedure of introducing a second stimulus to which the organism can be conditioned to respond is known generally as higher-order conditioning. The specific example above would be referred to as second-order conditioning. Although Pavlov was only ever able to go beyond third-order conditioning with his dogs, modern scientists accept that humans may be conditioned to higher orders. Such higher-order conditioning may play an important part in many of our emotional reactions.

Operant conditioning

The idea that certain basic phenomena such as classical conditioning may be used to explain the behaviour of a range of organisms from laboratory rats, pigeons or dogs to humans is one of the mainstays of the behaviourist tradition. The behaviourists began their work in the hope that by studying simple forms of learning in simple animals, it should be possible to uncover the basic laws and principles of learning. These could then be generalized and used to explain human learning and behaviour.

The most famous contemporary behaviourist, B. F. Skinner, is also often described as the most influential psychologist of this century. Skinner distinguished between two types of behaviour – respondent and operant. Respondent behaviour refers to the kind of behaviour shown during classical conditioning when a stimulus triggers a more or less natural reaction such as the salivation produced by Pavlov's dogs or other automatic responses like excitement, fear and sexual arousal. Operant behaviour (behaviour that operates on the environment) deals with the forms of behaviour that are not the result of simple, automatic responses. Most human behaviour in fact is operant behaviour – going to work, driving a car, solving a mathematical problem and playing tennis are all examples of operant behaviour. According to Skinner, such behaviour is learned and strengthened by a process of operant conditioning.

The major elements involved in operant conditioning are the stimulus, the response and reinforcement or reward. As an example of the operant conditioning process at work, consider an executive who is asked to speak at a management meeting. The stimulus is the request for the executive to speak. The executive responds by giving certain views and this response may be reinforced (rewarded) by nods and smiles from a senior manager. The effect of reinforcement is to increase the likelihood that the executive will respond with the same or similar views at future meetings. The learning involved is sometimes described as instrumental conditioning, because the response of the person or other organism involved is instrumental in obtaining the reinforcement.

Although the example given above involves human behaviour, much of the work on operant conditioning has been carried out with laboratory animals such as rats and pigeons. In some classic experiments, mostly with rats and pigeons, Skinner was able to show that by providing them with reinforcement (usually food) at appropriate points, animals could be taught to exhibit a wide range of behaviours. Many of the experiments were conducted with the aid of an operant chamber or "Skinner box". Reinforcement is provided when the animal in the box exhibits certain operant behaviours (e.g. pressing the lever, or pecking a certain region of the box).

Operant techniques, unlike classical conditioning, can be used to produce behaviour that is not normally part of the organism's repertoire. For example, pigeons have been taught to play ping-pong and "Priscilla the Fastidious Pig" was taught to turn on the radio, eat breakfast at table, drop dirty clothes in a washing hamper, vacuum the floor and select her sponsoring company's food in preference to brand X (Breland and Breland, 1951). According to Skinner, the same fundamental processes of operant conditioning are involved regardless of whether we are concerned with a pigeon learning how to obtain food in an operant chamber, a child learning to talk and write, or a subordinate learning how to deal with a difficult manager. Operant behaviours (pecking in the right spot, pronouncing a difficult word correctly or saying the appropriate thing at a committee meeting) produce reinforcement (food, the praise of parents or the manager), and as a consequence the behaviour that produced the reinforcement is learned and strengthened. The process of operant conditioning is often described with the aid of a three-term framework: Antecedents (A), Behaviour (B) and Consequence (C). Antecedents refer to the conditions or stimuli that precede the behaviour, and consequences refer to the reinforcing or punishing outcomes that the behaviour produces.

With animals, reinforcement often takes the form of food; but for humans, reinforcement may take a wide variety of forms – smiles, gifts, money, complimentary words – and a wide range of other things may provide reinforcement for behaviour. Broadly, reinforcement is anything which follows operant behaviour and increases the probability that the behaviour will recur. In many circumstances, of course, during our daily lives, we administer reinforcement to others in a fairly unsystematic and uncontrolled fashion. Smiles, nods, praise, etc., are all given with little thought for the consequences on the operant behaviour of others or the learning that we are unwittingly encouraging. A common example occurs when parents say no to a child's request for something and at first resist even when the child cries and makes them feel mean and unfair. Eventually, when they can stand it no longer, they give in and comply with the child's request, thus unwittingly reinforcing the child's crying.

The behaviourist research into operant learning has proved to be a rich source of information about certain types of learning experience; many of the basic principles have been applied in a wide range of organizational and other contexts. Over the next few pages some of the more important principles derived from behaviourist research are discussed.

Extinction

So far, we have looked at the effect that reinforcement has on strengthening behaviour. What happens when reinforcement is not produced as a result of behaviour? When reinforcement is withdrawn or perhaps never given at all, the operant behaviour associated with it will gradually cease to occur. In technical terms, it is extinguished. Learned behaviour will continue only if the person is being reinforced. For many things we learn during formal education, at work and in everyday life, reinforcement is so frequent and common that we do not notice it. Nevertheless, as Zohar and Fussfield (1981) point out, when operant techniques are used to change employees' behaviour in organizations, the new behaviour will sometimes extinguish quite rapidly if reinforcement is removed.

Schedules of reinforcement

Sometimes reinforcement takes place on a continuous basis. An employee who is rewarded every time a satisfactory piece of work is produced is being reinforced on a continuous basis. Most reinforcement at work and in everyday life, however, occurs on a partial basis: parents rarely praise their children every time they exhibit good manners, good work often goes unnoticed by superiors, people do not always laugh uproariously at our jokes! In general, behaviour that is based on a partial reinforcement schedule is much more persistent and likely to continue even when reinforcement is removed. This is true despite the fact that on partial reinforcement schedules less reinforcement is provided. In fact, the general rule is that the lower the percentage of correct responses that are rewarded, the more persistent the behaviour will be. An experiment reported by Lewis and Duncan (1956) helps to explain this apparent paradox. In their experiment people were allowed to gamble, using slot-machines. The machines were "rigged" so that some paid out on every trial (i.e. continuous reinforcement). Other machines paid out on a partial bias (as real slot-machines do). In the second part of the experiment, everyone played on a second machine – rigged so that it would never pay out. People who had been trained on the partial schedules were much more resistant to extinction and they continued to play long after people on a continuous schedule had stopped. In fact, the overall results conformed well with the idea mentioned above, that the lower the percentage of responses rewarded, the more resistant to extinction is the behaviour concerned, demonstrating the powerful effect of partial reinforcement schedules compared with continuous reinforcement.

Partial reinforcement may be given on either an interval or ratio schedule. Interval reinforcement occurs when a specified amount of time has passed. The next response that occurs will then produce reinforcement. For example, a telephone salesperson might be told to take a break by the supervisor as soon as the last call in any 45-minute period is completed. Ratio reinforcement is based, not on the passage of time, but on the number of responses that have occurred (e.g. a worker is given a break after every 50 components he has produced). Schedules of reinforcement can also either be fixed to occur regularly after every so many minutes or responses, or variable and occur, on average, every "*x*" minutes or responses, but the actual gap between each reinforcement is varied (see Fig. 9.1).

The reinforcement hierarchy

Some ideas concerning reinforcement, which seem particularly valuable within the context of organizational behaviour, have been proposed and developed by Premack (1965). Premack demonstrated by experiment that an event which serves as a reinforcer for some behaviour may not have a reinforcing effect on other, different behaviours. In addition, he demonstrated that reinforcers may sometimes change places with the behaviour which produces them. For example, a thirsty laboratory animal will run to obtain water; equally, an animal subjected to a long period of inactivity will drink in order to take an opportunity to run. In other words, drinking may reinforce running, but in some circumstances running may reinforce drinking. This simple example demonstrates the fact that the attraction of reinforcers may change as circumstances change. Premack has argued that there is, in effect, a hierarchy of reinforcement. The order of reinforcers in the hierarchy will change as circumstances change. Behaviours at the top of the hierarchy are things that we would like to engage in

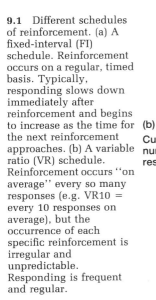

9.1 Different schedules of reinforcement. (a) A fixed-interval (FI) schedule. Reinforcement occurs on a regular, timed basis. Typically, responding slows down immediately after reinforcement and begins to increase as the time for the next reinforcement approaches. (b) A variable ratio (VR) schedule. Reinforcement occurs "on average" every so many responses (e.g. VR10 = every 10 responses on average), but the occurrence of each specific reinforcement is irregular and unpredictable. Responding is frequent and regular.

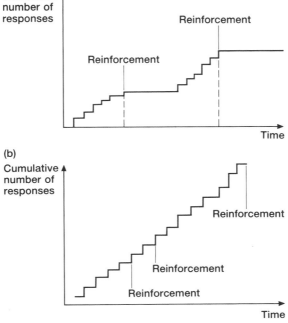

if given the opportunity – collecting £1 million from a bank, for instance. Behaviours at the bottom are those that we would rarely engage in even if the opportunity to do so were unlimited.

The reinforcement hierarchy may be used to influence or explain behaviours in many settings. Consider, for example, an employee who enjoys finishing work early and a long break from work at lunchtime. If the reinforcement provided by an early finish is further up the hierarchy than a lunchtime break, the employee may be persuaded to work through the lunch period for the reward of an early finish. In other words, one behaviour (early finish) may be used to reinforce another (work through lunch). Of course, if the employee in question had reason to attend a particularly important social event at lunchtime, the position of the two behaviours in the hierarchy might become reversed and the lunchbreak might act as a reinforcer for working late. This general principle can be used to great advantage in a wide variety of settings.

Punishment

Just as a reinforcement will increase the likelihood of a response, punishment (the use of aversive or unpleasant stimuli) will decrease the likelihood of the behaviour that immediately precedes it. At first sight, punishment may seem to be a useful means for suppressing or eliminating certain behaviours. It is – but only when correctly used.

Consider the case of a supervisor who always raises disciplinary problems at the company's weekly progress meetings and, in so doing, reveals that he has consistently made bad decisions and errors of judgement when supervising his staff. At first, at the meetings, his manager responds with tactful and diplomatic assistance and tries to point out the errors to the supervisor, suggesting how they might be avoided in future. Eventually, however, the manager becomes exasperated, loses her temper and punishes the supervisor with strong words and a public dressing down. For the next few months, there are no more reports of discipline problems and the manager begins to feel that the "short, sharp shock" has worked. Suddenly, however, the manager is confronted with a deputation of employees from the supervisor's department who claim that discipline has grown progressively worse and that their working conditions are now intolerable. What went wrong? Had the punishment not worked? The punishment had worked, but inevitably – as anticipated above – it had decreased the likelihood of the behaviour immediately preceding it, which in this case was the *reporting* of problems by the supervisor at the weekly meetings. The supervisor had learned that this was not a successful thing to do. Consequently, he deliberately neglected raising the issue at meetings and thus avoided the possibility of punishment occurring, which was not the outcome the manager had intended. On the contrary, the behaviour the manager had tried to punish had continued unchecked and the supervisor continued making errors of judgement.

In many cases, it is impractical to give punishment at the appropriate time. For this and many other reasons (e.g. a classically conditioned aversion to the punished, and the fact that avoiding punishment may provide a form of reinforcement and therefore encourage avoidance behaviour), most people feel that punishment is not a very effective means of controlling behaviour. Incidentally, punishment – the presentation of an aversive stimulus – should not be confused with negative reinforcement. Negative reinforcers are stimuli that have the effect of increasing the probability of occurrence of the response that precedes them when they are *removed* from the situation.

Fundamentals of conditioning: Contiguity and contingency

The general overview of the work of the behaviourists given above has illustrated their use of certain key concepts such as response, stimulus, reinforcement and extinction. The research on punishment mentioned immediately above illustrates two important concepts, one of which is contiguity, i.e. for conditioning to occur there should be only a small delay between behaviour and reinforcement (or punishment). In broad terms, the longer the gap between these two events, the less likely it is that the target behaviour will be strengthened or diminished. The other fundamental concept, not mentioned explicitly so far, is the idea of contingency: This emphasizes that reinforcement is contingent on response; in other words, for conditioning to occur, reinforcement should be provided only when the desired behaviour occurs.

Reinforcing other behaviours makes it likely that they will be influenced and that the intended behaviour will not be affected. Contiguity and contingency are seen as fundamental elements involved in understanding how conditioning takes place and, taken together with the concepts of stimulus, response, reinforcement and extinction, represent the core of the behaviourist position.

Organizational behaviour modification

The principle of operant conditioning and systematic procedures of behaviour analysis have been applied in educational and clinical settings for some time (Ulrich *et al.*, 1974; Rimm and Masters, 1979). More recently, they have also been used within organizational settings to modify behaviour. Comprehensive coverage of the application of operant techniques to Organizational Behaviour Modification (OB Mod) has been presented by Luthans and Kreitner (1975). The essence of the OB Mod approach involves focusing on critical behaviours that are important for satisfactory work performance and the application of reinforcement principles attempting to strengthen appropriate behaviour patterns. Luthans and Kreitner describe a five-step procedure for using OB Mod techniques:

1. Identify the critical behaviours.
2. Measure the critical behaviours.

3. Carry out a functional analysis of the behaviour.
4. Develop an intervention strategy.
5. Evaluate.

Critical behaviours represent the activities of the personnel within the organization that are influencing organizational performance and are to be strengthened, weakened or modified in some way. Such behaviour might be identified in a variety of ways, including discussion with relevant personnel, systematic observation or tracing the cause of performance or production deficiencies. An important point, however, is that only specific, observable behaviour is used. To say that it is critical to "have a positive attitude" would not be acceptable and the behaviour that demonstrated such qualities (low absenteeism, prompt responses to requests, instructions, etc.) would need to be identified.

Once the critical behaviours are identified, a baseline measure of their frequency of occurrence is obtained, either by direct observation or recording, or perhaps from existing company records. This baseline measure is important in two main ways. It provides an objective view of the current situation, indicating for example that the scale of a problem is much bigger or smaller than it was at first thought to be, and it provides a basis for examining any change that might eventually take place as a result of intervention.

Functional analysis involves identifying:

1. The cues or stimuli in the work situation (antecedent conditions) that trigger the behaviour.
2. The contingent consequences, i.e. the consequences in terms of reward, punishment, etc., that are maintaining the behaviour.

These can be examined using the A-B-C (Antecedent Behaviour Consequences) framework mentioned earlier. This stage is critical for the success of any programme of OB Mod, because it is essential to have an accurate picture of the antecedents and consequences that may be maintaining the behaviour in question. For example, an OB Mod programme may be considered by a sales manager as a means of encouraging sales personnel to make fewer visits to base – visits that are spent in unproductive chats with colleagues. The sales manager may be concerned about the behaviour because of the time-wasting involved and because the sales director keeps making comments about large numbers of the sales force "sitting at base together doing nothing". The apparent rewarding consequences of returning to base may be the opportunity to relax and avoid the pressures of being on the road. It could be, however, that the important consequence for the sales staff is the opportunity for social interaction with colleagues and that it is the reinforcing effect of this social interaction which is maintaining their undesirable behaviour. Any attempt to modify their behaviour by providing opportunities for relaxation away from base or by staggering their visits to base so that only small numbers are there at any time would be founded on an inaccurate view of the behaviour-consequence contingencies.

Once the functional analysis has been conducted, an intervention strategy designed to modify the behaviour concerned must be developed. The purpose of

Table 9.1 Possible rewards for use in organizational behaviour modification

Contrived on-the-job rewards				Natural rewards	
Consumables	Manipulatables	Visual and auditory	Tokens	Social	Premack
Coffee-break treats	Desk accessories	Office with a window	Money	Friendly greetings	Job with more responsibility
Free lunches	Wall plaques	Piped-in music	Stocks	Informal recognition	Job rotation
Food baskets	Company car	Redecoration of work environment	Stock options	Formal acknowledgement of achievement	Early time off with pay
Easter hams	Watches		Passes for films		
Christmas turkeys	Trophies	Company literature	Trading stamps	Invitations to coffee/lunch	Extended breaks
Dinners for the family on the company	Commendations Rings/tie-pins	Private office Popular speakers or lecturers	Paid-up insurance policies Dinner and theatre tickets	Solicitations of suggestions Solicitations of advice	Extended lunch period Personal time off with pay
Company picnics	Appliances and furniture for the home	Book club discussions	Holiday trips	Compliment on work progress	Work on personal project on company time
After-work wine and cheese parties	Home shop tools	Feedback about performance	Coupons redeemable at local stores	Recognition in house organ	Use of company machinery or facilities for personal projects
Beer parties	Garden tools Clothing Club privileges Special assignments		Profit-sharing	Pat on the back Smile Verbal or non-verbal recognition or praise	Use of company recreation facilities

Source: Luthans and Kreitner (1975).

the intervention strategy is to strengthen desirable behaviour and weaken undesirable behaviour. A major feature of human behaviour is the range and variety of rewards that might be used to provide reinforcement. Money provides an obvious example, but many other potential rewards can be identified – Table 9.1 provides some examples. It is worth noting that not all of the rewards involve the organization in direct costs, such as friendly greetings and compliments. Various intervention strategies may be used, but most involve the use of positive reinforcement in some way. Punishment appears to have had a lesser role in most studies, although it has received some attention (see Arvey and Ivancevich, 1980). It is also possible to make use of Premack's reinforcement hierarchy principle mentioned earlier, whereby employees are rewarded for engaging in behaviour low down in the hierarchy (e.g. working at a job until it is finished, even if it means staying late) by being allowed to engage in behaviours higher up (e.g. being given more challenging and responsible work). The choice of appropriate reinforcers is crucial for successful interventions, because the effects of specific potential rewards vary according to the people involved. To some people, for instance, the allocation of more challenging and responsible work would not be as rewarding as the opportunity to leave work on time every evening. Some people would find money more attractive than time off, etc.

OB Mod in practice

Table 9.2 illustrates the major consequences that can follow behaviour and gives references to some illustrative OB Mod studies. Although it is not an exclusively behaviourist concept, feedback is included in Table 9.2 because of its widespread usage in OB Mod studies, often in conjunction with reinforcers such as praise (Alavosius and Sulzer-Azaroff, 1986) or money and free gifts (Haynes *et al.*, 1982). Feedback is an important aspect of many other theoretical

Table 9.2   Consequences of behaviour and organizational behaviour modification

Consequence	Effect on preceding behaviour	Usage in OB Mod	Illustrative studies
Positive reinforcement	A consequence which, when introduced, *increases* the frequency of immediately preceding behaviour recurring	Widely used although praise and social reinforcers are more common than monetary reinforcers	Komaki *et al.* (1978) used feedback to improve safety Geller *et al.* (1983) used incentives (free dinners) to improve the usage rates of seat belts
Negative reinforcement	A consequence which, when *removed*, increases the frequency of the immediately preceding behaviour recurring	Not used explicitly very often, but may be a side-effect of intervention in some studies	Luthans *et al.* (1981; 1986) used cash awards and paid vacations to change behaviour Fox *et al.* (1987) used a token economy to reduce lost work and lost time in open-pit coal mines
Punishment	A consequence which, when introduced, *decreases* the frequency of the immediately preceding behaviour recurring	Usually avoided because of unintended side-effects	Karan and Kopelman (1987) used feedback to reduce vehicle accidents in a packaging forwarding facility
Extinction	The *absence* of any rewarding or punishing consequence. Causes the subsequent frequency of the preceding behaviour to *decrease*. Often difficult to differentiate from punishment (e.g. if a reinforcer is deliberately withdrawn in order to extinguish some specific behaviour)	Often explicitly or implicitly used in conjunction with positive reinforcement to strengthen desirable behaviour and weaken undesirable behaviour	
Feedback	Providing information about the outcomes of behaviour – or actual behaviour (e.g. how close behaviour is to a target behaviour)	One of the most frequently used intervention strategies	

positions and behaviour change strategies such as goal-setting (Locke and Latham, 1984). Within the behaviourist framework, feedback is construed as a consequence of behaviour and, because behaviour may be influenced by adjusting consequences, feedback may be used to help to shape behaviour. Despite this feedback and its role in helping to shape behaviour, it is a troublesome concept for pure behaviourism because it is difficult to see how it can have any influence on subsequent behaviour without the informational (i.e. cognitive) component of feedback being important (see Locke and Henne, 1986; Bandura 1986).

Behaviour modification has been used in a wide variety of settings to produce changes in many aspects of organizational behaviour. One of the earliest and best known studies (although it is not methodologically rigorous) was the Emery Air Freight study (at Emery Air Freight, 1973). One of the remarkable things about this study is that marked changes in behaviours related to work quality were brought about with the use of feedback and praise only.

This study and several other early studies focusing on work quality, absenteeism, supervisory training and other aspects of work behaviour showed that the operant-based systematic application of OB Mod techniques could produce important changes in behaviour (for further examples, see O'Brien *et al.*, 1982; Luthans and Martinko, 1987). An illustrative study involving the application of behaviourist principles is that of Zohar and Fussfeld (1981). This study was conducted in a textile factory in which noise levels were extremely high (106 dB). Despite these dangerously high levels of noise, the employees were reluctant to wear ear-defenders and only 35% wore them all the time. Zohar and Fussfeld first made contact with the personnel involved and established some reinforcers that the personnel found attractive (consumer durables, such as radios and TV sets). After taking baseline measures of the frequency of ear-defender usage, Zohar and Fussfeld than introduced a variable ratio token economy system. Under this scheme, tokens were secondary reinforcers, because they had no direct rewarding value themselves, which could be exchanged for the consumer durables, when an operative had collected enough tokens. The tokens were given to operatives by supervisors who distributed them on an irregular basis only to operatives who were wearing ear-defenders. The token economy had the almost immediate effect of increasing ear-defender usage from 35 to 90%. Furthermore, when the investigations collected follow-up data 9 months after the token economy (which ran for only 2 months) had been discontinued, ear-defender usage was still at 90%. This study is a good example of OB Mod at work, as it shows how a previously intractable problem – the company had already tried poster campaigns, etc., to improve ear-defender usage – may be resolved permanently at relatively little cost.

Evaluating the effect of OB Mod

Evaluation is an important element in the application of any OB Mod programme. Various designs can be used to conduct the evaluation phase of an OB Mod programme. The primary aim of the evaluation is, of course, to examine if, and to what extent, the intervention has modified the target behaviours. The most widely used designs are the reversal or ABAB design and the multiple baseline design. The reversal (ABAB) design involves alternating use of the OB Mod programme and removal of the programme over a period of time (see Fig. 9.2). In such a design, the frequency of the target behaviour is assessed before the programme begins. This provides a baseline (the A phase). The next phase involves intervening and using reinforcement, punishment, etc., to modify behaviour (the B phase). After the intervention has produced stable new rates for the behaviour, it is removed (the reversal) and conditions revert to baseline.

Usually, the behaviour will also revert, or at least show some return towards baseline levels. Although this design can provide impressive evidence of the effect of the intervention, there are obvious problems. The return to baseline may not always be desirable. Furthermore, the intervention may have been deliberately designed to ensure lasting behaviour change so that even when the specific reinforcers, etc., used in the intervention phase are removed, the behaviour should not revert to baseline levels (Zohar and Fussfeld, 1981).

The multiple baseline design can help to deal with these problems. In this design, baseline data are collected across two or more behaviours. Then a specific intervention strategy to change each behaviour in turn is introduced (see

9.2 The reversal (ABAB) design for evaluating an OB Mod programme.

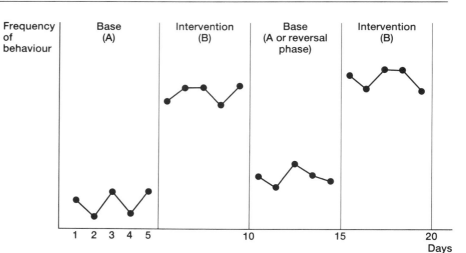

Fig. 9.3). Each behaviour should change only when the relevant intervention strategy is used. If this happens, it provides convincing evidence (without the need for reversals) that the intervention is causing the change. Further details on these and other methods may be found in Kazdin (1980), Luthans and Kreitner (1975) and Komaki and Jensen (1986).

Putting more thought into OB Mod

Despite its obvious success in bringing about useful behaviour change, traditional OB Mod has frequently been criticized (e.g. Locke, 1977) and its potential for theoretical growth and conceptual development has been constrained by the rigorous emphasis, in pure behaviourism, on directly observable and measurable phenomena. The difficulties encountered in trying to

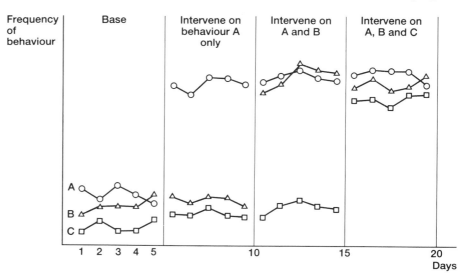

9.3 The multiple baseline design for evaluating an OB Mod programme.

incorporate such obviously cognitive concepts as feedback into such a reso-
lutely anti-mentalistic framework have already been mentioned. Problems
such as this, together with the theoretical developments which have extended
behaviourist theory into the cognitive domain (Bandura, 1986), have led to an
integration of OB Mod with more cognitive approaches.

The cognitive approaches of most relevance to contemporary organizational
behaviour and analysis are social cognitive theory (Bandura, 1986) and goal-
setting theory (Locke and Henne, 1986). Goal-setting is discussed in Chapter 10.
Essentially, goal-setting is a cognitively based theory which proposes that
specific, difficult goals, when they are accepted by the individual, will lead to
effective performance. Goals influence cognitions by directing attention. Feedback on goal attainment is necessary for goal-setting to be maximally effective.
Many behaviour change studies have made use of both goal-setting and feedback
and extremely effective interventions have been produced (e.g. Chokkar and
Wallin, 1984). A behaviourist interpretation of goals would see them as antecedent conditions. It has, however, become increasingly accepted by researchers
that *cognitive* states concerning goal commitment, acceptance and attributions
are important concepts in understanding how goal-setting works.

Case study 9.1   Improving attendance with OB Mod

Absenteeism at SJR Foods plant had been getting
steadily worse for many years. Radha El-Bakry,
the production manager, felt that it would be
worth investing some money in solving the
problem. In consultation with the company
unions, she developed and installed a lottery
scheme which involved the issuing of free
tickets to employees who attended work. Each

more than paying for itself in improved attendance (see Fig. 9.4).

At the same time, as she introduced the
lottery system, Radha had agreed a goal with the
employee representatives of 90% attendance. At
the end of each week, a chart in the canteen
(similar to Fig. 9.4) was completed, which
showed the attendance rate for that week.

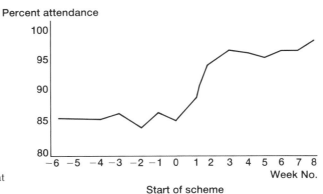

9.4 Attendance rates at
SJR Foods.

full day's attendance entitled the employee to
one free lottery ticket. Full attendance for a week
produced a bonus of two extra tickets. The lottery was drawn every Friday evening and prizes
were available for collection on the spot. Within
2 weeks of its introduction, the scheme was

Suggested exercises

1. Using the terminology and concepts of OB
   Mod, explain what had been done at SJR
   Foods.
2. Discuss the extent to which this intervention
   adopted a pure behaviourist approach.

Social cognitive theory does not reject the operant-based view of behaviour development which is at the heart of behaviourism. This theory does, however, extend the operant view and makes use of important additional cognitive concepts. The essence of social cognitive theory (earlier called social learning theory) is that the role of cognitive processes in determining behaviour is given prominence. Social cognitive theory accepts the basic tenets of the behavioural approach (i.e. reinforcement, contingency and contiguity, and the impact of schedules of reinforcement) but goes on to add further novel concepts. So one of these novel concepts involves significant departures from traditional operant approaches to behaviour. The overall framework within which these concepts are developed involves the concept of "reciprocal determinism" (see Fig. 9.5).

Social learning theory emphasizes the interaction of situation and person factors, and may be a better theoretical basis for organizational behaviour than the purely situational view based on operant conditioning only. Social learning theory differs from the traditional operant approach in many ways.

One of the important differences concerns the acceptance that internal cognitive processes are important determinants of behaviour. For example, whereas traditional reinforcement theory argues that behaviour is regulated by its immediate, external consequences only, social learning theory suggests that internal psychological factors such as expectancies about the eventual consequences of behaviour have a role in controlling behaviour. Bandura (1977, p. 18) expresses it as follows:

> Contrary to the mechanistic view, outcomes change behaviour largely through the intervening influence of thought. ... Anticipatory capacities enable humans to be motivated by prospective consequences. Past experiences create expectations that certain actions will bring valued benefits, and that still others will avert future trouble. ... Homeowners, for instance, do not wait until they experience the distress of a burning house to purchase fire insurance.

Social learning theorists also argue that, as well as responding to the influence of reinforcement in the environment, people often control and develop behaviour patterns through the use of self-reinforcement. "Self-appraisals of performance set the occasion for self-produced consequences. Favourable judgements give rise to rewarding self-reactions, whereas unfavourable appraisals activate punishing self-responses" (ibid., p. 133). Bandura and other social learning theorists argue that internal psychological events and processes such as self-reinforcement and expectancies help to determine behaviour. This behaviour will, to some extent, influence the situation surrounding the person, and in turn external situational factors, such as the

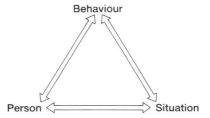

9.5 Reciprocal determinism.

behaviour of others, and help to determine expectancies and the other internal cognitive factors. In other words, there is a constant cycle of interaction between person and situation factors, a process described by Bandura as reciprocal determinism. This view is quite different from the traditional operant view that "A person does not act upon the world, the world acts upon him" (Skinner, 1971, p. 211).

Another important aspect of social learning theory is the proposal that people often develop their own patterns of behaviour by observing and then copying or modelling the behaviour of others. The concept of observational learning or modelling is difficult for those holding the traditional, operant behavioural view to explain. For example, the act of copying a model provides no direct reinforcement in itself. Social learning theorists argue that this sort of action can, however, be explained if we accept that the modelling occurred because the learner had expectancies about what might eventually occur as a consequence of modelling. Thus, junior members of an organization model their dress attitudes and behaviours on those of successful senior personnel, based on expectancies, goals and plans that they have about the eventual consequences of their behaviours. Luthans and Kreitner (1975) have provided a framework for OB Mod which is rooted firmly in the concepts of social cognitive theory.

In keeping with this convergence of behavioural and cognitive theories, more recent studies have often incorporated behavioural interventions within a cognitive framework. A study by Pritchard *et al.* (1988), for example, used a mixture of goal-setting, feedback and incentives. Their study conducted in a military setting involved a baseline period of 8–9 months followed by feedback (5 months); this was followed by the addition of goal-setting (5 months). Finally, incentives were then used (5 months). The results indicated an improvement in productivity over baseline of 50% for feedback, 75% for group goal-setting and 76% for incentives. Although the study did not provide conclusive proof of the different effects of the various interventions, the authors felt that incentives added little to the improvements brought about by feedback and goal-setting. This finding must, however, be set against the results obtained by Guzzo *et al.* (1985) in their meta-analytic (see Chapter 7) investigation of many studies, which showed that incentives do generally improve performance, although the effect depends on the method of application and circumstances.

As well as studies such as that of Pritchard *et al.* (1988), there are still examples of a more tightly prescribed, essentially operant-based approach to behaviour. Saari and Näsänen (1989), for example, used feedback to reduce accidents in a shipyard, achieving a reduction of 70–90% in accidents, persisting to a 3-year follow-up. This study is interesting in another sense, because it was conducted in Finland. Most of the research on behaviour change cited in this chapter has been conducted in the USA, and some authors (e.g. Hale and Glendon, 1987) have expressed the view that feedback techniques may not work as effectively in European cultures as they have done in the USA. One consistent champion of the operant approach in organizational settings is Komaki who, in her work, has extended the operant approach well beyond the straightforward attempts to manipulate behaviour into a variety of interesting and important areas such as leader behaviour and supervision (e.g. Komaki *et al.*, 1989; see also Chapter 13) and performance measurement (Komaki *et al.*, 1987).

Summary

In many ways, what people do (i.e. their behaviour) at work is the most important aspect of work psychology. Behaviourally orientated psychologists have developed concise and powerful frameworks which have been shown to be effective in changing behaviour in organizational settings. The work of Luthans and Kreitner (1975) and others has provided a range of examples of the use of behavioural techniques. Despite its success, even the major exponents of behaviour modification (based on purely behavioural frameworks) recognize that there are also theoretical and practical shortcomings. More recent work has shown that the inclusion of ideas from social cognitive theory provides a theoretically more advanced, yet still practical basis for bringing about behavioural change.

Case study 9.2   The effects of punishment on behaviour

Barry Cavanagh's new job as safety manager with Castell Construction was extremely challenging. The construction industry in general had one of the worst accident records of all industries in the country and although Castell's safety record was better than some companies, it was still a source of great concern. Barry felt that he understood the general causes of accidents very well: it was easier and quicker to take short-cuts when it came to safety. For example, when a small number of breeze blocks needed cutting down to a smaller size with a power cutter, it was inconvenient and time-consuming to get protective goggles, gloves and face mask from the stores. So the job would be done without protection. To make matters worse, because they were often under intense pressure from senior managers to work to agreed production targets, site managers and supervisors were often prepared to turn a blind eye to unsafe practices, if it meant that the job would get done on time.

Barry was a direct, no-nonsense kind of person and felt sure that it was a waste of time to try to educate the construction workers and to change their underlying attitudes to safety. He knew that to have any impact their *behaviour* needed to change. He also knew that various previous attempts to improve safety, initiated by his predecessor, had failed. These had included poster campaigns and talks from medical staff.

Barry decided that the best approach was to come down very heavily and severely on any examples of unsafe behaviour. Barry and his site managers began a campaign in which unsafe acts were punished severely with reprimands and other more severe forms of punishment such as loss of earnings. Most of their reprimands were given to accident victims or (when it was not the victim's fault) others involved in causing the accident.

At first, Barry's policy seemed to be working. He maintained a close watch on accident reports and even within the first weeks of the campaign there was a clear decrease, particularly in minor accidents. After a routine meeting with site managers Barry had been a little disappointed that they did not share his pleasure at the decrease in accident rates. After the meeting, one of the site managers took Barry to one side and explained why this was so and furthermore that the scheme was doing more harm than good. There had actually been no change in accident rates, but to avoid punishment operatives were covering up and not reporting all but the most serious and noticeable incidents! Not only was there no improvement in accidents, but the relationship between site managers and operatives had deteriorated. Site personnel were angered by the behaviour of managers, reprimanding operatives who were often still shaken and in pain after an accident.

Suggested exercises

1. Using the concepts and terminology of behaviour modification, explain what went wrong and why.
2. Make suggestions about how Barry might have gone about achieving his goal by a more successful route, using OB Mod techniques.

References

Alavosius, M. P. and Sulzer-Azaroff, B. (1986). The effects of performance feedback on the safety of client lifting and transfer. *Journal of Applied Behavior Analysis, 19*, 261–267.

Arvey, R. D. and Ivancevich, J. M. (1980). Punishment in organizations: A review, propositions and research suggestions. *Academy of Management Review, 5*, 123–132.

Bandura, A. (1977). *Social Learning Theory*. Englewood Cliffs, N.J.: Prentice-Hall.

Bandura, A. (1986). *Social Foundations of Thought and Action: A Social Cognitive Theory*. Englewood Cliffs, N.J.: Prentice-Hall.

Breland, K. and Breland, M. (1951). A field of applied animal psychology. *American Psychologist, 6*, 202–204.

Chokkar, J. S. and Wallin, J. A. (1984). A field study of the effect of feedback frequency on performance. *Journal of Applied Psychology, 69*, 524–530.

Davis, T. R. V. and Luthans, F. (1980). A social learning approach to organizational behavior. *Academy of Management Review, 5*, 281–290.

Fox, D. K., Hopkins, B.L. and Anger, W. K. (1987). The long-term effects of a token economy on safety performance in open-pit mining. *Journal of Applied Behavior Analysis, 20*, 215–224.

Geller, E. S., Davis, L. and Spicer, K. (1983). Industry-based incentives for promoting seat belt use: Differential impact on white-collar versus blue-collar employees. *Journal of Organizational Behavior Management, 5*, 17–29.

Guzzo, R. A., Jette, R. D. and Katzell, R. A. (1985). The effects of psychologically based intervention programmes on worker productivity: A meta-analysis. *Personnel Psychology, 38*, 275–291.

Hale, A. R. and Glendon, A. I. (1987). *Individual Behavior in the Control of Danger*. Amsterdam: Elsevier.

Haynes, R. S., Pine, R. C. and Fitch, H. G. (1982). Reducing accident rates with organizational behavior modification. *Academy of Management Journal, 25*, 407–416.

Karan, B. S. and Kopelman, R. E. (1987). The effects of objective feedback on vehicular and industrial accidents: A field experiment using outcome feedback. *Journal of Organizational Behavior Management, 8*, 45–56.

Kazdin, A. E. (1980). *Behavior Modification in Applied Settings*, revised edn. Homewood, Ill.: Dorsey Press.

Komaki, J., Barwick, K. and Scott, L. (1978). A behavioral approach to occupational safety: Pinpointing and reinforcing safe performance in a food manufacturing plant. *Journal of Applied Psychology, 63*, 434–445.

Komaki, J. L., Collins, R. L. and Temlock, S. (1987). An alternative performance measurement approach: Applied operant measurement in the service sector. *Applied Psychology: An International Review, 36*, 71–86.

Komaki, J. L., Desseles, M. L. and Bownam, E. D. (1989). Definitely not a breeze: Extending an operant model to effective supervision to teams. *Journal of Applied Psychology, 74*, 522–529.

Komaki, J. L. and Jensen, M. (1986). Within group designs: An alternative to traditional control-group designs. In M. F. Cataldo and T. J. Coates (Eds), *Health and Industry, A Behavioral Medicine Perspective*. New York: John Wiley.

Lewis, D. J. and Duncan, C. P. (1956). Effects of different percentages of money reward on extinction of a lever pulling response. *Journal of Experimental Psychology, 52*, 23–27.

Locke, E. A. (1977). The myths of behavior modification in organizations. *Academy of Management Review, 4*, 543–553.

Locke, E. A. and Henne, D. (1986). Work motivation theories. In C. L. Cooper and I. T. Robertson (Eds), *International Review of Industrial and Organizational Psychology, 1986*. Chichester: John Wiley.

Locke, E. A. and Latham, G. P. (1984). *Goal Setting: A Motivational Technique that Works*. Englewood Cliffs, N.J.: Prentice-Hall.

Luthans, F. and Kreitner, R. (1975). *Organizational Behavior Modification*. Glenview, Ill.: Scott-Foresman.

Luthans, F. and Martinko, M. (1987). Behavioral approaches to organizations. In C. L. Cooper and I. T. Robertson (Eds), *International Review of Industrial and Organizational Psychology, 1987*. Chichester: John Wiley.

Luthans, F., Paul, R. and Baker, D. (1981). An experimental analysis on salespersons' performance behaviours. *Journal of Applied Psychology, 66*, 314–323.

O'Brien, R. M., Dickinson, A. M. and Rosow, M. P. (1982). *Industrial Behavior Modification*. New York: Pergamon Press.

Premack, D. (1965). Reinforcement theory. In D. Levine (Ed.), *Nebraska Symposium on Motivation*. Lincoln, Nebr.: University of Nebraska Press.

Pritchard, R. D., Jones, S. D., Roth, P. L., Stuebing, K. K. and Ekeberg, S. E. (1988). Effects of group feedback, goal-setting, and incentives on organizational productivity. *Journal of Applied Psychology, 73*, 337–358.

Rimm, D. C. and Masters, J. C. (1979). *Behavior Therapy: Techniques and Empirical Findings*, 2nd edn. London: Academic Press.

Saari, J. and Näsänen, M. (1989). The effect of positive feedback on industrial housekeeping and accidents: A long-term study at a shipyard. *International Journal of Industrial Ergonomics, 4*, 201–211.

Skinner, B. F. (1971). *Beyond Freedom and Dignity*. New York: Knopf.

Skinner, B. F. (1974). *About Behaviorism*. New York: Knopf.

Ulrich, R., Strachnik, T. and Mabry, J. (Eds) (1974). *Control of Human Behavior*. Glenview, Ill.: Scott-Foresman.

Zohar, D. and Fussfeld, N. A. (1981). A systems approach to Organizational Behaviour Modification: Theoretical considerations and empirical evidence. *International Review of Applied Psychology, 30*, 491–505.

Approaches to work motivation

Introduction

Motivation is a key topic in work psychology. It is central to often-asked questions such as: "How can I get my people to work harder?" In this chapter, we examine the concept of motivation and explore some of its implications. We then look at some conflicting "common-sense" ideas about motivation. The chapter then turns to a description and evaluation of some key approaches to motivation, including need theories, the motivation to manage, expectancy theory, equity theory and goal-setting. Both theoretical and practical issues are covered. Theoretical developments have now started to integrate what seemed to be contradictory approaches to motivation. Goal-setting theory has acted as a trigger for such developments, which have also encompassed ideas not previously applied to motivation. This chapter therefore concludes with an examination of such integration. Behaviourist theories are also relevant to motivation, and are covered in Chapter 9. Attempts to enhance motivation by the careful design of people's jobs are examined in Chapter 17.

Overview of motivation

As with many important concepts in psychology, there is no single universally accepted definition of motivation. Nevertheless, the word itself gives us some clues. To use a mechanical analogy, the motive force gets a machine started and keeps it going. In legal terms, a motive is a person's reason for doing something. Clearly, then, motivation concerns the factors which push us or pull us to behave in certain ways. Specifically, it is made up of three components:

- *direction*, i.e. what a person is trying to do;
- *effort*, i.e. how hard a person is trying; and
- *persistence*, i.e. how long a person continues trying.

Some key points must be made immediately:

1. People are usually motivated to do *something*. Some folk try hard and long to avoid work – that is motivated behaviour! Hence we should always

remember the "direction" component (see above). What motivation usually means in the work context is motivation to tackle specified work duties.

2.   It is easy to make the mistake of thinking that motivation is the only important determinant of work performance. But what about ability? And, where a group is working together, what about co-ordination of group members' activities?

3.   Research on motivation occasionally uses persistence as the outcome of interest. More often it uses effort, and more often again, performance. But, as noted in 2, performance depends on other factors too.

One often-made distinction is between *content* theories and *process* theories of motivation. The former focus on *what* motivates human behaviour at work, whereas the latter concentrate on *how* the content of motivation influences behaviour. In fact, most theories have something to say about both content and process, but they do vary considerably in their relative emphasis.

"Common-sense" approaches to motivation

McGregor (1960), Argyris (1964), Schein (1980) and others have collectively identified three broad "common-sense" approaches to motivation which are endorsed by different individuals or even the same individual at different times. McGregor (1960) termed two of the three theory X and theory Y, though the reader should be clear that in neither case is the word "theory" used in its formal academic sense. Schein (1980) added what can be called the social approach. In all three cases, we are essentially uncovering a general perspective on human nature. Briefly, they run as follows:

1.   *Theory X*. People cannot be trusted. They are irrational, unreliable and inherently lazy. They therefore need to be controlled and motivated using financial incentives and threats of punishment. In the absence of such controls, people will pursue their own goals and these are invariably contrary to those of their work organization.

2.   *Theory Y*. People seek independence, self-development and creativity in their work. They can see further than immediate circumstances and are able to adapt to new ones. They are fundamentally moral and responsible beings who will strive for the good of their work organization if they are treated as such.

3.   *Social*. A person's behaviour is influenced most fundamentally by social interactions, which can determine their sense of identity and belonging at work. People seek meaningful social relationships at work. They are responsive to the expectations of people around them, often more so than to financial incentives.

As you can probably see, theory X and theory Y are in most respects opposites with the social approach different from both. Which of these "common-sense" approaches do you find most convincing? The authors' experience with business/management undergraduates is that, if forced to choose one, about 50% go for the social approach, about 40% for theory Y and about 10% for theory X. Interestingly, most of that 10% can usually be found right at the back of the lecture theatre!

None of these three "common-sense" accounts is universally correct. But as Schein (1980) points out, over time people may be socialized into their organization's way of thinking about motivation. Ultimately, managers can influence their staff to see motivation their way. Of course, they may also attract and select staff who are already inclined to see things their way. Nevertheless, none of the approaches can be forced on all of the people all of the time. The indiscriminate use of any could have disastrous results. Hence, although each of these approaches finds some expression in theories of motivation, the match between theory and common sense is not particularly close. So what are these theories? Let us now examine some of the most widely known and extensively researched.

Need theories

What are they?

These are based on the idea that there are psychological needs, probably of a biological origin, which lie behind human behaviour. When our needs are unmet, we experience tension or disequilibrium which we try to put right. In other words, we behave in ways which satisfy our needs. Clearly, the notion of need reflects the *content* of motivation as opposed to process. But most need theories also make some propositions about how and when particular needs become salient, i.e. process. The notion of need has a long history in general psychology. It has, for example, formed the basis of at least one major analysis of personality (Murray, 1938). Two major traditions have been evident in the work setting: first, there are models based on the notion of psychological growth and, secondly, there are various approaches which focus on a range of quite specific needs.

Need theories based on psychological growth

Easily the best known of these theories is that of Abraham Maslow (1943, 1970). Maslow was a humanistically orientated psychologist (see Chapter 2) who offered a general theory of human functioning. His ideas were applied by others to the work setting. Maslow proposed five classes of human needs. Briefly, these are as follows:

1. *Physiological*: the need for food, drink, sex, etc., i.e. the most primitive and obviously biological needs.
2. *Safety*: the need for physical and psychological safety, i.e. a predictable and non-threatening environment.

3. *Belongingness*: the need to feel a sense of attachment to another person or group of persons.

4. *Esteem*: the need to feel valued and respected, by self and significant other people.

5. *Self-actualization*: the need to fulfil one's potential, i.e. to develop one's capacities and express them.

Other psychologists came up with rather similar analyses. For example, Alderfer (1972) proposed three classes of needs: existence, relatedness and growth. Existence equated to Maslow's physiological and safety needs. Relatedness can be matched to belongingness and the esteem of others. Growth is equivalent to self-esteem and self-actualization. Both Maslow and Alderfer made propositions about how particular needs become more or less important to the person (i.e. process), but need theories are often thought of as examples of content theories because of their emphasis on describing needs.

For some years, need theories (especially Maslow's) dominated work motivation. Unfortunately, evaluations of them (e.g. Wahba and Bridwell, 1976; Salancik and Pfeffer, 1977; Rauschenberger *et al.*, 1980) revealed a number of fatal flaws, such as:

1. Needs did not group together in the ways predicted.

2. The theories were unable to predict when particular needs would become important.

3. There was no clear relationship between needs and behaviour, so that, for example, the same behaviour could reflect different needs, and different behaviours the same need.

4. Needs were generally described with insufficient precision.

5. The whole notion of need as a biological phenomenon is problematic. It ignores the capacity of people and those around them to construct their own perceptions of needs and how they can be met.

Hence these accounts of motivation based on needs have only very limited value. They offer interesting ways of thinking about human functioning, but their theoretical foundation is doubtful and they have offered no clear guidance to managers about how to motivate individuals.

Maslow's work has, however, provided a clear picture of the self-actualizing person. Maslow regarded self-actualization as the pinnacle of human growth and adjustment, but argued that few of us operate at that level. Examine Table 10.1 to see whether you do, and whether Maslow's description of a fully functioning person matches yours. To what extent do work organizations need self-actualizing people?

Achievement, power and motivation to manage

Rather more success has been enjoyed by need-based approaches to motivation which concentrate on a small number of more specific needs. Need for achievement was one of the 20 needs underlying behaviour proposed by Murray (1938).

Table 10.1 The self-actualizing person

1. *Perceives people and events accurately*, without undue interference from their own preconceptions
2. *Accepts self and others*, including imperfections, but seeks improvement where possible
3. *Is spontaneous*, especially in their thoughts and feelings
4. *Focuses on problems outside self*, rather than being insecure and introspective
5. *Is detached*, so that they are not unduly thrown off course by awkward events
6. *Is autonomous*, and remains true to self despite pressure to conform
7. *Appreciates good and beautiful things*, even if they are familiar
8. *Has peak experiences* of intense positive emotions of a sometimes mystic quality
9. *Has close relationships*, but only with a few carefully chosen people
10. *Respects others*, avoids making fun of people and evaluates them according to their inner qualities rather than race or social class
11. *Has firm moral standards*, and sense of right and wrong, though these may be different from many other people
12. *Is creative:* this is perhaps the most fundamental aspect of self-actualization, and is seen as the result of the other aspects listed above. By being open-minded and open to their experience, the self-actualizing person sees things in novel ways and can draw novel conclusions from established information

Based on Sugarman (1986, pp. 31–44).

It concerns the desire "to overcome obstacles, to exercise power, to strive to do something difficult as well and as quickly as possible" (Murray, 1938, pp. 80–81, quoted by Landy, 1985, p. 322). Typically, people with a high need for achievement seek fairly difficult, but not impossible, tasks. They like to take sole responsibility for them, and want frequent feedback on how they are doing. Need for achievement formed the basis of McClelland's (1961) theory of work motivation. McClelland argued that enhancing the population's need for achievement was essential for a country's economic prosperity, and that such enhancement could be achieved through appropriate training courses.

The need for achievement has attracted considerable attention in both theoretical and applied contexts (e.g. see Beck, 1983). It is not a simple construct, however. Cassidy and Lynn (1989) have identified six components:

1. *Work ethic*: the motivation to achieve based on the belief that performance is "good" in itself.

2. *Pursuit of excellence*: a desire to perform to the best of one's ability.

3. *Status aspiration*: a desire to climb the status hierarchy and dominate others.

4. *Competitiveness*: a desire to compete with others and beat them.

5. *Acquisitiveness*: for money and wealth.

6. *Mastery*: competitiveness against set standards (rather than against other people; see 4).

Other needs, such as affiliation and autonomy, have also been proposed and assessed (e.g. Steers and Braunstein, 1976). A need for dominance or power is sometimes included within need for achievement (see above), but sometimes treated separately.

McClelland and Boyatzis (1982) proposed that management success could be predicted from a manager's "Leadership motive pattern", which is indicated by moderately high need for power, low need for affiliation (i.e. for warm, empathic relationships with others) and high self-control. They found support for their proposition among general managers in the giant American telephone company AT & T.

John Miner (1964) developed the concept of motivation to manage, and also devised a measure of it (the Miner Sentence Completion Scale, or MSCS) which requires a person to complete 35 half-finished sentences. Their responses are then scored by a carefully trained expert on the various components of motivation to manage. These are shown in Table 10.2. The need for power, self-control and low need for affiliation probably underlie motivation to manage. So do some of the components of need for achievement identified by Cassidy and Lynn (1989). Miner and Smith (1982) reported that motivation to manage among undergraduate business students in the USA declined during the 1960s and 1970s and subsequently stabilized. The decline was most consistent for competitive situations and assertive roles. On a brighter note, Miner and Smith found that whereas females scored lower than males in the early 1960s, this was no longer true by 1980.

Miner regards levels of managerial motivation as having a substantial effect on a country's economic performance, and few have disagreed with him about that. However, Bartol *et al.* (1980) *have* disagreed with Miner's data. They found that motivation to manage generally increased among students during the 1970s, but that the sex difference remained. This led to a rather acrimonious exchange (Miner *et al.*, 1985; Bartol *et al.*, 1985) in which Miner accused Bartol of making erros in scoring the MSCS, with Bartol replying that Miner's scoring

Table 10.2 Components of motivation to manage

Component	Meaning
Authority figures	A desire to meet managerial role requirements in terms of positive relationships with superiors
Competitive games	A desire to engage in competition with peers involving games or sports
Competitive situations	A desire to engage in competition with peers involving occupational or work-related activities
Assertive role	A desire to behave in an active and assertive manner involving activities which are often viewed as predominantly masculine
Imposing wishes	A desire to tell others what to do and to utilize sanctions in influencing others
Standing out from group	A desire to assume a distinctive position of a unique and highly visible nature
Routine administrative functions	A desire to meet managerial role requirements of a day-to-day administrative nature

Adapted from Miner and Smith (1982, p. 298) with the permission of the American Psychological Association.

was not necessarily faultless, and anyway his initial data at the start of the 1960s were obtained from just one university.

Bartol and Martin (1987) subsequently reported work using the forced-choice version of the MSCS where the respondent has to choose one of six provided sentence completions rather than generate their own. They again found that males showed higher motivation to manage than females. They also found that taking a Masters degree in business administration (MBA) did not affect motivation to manage. Motivation to manage was unrelated to students' grades on the course, but it did predict salary after graduation. Whatever the truth about declines over two decades in motivation to manage among future managers, these results suggest that management education does not fire students with enthusiasm for management, at least in the USA.

Case study 10.1   The motivation to manage

Marie Herzog is an administrative assistant at a large packaging factory in Lyons. She had previously been promoted from the factory floor and is keen to go higher. Her boss, Simone Trouchot, is not so sure – how keen is Marie? Simone made the following observations. Marie seemed rarely to impose her will on her clerical subordinates, even when they were obviously in the wrong. She got on well with the higher managers at the factory, and seemed willing to work closely to the remit they gave her. On the other hand, Marie rarely volunteered her department for trying out experimental new ideas. She seemed uncomfortable when the spotlight was turned on her and her department, even if the attention was congratulatory. Marie seemed happiest dealing with routine administrative tasks she knew well. She was an accomplished athlete, and had recently been the Lyons 400 metres champion 2 years in succession. Marie was extremely keen to get her department working better than other similar ones, and to ensure she dealt with problems faster and better than others in similar jobs at the factory.

Suggested exercise

Consult Table 10.2 to judge the extent and nature of Marie Herzog's motivation to manage. Are there particular kinds of managerial roles in which she would feel particularly motivated?

Expectancy theory: What's in it for me?

Whereas need theories place heavy emphasis on the content of motivation, expectancy theory concentrates on the process. Originally proposed by Vroom (1964), expectancy theory (also sometimes called VIE theory or instrumentality theory) aimed to explain how people choose which of several possible courses of action they will pursue. This choice process was seen as a cognitive, calculating appraisal of the following three factors for each of the actions being considered:

1. *Expectancy*: If I tried, would I be able to perform the action I am considering?

2. *Instrumentality*: Would performing the action lead to identifiable outcomes?

3. *Valence*: How much do I value those outcomes?

Vroom (1964) proposed that expectancy and instrumentality can be expressed as probabilities, and valence as a subjective value. He also suggested that force to act is a function of the product of expectancy, instrumentality and valence: in other words, V, I and E are multiplied together to determine motivation. This would mean that if any one of the components was zero, overall motivation to pursue that course of action would also be zero.

If correct, VIE theory would have important implications for managers wishing to ensure that employees were motivated to perform their work duties. They would need to ensure that all three of the following conditions were satisfied:

1. Employees perceived that they possessed the necessary skills to do their jobs at least adequately (expectancy).

2. Employees perceived that if they performed their jobs well, or at least adequately, they would be rewarded (instrumentality).

3. Employees found the rewards offered for successful job performance attractive (valence).

How many managers can honestly claim that these conditions hold in their organization?

Although it looks attractive, VIE theory has not done especially well when evaluated in research (e.g. Schwab *et al.*, 1979). The following points can be made:

1. Research studies which have not measured expectancy, or have combined it with instrumentality, have accounted for effort and/or performance better than studies which assessed expectancy and instrumentality separately.

2. People often add the components rather than multiplying them.

3. The theory does not work where any of the outcomes have negative valence (i.e. are viewed as undesirable) (Leon, 1981).

4. The theory works better where the outcome measure is objective performance, or self-reported effort and performance, rather than effort or performance reported by another person.

5. VIE theory works best where the person is choosing between not less than 10 and not more than 15 outcomes.

6. Self-report measures of V, I and E have often been poorly constructed.

7. Most research has compared different people with each other, rather than comparing different outcomes for the same person. The latter would enable a better test of VIE theory.

Only the first three of these points reflect badly on VIE theory as a whole. The next two demonstrate some boundaries of its effectiveness, and the last two are limitations of research design rather than the theory itself. Nevertheless, as Schwab *et al.* (1979, p. 146) state:

... there is a nagging suspicion that expectancy theory overintellectualizes the cognitive processes people go through when choosing alternative actions (at least insofar as choosing a level of performance or effort is concerned). The results of the present review are consistent with this suspicion.

But it is still useful to identify the potential determinants of the motivation process, even if they do not combine as predicted by VIE theory. As Landy (1985, pp. 336–337) has put it:

> The cognitive nature of the approach does a good job of capturing the essence of energy expenditure. ... A manager can understand and apply the principles embodied in each of the components of the model. Instrumentalities make sense. The manager can use this principle to lay out clearly for subordinates the relationships among outcomes (e.g. promotions yield salary increases, four unexcused absences yield a suspension of one day). Similarly, the manager can affect effort – reward probabilities by systematically rewarding good performance.

Finally, notice how little attention VIE theory pays to explaining *why* an individual values or does not value particular outcomes. No concepts of need are invoked to address this question. VIE theory proposes that we should ask someone how much they value something, but not bother about *why* they value it. This is another illustration of VIE theory's concentration on process, not content.

Equity theory: Am I being fairly treated?

Equity theory is like expectancy theory in that it focuses on the cognitive processes which govern a person's decision whether or not to expend effort. But it suggests that people are motivated to obtain what they consider a fair return for their efforts rather than to get as much as they can. This strains the credulity of some students and managers, but let us suspend disbelief for the moment and consider the propositions of equity theory.

There are many variants of equity theory, but the most often cited is derived from propositions put forward by Adams (1965), originally in the context of interpersonal relationships. Huseman *et al.* (1987, p. 222) have described the propositions like this:

1. Individuals evaluate their relationships with others by assessing the ratio of their outcomes from and inputs to the relationship against the outcome/input ratio of a comparison other.

2. If the outcome/input ratios of the individual and comparison other are perceived to be unequal, then inequity exists.

3. The greater the inequity the individual perceives (in the form of either overreward or underreward) the more distress the individual feels.

4. The greater the distress an individual feels, the harder he or she will work to restore equity... . Equity restoration techniques include altering or cognitively distorting inputs or outcomes, acting on or changing the comparison other, or terminating the relationship.

In other words, a person is motivated to maintain the same balance between their contributions and rewards as that experienced by a salient comparison person or persons.

Laboratory experiments have generally provided reasonable support for equity theory. Because rewards and availability of comparison others are closely controlled by the experimenter, the only way that people participating in the experiment can establish equity is to increase or decrease the quantity or quality of their work. And this they do, on the whole (Pritchard, 1969). But out in the "real world" things are of course more complicated. People have much more choice of comparison other and of strategy to establish equity. As well as making it difficult to predict who will do what, this can also obscure whether people are trying to establish equity at all. Furthermore, Birnbaum (1983) has suggested that some people construe equity as equality of outcome rather than as equality of ratio between input and outcome.

Equity enthusiasts have therefore drawn back a little and done some more groundwork. Huseman *et al.* (1987) argue that some people are more sensitive to equity than others. Dornstein (1988, 1989) has established that people do indeed make comparisons with others: usually, it seems, similar workers outside their employing organization. Greenberg (1987) has put equity theory into the much wider context of organizational justice theories. Therefore, a revised equity theory may in time return to the fray. In the meantime, it is limited to the (admittedly important) observation that individuals do indeed notice and care about what happens to others when considering their own motivation.

Goal-setting theory

The theory

This approach to motivation has been pioneered in the USA by Ed Locke and his associates, starting in the 1960s and continuing with increasing strength and sophistication ever since. So much so, that by the end of the 1980s, well over half the research on motivation published in leading academic journals reported tests and/or refinements of goal-setting theory. As Locke *et al.* (1981, p. 126) put it: "A goal is what an individual is trying to accomplish; it is the object or aim of an action. The concept is similar in meaning to the concepts of purpose and intent."

Locke drew on both academic writings on intention (Ryan, 1970) and the much more practical management by objectives (MBO) literature in formulating his ideas. Figure 10.1 represents current goal-setting theory, and shows that characteristics of a goal and attitudes towards it are thought to be influenced by incentives, self-perceptions and the manner in which goals are set.

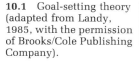

10.1 Goal-setting theory (adapted from Landy, 1985, with the permission of Brooks/Cole Publishing Company).

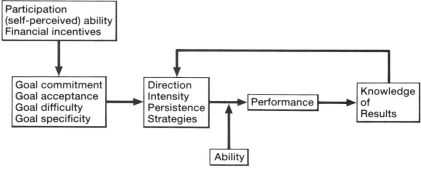

In turn, those goal characteristics and attitudes are thought to determine behavioural strategies, which lead to performance within the constraints of ability. Knowledge of results (also called feedback) is thought to be essential to the further refinement of behavioural strategies.

What does research say about goal-setting? Reviews by Locke *et al.* (1981), Locke and Latham (1990) and Mento *et al.* (1987) arrive at a number of conclusions, most of which fully or substantially support goal-setting theory. Most fundamental has been the overwhelming confirmation of the following phenomena:

1. Difficult goals lead to higher performance than easy goals, so long as they have been accepted by the person trying to achieve them. This follows from the fact that people direct their behaviour towards goal achievement, so that difficult goals produce more effective behaviour than easy ones.

2. Specific goals lead to higher performance than general "do your best" goals. Specific goals seem to create a precise intention, which in turn helps the person to shape their behaviour with precision.

3. Knowledge of results (feedback) is essential if the full performance benefits of setting difficult and specific goals are to be achieved. Locke *et al.* (1981) have pointed out that although feedback may exert its main effect through providing a person with information, it may also itself have motivating properties. Optimal timing, frequency and amount of feedback are at present somewhat uncertain.

These three findings establish the core of goal-setting and make it probably the most consistently supported theory in work and organizational psychology. Locke *et al.* (1981) observed that 90% of laboratory and field research studies produced results supporting the fundamental elements of goal-setting theory. Mento *et al.* (1987, pp. 74–75) reinforced that conclusion, and further commented that:

> If there is ever to be a viable candidate from the organizational sciences for elevation to the lofty status of a scientific law of nature, then the relationships between goal difficulty, specificity/difficulty and task performance are most worthy of serious consideration. [There is also] clear support of the efficacy of coupling feedback with hard specific goals. Both

knowledge and motivation, it would seem, are necessary for enhanced performance.

Some further comments can be made on the basis of research evidence. First, financial incentives can indeed enhance performance. Locke *et al.* (1981) report that this occurs either through raising goal level, or through increasing commitment to a goal. Secondly, and unsurprisingly, ability also affects performance. Thirdly, research on goal-setting has been carried out in a range of contexts. Much work has been done in laboratories using students who tackle tasks such as solving anagrams or brainstorming, but much has been conducted with groups such as truck drivers and lumberjacks in their work settings. Fourthly, goal-setting is magnificently clear about how managers can enhance the performance of their employees. Research results also show that goal-setting is worth doing – Locke *et al.* (1981) reported that in goal-setting field experiments, the median improvement in work performance produced by goal-setting was 16%.

Some continuing issues in goal-setting

John Hollenbeck and colleagues have focused on the concept of *goal commitment*. Hollenbeck and Klein (1987) defined commitment as the determination to try for a goal, which implies an unwillingness to reduce or abandon it. They distinguished between goal commitment and goal acceptance, the latter referring merely to use of a goal as an initial point of reference. Hollenbeck and Klein argued that although commitment to difficult goals has been viewed as necessary for effective performance, the proposition has never properly been put to the test. They further stated that if goal commitment is indeed important, we need to know what influences it – a point also made by Locke *et al.* (1988).

Hollenbeck *et al.* (1989) conducted a study in which students set or were assigned performance goals for their future marks on their course. Among those students who set (or were assigned) *difficult* goals, high goal commitment was associated with subsequent improvements in marks. Goal commitment was higher when the goal was made public (by communicating it to other students and a close relative) than when it was kept private. Those students with an internal locus of control (i.e. they had a general belief that people can control their fate) and a high need for achievement, tended to have higher goal commitment than the others. On the whole, goal commitment was unaffected by whether the goal was self-set by the student or assigned by the experimenter, though self-setting was better for students with a high need for achievement.

This clearly represents a useful start in an important area. In work organizations, some employees may need some encouragement to feel committed to goals, whether assigned or self-set. It is important that goal-setting research soon establishes ways of achieving that commitment.

A second continuing issue in goal-setting concerns participation. Locke *et al.* (1981) concluded that there was no evidence from published research that participation in goal-setting by the person attempting to achieve the goal produced better performance than if the goal was assigned to them by someone else. Mento *et al.* (1987) reported some evidence that participation was superior, but added that the evidence was far from conclusive.

Latham *et al.* (1988) have conducted a series of experiments designed to investigate whether participation in goal-setting is desirable. Over earlier years, Latham (working in the USA) had consistently found no effect of participation on performance. But Erez, who worked mainly in Israel, consistently found that participation in goal-setting enhanced greater goal commitment (and sometimes performance) than simply assigning goals.

Therefore, Latham and Erez, using Locke as an arbitrator, put their heads together and designed a series of experiments that would settle the matter. As they proudly pointed out, it is most unusual for scientific adversaries to work together in this manner. Hopefully it could set a trend for the future – recalling the section on motivation to manage earlier in this chapter, perhaps Bartol and Miner should try it!

Latham and Erez identified several differences in the way they conducted their earlier experiments. They tested the impact of each difference in their collaborative experiments. One in particular turned out to be important. In Latham's experiments, where a goal was assigned to subjects, an attempt was also made to "sell" the goal by encouraging them to believe it was attainable. But in Erez's work, the subjects were simply told what the goal was. Latham *et al.* (1988) found that this made all the difference. The goal commitment and self-efficacy of "tell and sell" subjects was very similar to that of those subjects who participated in goal-setting, and higher than that of the subjects in the "tell only" condition. A similar pattern, though less pronounced, was also evident for task performance. Thus it seems that (at least in laboratory experiments) participation in goal-setting is better than simply telling people their goal, but not better than assigning people a goal and attempting to justify it to them.

Possible limits to the effectiveness of goal-setting

Austin and Bobko (1985) identified four respects in which goal-setting theory had not been properly tested. First, goals which reflect quality of work (as opposed to quantity) were rarely set in goal-setting research. Yet in many people's work, quality is more important than quantity. Secondly, real jobs often have conflicting goals: achieving one may mean neglecting another. This could complicate or even undermine the application of goal-setting. Thirdly, goal-setting research has used goals for individual people and assessed the performance of individuals. In the world of work, however, group goals and group performance often matter more. Fourthly, Austin and Bobko argued that goal-setting had not adequately demonstrated its effectiveness outside laboratory settings. Whereas the last of these doubts may be unjustified (Mento *et al.*, 1987), the other three do indeed represent as yet relatively unexplored areas for goal-setting as Austin and Bobko claimed. One might also add that nobody has yet satisfactorily explained *why* goals have motivating effects. Most of the research on goal-setting concerns *how* that motivation is harnessed.

Some research has directly investigated the specific potential limitations of goal-setting. Meyer and Gellatly (1988) argued that one function normally served by an assigned goal is to signal what constitutes an appropriate level of performance, or *performance norm*. They manipulated subjects' beliefs about performance norms on a brainstorming (i.e. creative idea generation) task so that they were sometimes different from the goal set. They found that this affected performance and reduced the impact of goal-setting. The practical implication is that goal-setting may be undermined in the workplace where people already have clear ideas (perhaps widely held within a work group) about what constitutes acceptable performance.

Earley *et al.* (1989) suggested that goal-setting may be harmful where a task is novel and where a considerable number of possible strategies are available to tackle it. They asked students to undertake a stock market prediction task, and sure enough they found that people who were assigned specific, difficult goals performed *worse* than those assigned a "do your best" goal. They also changed their strategy more. It seems, then, that goal-setting can induce people to pay too much attention to task strategy and not enough to task performance itself. A major innovative piece of work by Kanfer and Ackerman (1989), which has combined motivation theories with cognitive ability theories, has drawn a similar conclusion. Kanfer and Ackerman (1989, p. 687) focused on skill acquisition as opposed to performance of established skills, and concluded:

> Our findings indicate that interventions designed to engage motivational processes may impede task learning when presented prior to an understanding of what the task is about. In these instances, cognitive resources necessary for task understanding are diverted towards self-regulatory activites (e.g. self evaluation). Because persons have few spare resources at this phase of skill acquisition, these self-regulatory activities can provide little benefit for learning.

So when someone is learning a task, don't get them fired up to achieve specific goals. Find ways of aiding learning, not performance, at that stage.

Case study 10.2   Goal-setting in a car repair shop

Giovanni Ronto was dissatisfied with the performance of the mechanics at his car repair workshop. He did not keep detailed records, but in his opinion too many customers brought their cars back after repair or servicing complaining they were still not right. Others found that their cars were not ready by the agreed time. The garage had recently become the local dealer for one of the smaller car manufacturers. The mechanics had been relatively unfamiliar with cars of that make, and were still often unsure how to carry out certain repairs without frequently checking the workshop manual. Giovanni had decided to introduce performance targets for the mechanics as a group. He told them that complaints and delays must be "substantially reduced", and to sweeten the pill he immediately increased the group's pay by 8%. The increase would continue as long as performance improved to what he regarded as a satisfactory extent. He promised to let the mechanics know each month whether he regarded their collective performance as satisfactory.

Suggested exercise

Use goal-setting theory and research to decide whether Giovanni Ronto's attempt at goal-setting is likely to succeed.

Integration of motivation theories

The reader may already have noted that goal-setting theory makes predictions which contradict, for example, expectancy theory. VIE theory predicts that – other things being equal – people will tend to be motivated by tasks where they feel certain they can succeed. Goal-setting, on the other hand, suggests that people are most motivated by difficult tasks where success is (presumably) not certain. In fact, Matsui *et al.* (1981) showed that the valence (i.e. value) attached to succeeding at a difficult task was sufficiently great to override lower expectancy of success, thus resolving the apparent inconsistency.

Subsequent research has increasingly incorporated expectancy and valence into the goal-setting framework. It has been suggested that when people set their own goals, they do indeed seek an optimal trade-off between expectancy and valence, and that people's perception of their task-specific ability influences the difficulty of self-set goals but not the expectancy of being able to achieve them (Hollenbeck and Brief, 1987).

It is also becoming apparent that although individual differences have traditionally held no clear role in goal-setting theory, this is starting to change. The need for achievement and self-efficacy (see also Chapter 9) are two variables which may influence one or more of goal difficulty level, goal commitment and value attached to successful performance. Quite possibly, other individual differences, including perhaps other needs apart from achievement, will also prove important. This underlines the fact that goal-setting does not work by magic: how people react to them and interpret them affects the outcomes of goals. Concepts drawn from other theories of motivation are proving useful in understanding these processes. So too are theories from outside the field of motivation. Klein (1989) has proposed that *control theory* forms the most appropriate basis for providing a "meta-theory" or general framework within which more specific theories can address particular motivation issues. Control theory proposes that behaviour is governed by a system where an organism's current state is compared with a referent standard (i.e. desired state), and if there is a discrepancy, behavioural strategies are employed to reduce it. Klein's "integrated control theory model of work motivation" is shown in Fig. 10.2.

Figure 10.2 needs a little explanation, but is simpler than it might at first seem. A goal (box 1) is a desired standard which elicits behaviour and performance. Feedback on the results of performance is compared with the standard by the so-called comparator (box 5). If there is no discrepancy or error (box 6), the previous behaviour is continued in order to keep things that way. If there *is* an error, two things can happen. If the situation is familiar to the person, they are likely to engage in an "unconscious scripted response" (box 8), which routinely produces more already-learned behaviour so that the error can be reduced. (The notion of script was briefly introduced in Chapter 2. It refers to cognitive structures that specify familiar sequences of events and behaviours.) Many work behaviours follow scripts or sometimes "plans", which are more general descriptions of slightly less familiar situations. If there is not an immediately obvious reason why there is a discrepancy between actual and

10.2 Klein's integrated control theory of work motivation (reproduced with permission from Klein, 1989).

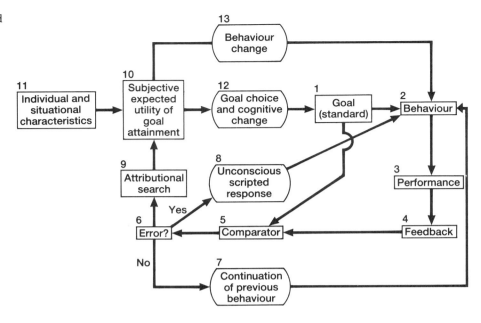

desired states, the person seeks to attribute a reason for it (box 9). The person considers questions like whether the cause of discrepancy is internal or external to self (see Chapter 11), whether the cause is long-term or short-term, and whether it is controllable.

Klein argues that the results of the attribution process determine the perceived attractiveness of the goal and the person's expectancy of achieving it. These are said to be multiplied to produce the subjective expected utility (SEU) of goal attainment (box 10). Personal characteristics (e.g. abilities, needs?) also influence SEU, as do situational ones (such as time available). Decisions about SEU can lead both to behaviour change (box 13) and change of goal, which brings us back to the start.

Klein's work is truly impressive. He has brought together attribution theory, control theory, expectancy theory, feedback theory, goal-setting theory and information-processing theory. Much of modern psychology is here. Klein also builds on other work which has covered some similar ground (e.g. Landy and Becker, 1987; Lord and Hanges, 1987; Taylor *et al.*, 1984). He makes no fewer than 33 propositions on the basis of his framework. Many of these are derived directly from one or another of the theoretical traditions Klein considers, and he claims they often address problems that other theories have been unable to explain.

No doubt many of Klein's ideas will soon be tested in the context of work motivation. There are certainly enough of them to keep an army of behavioural scientists happy for years. Some elements of Klein's framework are doubtless incorrect or incomplete. But it represents new thinking on motivation which uses past work profitably and selectively. This can only enhance our understanding of work motivation over the next few years.

Summary

Work motivation is a wide-ranging topic of considerable practical and theoretical importance. It concerns the direction, intensity and persistence of work behaviour. Some psychologists view motivation as a product of innate human needs. Others see it as a calculation based on the question "how can I maximize my gains?" Still others take the view that we are motivated to achieve what we perceive as a fair situation relative to that experienced by other people. But the most effective approach to motivation is goal-setting. It is based on the premise that intentions shape actions. If work goals (e.g. target levels of performance) are specific and difficult, and if they are accompanied by feedback on how well one is doing, work performance is usually enhanced. There are some circumstances, however, in which goal-setting is less effective. The most recent analyses of motivation use ideas from other theories to account for these limitations and thus further develop our understanding of motivation.

Case study 10.3   An unmotivated building inspector

Nobody at Kirraton Council planning department knew what to do about Simon Lucas. Simon was a building inspector. It was his job to approve proposals for small alterations to buildings (such as extensions and loft conversions) which did not need formal planning permission, and to check that the building work carried out was consistent with the approved plans. The trouble was, he didn't – at least, not often and not quickly. There had been a number of complaints about delays in approval of plans that were Simon's responsibility. He did not seem to keep up with the frequent changes in building regulations, which meant that he sometimes made decisions that contradicted them. He only rarely carried out site inspections. This meant that some of the less scrupulous builders got away with unauthorized changes to plans, and others who genuinely wanted his advice did not get it. However, it was difficult to pin Simon down. Council guidance was vague: plans should be dealt with "within a few weeks"; site inspection conducted "as and when necessary"; and decisions made "within the spirit", not the letter, of some of the less vital regulations.

Simon's boss, Katherine Walker, decided that she would check his records and unobtrusively observe him at work – it was an open-plan office, so this was feasible. She discovered that he was 26 years old, and had qualified as a building inspector 2 years earlier. Simon had been recruited by Katherine's predecessor, apparently partly because Simon had "come up the hard way". Rather than attending college full-time to obtain the necessary qualifications, he had worked for several years as an architect's draughtsman and attended college night classes. In fact, he had been one of the last people to qualify in that way. The building inspectors' professional institute had subsequently decided that part-time study could not develop the necessary skills and knowledge for work as a qualified building inspector. Katherine knew it was true that the part-time route was often seen as "second class". She heard it said that this had prevented Simon from getting a job in another area of the country where he very much wanted to live. Few senior building inspectors held the view of Katherine's predecessor that Simon's route into the profession was superior to full-time study.

Katherine observed that Simon often seemed not to be doing very much. He sat at his desk doodling quite a lot. He sometimes had to phone people more than once because he had forgotten to check something the first time. It took him a long time to find things on his shelves and desk. As far as she could tell, his home life was not a particular problem. Simon was married, apparently happily, and seemed to participate in many social and leisure activities judging from his lunchtime conversations, not to mention his phone calls to squash clubs, campsites, etc., during work time!

Simon's job was relatively secure. Ultimately, he could be sacked if he demonstrated continuing incompetence, but he had successfully completed his probationary period (Katherine wasn't sure how). Because Kirraton Council covered only a small area, and because Simon's job was a specialist one, he could not be moved to another town or department. Building inspectors' pay depended on age and length of service, with slightly higher rates for those with a relevant college degree. Outstanding performance could only be rewarded with promotion, and this was extremely unlikely for anyone with less than 10 years' service.

The other four building inspectors were quite a close-knit group of building sciences graduates who had worked together for several years before Simon's arrival. He had found it hard to establish a relationship with them, and now it was even harder because they felt his apparently poor performance reflected badly on them all. They did not involve him much in their activities, and nor did they appear to respect him. Katherine knew something had to be done, but what, and how?

Suggested exercises

1. What can (i) need theories, (ii) expectancy theory, (iii) equity theory and (iv) goal-setting theory contribute to our understanding of this situation?
2. What does each theory, plus control theory, suggest about what Katherine Walker should do? What further information would she need in each case?

References

Adams, J. S. (1965). Inequity in social exchange. In L. Berkowitz (Ed.), *Advances in Experimental Social Psychology*, Vol. 2. London: Academic Press.

Alderfer, C. P. (1972). *Existence, Relatedness and Growth: Human Needs in Organizational Settings*. New York: Free Press.

Argyris, C. (1964). *Integrating the Individual and the Organization*. Chichester: John Wiley.

Austin, J. T. and Bobko, P. (1985). Goal-setting theory: Unexplored areas and future research needs. *Journal of Occupational Psychology*, *58*, 289–308.

Bartol, K. M. and Martin, D. C. (1987). Managerial motivation among MBA students: A longitudinal assessment. *Journal of Occupational Psychology*, *60*, 1–12.

Bartol, K. M., Anderson, C. R. and Schneier, C. E. (1980). Motivation to manage among college business students: A reassessment. *Journal of Vocational Behavior, 17*, 22–32.

Bartol, K. M., Schneier, C. E. and Anderson, C. R. (1985). Internal and external validity issues with motivation to manage research: A reply to Miner, Smith and Ebrahimi. *Journal of Vocational Behavior, 26*, 299–305.

Beck, R. C. (1983). *Motivation: Theory and Principles*. Englewood Cliffs, N.J.: Prentice-Hall.

Birnbaum, M. H. (1983). Perceived equity of salary policies. *Journal of Applied Psychology, 68*, 49–59.

Cassidy, T. and Lynn, R. (1989). A multifactorial approach to achievement motivation: The development of a comprehensive measure. *Journal of Occupational Psychology*, *62*, 301–312.

Dornstein, M. (1988). Wage reference groups and their determinants: A study of blue-collar and white-collar employees in Israel. *Journal of Occupational Psychology, 61*, 221–235.

Dornstein, M. (1989). The fairness judgements of received pay and their determinants. *Journal of Occupational Psychology, 62*, 287–299.

Earley, P. C., Connolly, T. and Ekegren, G. (1989). Goals, strategy development and task performance: Some limits on the efficacy of goal-setting. *Journal of Applied Psychology, 74*, 24–33.

Greenberg, J. (1987). A taxonomy of organizational justice theories. *Academy of Management Review, 12*, 9–22.

Hollenbeck, J. R. and Brief, A. P. (1987). The effects of individual differences and goal origin on goal setting and performance. *Organizational Behavior and Human Decision Processes, 40*, 392–414.

Hollenbeck, J. R. and Klein, H. J. (1987). Goal commitment and goal-setting process: Problems, prospects, and proposals for future research. *Journal of Applied Psychology, 72*, 212–220.

Hollenbeck, J. R., Williams, C. R. and Klein, H. J. (1989). An empirical examination of the antecedents of commitment to difficult goals. *Journal of Applied Psychology, 74*, 18–23.

Huseman, R. C., Hatfield, J. D. and Miles, E. W. (1987). A new perspective on equity theory: The equity sensitivity construct. *Academy of Management Review, 12*, 222–234.

Kanfer, R. and Ackerman, P. L. (1989). Motivation and cognitive abilities: An integrative/aptitude–treatment interaction approach to skill acquisition. *Journal of Applied Psychology, 74*, 657–690.

Klein, H. J. (1989). An integrated control theory model of work motivation. *Academy of Management Review, 14*, 150–172.

Landy, F. J. (1985). *Psychology of Work Behavior*, 3rd edn. Homewood, Ill.: Dorsey Press.

Landy, F. J. and Becker, L. J. (1987). Motivation theory reconsidered. *Research in Organizational Behavior, 9*, 1–38.

Latham, G. P., Erez, M. and Locke, E. A. (1988). Resolving scientific disputes by the joint design of crucial experiments by the antagonists: Application to the Erez–Latham dispute regarding participation in goal setting. *Journal of Applied Psychology, 73*, 753–772.

Leon, F. R. (1981). The role of positive and negative outcomes in the causation of motivational forces. *Journal of Applied Psychology, 66*, 45–53.

Locke, E. A. and Latham, G. P. (1990). *A Theory of Goal Setting and Task Performance*. Englewood Cliffs, N.J.: Prentice-Hall.

Locke, E. A., Shaw, K. N., Saari, L. M. and Latham, G. P. (1981). Goal setting and task performance 1969–1980. *Psychological Bulletin, 90*, 125–152.

Locke, E. A., Latham, G. P. and Erez, M. (1988). The determinants of goal commitment. *Academy of Management Review, 13*, 23–39.

Lord, R. G. and Hanges, P. J. (1987). A control systems model of organizational motivation: Theoretical development and applied implications. *Behavioral Science, 32*, 161–178.

Maslow, A. H. (1943). A theory of motivation. *Psychological Review, 50*, 370–396.

Maslow, A. H. (1970). *Motivation and Personality*, 2nd edn. New York: Harper and Row.

Matsui, T., Okada, A. and Mizuguchi, R. (1981). Expectancy theory prediction of the goal theory postulate "the harder the goals, the higher the performance". *Journal of Applied Psychology, 66*, 54–58.

McClelland, D. C. (1961). *The Achieving Society*. Princeton, N.J.: Van Nostrand.

McClelland, D. C. and Boyatzis, R. E. (1982). Leadership motive pattern and long-term success in management. *Journal of Applied Psychology, 67*, 737–743.

McGregor, D. (1960). *The Human Side of Enterprise*. New York: McGraw-Hill.

Mento, A. J., Steel, R. P. and Karren, R. J. (1987). A meta-analytic study of the effects of goal setting on task performance: 1966–1984. *Organizational Behavior and Human Decision Processes, 39*, 52–83.

Meyer, J. P. and Gellatly, I. R. (1988). Perceived performance norm as a mediator in the effect of assigned goal on personal goal and task performance. *Journal of Applied Psychology, 73*, 410–420.

Miner, J. B. (1964). *Scoring Guide for the Miner Sentence Completion Scale*. Atlanta, Ga.: Organizational Measurement Systems Press.

Miner, J. B. and Smith, N. R. (1982). Decline and stabilization of managerial motivation over a 20-year period. *Journal of Applied Psychology, 67*, 297–305.

Miner, J. B., Smith, N. R. and Ebrahimi, B. (1985). Further considerations in the decline and stabilization of managerial motivation: A rejoinder to Bartol, Anderson and Schneier (1980). *Journal of Vocational Behavior, 26*, 290–298.

Murray, H. J. (1938). *Explorations in Personality*. Oxford: Oxford University Press.

Pritchard, R. D. (1969). Equity theory: A review and critique. *Organizational Behavior and Human Performance, 4*, 176–211.

Rauschenberger, J., Schmitt, N. and Hunter, J. E. (1980). A test of the need hierarchy concept by a Markov model of change in need strength. *Administrative Science Quarterly, 25*, 654–670.

Ryan, T. A. (1970). *Intentional Behavior*. New York: Ronald Press.

Salancik, G. R. and Pfeffer, J. (1977). An examination of need satisfaction models of job attitudes. *Administrative Science Quarterly, 22*, 427–456.

Schein, E. H. (1980). *Organizational Psychology*, 3rd edn. Englewood Cliffs, N.J.: Prentice-Hall.

Schwab, D. P., Olian-Gottlieb, J. D. and Heneman, H. G. (1979). Between-subjects expectancy theory research: A statistical review of studies predicting effort and performance. *Psychological Bulletin, 86*, 139–147.

Steers, R. M. and Braunstein, D. N. (1976). A behaviorally-based measure of manifest needs in work settings. *Journal of Vocational Behavior, 9*, 251–266.

Sugarman, L. (1986). *Life-span Development*. London: Methuen.

Taylor, M. S., Fisher, C. D. and Ilgen, D. R. (1984). Individuals' reactions to performance feedback in organizations: A control theory perspective. *Research in Personnel and Human Resources Management, 2*, 81–124.

Vroom, V. H. (1964). *Work and Motivation*. Chichester: John Wiley.

Wahba, M. A. and Bridwell, L. B. (1976). Maslow reconsidered: A review of research on the need hierarchy theory. *Organizational Behavior and Human Performance, 15*, 212–240.

Perceiving people

Introduction

How do we make judgements about other people? Do we do it well, and could we do it better? Although not often defined as a topic area in work psychology, person perception is clearly crucial to a wide range of activities in the workplace. That is why it is given its own chapter here. This chapter aims to introduce the reader to some common phenomena in person pereception and to apply them to work situations. It also aims to enable the reader to become as aware as possible of his or her own person perception. A brief introduction to the field is followed by coverage of stereotypes, implicit personality theories, impression management and attribution, as well as other more specific phenomena. The emphasis throughout is on how findings from social psychology can be used to understand and improve interpersonal communication in the workplace.

Overview of person perception

Person perception concerns how we obtain, store and recall information about other people in order to make judgements about them. In the 1980s, it became increasingly apparent that advances in person perception made by social psychologists were being largely ignored by work psychologists (Ilgen and Klein, 1989). There have been some exceptions, such as selection interviewing (see Chapter 7), performance appraisal interviewing (see Chapter 6) and leadership (see Chapter 13). But person perception is clearly relevant to many more work situations than these, including meetings, sales presentations, conferences, telephone conversations and even written material such as memos or reports.

Person perception can be considered at three levels:

- perceiving the *behaviour* of other people;
- perceiving the *personality* of other people; and
- perceiving the *causes* of events involving people.

Clearly, people who do these things well are at an advantage in the workplace, other things being equal. They will be more likely to relate well to others, get the best out of them, and manage social situations with skill. But aren't we all quite good at person perception? Isn't it just common-sense stuff that comes naturally? No. We frequently succumb to various biases and distortions that can impair our perception of others. There are two general sources of such problems:

1. *Motivation or emotion.* For reasons such as the protection of our own self-esteem, we may not even attempt to achieve accuracy in our perception of others. We may, however, *believe* that we are trying to be accurate.

2. *Information-processing limitations.* We may seek the truth, but lack the cognitive resources to weigh up information about other people in an optimal manner.

The first of these is loosely derived from psychoanalytic approaches to psychology, and the second from social cognitive approaches (see Chapter 2). Social psychologists working in both these traditions have spent 30 years or more concentrating on our imperfections when we perceive others. As Higgins and Bargh (1987, p. 371) put it:

> It sometimes appears as though the burden of proof is on demon-strating that people take environmental information into account, rather than on showing that they dismiss, discount or distort it in line with their prior theories.

But now the pendulum is swinging back. As we shall see, recent work tends to show that although we are not perfect, we are not half as bad at perceiving others as has sometimes been made out. But it is equally clear that we need to be aware of possible pitfalls in order to overcome them. To quote Higgins and Bargh (1987, p. 415) again: "... recognizing that one's own beliefs, inferences and memory are limited promotes the realization, 'I could be wrong' – a first step in tolerance, open-mindedness, and prudence".

Before we look further, two additional points should be made. First, much of the above discussion depends on the notion of accuracy in person percep-tion – that there is a right answer to the question "what is (s)he like?" if only we can find it. This seems a reasonable assumption when we are perceiving people's *behaviour.* It is less straightforward when applied to judgements of *personality* and personal responsibility. Neither of these can be observed directly (see Forgas, 1985, ch. 2).

The second point concerns method in social psychology. Most of what social psychologists know about person perception comes from experimental laboratory studies. People are often asked to make judgements about others which do not usually have significant consequences for either the perceiver or the perceived. They are normally made using dimensions provided by the psychologist, which are not necessarily those the observer would have chosen. The judgements are usually made by students because students are easily accessible to most experimenters. Of course, these are all common features of laboratory research in psychology, and there are compensatory advantages (see Chapter 3). But perhaps it is not surprising that some work psychologists have been reluctant to take the practical implications of that research at face value.

The remainder of this chapter is devoted to outlining some common phenomena in person perception. Guidance is offered about how to recognize them, avoid mistakes, and use them to good effect.

Stereotypes

What are stereotypes and how do they arise?

Stereotypes are generalizations about what people in a particular group are like. Groups can be defined on any number of criteria, but common ones are race, sex, occupation and age. Beliefs such as the following can be described as stereotypes:

- trade union officials are mostly militant ideologues;
- most police are violent authoritarians;
- managers in this company are honest;
- accountants are more stimulating than anybody else; and
- production managers usually speak their mind.

Clearly, then, stereotypes vary in their favourability. They also differ in their extremity. The third and fourth above do not allow for any exceptions, but the others do because they refer to "most" rather than "all". Sometimes they can have a grain of truth, in the sense that *on average* members of one group differ from another. On average, middle managers are doubtless more intelligent than building site labourers. But there is equally certainly a large overlap – some building site labourers are brighter than some middle managers.

We can also develop stereotypes of groups based on very limited information about them, perhaps confined to what we see on television. Other stereotypes can arise when a "generalization" is true of a very few people in one group and practically none in another group. Suppose for a moment that 1 in 500 shop stewards are members of revolutionary left-wing political groups, compared with 1 in 3000 of the general population. Would it be a good idea to expect that a shop steward you were about to meet for the first time would be a revolutionary left-winger? Clearly not. It is more probable that he or she holds such views than someone who is not a shop steward, but still not at all likely.

Stereotypes and group identity

Stereotypes are often thought to derive from a need to establish a clear "map" of our social world where our identity and that of others is defined in terms of group memberships. This is a fundamental premise of *social identity theory* (Tajfel and Turner, 1985), which has become enormously influential in European social psychology. This theory proposes that not only do we wish to create a social map, we wish to uphold the value of our own group (and thereby of ourselves too) relative to other groups. Some remarkable experimental work has shown that this happens even where groups are short-term, and defined on the basis of some apparently innocuous criterion such as preference for one painting rather than another, or even random allocation. Further, it seems that group members seek to maximize the *difference* between the rewards received by their own group and another group, even at the expense of absolute gain. Thus a reward of, say, £8.00 for own-group members and £3.00 for members of another group is usually preferred to £10.00 for each group.

Principles of social identity theory have been applied to work organizations by Ashforth and Mael (1989). They point out a real danger that people in different groups (e.g. departments, functions, levels) will perceive each other in terms of negative stereotypes, and use this to justify attempts to maintain or enhance their own superiority while minimizing collaborative activities. This tendency is especially marked where groups are in fact relatively similar, because that is when people most feel the need to establish their own distinctiveness. Groups of relatively low status are also more concerned than others to establish an identity, and the relative unconcern of higher-status groups simply serves to frustrate them.

So are stereotypes dangerous?

They can be. As some of the above discussion demonstrates, they can serve to handicap inter-group understanding with potentially negative consequences for work organizations and society in general. More optimistically, where group members feel that between-group differences in resources or status are legitimate, they form less negative views of members of other groups. Also, group members often arrive at a "compromise" where they see themselves and members of another group as possessing complementary virtues (van Knippenberg, 1984). Thus the accountant may acknowledge that the marketer has valuable creative flair, but argue that flair needs careful costing and control which only the accountant can provide. Fostering such beliefs about complementary strengths is an important task for managers who wish their organizations to function in an integrated fashion.

Much experimental research has demonstrated that we recall information consistent with a pre-existing stereotype better than information that is not consistent with the stereotype (e.g. O'Sullivan and Durso, 1984). As Higgins and Bargh (1987) point out, this fits well with the tendency for stereotypes and other beliefs (even weakly held ones) to resist change even in the face of disconfirming evidence. We also sometimes "remember" information about people which was in fact never presented, if that information is consistent with stereotype. Bodenhausen (1988) has produced experimental evidence that we process stereotype-consistent information more thoroughly than inconsistent information. Apparently, stereotypes do not influence our *interpretation* of what someone does; rather, they determine the thoroughness with which we notice and consider their action.

But the tendency to remember consistent information better is not universal (Hastie and Kumar, 1979). Information consistent with a pre-existing stereotype is remembered better than information irrelevant to that stereotype, but sometimes *worse* than information inconsistent with the stereotype. This seems to be the case where an observer is actively seeking to *test* the stereotype and is therefore open to contradictory information.

Overcoming stereotypes

Perhaps most of us like to think that we are free of stereotypes. If so, we are probably fooling ourselves. At the university where the authors are employed, a small number of students come each year from Norway. One of us (who shall remain nameless!) still catches himself feeling slightly surprised that many of these students are *not* blonde and tall – his stereotype of Scandinavians. Devine (1989) argues that we cannot avoid starting out with stereotypes. The difference between prejudiced and non-prejudiced individuals is that the latter deliberately inhibit the automatically activated stereotype and replace it with more open-minded thoughts:

> [This] can be likened to the breaking of a bad habit.... The individual must (a) initially decide to stop the old behaviour; (b) remember the resolution, and (c) try repeatedly and decide repeatedly to eliminate the habit before the habit can be eliminated (Devine, 1989, p. 15).

One other catch is worth noting. It seems that we interpret information about a person – a particular action, for example – as consistent with our stereotype of them if that action reaches a certain "threshold" level of consistency with the stereotype. In other words, we then exaggerate the extent to which the action matches the stereotype – a so-called assimilation effect. But if the action does not quite reach that threshold, the opposite happens. We interpret it as inconsistent with the stereotype, and in fact over-emphasize the inconsistency – a contrast effect (Manis *et al.*, 1988). So if we are not careful, as an observer we can actually end up perceiving someone as more different from our stereotype than they really are. From the viewpoint of the person being observed, this brings the hope that we do not have to behave in an extreme fashion in order to alter somebody's stereotypical perception of us.

Case study 11.1   Stereotyping and social identity

Pratik Rahim works in the medical records department of a large hospital. He takes a dim view of doctors: "The trouble is they are all so arrogant. They waltz in here and expect me to find patients' case notes immediately. It's not as simple as that – they could be almost any place in the hospital. They couldn't do their job properly if it wasn't for me, but they seem to forget that. One doctor actually comes in here and threatens to report me if I don't do what he wants right away. Another *always* finds me in the canteen during my lunch break and makes me come back here for an urgent file she needs. They don't all do things like that, but I bet they would if they thought they could get away with it. And, of course, I never get invited on to the wards to see what goes on there. I can only remember one doctor being really nice to me – and he had just been promoted! People say they notice doctors being friendly to me sometimes but I can't say I do. So I just do what they ask without wasting my breath to pass the time of day."

Suggested exercise

Study pp. 191–5 and find as many phenomena as you can which are reflected in this case study. Are there any others? Is there any hope of changing Pratik's view of doctors?

Implicit personality theories and prototypes

What are they?

Stereotypes are not the only way we form expectations about people. We also carry round our own "theories" about which personality characteristics tend to go with which others. We do not usually articulate these to ourselves: they are implicit rather than explicit – hence the term "implicit personality theories". Prototypes refer to our idea of what a "typical x" is like, where x is a personality type. Hence we probably have our own ideas about what a "typical extrovert", "typical worrier" or "typical snob" is like. In each case, of course, a prototype represents a partial summary of our implicit personality theories. Prototypes differ from stereotypes in that the latter concern the perceived characteristics of externally defined groups, whereas prototypes concern personality types, as noted above.

Different people have different implicit personality theories. To take a simple example, one of the authors presents students with the following dimensions drawn from the 16PF personality questionnaire (see Chapter 6):

- outgoing–reserved;
- stable–emotional;
- imaginative–practical;
- bold–shy;
- tender-minded–tough-minded;
- self-sufficient–group-tied; and
- tense–relaxed.

He invites the students to assume that a particular individual is outgoing as opposed to reserved. Then the students are asked: "Does your knowledge that the person is outgoing lead you to infer anything about their scores on any of the other personality dimensions shown here? If so, what?" Most students feel able to make some inferences. They feel they can identify certain personality characteristics which, in their own implicit personality theory, are associated with being outgoing. But they disagree a lot about which dimensions, and which ends of particular dimensions, are associated with being outgoing.

Some aspects of implicit personality theories are more widely shared. A classic experiment by Kelley (1950) showed that the dimension "warm–cold" seems to influence our judgements of people on many other dimensions, even after we have interacted with them. Kelley gave university students a description of a visiting lecturer, consisting of a brief paragraph about him. For half the students, the last sentence read: "People who know him consider him to be a rather cold person, industrious, critical, practical and determined." For the other half of the class, the words "rather cold" were replaced with "very warm". The students did not know they had received different descriptions.

The visiting lecturer then took the class for a short discussion. After he had left, the students completed anonymous evaluations of him. Relative to the "very warm" group, the "rather cold" group rated the lecturer considerably less sociable, and considerably more ruthless, self-centred and irritable among other things. And this was after they all participated in the same class! The "rather cold" group also contributed less to the group discussion than the "very warm" group.

Apart from highlighting the centrality of "warm–cold" in our implicit personality theories, this demonstrates again how our expectations of a person can influence our subsequent impressions of him or her. Where we have formed clear expectations, and where we do not seek to challenge them, we are in danger of forming biased judgements of others.

Confirming what we already believe

The students in Kelley's experiment had only a very limited opportunity to influence the behaviour of their visiting lecturer. In less formal situations, there is often more opportunity. So much so that some people have wondered whether we simply use our interaction with somebody to confirm our expectations about them. Snyder and Swann (1978) conducted some research which appeared to show exactly that. They asked women students to choose questions they would ask another person in order to determine whether that person matched an already supplied personality profile. The students received either an "introvert" or an "extrovert" profile. They were given a choice of 26 questions to ask. These varied according to whether they were considered (by independent judges) to be the sort asked by someone who already knows the target person to be extrovert (11), introvert (10) or neither (5). The results were clear. The students showed a strong tendency to choose questions which could only confirm the personality description they had already been given, especially for the extrovert description. Snyder and Swann also demonstrated that people who listened to tapes of the chosen questions being put to an interviewee judged the interviewee in ways consistent with the questions asked.

If generalizable, these results would have serious implications in the world of work. They would mean that we are rarely capable of proving our own expectations wrong. Fortunately, it has subsequently been shown that we rise well above the depths suggested by Snyder and Swann, although a preference for so-called "hypothesis matching" questions is clear enough. Other work (e.g. Trope *et al.*, 1984; Pennington, 1987) indicates that:

1. People almost never ask leading questions of the kind provided by Snyder and Swann when they can devise the questions themselves.

2. People usually prefer questions which are capable of testing their expectation, even if they are framed in a way which is consistent with that expectation.

3. Where people are able to choose their questions as their interaction with someone proceeds (rather than beforehand), they soon depart from a confirmatory strategy.

Case study 11.2　Expectations and social reality

The manufacturing firm where Brian Hall was personnel officer was looking for a new part-time industrial chaplain for their main factory. One of the local vicars, Peter Hinde, was interested. Brian took him for a thorough tour of the factory, chatting as they went. Brian had previously heard from one of Hinde's parishioners that he could be rather secretive, which was bad news because in his opinion a chaplain needed to be open, honest and sincere. On the way round the factory, he observed that Hinde laughed only occasionally and rarely cracked jokes, though when he did they were good ones. He talked to people in an intense way, but not for long. Each time he quickly moved on. Hinde commented a lot to Brian on the people they met on their tour and seemed to feel they were straightforward, open and honest. Especially in the early part of the tour, Hinde did not give much away about his religious beliefs, concentrating instead on *their* lives and points of view. He listened to what they had to say and never interrupted. Brian asked him some questions about how he handled situations when parishioners wanted him to give more information than he wanted. After Hinde left, Brian sat in his chair and sighed. Peter Hinde probably wasn't right for the factory. Just his luck! As if he wasn't fed up enough already, having only yesterday been turned down for a promotion that would have meant he could say goodbye to tasks like this.

Suggested exercises

1. What conclusions do you think Brian Hall drew about Peter Hinde as they toured the factory? Why did he come to those conclusions?
2. Suppose that Brian had got his promotion, and had heard that Peter Hinde was quite open in his dealings with people. How might he then have assessed Hinde's behaviour in the factory?

Are implicit personality theories accurate?

The possibility that we might after all be quite good at person perception is reinforced by Rothstein and Jackson (1984), who argued that an interviewer's implicit personality theories are typically used appropriately in judging interviewees. Borkenau and Ostendorf (1987) arrived at somewhat similar conclusions. In their experimental research, people estimated the extent to which they expected various categories of behaviour to occur together in a group discussion. Observation of real group discussions showed that the estimates were generally accurate. So were observers' recollections of what happened in the discussions. One persistent mistake was noted, however. Estimates ignored the base-rate frequency of behaviour. For example, let us take two behaviours: stealing a pencil from work and stealing a word processor from work. We might expect these behaviours to be associated. But presumably the second is rarer than the first – at least one hopes so! This means that someone who steals a word processor from work is also likely to steal a pencil. But the reverse is less true, simply because few people steal word processors from work. We seem to forget such "base-line" information when we form our expectations about what people are like. This mirrors our earlier point about shop stewards and stereotyping.

Some other phenomena in person perception

So far, much of this chapter has concerned how our prior expectations can colour our subsequent perceptions of people. But this, of course, neglects social interaction itself. Surely what actually happens must have some effect!

One important phenomenon is the so-called *primacy effect*. If we are not careful, first impressions are lasting impressions, and we place too much weight on early information about a person. If your first encounter with a new colleague is in the bar one evening when she is loud and excited, and she knocks a drink over your lap, it will take a great deal of sober and careful behaviour on her part over the following weeks to change your initial impression of her. Too much in fact – we tend not to revise that initial impression readily enough. This is analogous to the finding (Springbett, 1958) that selection interviewers often make up their mind about a candidate's suitability within the first few minutes of the interview. It is relatively easy to train people to avoid the primacy effect, though it then becomes important to guard against the *recency effect* – a tendency to give too much weight to the *last* information received about a person. In the context of training assessors for performance appraisal, it is possible to pay so much attention to such "technicalities" that basic accuracy suffers (Bernardin and Pence, 1980).

So-called *halo and horns effects* are also important. The halo effect refers to our tendency to assume that one desirable characteristic in a person means that they will also possess other desirable characteristics, even if we have no direct evidence for them. The horns effect refers to the same phenomenon, but with undesirable characteristics. Clearly, the halo and horns effects are close relatives of implicit personality theories. They are also undesirable in themselves, but like primacy and recency effects, too much concentration on avoiding them can deflect attention from accuracy in person perception (Bernardin and Pence, 1980).

What is the relative importance of *verbal and non-verbal behaviour* in determining our impression of a person? The answer to this depends partly on what impressions are involved, but often non-verbal behaviour is considerably more important. It's not what we say, it's the way we say it. Factors like eye contact, limb movement and positioning, body posture and voice intonation (this counts as non-verbal behaviour) all matter here (Argyle *et al.*, 1971). Often as observers we are not aware that our impressions are being affected by such factors, but they are. For example, Montepare and Zebrowitz-McArthur (1988) have shown that we make judgements about people's personality partly on the basis of the way they walk!

Are perceptions of other people affected by the perceiver's *mood*? We would hope that the perceiver can take their mood into account, but apparently this is not so. Baron (1987) among others has found that an interviewer's mood affects the positiveness of their judgement of an interviewee. This finding could not be attributed to the interviewer's mood affecting the candidate's behaviour, because this was held constant. It is worrying to think that when we are judged by someone in a bad mood, they may well take it out on us! On the other hand, this may not necessarily apply where perceiver and perceived already know each other well.

The target strikes back

It is easy to forget that the person being perceived (the "target person", to use the terminology of social psychologists) is not necessarily passive in the person perception process. Presenting a certain image of ourselves to the world is important to most of us, and is of course central to many jobs. This is often termed *impression management* (Schlenker, 1980). To some extent, then, the perceiver only perceives what the target wants him or her to perceive. Through techniques such as ingratiation, positive descriptions of self, apologies and selective description of events, we seek to create and maintain desired impressions of ourselves.

Snyder (1974) has coined the term "self-monitoring" to express the extent to which a person notices the self-presentation of others and uses that information to guide their own self-presentation. People who score high on self-monitoring are better able to change their behaviour to suit the situation or audience. They are therefore often better performers in jobs which require communication with a variety of people, though most managers are sufficiently sensitive to make some adjustment in their self-presentation strategies to fit different situations (Gardner and Martinko, 1988).

There are, of course, limits to the power of impression management. We cannot be "all things to all people" for very long without being found out. Nevertheless, it is clear that if our self-presentation is true to our self-concept, an observer is likely to be swayed by it (Swann and Ely, 1984). Some other experimental work has also shown that observers tend to be more influenced by a target person's claims about their own virtues than by what other people think of the target (Jones *et al.*, 1984). This phenomenon may depend partly on the perceived credibility and motives of those other people, but nevertheless it is interesting that what is probably the most biased source of information (the target) can be seen as reasonably credible.

It is therefore sometimes necessary for an observer to "see through" not only their own expectations but also the overt behaviour of a person they are trying to weigh up. This brings us to the final theme of the chapter: how do we decide what causes people to behave as they do?

Why did they do that?

Some principles of attribution theory

In the 1960s and 1970s, a school of thought developed in social psychology that has become known as *attribution theory*. Many people have pointed out that nowadays it is really too fragmented to be called a theory, but this should not detract from the value of its principles. Beginning with the observation that we are often more interested in the causes of events than the events themselves (Heider, 1958), attribution theorists have sought to uncover the principles we use in deciding why something happened. Naturally enough, psychologists have been most interested in events involving human action, which are in any case the sort of events we encounter most often in our day-to-day lives. People are normally viewed as "naive scientists" who seek the truth by weighing up all the evidence surrounding an event in order to establish a "theory" of what caused it. The most obvious possible causes are:

1. The *actor*: the person whose behaviour was the event.

2. The *entity*: the person or thing towards which the actor's behaviour was directed.

3. The *situation* in which the behaviour took place.

Several attribution frameworks have been proposed, but perhaps the most useful is that of Kelley (1971). An adaptation of his proposals is described in Table 11.1. This model assumes that the observer already has some familiarity with the actor. It is also clearly not the whole story. Deciding whether the actor, entity or situation caused the actor's behaviour does not in itself establish *what* about the actor, entity or situation was responsible. Even if we conclude that a sales assistant is rude to customers because of something about the assistant himself, we could still choose between impatience, intolerance, lack of social skill, lack of motivation, a persistently painful back problem, and plenty of other possibilities.

Let us take an example. Suppose a factory floor supervisor, Sarah, notices one of the shop-floor workers, Dave, becoming angry and frustrated with the machine he is working on. Before deciding what, if anything, to do about this, Sarah asks herself why Dave is behaving in this manner. If she follows the

Table 11.1   Attributing causes of behaviour

Any behaviour involves:

An *actor*: the person performing the behaviour

An *entity*: the person or thing towards whom/which the behaviour is directed

An observer examines the extent to which the actor's behaviour demonstrates:

1. *Distinctiveness*: does the actor do this only in the presence of that entity?

2. *Consistency*: does the actor do this consistently with this entity over time and different situations?

3. *Consensus*: do other actors behave in the same way towards that entity?

We decide that a relatively stable feature of the *actor* was responsible (i.e. make an *internal attribution*) when the answers to these questions are:

1. No   2. Yes   3. No

We hold the *entity* responsible when the answers to these questions are:

1. Yes   2. Yes   3. Yes

Other combinations of answers produce less certain answers, but attribution is often to some feature of the situation (other than the entity), especially where the answer to question 2 is "no" attributional principles shown in Table 11.1, she will address the following questions:

- Have I seen Dave reacting this way when working on other similar machines on the shop floor? (Distinctiveness)
- Have I seen Dave getting angry with this machine on other occasions? (Consistency)
- Do other people get angry with this machine when they work on it? (Consensus)

Suppose that Sarah *has* seen Dave reacting this way with this and other machines, but has not seen other people react in that way to that machine. She will feel confident in attributing the behaviour to Dave himself – that's the way he is. On the other hand, if Sarah recalls that both Dave and other people get angry with this machine, and that Dave does not react that way to other machines, she will attribute his reaction to the machine. It is playing up – better fetch one of the maintenance engineers to check it over.

We can see that the conclusions Sarah draws have real implications for her, Dave and the factory's productivity. The distinctiveness, consistency and consensus questions look like sensible ones to ask, though perhaps not the only ones. And indeed research has shown that people do consider these issues, albeit not necessarily in quite the way they are framed here. But is it that simple? Not quite. As ever, we introduce various biases and emphases into the attribution process. Some can be put down to faulty information processing; others have more to do with our desire to see the world in certain ways.

Some biases in the attributional process

There is considerable evidence that we have a basic tendency to attribute the cause of behaviour to the actor. A lot of research has demonstrated that even where an actor's behaviour is clearly constrained, observers are inclined to conclude that the behaviour reflects the actor's own attitudes or personality (though research by Fleming and Darley, 1989, also suggests that observers do look for evidence about the actor's emotional reactions to what they are having to do).

This tendency to attribute responsibility to the actor too readily is often termed the *fundamental attribution error*. Perhaps it is not a surprising phenomenon in cultures which emphasize individual responsibility for actions. On the other hand, we do not apply the same rules to explaining our own behaviour! When considering our own actions, we more often look to the situation for an explanation. Although in some respects we like to think of ourselves as distinct from others, when it comes to explaining our own behaviour we seem to believe that we did what any reasonable person would have done in the circumstances.

Another related phenomenon is our apparent tendency to under-use consensus information and indeed most other cues not immediately evident in the actor's behaviour. One such cue mentioned earlier in this chapter is the baseline frequency of different behaviours. Nevertheless, where consensus information is available and/or brought to the attention of the observer, it is used (Higgins and King, 1981).

A motivational bias in attribution can also be observed. Children tend to hold someone responsible for an act to the extent that it has important consequences. It seems that adults have something of the same tendency. For example, one experiment (Walster, 1966) showed that more blame is attributed to a car driver whose parked car rolls down a hill and causes lots of damage than to one whose car rolls down but fortuitously does little damage. Such scapegoating seems to be based on a desire to believe that serious events must happen for a reason, and preferably one that we can control. Related to this is the tendency to believe in a "just world" where people get what they deserve (Lerner, 1965).

Let us finally return to the case of the factory supervisor and the machine worker. If Sarah and Dave fit the phenomena described in this section, Sarah will tend to start from the position that Dave is responsible for his action, whereas Dave is likely to see things quite differently. Sarah may forget to ask herself whether other workers react in the same way to that machine (consensus) and find Dave accusing her of picking on him and ignoring others when they do the same as him. Sarah is more likely to hold Dave responsible if in his frustration he happens to break the machine than if the same actions happen not to cause a breakage.

Summary

The way we perceive somebody is usually influenced by our prior expectations of them. Those expectations may or may not be particularly accurate. We need to be aware of them, and consciously seek evidence that they are wrong rather than only seeing what we expect to see. We should also examine what our expectation is based on, and consider whether that is a sound foundation. Stereotypes of others based on their group membership are probably inevitable, but it is important to remember that other groups may have complementary virtues to our own. Our ideas about which personal characteristics are associated with which others may well be reasonably accurate. However, we cannot take this for granted. We must be careful to notice and remember behaviour which violates our assumptions, and avoid "remembering" behaviour which never actually occurred. It is necessary to guard against giving too much weight to first impressions of someone. A person being perceived can often manage the impression they give, and cannot be considered a sitting target just waiting to be perceived. Their own beliefs about what they are like are often adopted by the perceiver. In deciding causes of a person's behaviour, we should also find out as much about the situation as possible, and about what other people generally do in the same situation. We should also try to consider the behaviour independent of its consequences.

Case study 11.3   An interpersonal conflict at Homebuy

Stephanie Barnes had a problem. She was one of the two supervisors of a large team of clerks at the headquarters of Homebuy mail order shopping company. One of the clerks who reported to Stephanie, Martin Warner, was being very disruptive. He seemed to have a grudge against her. On checking her records, Stephanie was surprised to find that his time-keeping was as good as anybody's, and so was his work. But he could be very rude and abrupt toward Stephanie. She found conflict hard to handle at the best of times, and could not understand why Martin apparently disliked her so much. None of the other clerks seemed to find it necessary to behave like that towards her.

As far as Stephanie could see from observing Martin unobtrusively at his desk and in the canteen, he was perfectly civil and friendly to other people. He was, however, rather cold towards Michael Butcher, who was the other supervisor of Stephanie's grade. Interestingly, Martin seemed to be at his worst when she was trying to check a query about his work. At other times (e.g. when Stephanie was assigning him work or answering a question he asked) he didn't seem so bad.

Things looked different from Martin's point of view. This was the third job he had held since leaving school at the age of 17. In each of the previous two he had had trouble with his supervisor. In his experience, first-line managers were interfering bullies whose main aim was to make their subordinates feel small using all kinds of devious methods. It didn't help that in his first few weeks at Homebuy, Stephanie Barnes had repeatedly checked his work even though the tasks were quite straightforward and did not in his opinion need checking.

She seemed to do it less now, but still more often than he would like, and for all the types of work he handled, even the simple ones. She did not check up on the other clerks so often, and when she checked up on him she would pretend to be giving him a helping hand when she was really snooping. Michael Butler had supervised Martin for a few weeks when Stephanie had been on holiday or ill, but Martin had formed no particular impression of his supervisory style.

After almost a year of this, Stephanie had had enough. She felt that Martin was probably simply an aggressive young man with a chip on his shoulder. Yet somehow it did not all quite add up. Perhaps a quiet chat to show him she was not a threat would help. So Stephanie called Martin into her office. After carefully explaining what she saw as the problem, Stephanie asked Martin whether there was any particular reason why he was such an aggressive person. This provoked an angry response from Martin, so she tried a different tack. She asked him to describe his past experiences with bosses, and his relationships with people more generally. They parted an hour later with Stephanie feeling she had learned a little about Martin and sowed the seeds of a somewhat better relationship.

Suggested exercises

1. Use attribution theory to predict how Stephanie and Martin might see the cause of each other's behaviour. Are there any special problems where (to use attribution terminology) the observer is also the entity?
2. Examine the significance in this case study of: (i) expectations based on stereotypes; (ii) the primacy effect; (iii) the "horns" effect; and (iv) self-fulfilling hypotheses.

References

Argyle, M., Alkema, F. and Gilmour, R. (1971). The communication of friendly and hostile attitudes by verbal and nonverbal signals. *European Journal of Social Psychology*, *1*, 385–402.

Ashforth, B. E. and Mael, F. (1989). Social identity theory and the organization. *Academy of Management Review, 14*, 20–39.

Baron, R. A. (1987). Interviewer's moods and reactions to job applicants: The influence of affective states on applied social judgements. *Journal of Applied Social Psychology, 17*, 911–926.

Bernardin, H. J. and Pence, E. C. (1980). Effects of rater training: Creating new response sets and decreasing accuracy. *Journal of Applied Psychology, 65*, 60–66.

Bodenhausen, G. V. (1988). Stereotypic biases in social decision making and memory: Testing process models of stereotype use. *Journal of Personality and Social Psychology, 55*, 726–737.

Borkenau, P. and Ostendorf, F. (1987). Fact and fiction in implicit personality theory. *Journal of Personality, 55*, 415–443.

Devine, P. G. (1989). Stereotypes and prejudice: Their automatic and controlled components. *Journal of Personality and Social Psychology, 56*, 5–18.

Fleming, J. H. and Darley, J. M. (1989). Perceiving choice and constraint: The effects of contextual and behavioral cues on attitude attribution. *Journal of Personality and Social Psychology, 56*, 27–40.

Forgas, J. P. (1985). *Interpersonal Behaviour*. Oxford: Pergamon Press.

Gardner, W. L. and Martinko, M. J. (1988). Impression management: An observational study linking audience characteristics with verbal self-presentations. *Academy of Management Journal, 31*, 42–65.

Hastie, R. and Kumar, P. (1979). Person memory: Personality traits as organizing principles in memory for behaviors. *Journal of Personality and Social Psychology, 37*, 25–38.

Heider, F. (1958). *The Psychology of Interpersonal Relations*. New York: John Wiley.

Higgins, E. T. and Bargh, J. A. (1987). Social cognition and social perception. *Annual Review of Psychology, 38*, 369–425.

Higgins, E. T. and King, G. (1981). Accessibility of social constructs. In N. Cantor and J. F. Kihlstrom (Eds), *Personality, Cognition and Social Interaction*. Hillsdale, N.J.: Lawrence Erlbaum Associates.

Ilgen, D. R. and Klein, H. J. (1989). Organizational behavior. *Annual Review of Psychology, 40*, 327–351.

Jones, E. E., Schwartz, J. and Gilbert, D. T. (1984). Perceptions of moral expectancy violation: The role of expectancy source. *Social Cognition, 2*, 273–293.

Kelley, H. H. (1950). The warm–cold variable in first impressions of persons. *Journal of Personality, 18*, 431–439.

Kelley, H. H. (1971). *Attribution in Social Interaction*. Morristown, N.J.: General Learning Press.

Lerner, M. J. (1965). Evaluation of performance as a function of performer's reward and attractiveness. *Journal of Personality and Social Psychology, 3*, 355–360.

Manis, M., Nelson, T. E. and Shedler, J. (1988). Stereotypes and social judgement: Extremity, assimilation and contrast. *Journal of Personality and Social Psychology, 55*, 28–36.

Montepare, J. M. and Zebrowitz-McArthur, L. (1988). Impressions of people created by age-related qualities of their gaits. *Journal of Personality and Social Psychology, 55*, 547–556.

O'Sullivan, C. S. and Durso, F. T. (1984). Effect of schema-incongruent information on memory for stereotypical attributes. *Journal of Personality and Social Psychology, 47*, 55–70.

Pennington, D. C. (1987). Confirmatory hypothesis-testing in face-to-face interaction: An empirical refutation. *British Journal of Social Psychology, 26*, 225–236.

Rothstein, M. and Jackson, D. N. (1984). Implicit personality theory and the employment interview. In M. Cook (Ed.), *Issues in Person Perception*. London: Methuen.

Schlenker, B. (1980). *Impression Management*. Monterey, Calif.: Brooks-Cole.

Snyder, M. (1974). Self-monitoring of expressive behavior. *Journal of Personality and Social Psychology, 30*, 526–537.

Snyder, M. and Swann, W. B. (1978). Hypothesis-testing processes in social interaction. *Journal of Personality and Social Psychology, 36*, 1202–1212.

Springbett, B. M. (1958). Factors affecting the final decision in the employment interview. *Canadian Journal of Psychology, 12*, 13–22.

Swann, W. B. and Ely, R. J. (1984). A battle of wills: Self-verification versus behavioral confirmation. *Journal of Personality and Social Psychology, 46*, 1287–1302.

Tajfel, H. and Turner, J. C. (1985). The social identity theory of intergroup behaviour. In S. Worchel and W. G. Austin (Eds), *Psychology of Intergroup Relations*, 2nd edn. Chicago, Ill.: Nelson-Hall.

Trope, Y., Bassok, M. and Alon, E. (1984). The questions lay interviewers ask. *Journal of Personality, 52*, 90–106.

van Knippenberg, A. F. M. (1984). Intergroup differences in group perceptions. In H. Tajfel (Ed.), *The Social Dimension: European Developments in Social Psychology*, Vol. 2. Cambridge: Cambridge University Press.

Walster, E. (1966). The assignment of responsibility for an accident. *Journal of Personality and Social Psychology, 5*, 508–516.

Decisions and decision making at work

Introduction

Decisions concern choices between more than one possible course of action. For many people, work involves frequent decisions. Some are perhaps made almost automatically – so much so, that some writers (e.g. Hunt, 1989) have argued that the whole notion of deliberate, conscious choice has been paid too much attention by applied psychologists. Others disagree, contending that understanding how decisions (conscious or otherwise) are made in the workplace, and how they might be improved, is crucial to enhancing the performance of organizations and even national economies. This chapter therefore examines decision making by individuals and groups in the workplace from a psychological perspective. Important insights can indeed be gained. In some cases, psychologists have simply demonstrated particular phenomena, leaving it to individuals to work out what, if anything, to do about them. In other instances, psychologists have designed interventions aimed at improving decision making.

Decision making by individuals

Biases and heuristics

Much of psychologists' work on individual decision making has focused on how we deviate from strictly "rational" processes. Rather like person perception (see Chapter 11), some of it could be taken as demonstrating what a lot of mistakes we make. However, some writers (e.g. Eiser, 1986, ch. 7) have pointed out that often our "mistakes" merely represent ways of thinking which, while not strictly rational, usually reflect the real world.

"Rationality" is often defined as choosing the option that has the *highest expected value* among those potentially open to us. For example, suppose you can choose between a 40% chance of winning £2000 (with a 60% chance of winning nothing) and the certainty of winning £600. The expected value of the first option is £800 (40% × £2000), and that of the second is £600 (100% × £600). The "rational" decision would therefore be the 40% chance of winning £2000. Much research on decision making has used problems of this general kind. It is true, of course, that the first option is preferable, *other things being equal*. But suppose you had no money at all, and your bank manager had written telling you your debts would be called in (thus causing your business to fail) unless you paid at least £500 into your account immediately. In such circumstances, the "rational" decision could be argued to be the less attractive. This illustrates the general point that it can make more sense to consider total assets than gains or losses. It also brings to mind the adage "don't bet if you can't afford to lose". Also, of course, life rarely poses us with such clear-cut options where we know exactly the probabilities of various possible outcomes.

There are many systematic strategies for decision making apart from a thorough search for the maximum gain. For example, one can evaluate alternatives on a very limited range of important criteria. Ignoring less crucial criteria *may* not have important costs, but it is of course possible that the cumulative effect of those criteria would be significant. Another possible strategy is to search for an alternative which one considers good enough, and stop the search as soon as one is found. This approach has been termed "satisficing" and can be contrasted with maximizing. Clearly, strategies like these cut corners. But they may be justified if a person does not have the time and/or ability to use more thorough ones, or if the decision is less than crucial. Perhaps the key issue is what the person expects to gain from any particular strategy and decision. This expectation concerns subjective usefulness (utility), as opposed to objective value.

Using this notion of subjective expected utility (SEU), psychological research has uncovered some interesting phenomena. Much of this research has been conducted (often with students in laboratories) by Kahneman, Tversky and colleagues (Kahneman and Tversky, 1979, 1981, 1984; Tversky and Kahneman, 1981, 1986).

Certainty vs uncertainty

We seem to give great weight in our decisions to the difference between, for example, a 95% chance of a particular outcome, and a 100% chance of it, or that between a 5% chance and 0%. In both examples, this reflects the difference between absolute certainty and near certainty. We give less weight to a difference of similar magnitude between intermediate probabilities (e.g. 60% *vs* 55%). As Kahneman and Tversky (1984) point out, this means that we tend to find highly likely (but not certain) pleasant outcomes *less* attractive than we should. Similarly, we are likely to find highly unlikely pleasant outcomes *more* attractive than we should. Hence we tend to be less inclined to take a small risk for a gain, and more likely to back a long-shot, than is indicated by objective probability.

Gains vs losses

As Kahneman and Tversky put it, the attractiveness of a possible gain is less than the aversiveness of a loss of the same amount. This leads to risk-averse decisions concerning gains and risk-seeking decisions concerning losses. Thus, Kahneman and Tversky have pointed out that while most people prefer the certainty of winning £800 over an 85% chance of winning £1000, a large majority of people prefer an 85% chance of *losing* £1000 over a certain loss of £800. Such risk-seeking over losses has also been found in (laboratory) studies where non-monetary outcomes such as hours of pain or loss of human lives are at stake. This has some interesting implications. Unpopular governments facing an election may be more inclined to risk a new policy initiative which could lose votes than a popular government in the same position. Firms in financial difficulties may take more risks (because they are trying to eliminate losses) than firms doing well (which are dealing with gains) (Fiegenbaum and Thomas, 1988). Singh (1986) reported that among 64 American and Canadian companies, the performance of a firm was indeed negatively related to risk-taking organizational decisions. But the picture was not that simple, because poor-performing companies tended to centralize their decision making, which militated *against* risk-taking, thus masking the relationship between performance and riskiness of decisions.

Framing

The same information can be presented in different ways. This can affect decisions made on the basis of that information. Thus, for example, organizers of conferences often advertise a special low fee for people who register early rather than a surcharge for people who register late. The organizers may privately think in terms of the latter, but use the former to keep customer goodwill, and hopefully increase the number of attenders. There are also links here with the previous paragraph, because some choices can be framed in terms of either gains or losses. An often-used scenario in laboratory experiments concerns the choice of medical programmes to combat a killer disease. The potential benefits of these programmes are presented either in terms of the number of people who will be *saved* (equivalent to gains), or the number who will *die* (equivalent to losses). According to Kahneman and Tversky (1981), people tend to prefer a programme which might succeed completely or fail completely (i.e. a risk) over one with a guaranteed moderate success level, when the options are presented in terms of number of deaths. The reverse is true when the same figures are presented in terms of number of lives saved. However, Fagley and Miller (1987) found no such effect, and questioned its generality. Although their hypothetical scenario was not exactly like Kahneman and Tversky's, Fagley and Miller's results do indeed cast doubt on this particular aspect of framing.

Escalation of commitment

Some approaches to commitment (see Kiesler, 1971, and also Chapter 8 of this volume) emphasize that if a decision is made freely and explicitly, the person making it feels a need to justify it to themselves and others. They are committed to it, and seek retrospectively to find reasons why they "did the right thing". There is some evidence for this concerning choice of organization to work in (e.g. Mabey, 1986). It also seems to happen in political decisions, such as American involvement in the Vietnam War. Managerial decisions are also affected (Staw, 1981; Bazerman *et al.*, 1984). At least in laboratory simulations, people who are told that their own earlier financial investment decisions are unsuccessful allocate more additional funds to that investment than if the original decision was made by another member of their (imaginary) organization. We believe that ultimately our own wisdom will be demonstrated, but other people are more likely to think we are "pouring good money after bad". However, McCain (1986) showed that although we invest a lot in our own decisions for a time, we do give up after repeated failure of that investment.

Losses vs costs

We have already noted that the aversiveness of losses is greater than the desirability of gains of the same (objective) amount. This can, however, be overcome if losses are construed, or framed, as voluntarily paid costs. Insurance companies can benefit from this. Thus, for example, Slovic *et al.* (1982) found that only 20% of their subjects preferred a sure loss of US$50 to a 25% chance of losing US$200. But 65% said they were prepared to at least consider paying a US$50 insurance premium against a 25% risk of losing US$200!

Accounts

There is some evidence that we assign gains and losses to particular "accounts" in our minds. Thus, in considering whether to buy an article in the shop one is already in, or at another for a saving of (say) £10, a person is more likely to say they would go to the other shop if the article costs (say) £150 than £50, and irrespective of the total amount of other purchases made. The saving is considered in the light of the total amount being spent on that item. Another example is also instructive. Some experiments have posed subjects with something like the following scenario: "As you are about to enter a theatre to see a play, you discover that you have lost your ticket (or, for some subjects, lost a £10 note). Tickets for the play costs £10 – would you now buy one?" People who have lost their ticket are much *less* likely to say yes than those who lost a £10 note. It seems that the loss is posted to the "play account" by the former group. The "account" is now overdrawn, and cannot be further depleted by the purchase of a replacement ticket.

Heuristics

Heuristics are "rules of thumb" people use to simplify information processing and decision making (Eiser, 1986, p. 220). In their early work, Tversky and Kahneman (1974) identified three particularly common heuristics. The *representativeness* heuristic is analogous to the finding in person perception (see Chapter 11) that we ignore base-rate information. We judge someone or something purely according to how representative it appears of a particular category, and we ignore the naturally occurring probability of belonging to that category in the first place. The *anchoring* bias refers to our failure to change our views as much as we should in the light of new information. We seem "anchored" by our starting point. This too finds expression in person perception. Finally, the *availability* heuristic concerns our tendency to consider an event more probable if it can easily be imagined than if it cannot. Hence an industrial relations manager contemplating policy changes might overestimate the risk of a strike (vivid event) and underestimate the risk of a persistently resentful and not particularly cooperative workforce (less vivid).

Attention

Perhaps not surprisingly, our decision making can be affected by how much attention we pay to it. Some experimental work (e.g. Langer *et al.*, 1978) has shown that when deciding whether to grant a request, we seem to regard information which merely restates the request as a reason for it, but only if the issue is deemed relatively unimportant. Thus if someone asks us "can I go to lunch at 11.55 today because I would like to go early?", we are more likely to say yes than if asked "can I go to lunch at 11.55 today?" – provided of course we do not regard this as an important issue.

Case study 12.1   An upmarket move?

Three years ago, Harry Milento gave up a highly paid job in insurance in order to opt for a "quieter life" running his own guest house in a scenic coastal location. Redecoration and improvements to the large old house he purchased proved more expensive and time-consuming than he had expected. Business was not good: a difficult economic climate had adversely affected the holiday trade, and a new guest house like Harry's inevitably had trouble getting established. The result was that he was certain to make a loss for the third successive year, albeit one which would not exhaust his financial reserves. An established traditional hotel nearby had recently gone upmarket with some success, and Harry was considering the same strategy. After all, he could relate well to successful and wealthy people, having once been one himself. The area had historically offered middle-to-low budget family holidays rather than more luxurious ones, but maybe things were changing, Harry thought. But, for him, a move upmarket would need extensive further alterations to his premises, and these would swallow up his remaining reserves.

Suggested exercise

Use psychological findings about decision making to suggest what Harry Milento is likely to do. Is this what he *should* do?

Decision-making style

People differ in the way they go about making decisions, and the same person may make decisions in different ways in different circumstances. Arroba (1978) identified six decision-making styles from her sample of managers and manual workers:

1. *No thought.*
2. *Compliant*: with expectations from outside.

3. *Logical*: careful, objective evaluation of alternatives.

4. *Emotional*: decision made on basis of wants or likes.

5. *Intuitive*: the decision simply seemed right and/or inevitable.

6. *Hesitant*: slow and difficult to feel committed.

Arroba found that the logical style was much more often used for work-related decisions than personal ones. The "no thought" style was used more for unimportant decisions than for others, the emotional style for quite important decisions, and the intuitive style for very important decisions. Overall, the logical style was used most often, with no thought a distant second, and emotional third. Perhaps the use of intuitive style for very important issues was due to a lack of complete information on which to base a decision. Other (experimental) research has shown that as decisions become more important and irreversible, people adopt a logical approach, especially where they expect to be held responsible for the decision (McAllister *et al.*, 1979).

Other work on style has drawn on Jung's personality typology (see Chapter 2), and made the assumption that style is an aspect of (fairly stable) personality. In its simplest form, this distinguishes between "analytic" and "intuitive" decision makers. The former gather concrete information and evaluate it by rational thought. The latter gather more subjective information and rely on their feelings to evaluate it. This is similar, but not identical, to Arroba's distinction between logical and emotional styles. Hunt *et al.* (1989) found that people tend to choose advisers with similar styles to their own when evaluating hypothetical strategic business decisions. Using a similar but more sophisticated eight-fold classification, Nutt (1990) found that managers whose style emphasized feeling as opposed to thinking, and (to a lesser extent) intuition as opposed to sensing, were more inclined to adopt a hypothetical risky business venture. Nutt also found that top managers' decisions were more influenced by their style than were middle managers'.

Janis and Mann (1977, 1982) have identified five styles which (unlike the above) are directly related to decision quality. They argued that decisions by definition involve psychological conflict, and people have different ways of dealing with that. Specifically, these are:

1. *Unconflicted adherence*. The decision maker continues with the existing course of action, ignoring potential risks.

2. *Unconflicted change*. The decision maker embarks on whatever new course of action is in their mind at the time without evaluating it.

3. *Defensive avoidance*. The decision maker avoids the decision by delaying it or denying responsibility.

4. *Hypervigilance*. The decision maker desperately searches for a solution, and seizes on the first one that seems to offer quick relief.

5. *Vigilance*. The decision maker searches carefully for relevant information and weighs it up in an unbiased fashion.

Underlying these five coping strategies are three factors:

1. Awareness or otherwise of risks associated with an alternative.

2. Optimism or otherwise about finding an acceptable alternative.
3. Belief that there is, or is not, enough time in which to make the decision.

Clearly, vigilance is seen as the optimal strategy. Janis and Mann (1982) argued that defensive avoidance is both the most common defective strategy for making major decisions, and also the hardest to correct. They made a number of suggestions about how to encourage proper gathering and processing of information. The techniques included preparation for dealing with the negative aspects of a decision; forcing a person to attend to unwelcome information; and role-playing to explore situations likely to result from a particular decision. Janis and Mann examined these techniques in the context of counselling, but a determined person could probably use them without outside assistance.

Group decision making

Groups *vs* individuals

Although many people are very cynical about the value of meetings and committees, the fact is that their work tends to involve a lot of them. In work organizations, most major decisions and many lesser ones are made by groups of people. Hence they have attracted a lot of interest, an increasing proportion of which is from organizational psychologists (Levine and Moreland, 1990). If handled in the right way, decisions made by groups can evoke greater commitment than those made by individuals, because more people feel a sense of involvement in it. On the other hand, group decisions usually consume more time (and therefore money) than individual ones, so they need to justify the extra costs. One often-asked question is whether individual or group decisions are superior. At one extreme is the "many heads are better than one" school of thought, which holds that in groups people spot each other's mistakes. On the other hand, there is the "too many cooks spoil the broth" brigade, which contends that problems of communication, rivalry and so on between group members more than cancel out any potential advantage of increased total available brain-power. In fact it is not possible to generalize about whether individuals or groups are universally better. It depends on the abilities and training of the individuals and groups, and also on the kind of task being tackled (Hill, 1982).

McGrath (1984) identified eight different types of task groups can face. The four that directly concern decision making are:

● generating plans;
● generating ideas;
● solving problems with correct answers; and
● deciding issues with no identifiably correct answers at the time the decision is made.

The second and third of these provide the best opportunities for comparing group and individual performance. *Brainstorming*, for example, is a technique for generating ideas with which many readers will already be familiar. It was developed by Osborn (1957), who argued that if a group of people agree that the more ideas they think of the better, and that group members will be encouraged, not ridiculed, for producing even bizarre ideas, then the average person can think up twice as many ideas in a group than they could on their own. In fact, research indicates that lone individuals encouraged to think of as many ideas as possible generate almost twice as many ideas per individual than groups do (e.g. Lamm and Trommsdorff, 1973) – quite the reverse of Osborn's claim! A number of possible explanations have been suggested for this phenomenon. These include *evaluation apprehension*, where a person feels afraid of what others will think, despite the brainstorming instructions, and *free-riding*, where group members feel other group members will do the work for them. However, Diehl and Stroebe (1987) devised experiments to test alternative explanations, and came out in favour of *production blocking*. Simply, only one person at a time in a group can talk about their ideas, and in the meantime other members may forget or suppress theirs.

Psychologists have conducted a number of experiments comparing individual and group performance on problems with correct answers. For example, Vollrath *et al.* (1989) found that groups recognized and recalled previously presented material better than individuals. However, McGrath (1984) has pointed out that the extent to which the correct answer can be shown to be correct varies. On one hand, there are "Eureka" tasks, i.e. when the correct answer is mentioned, everyone suddenly sees it must be right. There are also problems where the answer can be proved correct with logic, even though it is not necessarily intuitively appealing. Then there are problems where the correct answer can only be defined by experts.

An example of the second kind of problem, often used in research, is the so-called "horse-trading task". A person buys a horse for £60 and sells it for £70. Then they buy it back for £80 and sell it again for £90. How much money does the person make in the horse-trading business? Many people say £10, but the answer is £20 – though strictly this assumes that the person does not have to borrow the extra £10 to buy back the horse, and it ignores the opportunity cost of using the £10 in that way rather than another!

Some early research with problems of this kind (e.g. Maier and Solem, 1952) produced several important findings. First, lower-status group members had less influence on the group decision than higher-status ones, even when they (the lower-status people) were correct. Secondly, even when at least one person in the group knew the correct answer, the group decision was by no means always correct. Thirdly, group discussion made people more confident that their consensus decision was correct, but unfortunately the discussion did *not* in fact make a correct decision more likely.

Subsequent work on groups has developed the concept of social decision schemes (SDSs) (Davis, 1982; Stasser *et al.*, 1989). These describe alternative criteria on which group decisions can be made. Some examples include:

1. *Truth wins*: if one person knows the correct answer, the group recognizes and adopts it.

2. *Truth-supported wins*: if two people know the correct answer, the group recognizes and adopts it.

3. *Majority wins*: any decision favoured by a majority of group members is adopted.

4. *Equipotentiality*: all decisions favoured by one or more group members have an equal chance of being adopted.

For problems like the horse-trading one, group decisions most closely match the "truth-supported wins" SDS. It typically needs two correct people, not one, to convince the rest of the group. Put another way, on average *the group is as good as its second-best member*. This could be taken to mean that, for solving problems with correct answers, groups are on average better than individuals, but inferior to the best individuals.

However, conclusions of this kind cannot be generalized. Many decisions in organizations do not have a provable correct answer, or even an answer which experts could agree on. Also, even if groups typically do badly, perhaps they can be improved. This latter issue has been the subject of much popular and academic debate, and we now turn to it.

Group deficiencies and overcoming them

Some social scientists have concentrated on identifying the context within which groups can perform well (e.g. Larson and LaFasto, 1989). They point out necessities such as having group members who are knowledgeable about the problem faced; having a clearly-defined and inspiring goal (shades of Locke's goal-setting here: see Chapter 10); having group members who are committed to solving the problem optimally; and support and recognition from important people outside the group. Other work has attempted to identify the roles group members should adopt in order to function effectively together (Belbin, 1981).

Other observers of groups have concentrated more on procedural factors (e.g. Rees, 1984, ch. 12). Prominent here are the practices of the chairperson in facilitating discussion and summing it up, ensuring that everyone has their say and that only one person speaks at a time, and making sure that votes (if taken) are conducted only when all points of view have been aired, and with clearly defined options, so that group members know what they are voting for and against.

Social psychologists have noted many features of the group decision-making process which can impair decision quality. Many of these underlie the practical suggestions noted above. Hoffman and Maier (1961) noted a tendency to adopt "minimally acceptable solutions", especially where the decision task was complex. Instead of seeking the best possible solution, group members often settle on the first suggested solution which everyone considers "good enough". In certain circumstances, this might be an advantage, but on most occasions it is probably not a good idea. Hackman and Morris (1975) pointed out that groups rarely discuss what strategy they should adopt in tackling a decision-making task (i.e. how they should go about it), but that when they do, they tend to perform better. In these authors' experience, simply telling groups to discuss their strategy before they tackle the problem itself is usually not enough – strategy discussion has to be presented as a separate task if it is to be taken seriously.

Motivational losses in groups can also be a problem. Experimental research has repeatedly shown that as the number of people increases, the effort and/or performance of each one often decreases – the so-called *social loafing* effect (e.g. Latane *et al.*, 1979). This motivational loss can, however, be avoided if each person in the group feels that their contribution can be identified, *and* that their contribution makes a significant difference to the group's performance (Williams *et al.*, 1981; Kerr and Bruun, 1983). Hence a group leader would be well-advised to ensure that each group member can see the connection between individual efforts and group performance both for themselves and other group members. Interestingly, there is some evidence that social loafing does not occur in collectivist societies. Earley (1989) found that whereas American management trainees exhibited this effect in a laboratory-based management task, trainees from the People's Republic of China did not. In collective societies, one's sense of shared responsibility with others (in contrast with individualistic Western cultures) is perhaps the source of this difference. Once again, this reminds us of the culture-specific nature of some phenomena in applied psychology.

Janis (1972; 1982a,b) has arrived at some disturbing conclusions about how some real-life policy-making groups can make extremely poor decisions which have serious repercussions around the world. He analysed foreign policy fiascoes of various governments at various times in history. One of these, for example, was the Bay of Pigs fiasco in the early 1960s. Fidel Castro had recently taken power in Cuba, and the new American administration under John F. Kennedy launched an "invasion" of Cuba by 1400 Cuban exiles who landed at the Bay of Pigs. Within 2 days, they were surrounded by 20,000 Cuban troops, and those not killed were ransomed back to the USA at a cost of US $53 million in aid. Janis argued that this outcome was not just bad luck. It could and should have been anticipated. He suggested that in this and other fiascoes, various group processes could be seen which collectively he called *groupthink*.

According to Janis, groupthink occurs when group members' motivation for unanimity and agreement overrides their motivation to evaluate carefully the risks and benefits of alternative decisions. This usually occurs in "cohesive" groups, i.e. those where group members are friendly with each other, and respect each other's opinions. In some such groups, disagreement is construed (usually unconsciously) as a withdrawal of friendship and respect. As a result of group members' desire to avoid such a fate, the following symptoms are often evident:

1. *Overestimation of the group's power and morality*: after all, group members have positive opinions of each other.

2. *Closed-mindedness*: including efforts to downplay warnings and to stereotype other groups as inferior.

3. *Pressures towards uniformity*: including suppression of private doubts, leading to the illusion of unanimity and "mindguards" to shield group members (especially the leader) from uncomfortable information.

Janis (1982b) has argued that certain measures can be taken to avoid group think. These include:

1. Impartial leadership (so that group members are not tempted simply to "follow the leader").

2. Each person in the group should be told to give high priority to airing doubts and objections.

3. Experts should be in attendance to raise doubts.

4. "Second chance" meetings should be held where each member expresses their doubts about a previously made but not yet implemented decision.

One might add the necessity of fostering a group norm that disagreement does *not* signal disrespect or unfriendliness.

Janis' work has not gone unchallenged (Longley and Pruitt, 1980; Moorhead and Montanari, 1986). It has been argued that the groupthink syndrome is really simply a collection of phenomena which do not occur together as neatly as Janis claims, and which anyway have already been identified. Also, Janis obtained much of his information from published retrospective accounts, which (some argue) may have been much too inaccurate and/or incomplete. Whyte (1989) has argued that so-called groupthink is a product of group risk-seeking when they perceive that losses are at stake (see pp. 208–9) and group polarization (see next section). All these criticisms have some force. Nevertheless, Janis has provided rich case studies which graphically illustrate many potential problems in group decision making, and which should dispel any belief we might cling to that really important decisions are always made rationally.

Some other features of group decision making

Group polarization

One often-voiced criticism of groups is that they arrive at compromise decisions. But in fact this is often not so. Instead, it seems that groups tend to make more extreme decisions than the initial preferences of group members (Myers and Lamm, 1976). This has most often been demonstrated with respect to risk. If the initial tendency of the majority of group members is to adopt a moderately risky decision, the eventual group decision is usually more risky than that. Conversely, somewhat cautious initial preferences of group members translate to more cautious eventual group decisions.

Psychologists have reduced no less than 11 possible explanations of group polarization down to just two, using systematic research (Isenberg, 1986). The *social comparison* explanation is that we like to present ourselves in a socially desirable way, and therefore we try to be like other group members, only more so. The *persuasive argumentation* explanation is that information consistent with the views held by the majority will dominate discussion, and (so long as that information is correct and novel) have persuasive effects. Both explanations are valid, though the latter tends to be stronger. While polarization is not in itself inherently good or bad, clearly group members need to ensure that they air all relevant information and avoid social conformity – back to groupthink!

Minority influence

Minorities within groups only rarely convert the majority to their point of view. But how can they maximize their chances? Many people say that they should gain the acceptance of the majority by conforming wherever possible, and then stick out for their own point of view on a carefully chosen crucial issue. Moscovici and colleagues have argued otherwise (Moscovici and Mugny, 1983; Moscovici, 1985). They have found that a minority needs to disagree consistently with the majority, including on issues other than the one at stake, if it is to exert influence. Minorities do not exert influence by being liked or being seen as reasonable, but by being perceived as consistent, independent and confident. Much debate has centred on why and how minorities in groups exert influence (Latane and Wolf, 1981; Nemeth, 1986; Kruglanski and Mackie, 1989). The predominant view is that minorities and majorities exert influence in different ways. Nemeth (1986) suggested that majorities encourage convergent, shallow and narrow thinking, whereas consistent exposure to minority viewpoints stimulates deeper and wider consideration of alternative perspectives. Nemeth (1986, p. 28) concluded from experimental data that:

> Those exposed to minority viewpoints ... are more original, they use a greater variety of strategies, they detect novel solutions, and importantly, they detect correct solutions. Furthermore, this beneficial effect occurs even when the minority viewpoints are wrong.

This emphasizes again that groups need to encourage alternative points of view, not suppress them.

Case study 12.2   A soft drink product decision

Rudi Lerner was managing director of a medium-sized soft drinks company. His father had founded and then managed the business for nearly 30 years before handing over to his son 4 years ago. Rudi felt he knew much more about the business than his colleagues on the top management team. They agreed about that, and they liked and respected their boss as well as each other. They usually went out of their way to avoid contradicting him. On the rare occasion they did so, they received a friendly but firm reminder from the chairman that he had been in the business much longer than they had. That was true, but the team members had not changed for 5 years now, so nobody was exactly ignorant. However, it was hard to argue – after all, the company had been successful relative to its competitors over the years. Rudi attributed this to frequent takeovers of competitors by people from outside the business. He rarely commissioned market research, relying instead on his "gut feeling" and extensive prior experience. Now a new challenge faced the company: should it go into the low-calorie "diet" drinks market and, if so, with what products? The demand for diet drinks was recent but might be here to stay.

Suggested exercise

How likely is it that Rudi and the rest of the management team will make a good decision about entering the "diet" market?

The wider organizational context

Decisions in organizations can be divided into various types, and each decision has various phases (Mintzberg *et al.*, 1976; Heller and Misumi, 1987). As regards types, there are:

1. *Operational decisions*: usually with short-term effects and of a routine nature.
2. *Tactical decisions*: usually with medium-term effects and of a non-routine nature but not going so far as reviewing the organization's goals.
3. *Strategic decisions*: usually with long-term effects and concerning the organization's goals.

In line with leadership research (see Chapter 13), it is also possible to distinguish between people-oriented and task-oriented decisions within each type. Phases of decision making include:

1. *Start-up*: when it is realized that a decision is required.
2. *Development*: when options are searched for and considered.
3. *Finalization*: when a decision is confirmed.
4. *Implementation*: where the finalized decision is put into operation or fails (Heller *et al.*, 1988).

Much attention has been focused on who in organizations really makes decisions, and how their influence is distributed across the decision types and phases described above (French and Raven, 1959; Pfeffer, 1981; Mintzberg, 1983; Heller *et al.*, 1988). The concept of *power* is frequently invoked. Power concerns the ability of an individual or group to ensure that another individual or group does what the first individual or group wishes. Power can be derived from a number of sources, including the ability to reward and/or punish; and the extent to which a person or group is seen as expert or otherwise morally entitled to have its way. These sources of power tend to go together (Greene and Podsakoff, 1981). Especially if these sources of power are in short supply, individuals and groups often use *organizational politics* to maximize their chances of getting their way. Politics consists of tactics like enlisting the support of others, controlling access to information, and creating indebtedness by doing people favours for which reciprocation is expected. In extreme forms, politics can also involve more deceitful activities such as spreading rumours. In general, however, the effectiveness and morality of power and politics depend on their intended goals. The distinction between the two goals of self-aggrandisement and organizational effectiveness is often blurred. After all, most of us probably construe ourselves as playing important and legitimate roles in our work organizations, and it is easy to jump from there to a belief that what is good for us must therefore also be good for the organization.

Several large studies over the years have examined who participates in organizational decisions. Heller *et al.* (1988), for example, conducted a detailed longitudinal study of seven organizations in three countries (the

Netherlands, the UK and Yugoslavia). Not surprisingly, they found that most decision-making power was generally exercised by top management. The lower levels and works councils typically were merely informed or at best consulted. The distribution of power did, however, vary considerably between organizations and also somewhat between countries, with Yugoslavia generally having the highest degree of participation by bottom organizational levels, and the UK the lowest. There was also some variation between types and phases of decision making. Top management were most influential in strategic decisions. Within tactical decisions, the workers had quite a lot of influence at the start-up phase of people-oriented decisions but little thereafter. This led to frustration. But for tactical task-oriented decisions, they had much influence in the finalization phase. This was often less frustrating, because the right of management to *initiate* decisions of this kind was rarely challenged (i.e. high legitimate power).

Finally, examinations of strategic decision making by management have been undertaken (e.g. Hickson *et al.*, 1986). Some interesting findings have emerged. For example, Fredrickson and Iaquinto (1989) found that comprehensive information search and option consideration assisted effective strategic decision making in stable economic environments, but the reverse was true in unstable environments. Participating firms were drawn from the US paint industry (said to be stable) and forest products industry (unstable). Eisenhardt (1989), working with firms in the unstable (or, as she called it, "high-velocity") environment of microcomputers, found that fast decisions were superior to slow ones. More surprisingly, perhaps, fast decision makers seemed to use *more* information and consider *more* alternatives, than slow ones. It could be that decision-making speed is simply an aspect of general competence, or that in some circumstances any decision is better than none.

Summary

Decisions by individuals and groups are influenced by many psychological phenomena. For individuals, the subjective evaluation of risks and rewards is rarely the same as an objective mathematical calculation. This does not necessarily imply that people are typically mistaken, although some features of decision making can be construed as biases or as ineffective in certain circumstances. Groups are typically more effective than the average individual, but less so than the best individual in decision-making tasks. However, the typical effectiveness of groups should not be viewed as the best they could do. Possible ways in which groups can improve include more advance consideration of the problem-solving strategy they wish to adopt, a clear expectation that group members should challenge each other, and an understanding that such challenges do not signal hostility or disrespect. The nature of decision-making tasks, their importance and their subject matter all have implications for the way they are handled.

Case study 12.3   To expand or not to expand?

The management team of the Fastsave retail chainstore company had a decision to make. Should they build a new store in Danesville, a medium-sized town in which it owned a suitable patch of land? Fastsave was doing quite well, and had more than enough financial resources to make the necessary investment in a town which did not currently have a major supermarket. On the other hand, there were two existing large superstores within 15 miles. It was agreed that there was no significant danger of substantial losses: the question was more whether the time and effort involved in expansion would be worth the return.

The management team consisted of the general manager (GM), finance manager (FM), marketing manager (MM), operations manager (OM), personnel manager (PM) and company secretary (CS). Each member of the team had been supplied with reports on the demographic make-up of the town, a market research survey, detailed costings of building the store, and the likely attitude of the local council planning authority.

Group members were accustomed to working together and there was rivalry (at present friendly) between them about which of them if any would succeed GM when she retired in about 3 years. At the outset of the meeting, GM made it clear she would act as an impartial chairperson, and not reveal her own opinions until the end. In the past, however, she had usually been cautious about business expansions. The following extract is representative of the group's deliberations:

MM: I suspect the time is not right. We are currently upgrading six other stores, and to start a completely new one would run the risk of spreading our resources too thin. In purely financial terms we can do it, but would we do a good job?

OM: Yes, we've certainly got our hands full at present. In fact, I would be in favour of reviewing two of our already planned store upgradings because I'm not sure they are really worth it either. Generally we're doing all right as we are – let's consolidate our position.

MM: I can't believe I'm hearing this! According to our market research report, the population of Danesville wants its own big supermarket, and what's more the 45+ age group particularly likes our emphasis on low prices rather than super deluxe quality.

CS: Come on, as usual you're taking an approach which could possibly pay off but could land us in trouble . . .

MM: Like what?

CS: Well, there has been a lot of housing development in Danesville, and the local council is under pressure to preserve what it sees as the charm of the town. It would be very bad public relations to be perceived as undermining that. And having a planning application refused wouldn't be much better.

FM: That's right, and being seen as an intruder would probably reduce sales too.

PM: I can't comment on that last point, but as a general principle we should not stand still. Our competitors might overtake us. If resources are spread too thin, we can recruit more staff: we have the money, and experience suggests that the labour force in the region has the necessary skills.

FM: You've had a rush of blood to the head, haven't you? You're normally telling us how difficult it is to manage expansion of staff numbers. I must say I share the concern about a couple of our existing upgrading plans, let alone building an entirely new store. Do those stores really need refitting yet? They are doing all right.

CS: I notice that Danesville has an increasingly young, mobile population these days. Despite the market research report, will they really be interested in a local store, especially with our position in the market?

MM: They can be made to be. Anyway, who says that a Danesville store should not go slightly more upmarket? Tesco seem to manage to have both upmarket and down-market stores.

OM: Well yes, but I don't think we are big enough to be that versatile.

Suggested exercises

Examine this case study from the following perspectives:
- the likely attitude to risk;
- group polarization; and
- minority influence.

Given this examination, what do you think the group is likely to decide? What is your opinion of that decision?

References

Arroba, T. Y. (1978). Decision-making style as a function of occupational group, decision content and perceived importance. *Journal of Occupational Psychology, 51,* 219–226.

Bazerman, M. H., Giuliano, T. and Appelman, A. (1984). Escalation of commitment in individual and group decision making. *Organizational Behavior and Human Performance, 33,* 141–152.

Belbin, R. M. (1981). *Management Teams: Why They Succeed or Fail.* Chichester: John Wiley.

Davis, J. H. (1982). Social interaction as a combinatorial process in group decision. In H. Brandstatter, J. H. Davis and G. Stocker-Kreichgauer (Eds), *Group Decision Making.* London: Academic Press.

Diehl, M. and Stroebe, W. (1987). Productivity loss in brainstorming groups: Toward the solution of a riddle. *Journal of Personality and Social Psychology, 53,* 497–509

Earley, P. C. (1989). Social loafing and collectivism: A comparison of the United States and the People's Republic of China. *Administrative Science Quarterly, 34,* 565–581.

Eisenhardt, K. M. (1989). Making fast strategic decisions in high-velocity environments. *Academy of Management Journal, 32,* 543–576.

Eiser, J. R. (1986). *Social Psychology: Attitudes, Cognition and Social Behaviour.* Cambridge: Cambridge University Press.

Fagley, N. S. and Miller, P. M. (1987). The effects of decision framing on choice of risky vs. certain options. *Organizational Behavior and Human Decision Processes, 39,* 264–277

Fiegenbaum, A. and Thomas, H. (1988). Attitudes toward risk and the risk return paradox: Prospect theory explanations. *Academy of Management Journal, 31,* 86–106.

Fredrickson, J. W. and Iaquinto, A. L. (1989). Inertia and creeping rationality in strategic decision processes. *Academy of Management Journal, 32,* 516–542.

French, J. R. P. and Raven, B. (1959). The bases of social power. In D. Cartwright (Ed.), *Studies in Social Power.* Ann Arbor, Mich.: Institute for Social Research.

Greene, C. N. and Podsakoff, P. M. (1981). Effects of withdrawal of a performance-contingent reward on supervisory influence and power. *Academy of Management Journal, 24,* 527–542

Hackman, J. R. and Morris, C. (1975). Group tasks, group interaction process and group performance effectiveness: A review and proposed integration. In L. Berkowitz (Ed.), *Advances in Experimental Social Psychology*, Vol. 8. London: Academic Press.

Heller, F. A. and Misumi, J. (1987). Decision making. In B. Bass, P. Drenth, and P. Weissenberg (Eds), *Advances in Organizational Psychology*. London: Sage.

Heller, F. A., Drenth, P., Koopman, P. and Rus, V. (1988). *Decisions in Organizations: A Three-country Comparative Study*. London: Sage.

Hickson, D., Butler, R., Gray, D., Mallory, G. and Wilson, D. (1986). *Top Decisions: Strategic Decision-making in Organizations*. Oxford: Blackwell.

Hill, G. W. (1982). Group versus individual performance: Are N + 1 heads better than one? *Psychological Bulletin*, *91*, 517–539.

Hoffman, L. R. and Maier, N. R. F. (1961). Quality and acceptance of problem solutions by members of homogeneous and heterogeneous groups. *Journal of Abnormal and Social Psychology*, *62*, 401–407.

Hunt, R. G. (1989). On the metaphysics of choice, or when decisions aren't. In R. L. Cardy, S. M. Puffer and J. M. Newman (Eds), *Information Processing and Decision-making in Organizations*. Greenwich, Conn.: JAI Press.

Hunt, R. G., Krzystofiak, F. J., Meindl, J. R., and Yousry, A. M. (1989). Cognitive style and decision making. *Organizational Behavior and Human Decision Processes*, *44*, 436–453.

Isenberg, D. J. (1986). Group polarization: A critical review and meta-analysis. *Journal of Personality and Social Psychology*, *50*, 1141–1151.

Janis, I. L. (1972). *Victims of Groupthink*. Boston, Mass.: Houghton Mifflin.

Janis, I. L. (1982a). *Groupthink*. Boston, Mass.: Houghton Mifflin.

Janis, I. L. (1982b). Counteracting the adverse effects of concurrence-seeking in policy planning groups: Theory and research perspectives. In H. Brandstatter, J. H. Davis and G. Stocker-Kreichgauer (Eds), *Group Decision Making*. London: Academic Press.

Janis, I. L. and Mann, L. (1977). *Decision-making: A Psychological Analysis of Conflict, Choice and Commitment*. New York: Free Press.

Janis, I. L. and Mann, L. (1982). A theoretical framework for decision counselling. In I. L. Janis (Ed.), *Counselling on Personal Decisions*. New Haven, Conn.: Yale University Press.

Kahneman, D. and Tversky, A. (1979). Prospect theory: An analysis of decisions under risk. *Econometrica*, *47*, 263–291.

Kahneman, D. and Tversky, A. (1981). The framing of decisions and the psychology of choice. *Science*, *211*, 453–458.

Kahneman, D. and Tversky, A. (1984). Choices, values and frames. *American Psychologist*, *39*, 341–350.

Kerr, N. L. and Bruun, S. E. (1983). Dispensability of member effort and group motivation losses: Free-rider effects. *Journal of Personality and Social Psychology*, *44*, 78–94.

Kiesler, C. A. (1971). *The Psychology of Commitment*. London: Academic Press.

Kruglanski, A. and Mackie, D. M. (1989). Majority and minority influence: A judgemental process analysis. In W. Stroebe and M. Hewstone (Eds), *Advances in European Social Psychology*. Chichester: John Wiley.

Lamm, H. and Trommsdorff, G. (1973). Group versus individual performance on tasks requiring ideational proficiency (brainstorming). *European Journal of Social Psychology*, *3*, 361–387.

Langer, E., Blank, A. and Chanowitz, B. (1978). The mindlessness of ostensibly thoughtful action: The role of "placebic" information in interpersonal interaction. *Journal of Personality and Social Psychology*, *48*, 605–607.

Larson, C. E. and LaFasto, F. M. J. (1989). *Teamwork: What Must Go Right/What Can Go Wrong*. London: Sage.

Latane, B. and Wolf, S. (1981). The social impact of majorities and minorities. *Psychological Review*, *88*, 438–453.

Latane, B., Williams, K. and Harkins, S. (1979). Many hands make light the work: The causes and consequences of social loafing. *Journal of Personality and Social Psychology*, *37*, 822–832.

Levine, J. M. and Moreland, R. L. (1990). Small group research. In *Annual Review of Psychology*, Vol. 41. Palo Alto, Calif.: Annual Reviews Inc.

Longley, J. and Pruitt, D. G. (1980). Groupthink: A critique of Janis' theory. In L. Wheeler (Ed.), *Review of Personality and Social Psychology*, Vol. 1. London: Sage.

Mabey, C. (1986). *Graduates Into Industry*. Aldershot: Gower Press.

Maier, N. R. F. and Solem, A. R. (1952). The contribution of a discussion leader to the quality of group thinking: The effective use of minority opinions. *Human Relations*, *5*, 277–288.

McAllister, D. W., Mitchell, T. R. and Beach, L. R. (1979). The contingency model for the selection of decision strategies: An empirical test of the effects of significance, accountability and reversibility. *Organizational Behavior and Human Performance*, *24*, 228–244.

McCain, B. E. (1986). Continuing investment under conditions of failure: A laboratory study of the limits to escalation. *Journal of Applied Psychology*, *71*, 280–284.

McGrath, J. E. (1984). *Groups: Interaction and Performance*. Englewood Cliffs, N.J.: Prentice-Hall.

Mintzberg, H. (1983). *Power In and Around Organizations*. Englewood Cliffs, N.J.: Prentice-Hall.

Mintzberg, H., Raisinghani, D. and Theoret, A. (1976). The structure of "unstructured" decision processes. *Administrative Science Quarterly*, *21*, 246–275.

Moorhead, G. and Montanari, J. R. (1986). An empirical investigation of the groupthink phenomenon. *Human Relations*, *39*, 399–410.

Moscovici, S. (1985). Social influence and conformity. In G. Lindzey and E. Aronson (Eds), *The Handbook of Social Psychology*, 3rd edn. New York: Random House.

Moscovici, S. and Mugny, G. (1983). Minority influence. In P. B. Paulus (Ed.), *Basic Group Processes*. New York: Springer-Verlag.

Myers, D. G. and Lamm, H. (1976). The group polarization phenomenon. *Psychological Bulletin*, *83*, 602–627.

Nemeth, C. J. (1986). Differential contributions of majority and minority influence. *Psychological Review*, *93*, 23–32.

Nutt, P. C. (1990). Strategic decisions made by top executives and middle managers with data and process dominant styles. *Journal of Management Studies*, *27*, 173–194.

Osborn, A. F. (1957). *Applied Imagination*, revised edn. New York: Scribner.

Pfeffer, J. (1981). *Power in Organizations*. London: Pitman.

Rees, W. D. (1984). *The Skills of Management*. London: Croom Helm.

Singh, J. V. (1986). Performance, slack, and risk-taking in organizational decision making. *Academy of Management Journal*, *29*, 562–585.

Slovic, P., Fischoff, B. and Lichtenstein, S. (1982). Response mode, framing and information-processing effects in risk assessment. In R. Hogarth (Ed.), *New Directions for Methodology of Social and Behavioral Science*. San Francisco, Calif.: Jossey-Bass.

Stasser, G., Kerr, N. L. and Davis, J. H. (1989). Influence processes and consensus models in decision-making groups. In P. B. Paulus (Ed.), *Psychology of Group Influence*, 2nd edn. Hillsdale, N.J.: Lawrence Erlbaum Associates.

Staw, B. M. (1981). The escalation of commitment to a course of action. *Academy of Management Review*, *6*, 577–587.

Tversky, A. and Kahneman, D. (1974). Judgement under uncertainty: Heuristics and biases. *Science*, *185*, 1124–1131.

Tversky, A. and Kahneman, D. (1981). The framing of decisions and the psychology of choice. *Science*, *211*, 453–458.

Tversky, A. and Kahneman, D. (1986). Rational choice and the framing of decisions. *Journal of Business*, *59*, 251–278.

Vollrath, D. A., Sheppard, B. H., Hinsz, V. B. and Davis, J. H. (1989). Memory performance by decision-making groups and individuals. *Organizational Behavior and Human Decision Processes*, *43*, 289–300.

Whyte, G. (1989). Groupthink reconsidered. *Academy of Management Review*, *14*, 40–56.

Williams, K., Harkins, S. and Latane, B. (1981). Identifiability as a deterrent to social loafing: Two cheering experiments. *Journal of Personality and Social Psychology*, *40*, 303–311.

Leadership

Introduction

Leadership is a topic of great importance to people who are leaders, who aspire to be leaders, or who are on the receiving end of leadership. That includes nearly everybody in work! This chapter examines what leaders in the workplace are like, what they do, and what they *should* do. It also looks at the different kinds of situation facing leaders and the various strategies available for dealing with them. It ends with an examination of leadership from the follower's point of view. The main aim throughout is to show the reader the essential factors in effective leadership, in so far as they can be identified. No current approach to leadership is substantially better than all the others, but several approaches offer useful insights. These are, however, usually confined to advising the leader what to do, and have less to say about how to do it well. Aspects of that latter issue tend to crop up more in motivation (see Chapter 10) and group decision making (see Chapter 12). After all, much of leadership is ultimately about motivating and deciding.

Defining leaders and leadership

A leader can be defined as the person who is given responsibility for monitoring and directing a group's activities *or* who takes principal responsibility for those tasks. This definition acknowledges the important truth that the formally appointed leader is not always the real leader. But it also confines the notion of leader to a group context. Unless we interpret the word "group" extremely flexibly, this excludes leaders of nations, large corporations and so on, except in so far as they lead a small group of senior colleagues. Work psychologists have examined leadership strictly within workgroups of 4–10 people.

So much for the leader. Leader*ship* can be considered to be the personal qualities, behaviours, styles and decisions of the leader. In other words, it concerns how the leader carries out his or her role. Hence, while the role of leader can be described in a job description, leadership is not so easily pinned down.

Important questions about leadership

Over the years, several distinct but related questions have been asked about leadership. These include:

- Who becomes a leader?
- How do leaders differ from other people?
- How can we describe their leadership?

It is, in fact, difficult to consider these questions without bringing in the notion of *good* leadership. So we can also ask:

- What are effective leaders like?
- How do effective leaders differ from ineffective ones?

The reader will not be surprised to learn that these effectiveness issues have occupied much attention in both theory and practice.

At this point, it is worth pausing to consider how we can tell whether or not a leader is effective. The most obvious method is to assess the performance of their group relative to other similar groups with different leaders. Quite apart from the assumption that such comparison groups will be available, there is also the problem that performance is often determined by many things other than leadership. The reader can probably think of several straight away. Sometimes, grievance rates against the leader, and/or group members' satisfaction with the leader, have been used as a measure of leader effectiveness. But who is to say that, for example, low grievance rates are a good thing? Perhaps a group needs "shaking up", and it could be argued that a good leader should ruffle a few feathers. Similar considerations apply to voluntary turnover among group members as a measure of leader effectiveness. In short, there is no perfect measure of leader effectiveness. Group performance is used most often, probably correctly. But we must remember not to expect an especially strong association with leadership: too many other factors come into play.

In recent years, further questions about leadership have been raised. When and why is leadership seen as being important? How do leaders come to be perceived as such? These two questions emphasize that leadership is an interpersonal issue as well as a personal one. The social psychology of relationships between pairs of people, and within groups, is seen as crucial. There is also a perception that theories which concentrate on leader effectiveness have tended to neglect adequate description of exactly what goes on between leader and subordinates. Hence this more recent approach is to some extent returning to a descriptive rather than an evaluative orientation. However, its sophistication ensures that it does not simply cover old ground.

The diversity of issues and approaches relevant to leadership has inevitably produced much varied work on the topic, too much to cover here. This chapter is therefore selective in its coverage. Selection is based on dual criteria of theoretical and practical importance.

Leader-focused approaches to leadership

It seems reasonable to look for the simple before resorting to the complex. This has indeed been the case in leadership research. Most theory and practice up until the 1960s, and plenty since then, has had two key features:

1. Description of the leader rather than the dynamics of the leader's relationship with subordinates.
2. Attempts to identify the characteristics/behaviour of a "good leader" regardless of the situation.

Leader traits

Some early work (reviewed by Stogdill, 1974; House and Baetz, 1979) found that leaders tended to be higher than non-leaders on:

- intelligence,
- self-confidence,
- dominance,
- activity level and
- knowledge of the task.

Many other traits (e.g. adjustment, extroversion) have also been found in some studies to be more characteristic of leaders than non-leaders. In addition, intelligence and sociability seem characteristic of emergent (as opposed to appointed) leaders.

Most writers (see, e.g., Yetton, 1984) assert that there is little conclusive evidence for an association between specific characteristics and leadership, let alone *effective* leadership. House and Baetz (1979) were more optimistic. They pointed out that many of the early studies which produced inconclusive findings involved leadership in children's groups. Research with adults has produced more clear-cut results. They argued that the very nature of the leadership role must mean that sociability, need for power and need for achievement are relevant. However, House and Baetz also acknowledged two insights which are nowadays accepted by many people involved in leadership:

1. Traits must be expressed in the leader's *behaviour* if they are to be important.
2. Different types of tasks will require somewhat different leader characteristics and behaviours.

Task orientation and person orientation

In the 1950s, attention turned from leader traits to leader behaviours. Just as traits had been assumed to be quite stable, so were leader behavioural styles. One research team at Ohio State University in the USA, and another at Michigan University, launched major projects on leadership. They worked more or less independently of each other, and approached the task in opposite directions. The Ohio group sought to uncover the central features of leader behaviour by asking subordinates, and to a lesser extent leaders themselves, to describe the leader's behaviour. From an initial list of almost 2000 questions, 10 dimensions of leader behaviour were identified. It was then discovered that two general dimensions underlay the 10. These two have consistently emerged in subsequent work, and have been described (Fleishman, 1969) as follows:

1. *Consideration*. The extent to which a leader demonstrates trust of subordinates, respect for their ideas and consideration of their feelings.

2. *Structure*. The extent to which a leader defines and structures his or her own role and those of subordinates towards goal attainment. The leader actively directs group activities through planning, communicating information, scheduling, criticizing and trying out new ideas.

The Michigan team started by classifying leaders as effective or ineffective. They then looked for behaviours which distinguished between the two groups. One distinction was that effective managers seemed concerned about their subordinates, whereas ineffective ones were concerned *only* with the task. Clearly, this bears considerable resemblance to the distinction between consideration and structure described above. It seemed that consideration was a good thing, and structure a bad one if it was not accompanied by consideration. Blake and Mouton's (1964) much-used Managerial Grid encourages leaders to examine their own style on these two dimensions. It assumes that leaders can be high on both, low on both or high on one and low on the other. Blake and Mouton proposed that it is best to be high on both.

How realistic is all this? It seems that leaders see consideration and structure as quite separate when thinking about their own behaviour. However, subordinates tend to report that their leader is either person-orientated *or* task-orientated, not both (Weissenburg and Kavanagh, 1972). Research suggests that in many situations a certain level of consideration is essential for maintenance of satisfactory relations between leader and group. However, where group performance is the outcome measure, it is far from clear whether consideration and structure are always good, bad or indifferent.

How universal are the consideration and structure dimensions? Some work in the late 1980s (Smith and Peterson, 1988; Smith *et al.*, 1989) has sought to discover whether leader styles are described using the same dimensions across different cultures. Using data from electronics firms in the UK, the USA, Japan and Hong Kong, Smith *et al.* (1989) conclude that what they call maintenance and performance leadership styles (approximately equivalent to consideration and structure, respectively) do indeed exist in different cultures. However, they also stated that "... the specific behaviours associated with those styles differ markedly, in ways which are comprehensible within the cultural norms of each setting" (p. 97). For example, one of the questions asked by Smith *et al.* was: "When your superior learns that a member is experiencing personal difficulties, does your superior discuss the matter in the person's absence with other members?" In Hong Kong and Japan, this behaviour is seen as highly characteristic of maintenance (consideration). In the UK and the USA, it is not – probably most Western subordinates would regard this as "talking about me behind my back". Not that all other UK and US perceptions were identical. As Smith *et al.* (1989) noted, in the UK, consideration can be expressed by talking about the task, but this is not so in the USA.

These insights are very important as work organizations become increasingly international. Assuming that leaders can identify which style they wish to adopt, they need to make sure they do things which are interpreted as consistent with that style. Those behaviours differ somewhat between countries and cultures.

Participation

Another dimension of behavioural style which has received much attention is participativeness. This concerns the extent to which the leader is democratic or autocratic. It is clearly related to the dimensions already discussed, but arguably not identical. For example, the definition of structure given earlier does not necessarily exclude subordinates from influencing the direction given by the leader. Maier (1970) has identified some key features of participative leadership, with particular reference to decision making. These include sharing information with subordinates, encouraging suggestions and helping subordinates communicate with each other.

In the aftermath of the Second World War, it was hoped and believed that democratic leadership was superior to autocratic. There is some evidence for this, though it is strongest where subordinates' satisfaction with the leader is the outcome measure. Sometimes, the evidence is weaker where performance is the outcome. As Filley *et al.* (1976) observed, where the job to be done is clearly understood by subordinates, and within their competence, participation is not going to make much difference because there is little need for it. On the other hand, in many less straightforward situations, participation does aid group performance (see also Chapter 12).

Participation is not an "all or nothing" phenomenon. It comes in degrees. One way of describing points on the autocratic–democratic continuum is:

- *Tells*: the leader makes a decision and announces it.
- *Sells*: the leader makes a decision and seeks to convince subordinates it is a good one.
- *Consults*: the leader asks for subordinates' opinions before deciding.
- *Delegates*: the leader allows subordinates to make a decision.

We will encounter another way of dividing up that continuum later in this chapter.

Performance monitoring and performance consequences

There have also been more recent attempts to identify key features of leader behaviour. Working from a behaviourist perspective, US psychologist Judith

Table 13.1 Definitions and examples of categories in Komaki's Operant Supervisory Taxonomy and Index (OSTI)

Category	Definition
Performance consequences	Indicates knowledge of someone else's performance
Performance monitoring • work sampling (i.e. observing subordinate's work) • asking subordinate about their performance • asking somebody else about subordinate's performance	Collects information about an individual's performance
Performance antecedents	Instructs, reminds or conveys an expectation of performance
Own performance	Refers to his or her own performance
Work-related	Refers to the work but not to performance
Non-work-related	Does not refer to work issues or concerns
Solitary	Occasions on which the supervisor is not interacting

Adapted from Komaki (1986) with the permission of the American Psychological Association.

Komaki and her colleagues have developed an observational measure of leader behaviour called the Operant Supervisory Taxonomy and Index (OSTI) (Komaki *et al.*, 1986). The main categories of leader behaviour, together with definitions and examples, are shown in Table 13.1. Komaki (1986) compared the behaviour of highly effective and marginally effective supervisors in US insurance companies. Supervisor effectiveness was assessed by the supervisors' own bosses.

Komaki (1986) hypothesized that the behavioural categories of performance consequences and performance monitoring (see Table 13.1) would distinguish between the highly and marginally effective leaders. She argued that this would especially be the case where performance was monitored using work sampling, as that is likely to produce the most accurate judgements of subordinate performance. This expectation was based on operant conditioning (see Chapter 9): in order to administer rewards contingent on appropriate behaviour, supervisors need to know what subordinates have done, and make it clear that they know to those concerned. In fact, observation of the supervisors' behaviour showed that performance monitoring (especially work sampling) but not performance consequences, distinguished between highly effective and marginally effective supervisors. The better supervisors did more performance monitoring, though even they only spent about 3% of their time doing it, compared with 2% for the marginally effective ones. For both groups, most time was spent in solitary work-related behaviours (about 40% each). Perhaps leaders in some organizations do not have the power or opportunity to carry out performance monitoring and performance consequences.

Komaki confesses herself a yachting enthusiast, and in subsequent research

(Komaki *et al.*, 1989) she has combined business with pleasure by testing her ideas about leadership in a specially arranged yachting regatta! She and her colleagues observed skippers' behaviour over 19 races. Crews were rotated around skippers to avoid some skippers always getting the best crews. The skippers' performance monitoring and performance consequences behaviour both predicted their standing over the 19 races. The more of both, the better the performance.

Komaki's approach represents real progress. Her methods ensure that leaders' actual behaviours are recorded, rather than subordinates' perceptions of them. Her results suggest that key leader behaviours are not in fact very frequent and must therefore be carefully watched and developed. As Locke (1980) has pointed out, as well as having roots in operant conditioning, Komaki's approach is also relevant to the goal-setting theory of motivation (see Chapter 10).

Transactional and transformational leadership

You may have noticed that none of the approaches to leadership described so far have included the notion of *charisma*. The leader has been construed as a strategist, not as an inspirational figure. Yet real leaders in business and politics (not to mention fictional leaders in films and literature) are frequently portrayed as heroes and heroines. They unite and motivate their followers by offering shared goals usually based on a better tomorrow. Leaders deemed to be non-charismatic (e.g. US Vice-President and then President George Bush) are often seen as lacking what it takes – though of course that did not prevent Bush's rise to the top.

In the 1980s and 1990s, psychologists have been correcting their earlier omission. They have used a distinction between so-called transactional and transformational leadership (Burns, 1978). *Transactional* leaders use styles and techniques of the kind already described to clarify task requirements and ensure that subordinates are rewarded for appropriate behaviour. *Transformational* leaders, on the other hand, concentrate on:

> ... articulating a vision and mission, and creating and maintaining a positive image in the minds of followers and superiors ... these leaders challenge their followers and provide a personal example by behaving in a manner that reinforces the vision and the mission of the leader (Fiedler and House, 1988, p. 78).

Bass (1985) has developed a questionnaire called the Multifactor Leadership Questionnaire (MLQ) to assess the extent to which subordinates feel that their leader exhibits transformational and transactional leadership. In the MLQ, transformational leadership has three components:

1. *Charisma*: the leader transmits pride and a sense of mission, and can get to the heart of the matter.
2. *Individual consideration*: the leader treats each follower on their own merits, and seeks to develop them through delegation of projects and coaching/mentoring.
3. *Intellectual stimulation*: the leader encourages free thinking, and emphasizes reasoning before any action is taken.

There are two aspects to transactional leadership:

1. *Contingent reward*: the leader provides rewards if, and only if, subordinates perform adequately and/or try hard enough.
2. *Management-by-exception*: the leader does not seek to change the existing working methods of subordinates so long as performance goals are met.

These two forms of leadership are not entirely mutually exclusive: leaders are not necessarily one or the other, or indeed either! It has been shown that transformational leadership is not confined to the upper echelons of organizations. There is also evidence that leaders who use transformational leadership are viewed more positively by their subordinates than those who do not. The same is true of transactional leadership, but to a lesser extent. Leaders who use transformational techniques (especially the first two) also seem to be more successful in their own careers (Hater and Bass, 1988).

The distinction between transactional and transformational leadership looks like an important one. More evidence is needed on just how useful transformational leadership is, how it works and whether leaders can be trained to use it. But it looks as though it matters. Even in our sophisticated modern world (perhaps *especially* in our sophisticated modern world) we need a leader we can believe in.

Case study 13.1 Transactional and transformational leadership

Marc LeBlanc is manager of the claims department of a medical insurance company. The department's job is to process claims by clients who have spent time in hospital. Marc considers himself scrupulously fair with his staff of 17 administrative and clerical staff. He thinks that if something (such as a training course) is good for one of them, then it is good for all. He has successfully resisted senior management's wish for performance-related pay, arguing that group solidarity will ensure that everyone pulls their weight. Marc thinks of his job as making sure the department knows where it is going and why. In contrast to his predecessor, he never tires of telling his staff that their job is to "play a proper part in the client's return to good health", rather than contest every doubt, however tiny, about a client's claim. He has a noticeboard for displaying complimentary letters from clients grateful for prompt and trouble-free processing of their claims. He frequently emphasizes the need to look at things from the client's point of view. He tells his staff to focus on certain key aspects of the long and complicated claim form, and only briefly inspect most of the rest of it. Marc checks on whether they are doing this, but only when a complaint is received from a client or the company's own internal claims auditors. In such cases, he defends his staff, provided they have conformed to the department's way of doing things. He is less sympathetic if they have taken decisions about claims on other criteria, even if those claims have some unusual features.

Suggested exercises

1. Marc LeBlanc scores high on just one aspect of transformational leadership. Which one?
2. He scores high on one aspect of transactional leadership. Which one?
3. The performance of the claims department could be measured with more than one criterion. Think of one respect in which Marc's style *enhances* the department's performance, and one respect in which his style *hinders* performance.

From leader-focused approaches to contingency theories

The above approaches to leader behaviour vary in their sophistication. They have all left their mark, and each contributes something to our understanding of what leaders actually do and what it is best for them to do. In their original forms, they have an important feature in common. They all seek to describe leader behaviour without considering the wider context. In essence, they are stating that in order to be effective, leaders need to perform certain behaviours and do so whatever the situation.

In fact, concepts like consideration, structure, participation, performance monitoring, performance consequences and transactional and transformational leadership can all be used more flexibly. Indeed, some of them have been. The greater flexibility involves arguing that in certain kinds of situations particular leader behaviours are optimal, whereas in others different behaviours are required. Do we really need a leader high on consideration and low on structure in an emergency such as a bomb scare? Probably not – we need someone who will quickly tell us where to go, and what to do. We can do without a leader who asks us, at that moment, how we feel about the bomb scare. On the other hand, if a leader is responsible for allocating already well-defined tasks to a group of junior managers, we might hope for some sensitive consideration of the managers' preferences, career development plans, etc.

This brings us to contingency theories, so-called because they assume that optimal leader behaviour is contingent upon (i.e. depends upon) the situation. Contingency theories are necessarily fairly complex. Their task is not easy. They have to specify not only which leader behaviours are crucial, but also which aspects of the situation matter most, and how leader and situation interact. Needless to say, there is plenty of room for disagreement here. We will now take a look at the most influential and controversial contingency theories.

Contingency theory I: Fiedler

Fred Fiedler first put forward his theory of leadership in the 1960s (Fiedler, 1967). He built his theory from data collected over the previous decade. It is still being tested and disputed today. Fiedler argued that each leader has fairly stable personal characteristics which in turn lead to a characteristic style which they (and their subordinates) are stuck with. For Fiedler, the key personal characteristic concerns how positively the leader views their least preferred co-worker. He has developed a questionnaire measure of this concept called LPC (which stands for least preferred co-worker). The measure consists of 16 dimensions such as pleasant–unpleasant, boring–interesting and insincere–sincere. The leader describes their least preferred co-worker on these dimensions. A high LPC score signifies a positive view of the least preferred co-worker, whereas a low LPC score indicates a negative opinion.

There is some dispute about exactly what a leader's LPC score means. It could be pretty similar to consideration (high LPC) and structure (low LPC), though this assumes that consideration and structure are opposite ends of the same continuum rather than independent constructs. Indeed, high LPC leaders are often referred to as being person-orientated – after all, they must be if they can even be nice about people they do not like! Low LPC leaders are often thought of as task-orientated. There is no doubt considerable overlap between LPC on the one hand and consideration and structure on the other. But Fiedler and others have argued that LPC also reflects the leader's deeper pattern of motivation. Some have suggested that LPC involves cognitive complexity. High LPC leaders are sometimes said to be more cognitively complex than low LPC leaders, because they can differentiate between a person's inherent worth and their work performance.

Whatever LPC is, Fiedler argues that in some situations it is best to have a high LPC leader at the helm, while in others a low LPC leader is preferable. Specifically, Fiedler proposes three key aspects of the situation which together define its favourableness to the leader. In descending order of importance, these are:

1. *Leader–member relations*: whether or not the subordinates trust and like their leader.

2. *Task structure*: the extent to which the group's tasks, goals and performance are clearly defined.

3. *Position power*: the extent to which the leader controls rewards and punishments for subordinates.

If we divide each of these three into high and low, we arrive at $2 \times 2 \times 2 = 8$ types of situation. The most favourable is where leader–member relations are good, and task structure and position power are high. The least favourable is where leader–member relations are poor, and task structure and position power are low.

The key features of Fiedler's theory are shown in Table 13.2. From his early data, he concluded that in highly and fairly favourable situations, and in very unfavourable ones, group performance was better if the leader had a low LPC score (i.e. was task-orientated). In situations of moderate to low favourability, high LPC scores were best (i.e. person-orientated).

Table 13.2 Fiedler's theory of leadership

	Situation highly favourable							Situation highly unfavourable
	I	II	III	IV	V	VI	VII	VIII
Leader–member relations	Good	Good	Good	Good	Poor	Poor	Poor	Poor
Task structure	Structured	Structured	Unstructured	Unstructured	Structured	Structured	Unstructured	Unstructured
Leader position power	Strong	Weak	Strong	Weak	Strong	Weak	Strong	Weak
Desirable leader LPC score	Low	Low	Low	High	High	High	High	Low

It is not altogether clear why this should be so. However, one common-sense explanation is plausible. Where the situation is good, the leader does not *need* to spend time on interpersonal relationships. Where the situation is bad, things are so difficult that it is not *worth* spending time on interpersonal relationships. In both cases, forging ahead with the task is best. But where the situation falls between the two extremes, keeping group members happy becomes more important. A leader needs high LPC to hold the group together so that its tasks can be tackled. One problem with this explanation arises from its emphasis on leader–member relations. An inspection of Table 13.2 shows that the switch from low LPC to high LPC occurs between situations III and IV, in both of which leader–member relations are good.

Fiedler's theory asserts that because leaders have a fairly stable LPC score, there is little point trying to train them to cope with different situations. They cannot change their style. Instead, he argues (Fiedler and Chemers, 1984) that it is important to match leader to situation. Placement is more useful than training. So if you are a high LPC leader, you cannot expect to be placed in the most favourable leadership situations!

Many problems with Fiedler's theory have been pointed out. Apart from the unclear nature of LPC, there is doubt about whether the LPC score is as stable as Fiedler assumes. Also, perhaps it depends too much on just how undesirable the leader's least preferred co-worker really is. Another issue concerns Fiedler's concept of the situation. For example, in the medium- and long-term, leader–member relations are perhaps a function of the leader and subordinates themselves. Is it therefore valid to treat leader–member relations as part of the situation? This has important implications. Suppose for a moment that a leader and group find themselves in situation V (see Table 13.2). If they succeed in improving their relationship, the situation becomes I. This in turn would mean that a different kind of leader is required. Would moving the leader to another group be an appropriate reward for the improvement in leader–member relations?

Despite these doubts, it is clear that Fiedler is on to something. Peters *et al.* (1985) reported a thorough meta-analysis of tests of Fiedler's theory. They observed that the data on which the theory was originally based support it very well. Hence the theory was appropriately constructed given the then available data. Subsequent research that has tested the theory gives it partial support.

Laboratory-based studies have produced results more consistent with the theory than field studies. Situation II seems to be a particular problem because recent research has generally found that a high LPC score is best, rather than a low one. Peters *et al.* (1985) concluded that the theory fits moderately well with research data, but probably more features of the situation need to be taken into account. For example, Bryman *et al.* (1987) suggested organizational transience. In a study of construction sites, they found that low LPC leaders were an advantage on short-term sites, but not on longer-term ones. The longer a team is together, the more person-orientation is needed.

Fiedler himself has built on his earlier work (Fiedler and Garcia, 1987). His cognitive resource theory (CRT) examines leader intelligence and experience. He argues that in situations of low interpersonal stress (perhaps equivalent to high favourability: see Table 13.2), leaders use their intelligence more than their experience. But in situations of high stress (low favourability), they use their experience more than their intelligence. In fact, in such situations intelligence can be a positive disadvantage. It seems that stress disturbs cognitive functioning, and perhaps those who are most accustomed to high-level thinking find this disruption hardest to deal with.

Thus Fiedler is now introducing more characteristics of the leader over and above LPC. As he points out, experience and intelligence are often key criteria in selecting leaders. His recent work suggests that the concept of matching leader to situation must be based on the leader's intelligence and experience as well as LPC and situational characteristics. But the basic practical implication remains the same. Try to determine the characteristics of the situation you are selecting a leader for, and thereby specify the characteristics you most desire in the leader.

Case study 13.2   Using Fiedler's theories of leadership

For the last year, Debbie Walsh has been head of the 10 staff of the market analysis department of a garden furniture company. The company sells its produce through selected garden centres and do-it-yourself shops. The department's tasks are well-established. For example, it monitors sales of each product at each outlet. It evaluates the viability of potential alternative outlets. It checks the products and prices of competitors. Debbie is a "high-flyer" academically, having obtained a first-class honours degree and an MBA with distinction. The managing director has great faith in her, and has given her complete discretion over awarding salary increases to her staff and most other aspects of people management in the market analysis department. This is Debbie's first marketing job: most of her previous 4 years' work experience were spent in general management at a knitwear company. Other staff do not resent Debbie. They feel her appointment demonstrates the truth of the company's pledge to put ability ahead of experience in promotion

decisions. They may in future benefit from that policy themselves, because most of them are young and well-qualified. Debbie takes a "no-nonsense" approach to her work and colleagues. She responds well to businesslike people who come straight to the point. She has little patience with those who are slower to get to the heart of a problem, or who do not share her objectives. Most of her present staff have a similar approach to hers. But in one of Debbie's previous jobs, her hostility towards several slow and awkward colleagues was a major factor in her decision to leave that job.

Suggested exercises

1. Which of Fiedler's eight situation types is portrayed here?
2. Using Fiedler's contingency and cognitive resources theories decide whether Debbie is well-suited to her situation.

Contingency theory II: Vroom and Jago

Vroom and Yetton (1973) proposed a contingency theory of leader decision making. This has been updated and extended by Vroom and Jago (1988). They suggested that leaders are perfectly capable of changing their behaviour from situation to situation. Certainly most leaders say they do. The theory identifies five styles of leader decision making, ranging from the most autocratic to the most democratic:

- AI: The leader decides what to do, using information already available.
- AII: The leader obtains required information from subordinates, and then makes the decision him or herself. The leader may or may not tell the subordinates what the problem is.
- CI: The leader shares the problem with each subordinate individually, and obtains their ideas. The leader then makes the decision.
- CII: The leader shares the problem with subordinates as a group, and obtains their ideas. The leader then makes the decision.
- GII: The leader shares the problem with subordinates as a group. They discuss alternatives together and try to reach collective agreement. The leader accepts any decision supported by the group as a whole.

Vroom and Jago (1988) then proposed some key features of problem situations that leaders should consider:

1. *Quality requirement*: how important is it that a good decision is made?
2. *Commitment requirement*: how important is it that subordinates feel committed to the decision?
3. *Leader information*: does the leader have enough information to make a high-quality decision?
4. *Problem structure*: is it clear what the current situation is, what one wants to achieve, and what alternative paths to the goal are available?
5. *Commitment probability*: if the leader alone made the decision, would the subordinates feel committed to the decision?
6. *Goal congruence*: do subordinates share the organization's goals in solving this problem?
7. *Subordinate conflict*: is conflict likely among subordinates concerning which solution is best?
8. *Subordinate information*: do subordinates have enough information to make a good decision?
9. *Time constraint*: is time too short to involve subordinates in decision making?
10. *Geographical dispersion*: would it be too expensive to bring together geographically dispersed subordinates?

Also, Vroom and Jago (1988) argued that two further factors are relevant: the importance to the leader of minimizing decision time, and of maximizing opportunities for subordinate development.

In Vroom and Yetton's (1973) original model, only the first seven questions above were used. A "yes" or "no" answer to each question was required for any given decision situation. According to the answer to each question, a path was traced through a decision tree, and the optimal leader style or styles were specified. In many cases, several styles were considered optimal. Vroom and Jago's (1988) model has increased the number of questions to reflect more aspects of the situation (see above), and also asks for answers to most of them on a 5-point scale rather than simply yes or no. Further, by using some mathematical formulae, the one best style for any given decision problem can be specified.

Thus the revised model is more complex, more sensitive to situational differences, and more specific than the original. Computer software has been developed which allows a person to input their answers to the questions listed above, and then calculates an overall "suitability score" for each possible style.

Some general rules of thumb governing use of the leader styles in Vroom and Jago's model include the following. First, where subordinates' commitment is important, more participative styles are better. Secondly, where the leader needs more information, AI should be avoided. Thirdly, where subordinates do not share organizational goals, GII should be avoided. Finally, where both problem structure and leader information are low, CII and GII tend to be best. It should however be apparent that, in some cases, other factors such as time constraints or staff development needs can override those rules of thumb.

Vroom and Yetton's original model received some support from research (Crouch and Yetton, 1987). But there was also evidence that the skill with which leaders put their style into action was at least as important as choosing a style deemed appropriate in the first place (Tjosvold *et al.*, 1986). Vroom and Jago's new model has yet to receive the same examination, but looks promising. It is based on 15 years of research and development by its originator as well as an original model having some validity, so it should have considerable value. On the other hand, its complexity makes it difficult for leaders to use quickly and easily, even with computer support. Vroom and Jago (1988) have expressed the hope that knowledge of its general principles, including those presented here, will often be enough.

Other contingency approaches: Is a leader really necessary?

In their Situational Leadership Theory (SLT), Hersey and Blanchard (1982) have argued that leader effectiveness depends on the interplay between leader style and follower maturity. They considered two leader styles: relationship orientation and task orientation. These are more or less equivalent to consideration and structure, respectively. Follower maturity refers to the subordinates' understanding of the job and commitment to it, but length of time in the job is often used to measure it.

Vecchio (1987, p. 444) has explained the theory as follows:

During the early stages of an employee's tenure, a low level of relationship orientation coupled with high task orientation is considered to be ideal. As an employee (or group of employees) gains in maturity, the need for supervisory social-emotional support increases, while the need for structuring declines. At the highest levels of employee maturity, supervisory task and social behaviours become superfluous to effective employee performance.

In other words, employees first need to be introduced to their tasks. Then, as they are coping with tasks, they need sympathetic help and advice. After that they should have come to grips with both task and social relationships, and are best left to get on with it.

Vecchio (1987) declared that SLT is much used by managers but rarely tested. He found that among 303 teachers in the USA, the theory's predictions were pretty accurate for subordinates with low maturity, reasonably accurate for those with moderate maturity, and not at all accurate for those with high maturity. His measure of maturity was school principals' ratings of teachers' task-relevant and psychological maturity.

Perhaps the crucial message of Vecchio's results is that even when subordinates are mature, it is not a good idea for their leader to neglect both task and relationships. This rather argues against an extension of SLT principles proposed by Kerr and Jermier (1978). They developed the idea that in some circumstances leaders are unnecessary. Their approach has been termed "substitutes for leadership", though it also includes the notion that some factors can neutralize the impact of leadership (as opposed to substitutes, which do the leadership job for the leader). Examples of proposed substitutes for leadership include: intrinsically interesting tasks; ability, experience, training and knowledge of subordinates; and availability of senior staff other than subordinates' own leader.

Consistent with Vecchio (1987), research has tended to find that the presence of substitutes for leadership does not eliminate effects of leadership style on subordinate satisfaction and performance. This may be partly because measures of substitutes for leadership are not very good (Williams *et al.*, 1988). However, it is hard to escape the conclusion that leadership *does* matter. The apparent lack of efficacy of substitutes for leadership suggests either that leadership tasks cannot easily be distributed around a group, or that we have an inbuilt psychological need for a leader. We now turn to further consideration of that latter possibility.

Perceiving leadership

In recent years, increasing attention has been paid to how and when we perceive leadership to be important. A related issue is how we identify someone as leader. Many of the principles of person perception apply here (see Chapter 11).

In an article appropriately entitled "The romance of leadership", Meindl *et al.* (1985, p. 79) argued that:

> ... we may have developed highly romanticized, heroic views of leadership – what leaders do, what they are able to accomplish, and the general effects they have on our lives. One of the principal elements in this romanticized conception is the view that leadership is ... the premier force in the scheme of organizational processes and activities.

Meindl *et al.* (1985) further argued that our conception of leadership as important and influential should lead us to consider leadership as a key factor where performance is *either* very good *or* very bad. When things go really well, we attribute it to the leader's skill. When things go really badly, we blame the leader's ineptitude. But, when things go averagely well, we are unlikely to say it was primarily due to average leadership. This is because we see leadership as a big concept which has big effects, not moderate ones.

Meindl *et al.* (1985) produced support for their point of view in a number of interesting ways. First, they searched *The Wall Street Journal* (*WSJ*) between 1972 and 1982 for articles about 34 firms representing a range of US industries. They then related the proportion of *WSJ* articles about each company which mentioned top management to the company's performance. Sure enough, they found that a higher proportion of "leadership" articles appeared when firms were doing especially well or especially badly – particularly the former. Secondly, they surveyed dissertations by postgraduate students and related that to overall US economic performance. Increasing numbers of dissertations about leadership were associated with downturns in the US economy 2–4 years earlier (it usually takes 2–4 years to produce a dissertation). Thirdly, they conducted a similar analysis with business journals, where the articles generally take less time to produce than dissertations. In this case, upturns in the US economy were associated with increasing numbers of articles about leadership. Perhaps academics want to understand what goes wrong, whereas business people want to understand (and presumably copy) what goes right. Lastly, Meindl *et al.* conducted a series of laboratory experiments where case studies of corporate success and failure were presented, and students were asked to rate the importance of various possible causes, including leadership. Again, leadership was seen as a more important cause of extreme (especially good) performance than of medium performance. Alternative causes were generally seen as less important than leadership, and at a fairly constant level of importance across the range of performance outcomes.

All this seems like very good evidence for a "romanticized" view of leadership. It is tempting to assume that, by adopting this romanticized view, we are kidding ourselves. Not necessarily. Meindl *et al.* (1985) did not demonstrate that we are wrong to make these attributions about leadership, only that we do.

How do we decide *who* is leader? Lord *et al.* (1984) suggested that our prototype (see Chapter 11) of a leader is someone who is decisive, intelligent and industrious. According to Lord *et al.* (1984), when we observe someone who fits that description we tend to think of them as a leader. We may well later detect in that person other features of leadership because, and only because, we have "filed" that person away in our memory as a leader.

Other psychologists (e.g. Calder, 1977) have used principles of attribution theory (see Chapter 11) to explain how observers identify leaders. They have argued that a person's behaviour has to be of the right kind, but also different from that of other group members, in order for that person to be identified as leader. In the terminology of attribution theory, there has to be low consensus. Low consensus normally leads observers to make a dispositional attribution, i.e. to infer that the person's behaviour reflects something about them. This of course leads the observer to believe that not only is the person behaving like a leader, but that they also have inherent leadership qualities.

Research suggests that we use the prototype approach more often and more readily then attribution, possibly because attribution involves greater mental effort (Cronshaw and Lord, 1987). Whatever the truth of this, the use of prototypes and attribution theories in one sense brings us full circle. We are back to trait approaches to leadership. After all, if most people who appoint leaders have a similar prototype in their head of the traits they are looking for, it would not be surprising to find that leaders tend to possess those traits.

Summary

This chapter has examined many approaches to leadership. Consideration, structure, cognitive complexity/intelligence, participativeness, monitoring and rewarding performance, and charisma have been identified as some key leader behaviours. There is considerable overlap between these concepts, and some tidying up and increased precision is needed. The same is true of the various situational variables proposed by contingency theorists. For example, take another look at Vroom and Jago's questions. At least two relate closely to Fiedler's notions of leader–member relations and task structure. The theories are in some respects more similar than they might seem. It is therefore not surprising that several of them are equally (and moderately) good at explaining leadership phenomena. Several approaches, especially Vroom–Jago, Komaki and so-called transformational leadership contain useful practical guidance about how to go about being a leader. The prototype and attribution literatures say something useful about how to get yourself recognized as a leader. Future theory and practice in leadership needs to combine concepts from the better theories in a systematic way. Greater attention must also be paid to whether and how leaders can be trained or selected not only to do the desirable things, but also to do them well.

Case study 13.3   Leadership and policy implementation

It was a turbulent time in the health and safety department of Super Chem's Hamburg plant. The multinational chemical company had recently adopted a policy of developing managers by giving them international experience. A consequence of this policy had been that a 32-year-old Spaniard, Jose Ispaldo, had been put in charge of the department. Jose's German was more than adequate for the task, but this was his first assignment outside Spain, a country seen by many in the company as peripheral to its operations. He had much to learn when he first arrived, especially about German health and

safety legislation. He was, however, an experienced health and safety manager, having been head of health and safety at two smallish plants in Spain for 2 years each.

Almost as soon as he arrived, Jose was pitched into an interesting situation. Two major accidents at other plants had caused a high-level health and safety policy review. The resulting report had come out in favour of more stringent inspection and a tougher approach from company health and safety departments. The recommendations were clear and specific.

Jose knew that his presence was resented by

his six staff, who had worked together for some time and tended to think alike. They felt they had more specialist knowledge than he did. Most were older than him, and they could not understand why the deputy head, Gunter Koenig, had not been promoted. Koenig himself was understandably especially bitter. Jose felt that he could not follow his staff around as they inspected the plant: it would look too much like snooping. On the other hand, he needed to tap into his staff's knowledge of the plant and of how things had always been done there. Existing policy documents were too vague to be much help.

Jose had reason to believe that his staff typically adopted a collaborative approach with the managers whose areas they inspected. They preferred to use friendly persuasion and gentle hints rather than the precise written reports and threats for non-compliance required by the new policy. It had always worked at that plant they said, and it would continue to do so. Yet Jose knew that exactly the same had been said at the plants where major accidents occurred. What was worse for Jose, it was fairly clear that the plant manager privately agreed with Jose's staff. Jose's position was all the more difficult because he was known to be on a 2-year secondment, after which the previous head (who had herself been seconded elsewhere) was expected to return in his place. Therefore, he was not in a position to exert a long-term influence on the careers of his staff. But Jose himself was answerable not only to the plant manager but also to the company health and safety chief, who was the chief proponent of the new policy.

Jose knew that he was not a particularly creative or imaginative individual. He enjoyed the precision and rules and regulations of health and safety work. He was usually inclined to draw up detailed plans of work for himself and others, and to keep a careful check on the implementation of those plans. At the same time, he could understand how his staff felt: he had been landed with an unwelcome boss himself a few years earlier. He did not blame them for their attitude and, characteristically, he was always keen to emphasize what he genuinely saw as the many strengths of his subordinates.

Despite the complicated situation, Jose felt his task was clear enough. A decision had to be made about how, if at all, the department's practices would need to change in order to implement the new health and safety policy. Also, it had to be made in time for a visit by the health and safety chief 6 weeks later.

Suggested exercises

1. Analyse this case study using Fiedler's theories. What kind of situation is it? How well suited to it is Jose Ispaldo? What should he do next? What important features of this case study, if any, are neglected by Fiedler's ideas?
2. Analyse this case study using Vroom and Jago's theory. What kind of situation is it? What should Jose Ispaldo do next? What important features of this case study, if any, are neglected by Vroom and Jago?

References

Bass, B. M. (1985). *Leadership and Performance: Beyond Expectations.* New York: Free Press.

Blake, R. R. and Mouton, J. S. (1964). *The Managerial Grid.* Houston, Tx.: Gulf Publishing.

Bryman, A., Bresnen, M., Ford, J., Beardsworth, A. and Keil, T. (1987). Leader orientation and organizational transience: An investigation using Fiedler's LPC scale. *Journal of Occupational Psychology, 60,* 13–19.

Burns, J. M. (1978). *Leadership.* New York: Harper and Row.

Calder, B. (1977). An attribution theory of leadership. In B. H. Staw and G. R. Salancik (Eds), *New Directions in Organizational Behavior.* Chicago, Ill.: St Clair Press.

Cronshaw, S. F. and Lord, R. G. (1987). Effects of categorization, attribution and encoding processes on leadership perceptions. *Journal of Applied Psychology, 72,* 97–106.

Crouch, A. and Yetton, P. (1987). Manager behavior, leadership style and subordinate performance: An empirical extension of the Vroom–Yetton conflict rule. *Organizational Behavior and Human Decision Processes, 39,* 384–396.

Fiedler, F. E. (1967). *A Theory of Leadership Effectiveness.* New York: McGraw-Hill.

Fiedler, F. E. and Chemers, M. M. (1984). *Improving Leadership Effectiveness: The Leader Match Concept,* 2nd edn. New York: John Wiley.

Fiedler, F. E. and Garcia, J. E. (1987). *New Approaches to Effective Leadership: Cognitive Resources and Organizational Performance.* New York: John Wiley.

Fiedler, F. E. and House, R. J. (1988). Leadership theory and research: A report of progress. In C. L. Cooper and I. T. Robertson (Eds), *International Review of Industrial and Organizational Psychology, 1988.* Chichester: John Wiley.

Filley, A. C., House, R. J. and Kerr, S. (1976). *Managerial Process and Organizational Behavior.* Glenview, Ill.: Scott, Foresman.

Fleishman, E.A. (1969). *Leadership Opinion Questionnaire Manual.* Henley-on-Thames: Science Research Associates.

Hater, J. and Bass, B. M. (1988). Superiors' evaluations and subordinates' perceptions of transformational and transactional leadership. *Journal of Applied Psychology, 73,* 695–702.

Hersey, P. and Blanchard, K. (1982). *Management of Organizational Behavior,* 4th edn. Englewood Cliffs, N.J.: Prentice-Hall.

House, R. J. and Baetz, M. L. (1979). Leadership: Some empirical generalizations and new research directions. In B. M. Staw (Ed.), *Research in Organizational Behavior,* Vol. 1. Greenwich, Conn.: JAI Press.

Kerr, S. and Jermier, J. M. (1978). Substitutes for leadership: Their meaning and measurement. *Organizational Behavior and Human Performance, 22,* 375–403.

Komaki, J. L. (1986). Toward effective supervision. *Journal of Applied Psychology, 71,* 270–279.

Komaki, J. L., Zlotnick, S. and Jensen, M. (1986). Development of an operant-based taxonomy and observational index of supervisory behavior. *Journal of Applied Psychology, 71,* 260–269.

Komaki, J. L., Desselles, M. L. and Bowman, E. D. (1989). Definitely not a breeze: Extending an operant model of effective supervision to teams. *Journal of Applied Psychology, 74,* 522–529.

Locke, E. A. (1980). Latham versus Komaki: A tale of two paradigms. *Journal of Applied Psychology, 65,* 16–23.

Lord, R. G., Foti, R. J. and De Vader, C. L. (1984). A test of leadership categorization theory: Internal structure, information processing and leadership perceptions. *Organizational Behavior and Human Performance, 34,* 343–378.

Maier, N. R. F. (1970). *Problem–solving and Creativity in Individuals and Groups.* Belmont, Calif.: Books/Cole.

Meindl, J. R., Ehrlich, S. B. and Dukerich, J. M. (1985). The romance of leadership. *Administrative Science Quarterly, 30,* 78–102.

Peters, L. H., Hartke, D. D. and Pohlmann, J. T. (1985). Fiedler's contingency theory of leadership: An application of the meta-analysis procedures of Schmidt and Hunter. *Psychological Bulletin, 97,* 274–285.

Smith, P. B. and Peterson, M. F. (1988). *Leadership, Organizations and Culture.* London: Sage.

Smith, P. B., Misumi, J., Tayeb, M., Peterson, M. and Bond, M. (1989). On the generality of leadership style measures across cultures. *Journal of Occupational Psychology*, *62*, 97–109.

Stogdill, R. M. (1974). *Handbook of Leadership: A Survey of Theory and Research*. New York: Free Press.

Tjosvold, D., Wedley, W. C. and Field, R. H. G. (1986). Constructive controversy, the Vroom–Yetton model, and managerial decision-making. *Journal of Occupational Behaviour*, *7*, 125–138.

Vecchio, R. P. (1987). Situational leadership theory: An examination of a prescriptive theory. *Journal of Applied Psychology*, *72*, 444–451.

Vroom, V. H. and Jago, A. G. (1988). *The New Leadership: Managing Participation in Organizations*. Englewood Cliffs, N.J.: Prentice-Hall.

Vroom, V. H. and Yetton, P. W. (1973). *Leadership and Decision Making*. Pittsburgh: Pittsburgh Press.

Weissenburg, P. and Kavanagh, M. J. (1972). The independence of initiating structure and consideration: A review of the evidence. *Personnel Psychology*, *25*, 119–130.

Williams, M. L., Podsakoff, P. M., Todor, W. D., Huber, V. L., Howell, J. P. and Dorfman, P. W. (1988). A preliminary analysis of the construct validity of Kerr and Jermier's "substitutes for leadership" scales. *Journal of Occupational Psychology*, *61*, 307–334.

Yetton, P. W. (1984). Leadership and supervision. In M. Gruneberg and T. Wall (Eds), *Social Psychology and Organizational Behaviour*. Chichester: John Wiley.

Training and learning at work

Introduction

People in organizations develop and change as time passes. Some of this development occurs in a rather unsystematic fashion and takes place as people learn from each other and learn how to integrate themselves into the organization. Other development and change takes place, in a more controlled and planned fashion, when programmes of planned training and development are organized in attempts to improve the knowledge and skills that people have. In most modern organizations, such programmes represent an important component in their success and have significant cost/benefit implications. Figure 14.1 represents an outline of the major elements involved in the training and development process, and during the remainder of this chapter each of the elements will be described in some detail.

The training process

As Fig. 14.1 shows, the training and development process moves from an assessment of need through the development of programmes to validation and evaluation of what has taken place. It is important to recognize that, although Fig. 14.1 presents the elements involved in an orderly sequence, in practice there are many links and interactions between these elements, and often parts of various elements will be taking place in parallel or in a different order from the one shown. Although this chapter covers the major factors involved in the training process itself, other chapters present material of considerable importance to the training process including, in particular, job analysis and personnel selection (see Chapters 6 and 7).

Assessing needs

Before setting in motion any systematic training or development within any organization, those responsible should satisfy themselves that such activity is

14.1 The training process.

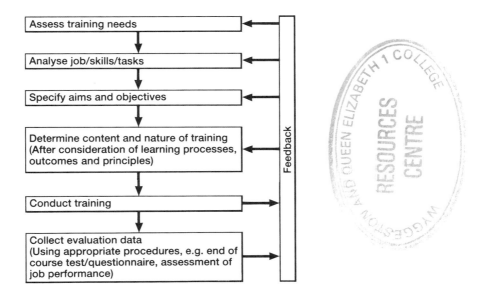

going to produce worthwhile results and is therefore necessary. On occasions, in some organizations, it is clear that programmes of training and development can take on a more or less independent "life of their own" and various activities will take place regardless of any clear and established need for them. Without adequate systems for staff training and development, an organization cannot function effectively, but as Davies (1972) has pointed out, both too little and too much training can cause problems. Davies noted that the penalties of too little training might include:

- unnecessary "on the job" learning;
- production shortfalls;
- errors and wastage;
- unsafe working practices; and
- dissatisfaction with the work itself.

On the other hand, too much training might result in:

- wasteful excessively long courses;
- unnecessary instructors, equipment and accommodation;
- unnecessary failure of trainees; and
- job dissatisfaction resulting from "overtrained" employees not being able to use all their skills.

Thus a systematic assessment of training needs is a necessary first step in the development of any programme.

It is customary and useful to consider the assessment of training needs at three different levels of analysis: organizational analysis, task analysis and person analysis (see McGhee and Thayer, 1961; Boydell, 1973). Such a framework still forms the basis for contemporary views of training needs assessment (Latham, 1988).

At the organizational level, the first step in the assessment of need is to examine and identify the aims and objectives of the organization. These can often be identified in general terms by examining plans and statements of policy and by discussion with senior personnel in the organization. Very broadly, organizational training needs exist when there is, or is likely to be, some sort of barrier hindering the achievement of organizational aims and objectives (either now or at some predicted future occasion). Symptoms might include output problems caused by bottlenecks in production, excessive errors or wastage, stress and related problems caused by a lack of ability on the part of some people or overload on other fully trained individuals. It is important to stress, however, that such problems represent training needs only if the barrier to the achievement of aims and objectives might be best removed by training rather than some other activity. Production problems, for example, might well be solved more effectively by redesigning the job or equipment, improving recruitment and selection procedures, or providing job aids. Recent emphasis in organizational level training needs assessment has stressed the kind of system-wide thinking embodied in the above description of organizational analysis in which consideration of the link between training activities and organizational goals is important (e.g. Goldstein, 1986). This systems view is also evident in more general work on strategic human resources management.

To bring about any form of training it is important to have a clear understanding of the target behaviour that is to be developed, and in most organizational settings this means a clear grasp of the main job components or activities that are involved. The closely related techniques of job analysis, skills analysis and task analysis have an important role here.

Job analysis

A great deal of job analysis is carried out in organizations in order to produce job descriptions. Such descriptions include information about the conditions of work, salary, physical surroundings, etc., but provide only a general description of the tasks involved in the job and of the skills required; as such, they are of very limited value in a training context. Some of the methods for job analysis can be useful for training purposes, e.g. the Position Analysis Questionnaire (PAQ) of McCormick *et al.* (1972) (see Chapter 6). However, even techniques such as the PAQ provide information that, although comprehensive, is often not detailed enough to allow for the construction of specific exercises and programmes of planned training.

Skills analysis

This term is usually reserved for procedures and methods of analysis similar to the technique described by Seymour (1966). Essentially, such techniques call for detailed analysis of the skilled physical movements involved in manual operations, and although they are useful in some training situations, their range of application is limited.

Task analysis

This is probably the most important from of analysis for training purposes. The technique focuses on the objectives or outcomes of the tasks that people perform and provides an extremely flexible and useful method for analysis. The main unit of analysis is the operation. An operation is defined by Annett *et al.* (1971) as follows: "Any unit of behaviour, no matter how long or short its duration and no matter how simple or complex its structure which can be defined in terms of its objective."

One of the important features of the procedures developed by Annett *et al.* (1971) is that tasks are analysed and broken down into increasingly specific operations in a hierarchical fashion. Because of this approach to analysis, the technique is known as Hierarchical Task Analysis (HTA). The starting point for HTA involves a general description of the main operation(s) involved in the job or job components being analysed. These operations are then divided into sub-operations and, in turn, the sub-operations themselves may be subdivided. Consider an example of a task that many of us have had to contend with, that of "knock-flat" furniture. Figure 14.2 shows how this may be described in task analysis terms.

The analysis begins with a fairly high-level description of the main operation involved, i.e. assemble table, which is then subdivided into further operations at increasingly specific levels of analysis. It is important to remember that an operation is a very flexible unit, and at the beginning of the process the analyst will not have any fixed ideas about how many operations are involved nor about the number of levels of analysis that will be needed. An analysis conducted in this way could continue to break down the operations involved until they are describing very tiny units of behaviour, and obviously at some point it is necessary to be able to decide that the analysis has reached a sufficiently specific level of detail. Two factors may be taken into account to help with this decision. The first of these is the probability that an untrained person

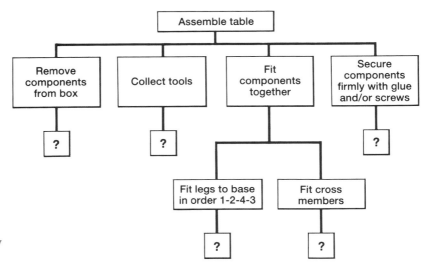

14.2   Part of a task analysis for the assembly of a "knock-flat" table.

would fail to carry out the operation successfully (P). The second is the cost to the system that would be incurred if the operation was carried out inadequately (C). Each operation in the analysis is examined with these two factors in mind in order to determine whether the operation needs to be divided further.

An operation needs to be analysed in more detail if the product of $P \times C$ is unacceptably high. The rationale for this is fairly straightforward. If the probability of failure is high, the operation will probably need to be described in more detail before the analysis can be used as a basis for developing training, unless the cost of failure is minimal. If the cost of failure (C) for a particular operation is high, more detail will be needed, unless the operation is easy for even an untrained person to perform. In other words, difficult operations with important cost consequences need to be analysed further until $P \times C$ becomes acceptably low. Additional information about the analytical techniques and recording procedures for HTA may be found in Annett *et al.* (1971), Duncan (1972) and Shepherd (1976), and a useful introduction to the technique is given in Stammers and Patrick (1975). Other researchers have developed similar procedures (see Goldstein and Gessner, 1988).

Person analysis essentially involves identifying who needs training and what kind of training they need. The methods available for answering these questions are not particularly sophisticated and most rely on the administration of interviews or questionnaires to collect the opinions of key individuals. A note of caution on the interpretation of such surveys is in order in view of the findings of studies comparing the perceived needs of job-holders and their supervisors. Both McEnery and McEnery (1987) and Staley and Shockley-Zalabak (1986) found little agreement between job incumbents and their supervisors. McEnery and McEnery (1987) also found that supervisors' assessments of their subordinates' needs correlated more closely with their (the supervisors) assessment of their own needs than the subordinates' own need assessment!

Defining aims and objectives

Training and development activities are designed to bring about changes in people's behaviour and the success of such endeavours is determined by how effectively these changes are instituted. Developing a clear grasp of the operations involved in the relevant jobs by the use of techniques such as HTA is an essential step in the process. Before training begins, however, the results of such analyses need to be used in order to provide a clear statement of the outcomes or targets of training. As Mager (1962) put it: "If you don't know where you're heading you'll probably end up someplace else."

A useful distinction can be made between the aims and the objectives of training. Aims involve general statements of intent: examples might be that a programme sets out to provide participants with "a grasp of the basic principles of management accountancy" or "an awareness of the relevance of industrial psychology to the management process". By contrast, objectives are much more specific and precise. In their most explicit form, objectives are sometimes expressed in the following, three-component form:

1. The terminal behaviour. A statement of what the trainee should be able to do at the end of training. Because of this emphasis on terminal behaviour, objectives expressed in this way are often referred to as behavioural objectives.

2. The conditions under which the behaviour is to be exhibited.

3. The standard performance of the behaviour.

It is important to recognize that objectives specify what the person will be able to do at the end of training; they do not describe what will happen during training. The statement that participants will gain experience of various personnel selection interviewing techniques would not be acceptable as an objective. It says what will happen on the course but not what the outcomes will be.

In many practical training situations, a full description of the expected outcomes of training is not provided in the form described above. Sometimes competence at the end of training is assessed by the use of various tests, or job simulation exercises. The behaviour that will produce satisfactory performance on these exercises represents the targets for the programme of training. Regardless of whether behavioural objectives or other methods are used to define these targets, it is important that the desired outcomes of training are clear at an early stage, so that programmes can be designed to enable trainees to reach the targets. Of course, in some circumstances, it is legitimate for the objectives of a programme to be relatively general and not expressed in the precise way described above. For example, many experiential learning exercises such as T-groups are conducted within organizations and have quite general aims concerned with the psychological awareness and growth of participants. To attempt to express precise objectives for such experiences would be completely counter to their purpose, because the learning that takes place for each individual is of a highly personal and often emotional nature and each person acquires different things from such experiences.

Types of learning capability

The type of learning that takes place as a result of training and development programmes is quite varied and it is traditional to make distinctions between the development of knowledge, skills and attitudes. Rather confusingly, contemporary US industrial/organizational psychologists use the term KSAs to refer to knowledge, skills and *abilities*. According to this distinction, knowledge is concerned with the recall and understanding of facts and other items of information. Skills may be used with reference to the psychomotor movements involved in practical activities such as operating equipment or machinery, but also incorporate higher-order cognitive or interpersonal processes. Attitudes refer primarily to the emotional or affective feelings and views that a person has, although attitudes also have other components (see Chapter 8). For example, a person might be able to operate a drilling-machine (skill) and might also be aware that certain safety procedures should be observed (knowledge), but feel that observing such procedures was time-wasting and unnecessary (attitude). This very simple distinction between knowledge, skills and attitudes is a useful starting-point for identifying different types of learning but is inadequate in many ways. For example, the distinction between knowledge and skill is not as clear as it might at first seem. At first sight, the job of a car mechanic might seem to be largely skill-based and that of a medical practitioner largely knowledge-based. Consider what happens, however, when the car mechanic is confronted with a car that is making a peculiar noise. The mechanic will make use of various fault-finding strategies in an attempt to establish what is causing the noise. These strategies are based on the application of various rules for finding faults, probably developed from direct experience and training. In much the same way, the medical practitioner will attempt to diagnose the cause of a patient's symptoms. Both of them are exhibiting a form of skill, but the skill in question is not dependent on co-ordinated physical movements, though the mechanic may need these as well; rather, it is an intellectual skill involving the use of rules and analysis to guide behaviour.

The categories of different types of learning developed by Gagné (1977) provide a much more comprehensive description than the knowledge/skills/attitudes distinction. Gagné identifies the following five types of learning, which he calls capabilities.

1. *Basic learning*. Stimulus–response associations and chains. This represents the formation of simple associations between stimuli and responses such as those that occur during classical conditioning (see Chapter 9).

2. *Intellectual skills*. These are divided into the following hierarchy:
   • *discriminations*: being able to make distinctions between stimulus objects or events;
   • *concrete concepts*: the classification of members of a class, by observation, e.g. red, circular;
   • *defined concepts*: classification by definition, e.g. mass, square roots;
   • *rules*: the use of a relation or association to govern action; and
   • *higher-order rules*: the generation of new rules, e.g. by combining existing rules.

3. *Cognitive strategy*. Skills by which internal cognitive processes such as attention and learning are regulated (e.g. learning how to learn or learning general strategies for solving problems).

4. *Verbal information*. An ability to state specific information.

5. *Motor skills*. Organized motor acts.

6. *Attitude*.

The benefit to be gained from identifying learning capabilities involved in a training programme is that it can often provide guidance on the methods or sequences of training that might be most useful. Guidance about training methods and sequence can thus be arrived at by moving from task analysis to learning capabilities to sequence and method of instruction.

Another system for categorizing types of learning has been developed by the Industrial Training Research Unit (1981). Its work has been designed specifically to provide guidance on the type of training method that is appropriate, for the type of learning involved. The learning types involved in the

Industrial Training Research Unit system can be summarized by the word CRAMP:

1. *Comprehension*: knowing why, how and when things happen.
2. *Reflex skills*: skilled physical movement and perceptual capacities.
3. *Attitude*.
4. *Memorization*: committing information to memory.
5. *Procedural*: following a procedure, e.g. operating a petrol-pump.

Once the type of learning has been identified, the CRAMP algorithm (see Fig. 14.3) can be used systematically to identify the training method(s) or the conditions for learning that might be appropriate.

Some relevant research has been conducted to develop methods for assessing the extent to which training content reflects the important knowledge and skill requirements of the job. Ford and Wroten (1984) showed how procedures developed by Lawshe (1975) could be used to assess the correspondence between elements covered in the training course and the importance of these elements in the job. An alternative procedure developed by Goldstein (1986) involves using two independent sets of subject matter experts, one to rate a predetermined set of knowledge, skills and abilities (KSAs) for criticality in the job, the other to rate the degree to which the training emphasizes each KSA. Comparisons between the ratings then provide information about the job–training match.

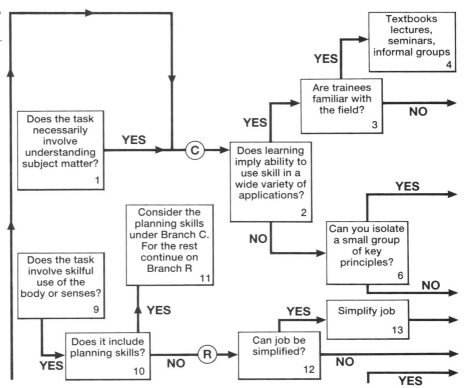

14.3 Part of the CRAMP algorithm for training design (from ITRU, 1981).

Training methods

One of the more frequent problems which arises with training programmes is that the method of instruction to be used is the first decision that is taken. It should be obvious from the previous pages that methods should be chosen or developed as a consequence of the desired targets of training and not the other way round. An enormous range of possible training methods is available. The ITRU CRAMP booklet, for example, provides information on over 30 methods. Gagné's ideas, the CRAMP algorithm and other ideas are helpful but there is no clear, scientific procedure for making the step from tasks to training method and the choice of method is eventually a partly subjective decision.

To discuss training methods as if they were separate and clearly defined techniques is inappropriate, because even the most widely used and well-known methods such as lectures, case studies, demonstration and practice show wide variation in use depending on factors such as instructors and trainees involved and the task being learned. Methods are adapted and combined in an almost infinite variety of ways. The use of closed-circuit television (CCTV) as a training method provides a good illustration. CCTV is often used to provide trainees with feedback on their own behaviour so that, with the aid of a trainer, they can observe their own behaviour and assess their strengths and weaknesses. Recently, however, a number of researchers using social learning theory (Bandura, 1986) as a basis have shown that such training might be carried out more effectively by using films or CCTV to present model behaviour that the trainees should attempt to emulate (Decker and Nathan, 1985). Thus, although both approaches use CCTV as "the method", because of developments in underlying ideas about how learning takes place the two approaches are quite different. From the training and development viewpoint, an understanding of the general process involved in learning and some grasp of the theoretical background is likely to provide a much more useful framework than detailed examination of specific methods.

One major problem in providing an overview of the effectiveness of different training methods is that much of the literature on training is theoretical rather than based on sound concepts, and descriptive rather than evaluative. Much of this literature is contained in various practitioner-orientated magazines and books. The scientific literature of work psychology does not contain such an extensive array of material but, in general, the material is more rigorous and analytical. Within this narrower range of literature, there are relatively small numbers of studies which provide a thorough evaluation of the effectiveness of a training method or methods. Before considering the research literature on the evaluation of different training methods and techniques, this chapter will provide coverage of the methods and concepts involved in the evaluation process itself.

Training evaluation

It has already been emphasized that the development of successful programmes of training and development is a difficult and uncertain process and frequently programmes will need to be modified or redesigned as a result of experience. Techniques for the validation and evaluation of training provide a means of examining the success of programmes and identifying areas where change is needed. Examining the validity of a training programme involves assessing the extent to which trainees have reached the objectives of the training and can be established properly only by examining trainees' capabilities after training. Goldstein (1978) has identified different types of validity that training programmes might show. For example, if trainees reach the objectives at the end of the course assessment, this demonstrates internal or training validity. But external or performance validity is achieved only when it can be demonstrated that trainees' work performance is up to the desired standard.

The evaluation of training is usually taken to be a much broader concept than validation, dealing with the overall benefits of a training programme (often including validity). Warr *et al.* (1970) identified four major types of evaluation data: context, input, reaction and outcome (CIRO).

Reaction evaluation involves gaining and using information about trainees' reactions. Many training designers collect this sort of information, sometimes without asking for it! It is undoubtedly useful to collect trainees' comments, but unfortunately in many cases this is the only information that is collected (see, e.g., Cantalanello and Kirkpatrick, 1968).

Outcome evaluation involves examining the validity of the training by collecting information about the extent to which learning objectives have been met (i.e. validity) and/or the amount of change that has occurred, usually with the aid of pre- and post-course measures. Most training is designed to bring about changes in the way people behave at work, and ideally outcome data should be collected to examine trainees' performance not only at the end of training (i.e. internal validity) but back in the work situation (external validity). In many circumstances, the learning that takes place during a course does not transfer satisfactorily to the work situation. An external validity study using appropriate criteria to measure work behaviour is the only way to check whether or not this is occurring. Unfortunately, such studies are not conducted as a matter of routine. A study by Campbell *et al.* (1970) showed that of a total of 73 management training programmes studied, only 21 made use of external criteria.

As well as deciding whether a training course is meeting its objectives or not, it is important to examine the relevance and value of the objectives even if they are being met. Warr *et al.* (1970) describe this as context evaluation. It provides an answer to the question, in this context (organization) what training should we be doing?

Finally, input evaluation involves obtaining and using information about possible training resources so that a choice can be made between alternative "inputs" (methods, media, training personnel, etc.) that might be used.

Probably the most popular framework for training evaluation studies is that of Kirkpatrick (1967), which involves four main levels of data collection: reaction, learning, behaviour and results.

Collecting reaction data represents the minimal level of evaluation for a training programme. As with Warr *et al.*'s (1970) CIRO framework, reaction data in Kirkpatrick's (1967) scheme are concerned with trainees' views of the training. Obviously, trainees' views are valuable but may easily give a misleading impression of the value of a training programme. Trainees' views inevitably provide an incomplete view of training effectiveness. Trainees may, for example, be very enthusiastic about a training programme because it was fun and an interesting break from routine. Equally, they may give poor reports on training during which they had to work extremely hard or which involved an unpopular instructor. None of these items of feedback tells us whether the training was actually effective in promoting new learning or not.

The collection of learning data represents a considerable improvement over the use of reaction data only. Learning criteria are concerned with whether or not the trainees' show evidence that they have attained the immediate learning objectives of the programme. To examine this question may, for example, involve administering pre- and post-programme written tests to check participants' understanding of the material covered during training. Learning results are usually collected immediately after training is over. Like reaction data, learning data are useful but incomplete. Trainees may react well to material and understand it perfectly well but may not behave effectively when they return to work. This problem of the transfer of learning from the training course to the workplace is the focus of the next level of evaluation, i.e. behaviour. Trainees may perform well at the end of training but fail to transfer their learning to the workplace for a variety of reasons, including a fear of looking foolish (in the eyes of their established work colleagues who may not have been exposed to the training) or a belief that the old methods are more effective. Behaviour evaluation involves assessing the impact of the training on behaviour. Trainees' behaviour may be examined in a variety of ways but the main point of concern, for evaluation purposes, is to gain a clear indication of trainees' post-training behaviour. This, after all, is the reason for training in the first place. If trainees' behaviour does not change, then positive views about the training (reaction) and abundant new knowledge (learning) will count for nothing. The methods and procedures used to examine behaviour are similar to the methods described for examining job performance in Chapter 6, which is concerned with personnel selection.

Finally, results level evaluation involves assessing the extent to which the training has had an impact on the organization's effectiveness. In other words, the focus here is on the organizational needs identified during the initial training needs assessment. Results criteria, although conceptually clear, are extremely difficult to assess in a controlled fashion, and it is often more or less impossible to be certain whether or not changes in organizational effectiveness have been brought about by the effect of training, or whether some other factors may also be partly or entirely responsible. Sales figures, for example, may be improved as a consequence of improved sales training or by events in the external economic situation. Productivity can be improved by operator training, better equipment, improved industrial relations, social factors on the factory floor, etc.

Threats to accurate evaluations

The problem of whether or not training is actually responsible for observed changes is one that makes the effective evaluation of training a technically complex and extremely time-consuming endeavour. The most thorough consideration of experimental designs that can be used by evaluators to examine the effectiveness of training programmes has been presented by Campbell and Stanley (1963) and Cook and Campbell (1979). Fundamentally, the goal of training evaluation is to provide the training designer with information about effectiveness that can be *unambiguously* interpreted and is *relevant* to the question of training effectiveness. To illustrate the problems involved in conducting good evaluation work, we will consider some of the common difficulties that may arise. These may be divided broadly into two categories: internal and external. These difficulties are usually referred to as internal or external threats to *validity*, because they affect (or threaten to affect) the validity of conclusions that can be drawn from the evaluation.

Threats to internal validity are concerned with the factors or problems that can cause the appearance that a training programme has been responsible for changes in learning, behaviour or results, when in fact the changes were caused by some other factors. For example, a group of new entrants to an organization may be given a pre-training test of knowledge of the organization's rules and procedures. After a period of induction training (1 hour per day for their first week), they may be tested again. If their test scores have improved, does this mean that the induction training was responsible? Of course not, the improved knowledge could have been gained in the 6 or 7 hours per day spent in the organization outside the induction training course. An obvious solution to this problem is to administer the tests immediately before and after training. Would any differences now be attributable to the training? It seems more likely now but, for example, there is the possibility that trainees might benefit from the formal training only when they have spent some of the previous day doing their normal duties in the organization. This could be important, for example, if for any reason the organization wanted to run the induction training in one block all at once, instead of spreading it over the first week. The question here is partly one of internal validity: did the training bring about the change? It is also partly a question of external validity: will the programme be effective for different trainees in different circumstances? Questions of external validity are to do with the extent to which the training will generalize to subsequent groups of trainees and settings.

Evaluation designs

In an attempt to control various threats to the validity of training evaluation, investigators will often make use of experimental designs. Most training evaluation has to be conducted within real organizational settings and under these circumstances it is often not possible to obtain the conditions necessary for perfect experimental designs. In such circumstances, it is common for what Campbell and Stanley (1963) have called quasi-experimental designs to be utilized. Campbell and Stanley (1963) also describe what they term pre-experimental designs. Such designs are unfortunately commonplace in the training world, although they produce results with so many threats to validity that they are uninterpretable and not capable of providing clear findings about training effectiveness (see Wexley, 1984, pp. 538–539). Two of the most well known pre-experimental designs are shown in Fig. 14.4, together with more complex designs which overcome *some* of the problems inherent in the pre-experimental designs.

Clearly, one-group, post-test-only designs control for none of the possible threats to internal or external validity and it is quite impossible to interpret the data. It is impossible to tell whether scores are better after training than before, let alone whether training or some other factor is responsible for any changes. The one-group, pre- and post-measure design goes some way towards resolving the problems by making it possible to measure change. Nevertheless, it is not possible with this design to assess whether training may have caused any difference. This may only be done if there is also an untrained control group, who are similar to the trained group and whose performance has also been measured at the appropriate times. To conduct a true experiment, trainees should be assigned to the experimental and control groups on a random basis, because systematic differences between groups before the experiment could bias the results. Often this degree of control is impossible in field research and the kind of quasi-experimental design shown in the non-equivalent control group example of Fig. 14.4 is the best that can be done. Typically, pre-existing groups in the organization, such as all the members of a particular job group, region or unit form the groups. This is obviously administratively much more convenient than random assignment and does control for some of the main threats to validity. Even the pre- and post-measure control group design is subject to some threats to validity and for totally unambiguous results more complex designs are needed (see Campbell and Stanley, 1963).

One group, post-measure only

$$X \Longrightarrow M_2$$

One group, pre-measure/post-measure

$$M_1 \Longrightarrow X \Longrightarrow M_2$$

14.4 Pre-experimental, experimental and quasi-experimental designs for training evaluation studies. *Key:* M_1 = pre-measure (administered prior to training); M_2 = post-measure (administered after training); X =training programme; R = random assignment of people to groups.

Pre-measure/post-measure control group

$$R \Longrightarrow M_1 \Longrightarrow X \Longrightarrow M_2$$
$$R \Longrightarrow M_1 \Longrightarrow M_2$$

Non-equivalent control group

$$M_1 \Longrightarrow X \Longrightarrow M_2$$
$$M_1 \Longrightarrow M_2$$

Case study 14.1   Assessing the effectiveness of training

The Midlands and Provincial Bank was going through a difficult period. Changes in the status and aims of many financial services organizations, such as building societies, meant that competition for business was becoming tougher. Like many banks, Midland and Provincial was a fairly traditional organization and most of its longer-serving employees had spent their careers in an industry where competition was restrained and relationships with customers were of less significance than financial acumen. In recent years, this had all changed and attracting and holding customers was of increasing importance. Interpersonal skills, customer care programmes and sales and marketing know-how were crucial qualities for the bank's employees to develop.

The bank's senior management team decided that the only way forward was to invest heavily in training in order to develop the required characteristics in their staff. Several commercial training consultancies were invited to discuss the situation with the board and three were invited to tender for the job of retraining the bank's personnel. The board of the bank were impressed with all of the proposals and found it very difficult to choose between the two consultants who submitted the best tenders.

Eventually, the decision was delegated to a small working group involving the personnel director, the controller of training and the head of human resources. The working group invited each consultant to prepare and run one pilot training course for branch managers in two different regions of the country. The personnel director visited both courses and at the end of the course conducted private (i.e. without the consultants) interviews with the course participants. He felt that the branch managers trained by one of the consultants had gained much more from the course and eventually the steering group awarded the contract to this consultancy.

Suggested exercise

Decide whether or not you feel that the steering group adopted a suitable procedure for choosing between the consultants. Explain why. Suggest ways in which the choice could have been made more effectively.

Evaluation research findings

The procedures for training evaluation described above are complex and difficult to administer and it is therefore not surprising that there are so few thorough evaluation studies available; some very good examples do however exist, and may serve as models for future research (see, e.g., Latham and Saari, 1979).

Training evaluation research has tended to concentrate on a limited set of training procedures which have been of theoretical importance or felt to have significant promise. The procedures in this category include Fiedler's Leader Match Training (Fiedler, 1967), a self-instructional programmed text (Fiedler *et al.*, 1976). Rater learning (i.e. training people to improve their ability to make accurate ratings of others) has also attracted quite a lot of attention, presumably because of the ubiquitous use of ratings in many areas of work psychology.

Behaviour-modelling

One approach to training which has attracted a great deal of attention in recent years, is behaviour-modelling training. Behaviour-modelling training is based on the theoretical ideas of social learning theory (SLT: Bandura, 1977), more recently referred to as social cognitive theory (SCT: Bandura, 1986 – see Chapter 9 of this volume). Behaviour-modelling may be more promising than other training "fads" because of its strong theoretical base. Ideas from SCT concerning how the vicarious learning process takes place form the basis for behaviour-modelling training. Vicarious learning is one of the major ways in which SCT differs from classical ideas of operant conditioning and allows for the fact that, in addition to learning from direct experience, people may learn from observing the behaviour of others (i.e. second-hand or vicariously). In other words, trainees may learn new ways of behaving from observing the behaviour of models, hence the term behaviour-modelling training.

Early work in behaviour-modelling training was conducted in clinical settings (e.g. treating people with phobias). In 1974, Goldstein and Sorcher published a book describing their procedures for applying SLT and developing industrial behaviour-modelling programmes. Essentially, behaviour-modelling training involves using Bandura's ideas about the component processes of vicarious learning as the basis for a training sequence. According to Bandura (1977), the main components of vicarious learning are (1) attention (to a model), (2) retention and mental organization of the model's behaviour, (3) motor reproduction of the model's behaviour and (4) motivation processes which serve to reinforce and strengthen the modelled behaviour. More succinctly, (1) notice the model, (2) remember the behaviour, (3) try it out and (4) the trainee needs to have some reason to adopt the model's behaviour (see Table 14.1).

Early research on behaviour-modelling training (BMT) in industry laid the foundations for using the approach but did not provide the systematic control and experimental rigour necessary to evaluate the effectiveness of the technique.

Table 14.1 Behaviour-modelling theory and practice

Vicarious learning process	Behaviour-modelling practice
Attention	Use senior figures in organization to indicate salient learning points and introduce material
Retention	Show trainees a realistic but simple version of a model displaying an example of desirable behaviour. Support this with specific learning points
Motoric reproduction	Provide trainees with an opportunity to practice and develop mastery of the material (usually involves role-play of realistic work experiences)
Motivation	Ensure that trainees receive or anticipate positive reinforcement contingent on target behaviours

Some classic, well-designed studies have subsequently examined the over-all effectiveness (using all four of Kirkpatrick's levels) of BMT in industrial settings (e.g. Latham and Saari, 1979). More recent work (Russell *et al.*, 1984) suggests that factors concerned with the post-training work environment are crucial to the effectiveness of BMT. Several studies have examined the effectiveness of particular aspects of BMT. Most research has focused on retention processes and the use of various techniques designed to aid retention (e.g. Decker, 1982; Hogan *et al.*, 1986). Research on other features of the vicarious learning process, e.g. motor reproduction or motivation, is less extensive. Taken overall, BMT has a record of reasonable success. It is clear that trainees are enthusiastic about the approach and can learn from it; nevertheless, the extent to which BMT can cause real changes in behaviour at work is in need of further confirmation.

Decker and Nathan (1985) have provided a review and summary of much of the industrial behaviour-modelling work.

The uncertain conclusions concerning the effectiveness of BMT are reflected in many other areas of research into training effectiveness. Burke and Day (1986) conducted a quantitative analysis of 70 managerial training studies involving a variety of content areas and instructional techniques. In general, the results showed that management training techniques were effective but the authors warn that further well-designed research is essential before more conclusive statements can be made.

Summary

Constant social and technological change provides the context for organizational life. This, coupled with individual growth and career development, means that training has a key role in many organizations. The adequate analysis of training needs (at organization, task and personal levels) provides the basis for training activities. Although the analysis of needs, together with a clear statement of training aims and objectives, is important, there is still a certain degree of judgement involved in choosing appropriate training methods. This essential subjectivity can be checked and evaluated by the application of systematic procedures for evaluating the effectiveness of training. Evaluation at reaction, learning, behaviour and results levels provides a way of determining the overall value of training and assessing necessary improvements. In general, research has shown that training is an effective way of bringing about behaviour change, although there are often problems in ensuring that the potential for change provided by training activities actually transfers to the work setting.

Case study 14.2   Training and organizational change

Premier TV had undergone enormous changes in the last few years. The most important of these concerned the new agreement that had been reached between management and unions. This provided a much more flexible rostering system so that unit managers could use people's time more effectively. The previous system had involved fixed rosters and set numbers of personnel for specific tasks. All this was now history, and managers (in consultation with programme makers) could decide who should work on which job and how many people were needed. However, the new agreement had been achieved at a cost and it was only after severe management pressure, which included threats of compulsory redundancy, that the unions agreed to the new agreement. This had left smouldering bad feeling between many employees and the company's senior managers.

Other changes in the organization structure of the company had also taken place. Financial controls on what was spent to make programmes were now much tighter and each department or unit was accounted for as a separate cost centre and was expected to operate at a profit by selling its services to other units within Premier TV or to outside companies.

During the period of change, the human resources staff at Premier had had little opportunity to assess training needs or to organize training events. Therefore, apart from induction training and some specialist technical training, nothing had taken place for the last 5 years. Kathy Lamb, the Human Resources Manager, was well aware that this could not continue and resolved to take some positive action.

Suggested exercise

Decide what Kathy Lamb should do. Explain why.

References

Annett, J., Duncan, K. D., Stammers, R. B. and Gray, M. J. (1971). *Task Analysis.* Training Information Paper No. 6. London: HMSO.

Bandura, A. (1977). *Social Learning Theory.* Englewood Cliffs, N.J.: Prentice-Hall.

Bandura, A. (1986). *Social Foundations of Thought and Action: A Social Cognitive Theory.* Englewood Cliffs, N.J.: Prentice-Hall.

Boydell, T. (1973). *The Identification of Training Needs.* London: British Association of Commercial and Industrial Education.

Burke, M. J. and Day, R. (1986). A cumulative study of the effectiveness of managerial training. *Journal of Applied Psychology, 71,* 232–245.

Campbell, D. T. and Stanley, J. C. (1963). *Experimental and Quasi-experimental Designs for Research.* Chicago, Ill.: Rand McNally.

Campbell, J. P., Dunette, M. D., Lawler, E. E. and Weick, K. E. (1970). *Managerial Behavior, Performance and Effectiveness.* New York: McGraw-Hill.

Cantalanello, R. F. and Kirkpatrick, D. L. (1968). Evaluating training programmes – the state of the art. *Training and Development Journal,* May, p. 9.

Cook, T. D. and Campbell, D. T. (1979). *Quasi-experimentation: Design and Analysis Issues for Field Settings.* Chicago, Ill.: Rand McNally.

Davies, I. K. (1972). *The Management of Learning.* London: McGraw-Hill.

Decker, P. J. (1982). The enhancement of behavior modeling training of supervisory skills by the inclusion of retention processes. *Personnel Psychology, 35,* 323–332.

Decker, P. J. and Nathan, B. R. (1985). *Behavior Modeling Training.* New York: Praeger.

Duncan, K. D. (1972). Strategies for analysis of the task. In T. Hartley (Ed.), *Strategies for Programmed Instruction: An Educational Technology*. London: Butterworth.

Fiedler, F. (1967). *A Theory of Leadership Effectiveness*. New York: McGraw-Hill.

Fiedler, F., Chemers, M. M. and Mahar, L. (1976). *Improving Leadership Effectiveness: The Leader Match Concept*. New York: John Wiley.

Ford, J. K. and Wroten, S. P. (1984). Introducing new methods for conducting training evaluation and for linking training evaluation to program redesign. *Personnel Psychology, 37*, 651–666.

Gagné, R. M. (1977). *The Conditions of Learning*, 3rd edn. New York: Rinehart and Winston.

Goldstein, A. P. and Sorcher, M. (1974). *Changing Supervisory Behavior*. New York: Pergamon Press.

Goldstein, I. L. (1978). The pursuit of validity in the evaluation of training programs. *Human Factors, 20*, 131–144.

Goldstein, I. L. (1986). *Training in Organizations: Needs Assessment, Development and Evaluation*. Monterey, Calif.: Brooks/Cole.

Goldstein, I. L. and Gessner, M. J. (1988). Training and development in work organizations. In C. L. Cooper and I. T. Robertson (Eds), *International Review of Industrial and Organizational Psychology, 1988*. Chichester: John Wiley.

Hogan, P. M., Hakel, M. D. and Decker, P. J. (1986). Effects of trainee-generated versus trainer-provided rule codes on generalization in behavior-modeling training. *Journal of Applied Psychology, 71*, 469–473.

Industrial Training Research Unit (1981). *CRAMP: A Guide to Training Decisions. A User's Manual*, revised edn. Cambridge: ITRU.

Kirkpatrick, D. L. (1967). Evaluation of training. In R. L. Craig and L.R. Bittel (Eds), *Training and Development Handbook*. New York: McGraw-Hill.

Latham, G. P. (1988). Human resource training and development. *Annual Review of Psychology, 39*, 545–582.

Latham, G. P. and Saari, L. M. (1979). Application of social learning theory to training supervisors through behavioral modeling. *Journal of Applied Psychology, 64*, 239–246.

Lawshe, C. H. (1975). A quantitative approach to content validity. *Personnel Psychology, 28*, 563–575.

McCormick, E. J., Jeanneret, P. and Meacham, R. C. (1972). A study of job characteristics and job dimensions as based on the position analysis questionnaires. *Journal of Applied Psychology, 36*, 347–368.

McEnery, J. and McEnery, J. M. (1987). Self-rating in management training needs assessment: A neglected opportunity. *Journal of Occupational Psychology, 60*, 49–60.

McGhee, W. and Thayer, P. W. (1961). *Training in Business and Industry*. New York: John Wiley.

Mager, R. F. (1962). *Preparing Objectives for Instruction*. Belmont, Calif.: Fearon.

Russell, J. S., Wexley, K. E. and Hunter, J. E. (1984). Questioning the effectiveness of behavior modeling training in an industrial setting. *Personnel Psychology, 37*, 465–481.

Seymour, W. D. (1966). *Industrial Skills*. London: Pitman.

Shepherd, A. (1976). An improved tabular format for task analysis. *Journal of Occupational Psychology, 47*, 93–104.

Staley, C. C. and Shockley-Zalabak, P. (1986). Communication proficiency and future training needs of the female professionals: Self assessment vs. supervisors' evaluations. *Human Relations, 39*, 891–902.

Stammers, R. and Patrick, J. (1975). *The Psychology of Training*. London: Methuen.

Warr, P. B., Bird, M. W. and Rackham, N. (1970). *The Evaluation of Management Training*. London: Gower Press.

Wexley, K. N. (1984). Personnel training. *Annual Review of Psychology*, *35*, 519–551.

Career choice and development

Introduction

Individuals and organizations are paying increasing attention to planning and managing careers. Ideas and perspectives from psychology play a central part. In this chapter, we examine definitions of career, approaches to career choice and career development and some of the practical applications arising from them. We also cover starting work and subsequent work-role transitions, and career planning and management within work organizations. The chapter aims to help the reader understand career theory and practice, and to apply key concepts to their own careers and also the careers of other people.

The foundations of career theory

Work psychologists have put forward many competing definitions of career. For our purposes, we can consider a career as "Any sequence of attitudes and behaviours associated with work-related experiences and activities over the span of the person's life" (Hall, 1986). Several points arise from this definition:

1. A career concerns the *pattern* of attitudes and behaviours over potentially long periods of time, e.g. their change and stability.

2. The inclusion of *attitudes* and *experiences* emphasizes that careers are subjective as well as objective. Hence, for example, a person's definition of success in their own career may differ from an "objective" assessment of success.

3. Careers are not confined to professional and managerial occupations, nor to "conventional" career paths involving promotion within a single occupation.

Sonnenfeld and Kotter (1982) have identified a series of theoretical perspectives that have been applied to careers. In rough historical order, starting with the oldest, these are as follows:

1. *Social class.* From this sociological perspective, careers are governed by a person's position in the social structure. This position determines the

opportunities that are made available to the person. More subtly, it also determines the socialization to which the growing person is exposed, so that they come to view their career in ways consistent with their social class origins.

2. *Static personality differences.* This approach assumes that people's personalities are relatively stable over time, and that people differ one from another. Careers are determined by personality: people choose (or should choose) careers which match their personality. The emphasis is therefore on theories and assessment devices which facilitate the matching process.

3. *Career stages.* From this perspective, the career can be divided into distinct phases or stages. The issues and concerns of most importance to a person are said to vary systematically with stage. The aim is therefore to identify the stages and the personal concerns associated with each.

4. *Life-cycle.* In many respects, this is an extension of the career stages approach. It acknowledges the importance of biological and cultural factors outside the work setting as influences on a person's career. The notion of stages remains, but is used more flexibly and is not confined to career. The aim is to define key life roles and to identify their interplay over time.

Sonnenfeld and Kotter (1982) point out that each perspective offers something useful in careers, and that none has been shown to be entirely wrong. For example, the assertion of the social class approach that job opportunities partly depend on position in the social structure cannot be denied (Roberts, 1981). However, most psychologists maintain that an individual's self-concept plays an important part in the careers of people in all social classes (Daws, 1981; Kidd, 1982). The argument then focuses on whether self-concepts are simply a consequence of social class, and whether by concentrating on them psychologists are inadvertently reinforcing the social status quo.

Many writers believe that the careers field is fragmented and has serious weaknesses (Collin and Young, 1986; Schein, 1986; Driver, 1988). They argue that people working from different perspectives scarcely take any notice of each other's work. As Schein (1986) has emphasized, this is perhaps appropriate in the early stages of development, but not after that. He also stressed the need for an accurate *description* of careers, especially concerning how they are viewed within work organizations. Differences between organizations would, he said, mean that any single perspective on careers could not have universal applicability.

On a similar theme, Collin and Young (1986) argued that people's accounts of their careers, and also the social environment in which they unfolded, needed more analysis. This latter point was acknowledged by Sonnenfeld and Kotter (1982). Further problems with existing career theory concern its concentration on white, Western, middle-class males. However, regarding gender, knowledge is now accumulating concerning women's careers (e.g. see *Applied Psychology: An International Review*, April 1988; and Gutek and Larwood, 1987).

Although the distinction is to some extent artificial, work on careers can be divided between career choice and career development. The former concerns the nature and process of choice by (usually) young people, while the latter involves subsequent changes and adjustment. The difference is reflected in the distinction between on the one hand the social class and static personality differences approaches (career choice), and on the other career stage and life-cycle approaches (career development). Its partial artificiality is due to the fact that choices made in early adulthood nowadays often become obsolete, and have to be re-made in the light of subsequent developments. It should also be noted that despite the broad definition of career given earlier, when psychologists speak of career choice they usually mean choice of a particular occupation or family of occupations.

Career choice

Holland's theory

John Holland (1985) has developed over many years an influential theory of career choice. In the course of his earlier work as a careers counsellor in the USA, he thought he could discern six pure types of vocational personality. He also felt he could see the roots of these types in traditional personality theory. Clearly, then, Holland's theory belongs to the static personality differences tradition identified by Sonnenfeld and Kotter. Throughout the 1960s, he developed his concepts and measures of them. Subsequent work has sought to validate these, and to test Holland's hypotheses about career choice (see below). Very briefly, Holland's six personality types are:

1. *Realistic.* Outdoor-type. Tend to like, and be good at, activities requiring physical strength and/or co-ordination. Not keen on socializing.

2. *Investigative.* Interested in concepts and logic. Tend to enjoy, and be good at, abstract thought. Often interested in the physical sciences.

3. *Artistic.* Tend to use their imagination a lot. Like to express their feelings and ideas. Dislike rules and regulations; enjoy music, drama, art.

4. *Social.* Enjoy the company of other people, especially in affiliative (i.e. helping, friendly) relationships. Tend to be warm and caring.

5. *Enterprising.* Also enjoy the company of other people, but mainly to dominate or persuade rather than help them. Enjoy action rather than thought.

6. *Conventional.* Like rules and regulations, structure and order. Usually well-organized, not very imaginative.

Holland proposed that the types can be arranged in a hexagon in the order described above to express their similarity to each other (see Fig. 15.1). Each type is placed at a corner of the hexagon. Types on opposite corners of the hexagon (i.e. three corners apart) are in many senses opposites. Types on adjacent corners (e.g. realistic and conventional) are quite similar. No single type exactly matches any individual, but nevertheless some types are more similar than others to any given person. In fact, Holland suggests that people are most

15.1 Holland's six types
of vocational personality.

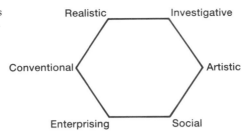

usefully described in terms of three types that resemble them most, in descending order of similarity. Hence, for example, for an ISE person, the investigative type comes closest to describing them, the social type comes next and enterprising third.

Holland proposed that occupations can also be described in terms of the six types. He has argued that any environment exerts its influence through the people in it. Hence occupations are described in terms of the people in them, using the three most prevalent types in descending order. In the USA, Holland's classification of occupations has been widely applied in, for example, the *Dictionary of Occupational Titles* (US Department of Labor, 1977).

Holland's fundamental hypothesis is that people will be most satisfied, and most successful, in occupations which are congruent with (i.e. match) their personality. Spokane (1985) and Holland (1985) have reviewed the large volume of research on this and other aspects of Holland's theory. Several conclusions can be drawn:

1. Holland's vocational personality types are rooted in basic personality dimensions, as indeed they should be. Also, the hexagonal arrangement, while not a perfect representation of the relative similarities of the types, is nevertheless a good approximation.

2. There is some evidence that congruence is correlated with satisfaction and success. However, this evidence is often cross-sectional, so we cannot be sure that congruence *leads* to satisfaction and success. Also, using three types in establishing codes may be unnecessary. One or two may well suffice.

3. Some research has examined the congruence between a person and their career *choice*, rather than the person and their actual career or educational environment. A choice is not an environment, and is therefore an inappropriate basis for assessing congruence.

4. Much research has relied entirely on pencil-and-paper measures rather than behavioural ones. Thus, people often complete one questionnaire about their personality, another about their occupational or educational preferences and yet another about, for example, their satisfaction. Behavioural outcomes like absence, rate of promotion and performance should be examined more often.

Holland's approach to personality assessment is interesting. He has developed the *Self-directed Search* (Holland, 1979), which asks the respondent about their preferred activities, their reactions to occupational titles, their abilities, competences and even daydreams. People can score their own SDS, establish their three-letter code, and then examine an "Occupations Finder" to check which occupations might be appropriate for them. They are encouraged to try various permutations of their three-letter code, especially if their three highest scores are of similar magnitude. All this is unusual in a number of respects. First, it is rare for questions about both abilities and interests to be included in a vocational guidance instrument. Secondly, the SDS is deliberately transparent – people can see what it is getting at (Holland and Rayman, 1986). Thirdly, it is rare for psychologists to allow the people they assess to score and interpret their own data. Holland feels that most people simply need reassurance that their career ideas are appropriate, and that the SDS generally provides this much more quickly and cheaply than careers counselling.

More generally, there are many tests of occupational interests on the market – some paper and pencil, others computerized. Few have such a strong theoretical and empirical basis as Holland's. One long-established test, the *Strong–Campbell Interest Inventory* (Hansen, 1985), has, however, been revised to reflect the Holland types, and data from it have contributed to the classification of occupations in Holland's terms.

Making career decisions

Theories such as Holland's describe the *content* of actual and ideal decisions, but not the *process*. How can a person make an effective career decision? A variety of factors are relevant.

Self-awareness

First, a person needs to have an accurate appraisal of his or her own strengths and weaknesses, values, likes and dislikes. Numerous exercises and techniques are available for this, some in published books (e.g. Ball, 1989; London and Stumpf, 1982, ch. 3) and others homegrown in, for example, college careers advisory services. Most are designed to help a person to examine systematically their experiences in the work setting and outside it, in order to arrive at the most accurate and complete self-assessment that their past experience allows. The importance of examining emotions as well as thoughts and negative experiences as well as positive ones, is usually stressed. Theoretical work (e.g. Mabe and West, 1982; Farh and Dobbins, 1989) has shown that self-assessments often fail to agree with assessments by objective tests or by other people. Mabe and West (1982) did, however, find that past experience of self-assessment and comparing oneself with other people contributed to accuracy. All this assumes, of course, that there is one and only one concept of self possessed by each person – an assumption that has been challenged on various grounds (Schein, 1971a; Sampson, 1989).

Knowledge of occupations

Again, there are many workbooks which give guidance on how to find out about occupations (e.g. London and Stumpf, 1982, ch. 2; Greenhaus, 1987, ch. 3).

Apart from reading published information, methods include talking to a person in that occupation, and "shadowing" such a person for a period of time in order to see what they actually do. Emphasis is placed on avoiding stereotypes of occupations, and ensuring that one pays attention not only to positions one might ultimately occupy in an occupation, but also to those one will have to fill *en route*.

Putting self-knowledge and occupational knowledge together

Often, this is surprisingly difficult (Yost and Corbishley, 1987, ch. 5), because the two are rarely defined in the same terms. However, it is clearly crucial to map one onto the other. In doing so, it is important to have information about both which is transferable, i.e. meaningful beyond the context in which it was gathered.

Readiness for effective career decision making

Some questionnaire measures have been developed to assess this. One is called the Career Exploration Survey (CES: Stumpf *et al.*, 1983). This is designed principally for students and other young people, and examines the extent to which they have engaged in various exploratory activities. Other workers have come up with measures of what they call *career maturity*. These are derived from developmental (career stage, life-cycle) approaches to careers, as the term "maturity" suggests. For example, Donald Super's *Career Development Inventory* assesses five constructs:

- extent of career planning;
- use and evaluation of resources in exploration;
- knowledge and use of decision-making principles;
- knowledge of career development principles; and
- information about the world of work (including preferred occupation).

The first two are *attitudinal*, i.e. they reflect the young person's approach. The latter three are *cognitive*, i.e. they concern the young person's knowledge and/or ability. In fact, there is some debate about whether career maturity is a viable concept, and about whether career maturity measures have sufficient reliability and validity (Crites *et al.*, 1985; Westbrook, 1985). Suspicions remain that career maturity may largely boil down to intelligence, and that it has middle-class bias (Kidd, 1981). However, Super (1985) has provided some evidence that career maturity among American males aged 14 or 15 predicts career progression and satisfaction 10 years later.

Decision-making styles

Much relevant work on decision making is described in Chapter 12. Specifically regarding *career* decision making, Phillips *et al.* (1984) have identified three styles: *rational*, where advantages and disadvantages of various options are considered logically and systematically; *intuitive*, where various options are considered and the decision is made on "gut feeling"; and *dependent*, where the person essentially denies responsibility for decision making and waits for other people or circumstances to dictate what they should do. Not surprisingly, it seems that the dependent style is least successful. The other two are about equally successful when aggregated across large numbers of individuals, though one or the other may suit any particular person best.

Self-esteem and self-efficacy

Some evidence has suggested that people with high *self-esteem* make better career decisions than those with low self-esteem (e.g. Korman, 1966). Debate has centred on why this might be (Dipboye, 1977). Korman suggested that people with low self-esteem are motivated to fail so that they can maintain a consistent picture of themselves as useless. However, the research data suggest a less extreme explanation – people with high self-esteem are more confident about putting the most valued aspects of self to the test. Although this risks painful failure, it also permits a fulfilling career. *Self-efficacy* refers to a person's belief that they can accomplish certain tasks. Seminal work by Betz and Hackett (1981) found that women feel less self-efficacy for male-dominated careers than for female-dominated ones, whereas men felt equal (and quite high) self-efficacy across the two types of career. Betz and Hackett argued that women were therefore unlikely to choose male-dominated careers, though Clement (1987) subsequently found that women's lower self-efficacy did not in fact deter them from considering traditionally male careers. Also, it seems that there may be little or no difference between the sexes in self-efficacy for the actual task of career decision making (Taylor and Betz, 1983).

Case study 15.1   Your own career decision making

1. How clear are you about your abilities and interests? How specific can you be about this? For example, it is not much good simply saying you like being with people. In what situations, and for what purposes, do you like being with people? If you are not clear, you might like to reflect further on your past experiences, or seek new ones to find out more about yourself.

2. How much do you know about different occupations? How clear are you about what people in particular occupations actually do, and the conditions (hours, pay, environment) in which they work? If you are not clear, you might like to read more about certain occupations, and/or ask people working in them to tell you about what they do.

3. What is your typical decision-making style – rational, intuitive or dependent? How successful have your decisions been in the past? If you tend to make decisions in a dependent manner, you might try to develop one of the other styles, perhaps by practising with small decisions.

Career development

Career and life stages

Many social scientists have sought to map out human development in adulthood (Sugarman, 1986). They have often identified age-linked stages of development, each with its own specific concerns and tasks for the person. For example, Erikson (1963), working originally from a psychoanalytic perspective, identified four stages of adult life, each with its own task that had to be satisfactorily resolved before the person could move on to the next stage:

1. *Adolescence*: The key task is achieving a sense of identity. The dangers are either remaining unclear about one's self-concept, or, at the opposite extreme, developing a rigid, inflexible sense of self. Typical age: 15–24.

2. *Young adulthood*: The key task is to develop intimacy and involvement with, for example, another person, an organization or a cause. The dangers are isolation on the one hand, and losing one's individuality on the other. Typical age: 25–34.

3. *Adulthood*: The key task is to accomplish something of lasting value: preferably something that will remain after the person has gone. The main danger is achieving nothing lasting. Typical age: 35–64.

4. *Maturity*: The key task here is to feel satisfied with one's life, choices and actions. The main danger is having too many regrets about things it is too late to rectify. Typical age: 65+.

Donald Super (1957) identified four career stages similar but not identical to Erikson's life stages:

1. *Exploration*: of both self and world of work in order to clarify the self-concept and identify occupations which fit it. Typical age: 15–24.

2. *Establishment*: perhaps after one or two false starts, the person finds a career field which suits them, and makes efforts to prove their worth in it. Typical age: 25–44.

3. *Maintenance*: the concern now is to hold onto the niche one has carved for oneself. This can be a considerable task, especially in the face of technological changes and vigorous competition from younger workers. Typical age: 45–64.

4. *Decline*: characterized by decreasing involvement in work – a tendency to become an observer rather than a participant. Typical age: 65+.

Clearly, there are some parallels between Erikson and Super. Both see the late teens and 20s as a time of exploration and self-concept clarification. Both see the following years as a time when the person "gets stuck in" and makes themselves indispensable. But there are differences too. Super sees this "getting stuck in" as achievement-orientated, whereas Erikson concentrates more in terms of involvement. Super's view of middle-age essentially concerns hanging on, whereas Erikson's emphasizes creative striving.

Some work has examined whether people's career concerns do indeed match Super's stages (e.g. Veiga, 1983; Isabella, 1988). The results suggest some distinctions between stages, but they are not very clear-cut. As Hall (1986, ch. 4) has pointed out, it is difficult to identify what career stage a person is in, especially if, for example, they enter a career relatively late in life. In fact, Super (1980, 1986) has acknowledged this, and has developed a much more flexible framework for mapping a person's life and career. He identified six roles people typically perform in Western societies: homemaker, worker, citizen, leisurite, student and child. The importance of each of these roles in a person's life can rise and fall over time. Also, at any given time, a person can be at different stages (exploration, establishment, etc.) in different roles. These insights do not in themselves create a theory, but they do help people to consider their lives in a systematic way (Super, 1986). Some self-assessment devices such as the Adult Career Concerns Inventory (Super *et al.* 1985) and the Salience Inventory (Super and Nevill, 1985) have been developed to assist in this process.

Of the many other attempts to map out adult life, Levinson *et al.*'s (1978) is perhaps the most influential. This is perhaps surprising, given that Levinson and his colleagues conducted interviews (albeit in-depth ones) with only 40 US-born men between the ages of 35 and 45. Nevertheless, Levinson came up with some interesting conclusions. He proposed that in each of three eras of adulthood (early, middle and late) there are alternating stable and transitional periods. For example, early adulthood (age 17–40) begins with the *early adult transition* (age 17–22) where the person seeks a niche in the adult world. Then comes a stable phase *entering the adult world* (age 22–28), where the task is to explore various roles while keeping one's options open. Next, between 28 and 33, comes the *age 30 transition*, where the person appraises their experiences and searches for a satisfactory lifestyle. This is followed by a stable settling down phase, when that lifestyle is implemented.

However, the *mid-life transition* (age 40–45) identified by Levinson has often been considered the most significant aspect of his work. He argued that lifestyle is reappraised at this age, often with considerable urgency and emotion. So much so, that some people refer to the "mid-life crisis". The person realizes that their life is probably at least half over and this concentrates their minds on what they should be doing with it. Often their children are growing up and see the parent as a symbol of authority rather than the image of the up-and-coming young adult that the parent prefers. Physical signs of ageing become unmistakable. There are by now clear indications of whether or not earlier career ambitions will be achieved. Together, these factors can lead to substantial life changes, e.g. a change of career or a change of spouse. Alternatively, the person may reaffirm their commitment to their current lifestyle, and increase their inputs and achievements.

After the mid-life transition comes *entering middle adulthood* (45–50), then the *age 50 transition* (50–55), then the *culmination of middle adulthood* (55–60). These all concern implementing and living with mid-life decisions. The *late adult transition* and *late adulthood* follow. Here, as at some other stages, Levinson's work bears considerable similarity to Erikson's. There are also similarities with Super's work. Ornstein *et al.* (1989) found moderate support for both Levinson and Super in a study of 535 (96% male) sales staff.

These approaches to adult development have implications for career management in organizations. In early career, people must be given the opportunity to integrate themselves into an organization and/or career, and demonstrate their worth to themselves and others. This may involve special efforts to give the newcomer significant work assignments and social support. In mid-career, it may be necessary to provide opportunities for some people to retrain, perhaps in response to a mid-life reappraisal. They could also be given opportunities that allow them to keep up-to-date in their chosen field. It may be helpful to give people in their mid- to late career a chance to act as mentor or guide to younger employees – this is, after all, a way of handing on one's accumulated wisdom and thereby making a lasting impression.

Case study 15.2   Career stages

Jenny Peterson was 36 years old and had been working in the sales function of a large retailer since she was 18. She had found her early years quite tough, and for a time wondered how she had ended up in the job. During those years, however, she gradually found that she could handle the tasks, and that some of them were quite enjoyable. By the time she was 23, she felt confident that she could cope with anything that came her way, but wondered whether she really wanted to work for the company. She thought a great deal about whether or not she liked its people and philosophy. Over the next decade, she slowly but surely found herself feeling more attached to both. Now a different matter was bothering her. Some of the younger staff seemed to know more than she did about sales techniques and marketing strategies. Was she already obsolete at age 36, she wondered?

Suggested exercise

Consider the extent to which Jenny Peterson's career so far is consistent with Super's and Erikson's stages.

Socialization and innovation

Career and life-stage approaches neglect individual differences in work experiences. Yet surely people are changed by, and change, their work environments. Some sociologists have focused on people's orientation to their work-role. For example, Schein (1971b) proposed three such orientations: *custodianship*, where the person accepts their job requirements as given; *content innovation*, where the person accepts the goals of their job but adopts their own ways of achieving them; and *role innovation*, where the person redefines the goals of their job. In the long-run, role innovators are probably vital for societal advance. In the short-term, many work organizations claim to value content innovators (though they would not use that term) but probably in truth many reward custodians more highly.

Van Maanen and Schein (1979) specified some key aspects of organizational "people-processing" strategies which would, they proposed, influence whether a person became a custodian or an innovator. These dimensions all concerned the formality or informality of organizational socialization strategies. For example, formal approaches to the training of newcomers would involve sending them on structured training courses (as opposed to on-the-job training) together as a group, and separate from other members of the organization. Such formal approaches tend to lead to a custodial orientation, though less so for people with high self-efficacy than for those with low self-efficacy (Jones, 1986).

Nicholson (1984) proposed that the extent to which a person changes their work-role (i.e. innovation) and is changed by it (i.e. socialization) depends on several factors. Increases in discretion (i.e. the amount of freedom in the work-role) will tend to lead to low innovation. Decreases in discretion foster high innovation. This is because in the latter case the person will be accustomed to doing things their way (through higher discretion in their previous work), and will seek to do the same in their present role. Work demands which are novel to the person lead to high personal change because novelty tends to produce new insights about oneself. By the same token, low novelty leads to low personal change. Nicholson also suggested that certain personality characteristics influence role orientation. People with a high need for control are hypothesized to be greater innovators than those with a low need, and those with a high need for feedback are thought to experience more personal change than those with a low need. Some evidence in support of these propositions in a large managerial sample has been reported by Nicholson and West (1988, ch. 6).

There is also clear evidence that people's personality, self-concept and cognitive functioning are influenced by the characteristics of their work. Brousseau (1978) showed that some of the task characteristics identified by Hackman and Oldham (1976; see Chapter 17, this volume) can change people's personality to a limited extent. Kohn and Schooler (1983), in a series of huge and carefully constructed studies, have shown that jobs with high amounts of discretion foster enhanced intellectual functioning. Mortimer *et al.* (1986) found that people tend to increase the importance they attach to certain work characteristics (e.g. autonomy, income) if their jobs offer high levels of such characteristics.

On the other hand, it is also clear that the amount of personal change in adult life is normally fairly small. People bring their own dispositions with them to work, and this probably influences work attitudes such as job satisfaction (Staw *et al.*, 1986). Nevertheless, change does happen. In a large longitudinal study of managers in the giant company AT & T, Howard and Bray (1988) found that, over 20 years, the managers became less ambitious but more autonomous.

One important caution is required here: much of the research described in this section has involved males only. The reason given is usually that women spend less time in work, surely a weak justification as quite apart from the inherent importance of women's experiences, this could provide an opportunity to find out *how much* time in work is required to produce certain effects on people.

Work-role transitions

Since the start of the 1980s, increasing attention has been paid to the processes involved in changing jobs (Latack, 1984; Sokol and Louis, 1984). Such attention is much-needed. In their study of managers in the UK, Nicholson and West (1988) showed that the frequency of job moves was increasing, with 3 years the average time spent in any single job. Equally important, the most common job moves involved changes in both status and function (27.6% of job changes) or all three of employer, status and function (24.6%). In other words, job changes were frequently quite dramatic. Furthermore, it appeared that many managers were unable to predict their occurrence very well even only a few months ahead.

Nicholson and West proposed a transition cycle model of job change. The cycle consists of four stages: preparation, encounter, adjustment, stabilization and then back to preparation. As they pointed out, in fast-moving work environments, the preparation stage may be very short, and the stabilization stage rarely reached, before the person moves on. Job changes were not generally experienced as especially stressful by the managers in Nicholson and West's study, which led Nicholson and West to reject the stress-coping approaches to job change advocated by some (e.g. Nelson, 1987). Nevertheless, this does not mean that job changes are typically handled well by work organizations. Nicholson and West (1988) and Louis (1982) among others have pointed out the need to prepare people for the possibility of change, to train them in how to use formal and informal resources when settling into their new job, and to train supervisors in how to orientate new arrivals.

One frequently considered job change is the first one – starting work for the first time (Arnold, 1990). It seems that early work experiences can have quite long-lasting effects, and in the initial stages it is important for the newcomer to feel a sense of belonging and a sense of competence. This can be achieved by social support and "psychological success" (Hall, 1971). The latter comes about through independent effort towards challenging work goals in a role of real significance to the organization. It is also important to provide experiences which help the young person learn how the organization really works and how they fit into it (Schein, 1978).

In reality, it seems that while newcomers are often pleasantly surprised by the friendliness of their new colleagues, they often feel a lack of supervision (Arnold, 1985). Also, they often have high expectations of work, perhaps inflated by their organization's attempts to sell itself to them during the recruitment process. This can lead to early disillusionment, accompanied by loss of motivation and an intention to leave the organization. Realistic Job Previews (RJPs) are designed to overcome some of these problems. RJPs describe jobs "warts and all" to potential recruits, rather than making them seem excellent in every respect, which of course they rarely are. Organizations which use RJPs can expect small but significant reductions in the proportion of newcomers leaving. There are sometimes attitudinal and even work performance benefits too (Premack and Wanous, 1985).

Career types

Some writers have tried to identify the different paths careers can take. For example, Driver (1982) specified four types of career:

1. *Steady state*: a career choice represents a life-time's commitment to an occupation.
2. *Linear*: the person moves "up the ladder" in one particular occupation.
3. *Spiral*: the person remains in an occupation for 7–10 years and then chooses another which builds on past skills and experience.

4. *Transitory*: choice of career changes frequently, with variety being the main driving force.

Driver (1988) commented that now the post-war "baby boom" generation in the West has reached middle age, and relatively senior positions at work, young people who subscribe to the linear career concept are having a tough time. Promotion opportunities are few and far between. The fast pace of societal and technological change generally favours the spiral and transitory career concepts, but these have not historically been seen as normal or legitimate patterns. The focus is shifting from long-term to short-term, from one career to several careers, from advancement to accomplishment, and from one-career families to dual-career families (Campbell and Moses, 1986).

Other writers have sought to identify themes which govern career paths, rather than the paths themselves. The most notable is Schein (1978). He specified five career "anchors" which managers and perhaps others may develop in early career:

1. *Managerial*: the person is chiefly concerned with managing others. They wish to be a generalist, and regard specialist posts purely as a short-term means of gaining some relevant experience.

2. *Technical*: the person is keen to develop and maintain specialist skills and knowledge in their area of expertise.

3. *Security*: the person is chiefly concerned with a reliable, predictable work environment.

4. *Autonomy*: the person wishes most of all to be free of restrictions on their work activities.

5. *Entrepreneurial*: the person is most concerned to create a product, service and/or organization of their own.

Schein (1978) argued that after a few years of work, it was possible to identify for most individuals which career anchor had become dominant. However, the process by which young people adopt one anchor rather than another is far from clear. Nevertheless, organizations need to be aware of their existence, and try to cater for people with different anchors. This is not always easy. For example, in many organizations, scientists and engineers complain that they cannot rise very high unless they abandon their technical skills and become managers. In other words, in some organizations, people with technical career anchors have fewer promotion opportunities than those with managerial anchors.

Managing career development in organizations

Organizations, especially large ones, possess a range of jobs of different types and different levels. Who gets which ones and how? Organizations need to develop systems to ensure that the flow of personnel is managed well. Some researchers have mapped out key concepts. For example, Gunz (1989) has introduced the notion of the "career climbing frame" in organizations. People can climb up it, along it or down it. They can start from more than one position at the bottom of the frame, and in principle move in almost any combination of directions thereafter. Of course, the organization makes some moves easier than others. Gunz has identified three orientations that individuals may adopt towards the climbing frame:

1. *Building*: willing to climb the frame by the approved route.
2. *Searching*: choosing to abandon the climbing frame and search for something one would prefer to do.
3. *Subsisting*: unwilling to climb the frame, but prepared to hang on for survival (i.e. keeping a job).

These orientations crucially affect the sort of career opportunities employees seek and/or are prepared to take.

Nigel Nicholson has identified four common shortcomings of organizational career development systems which can limit their effectiveness (Nicholson and Arnold, 1989):

1. *Restricted*: some restrictions are inevitable, but organizations often create unnecessary ones, especially concerning non-promotional transfers between functions.
2. *Political* (see also Chapter 12): career opportunities can be made or blocked by managers seeking to advance their own interests rather than those of the organization or the person whose career is at stake.
3. *Mechanistic*: career moves are governed by rules and regulations which allow no exceptions and often fail to change in response to changing conditions.
4. *Neglected*: possible career paths and means of treading them are simply not identified, so that nobody can see where they are going.

Organizations are becoming increasingly aware of the need to ensure that they offer appropriate support and opportunities for their employees' careers and thereby avoid mistakes such as those mentioned above. Many nowadays offer some or all of the following (Gutteridge, 1986):

- *self-assessment tools*, e.g. career planning workshops;
- *individual counselling* by internal staff or external specialists;
- *information on the organization's internal labour market*, e.g. internal vacancy lists, skill requirements of particular posts, career path planning;
- *assessment of future potential*, e.g. succession planning, psychological testing; and
- *developmental programmes*, e.g. mentoring systems, job rotation/sharing, time off or financial assistance for an educational course.

London and Stumpf (1982, ch. 5) presented a set of guidelines for ensuring that measures like these work well. They stressed the importance of establishing career paths, keeping information complete and up-to-date, and ensuring that there is a system for matching people to jobs. Guidelines such as these are important. Some people see career development systems as a waste of resources, so if such a system is to work, it must be managed well. It must not be purely the creation of one enthusiast. If it is, it will die when that person moves on (Gutteridge, 1986). It also needs to be integrated with other human resources functions such as selection and training (Gerstein and Amos, 1986). Even then, there is no guarantee that the systems will improve employee satisfaction and commitment; indeed, they may simply demonstrate to some people that there is nowhere in the organization for them to go (Granrose and Portwood, 1987). Nevertheless, satisfaction and commitment are not the only desired outcomes of career development systems. Others include a good match between people and their jobs, and an improved pool of valuable skills and experience within the organization.

Summary

Careers concern the sequence of jobs people hold, and the attitudes and behaviours associated with them. Perspectives brought to bear on careers have included sociological, static personality differences, career stages and life-cycle. The second of these forms the basis of several theories and assessment tools concerning initial career choice. However, it is increasingly recognized that choices frequently have to be re-made later in people's careers, and that between choices many significant developments can occur. Much career development theory and practice is therefore based on people's concerns at different stages of their lives. It also increasingly examines attempts by organizations to facilitate the career development of their employees. Current trends are towards increasing flexibility of career structures, and towards identifying how career development systems can be implemented and maintained successfully within organizations.

Case study 15.3   A successful laboratory technician

Pauline Ware was deputy chief laboratory technician at the main factory of a medium-sized agrochemicals company. She had worked there for 11 years, ever since joining from school. This is her story:

When I left school I didn't really know exactly what I wanted to do. I took my exams, mainly in sciences. I passed but did less well than I had hoped. I had really wanted to be a science teacher, but I wasn't sure whether my grades were good enough to get into a teacher training course, and somehow I never got round to finding out. Also, I wasn't very confident about my abilities at that time, and wondered whether I could really handle lots of youngsters.

Mind you, I had helped one of my teachers with one of his classes of younger children a few times, and that seemed to go quite well.

Anyway, I saw an advert in the local paper for a trainee lab technician job here. It sounded good. They said the person selected would be able to choose which project they wanted to work on, and that in the long-term there would be chances to take extra courses and get promotion to a job as development scientist. I was also told that most of my work would be quite skilled, and that other people were employed to do the most boring bits. Well, they offered me the job and I took it. I soon found out that things weren't quite as I'd imagined. There was no choice of project at that time, the budget for technician education was small, nobody could remember anyone being promoted from technician to scientist, though it was possible in theory, and I found I *was* expected to do many unskilled tasks like sweeping the floor. I complained to Personnel or Human Resources as they are called these days. They were quite surprised, and said that the laboratory must have failed to implement the changes in technician's job descriptions agreed several months earlier.

So I was quite fed up, but I didn't leave. That was partly because I couldn't think of anything better, and partly because I was planning to get married, and somehow work didn't seem very important. And I did learn quite a lot in that first job. I got little training, and there were no other new technicians joining at the same time as me, so it was a bit scary at first, but I learned my own way of doing things. That stood me in good stead 4 years later when I was moved to another lab. I soon found out that my predecessor there had not been very effective. Although it was a different lab, I knew more or less what to do. I changed a lot of things for the better, and that got me noticed. In the next 6 years I was promoted three times. So now here I am as deputy chief technician.

You'd think that was fine, but actually I'm not so sure. I don't really know where to go next. I wouldn't want the chief's job. She has to go to lots of meetings, argue over financial alloca-tions, draw up 5-year plans and all that. Myself, I have to make sure we are getting the right equipment at the right time, and I look after the training of the technicians – so in a way I'm a teacher after all! The point is that I'm still using my scientific know-how.

In the last 5 years three chiefs have left because the chief's job does not involve tech-nical work. So have two deputies who can't see any future for them in the chief's work. I have the same problem: I like my work, but I think in a couple of years I will have done all I can in this role. Then what? Nobody knows, least of all me. I want to prove I can handle a higher job because nowadays I feel confident about my abilities. Yet this company has never said anything about where you can go from here. In fact, I'm seeing Human Resources about it next week. Mind you, I still haven't forgotten how out of touch they were when they advertised my job.

Suggested exercises

1. Examine the role in this case study of (i) self-esteem, (ii) career exploration, (iii) Realistic Job Previews, (iv) socialization and innova-tion and (v) career anchors.
2. If you were the Human Resources Manager, what plans, if any, would you be making con-cerning the career development of laboratory technicians in the company?

References

Applied Psychology: An International Review (1988). Special issue on women's occupa-tional plans and decisions, April.

Arnold, J. (1985). Tales of the unexpected: Surprises experienced by graduates in the early months of employment. *British Journal of Guidance and Counselling*, *13*, 308–319.

Arnold, J. (1990). From education to labour market. In S. Fisher and C. L. Cooper (Eds), *On the Move: The Psychological Effects of Change and Transition*. Chichester: John Wiley.

Ball, B. (1989). *Manage Your Own Career: A Self-help Guide to Career Choice and Change*. London: British Psychological Society/Kogan Page.

Betz, N. E. and Hackett, G. (1981). The relationship of career-related self-efficacy expectations to perceived career options in college women and men. *Journal of Counseling Psychology*, *28*, 399–410.

Brousseau, K. R. (1978). Personality and job experience. *Organizational Behavior and Human Performance, 22,* 235–252.

Campbell, R. J. and Moses, J. L. (1986). Careers from an organizational perspective. In D. T. Hall (Ed.), *Career Development in Organizations.* London: Jossey-Bass.

Clement, S. (1987). The self-efficacy expectations and occupational preferences of females and males. *Journal of Occupational Psychology, 60,* 257–265.

Collin, A. and Young R. A. (1986). New directions for theories of career. *Human Relations, 39,* 837–853.

Crites, J. O., Wallbrown, F. H. and Blaha, J. (1985). The Career Maturity Inventory: Myths and realities. A rejoinder to Westbrook, Cutts, Madison and Arcia (1980). *Journal of Vocational Behavior, 26,* 221–238.

Daws, P. P. (1981). The socialisation/opportunity-structure theory of the occupational location of school leavers: A critical appraisal. In A. G. Watts, D. E. Super and J. M. Kidd (Eds), *Career Development in Britain.* Cambridge: Hobson's Press.

Dipboye, R. L. (1977). A critical review of Korman's self-consistency theory of work motivation and occupational choice. *Organizational Behavior and Human Performance, 18,* 108–126.

Driver, M. (1982). Career concepts: A new approach to career research. In R. Katz (Ed.), *Career Issues in Human Resource Management.* Englewood Cliffs, N.J.: Prentice-Hall.

Driver, M. (1988). Careers: A review of personal and organizational research. In C. L. Cooper and I. T. Robertson (Eds), *International Review of Industrial and Organizational Psychology, 1988.* Chichester: John Wiley.

Erikson, E. H. (1963). *Childhood and Society,* revised edn. Harmondsworth: Penguin.

Farh, J. and Dobbins, G. H. (1989). Effects of comparative performance information on the accuracy of self-ratings and agreement between self and supervisor ratings. *Journal of Applied Psychology, 74,* 606–610.

Gerstein, M. and Amos, M. A. (1986). Implementation and evaluation of adult career development programs in organizations. *Journal of Career Development, 12,* 210–218.

Granrose, C. S. and Portwood, J. D. (1987). Matching individual career plans and organizational career management. *Academy of Management Journal, 30,* 699–720.

Greenhaus, J. H. (1987). *Career Management.* London: Dryden Press.

Gunz, H. (1989). *Career and Corporate Cultures: Managerial Mobility in Large Corporations.* Oxford: Blackwell.

Gutek, B. and Larwood, L. (Eds) (1987). *Women's Career Development.* London: Sage.

Gutteridge, T. G. (1986). Organizational career development systems: The state of the practice. In D. T. Hall (Ed.), *Career Development in Organizations.* London: Jossey-Bass.

Hackman, J. R. and Oldham, G. R. (1976). Motivation through the design of work: Test of a theory. *Organizational Behavior and Human Performance, 16,* 250–279.

Hall, D. T. (1971). A theoretical model of career subidentity development in organizational settings. *Organizational Behavior and Human Performance, 6,* 50–76.

Hall, D. T. (1986). Breaking career routines: Midcareer choice and identity development. In D. T. Hall (Ed.), *Career Development in Organizations.* London: Jossey-Bass.

Hansen, J. I. (1985). *The Strong–Campbell Interest Inventory.* Palo Alto, Calif.: Consulting Psychologists Press.

Holland, J. L. (1979). *Professional Manual for the Self-directed Search.* Palo Alto, Calif.: Consulting Psychologists Press.

Holland, J. L. (1985). *Making Vocational Choices,* 2nd edn. Englewood Cliffs, N.J.: Prentice-Hall.

Holland, J. L. and Rayman, J. R. (1986). The self-directed Search. In W. B. Walsh and S. H. Osipow (Eds), *Advances in Vocational Psychology*, Vol. 1. London: Lawrence Erlbaum Associates.

Howard, A. and Bray, D. W. (1988). *Managerial Lives in Transition*. New York: Guilford Press.

Isabella, L. A. (1988). The effect of career stage on the meaning of key organizational events. *Journal of Organizational Behavior*, *9*, 345–358.

Jones, G. R. (1986). Socialization tactics, self-efficacy and newcomers' adjustments to organizations. *Academy of Management Journal*, *29*, 262–279.

Kidd, J. M. (1981). The assessment of career development. In A. G. Watts, D. E. Super and J. M. Kidd (Eds), *Career Development in Britain*. Cambridge: Hobson's Press.

Kidd, J. M. (1982). *Self and Occupational Concepts in Occupational Preferences and the Entry into Work: An Overlapping Longitudinal Study*. Unpublished PhD thesis, Hatfield Polytechnic.

Kohn, M. L. and Schooler, C. (1983). *Work and Personality*. Norwood, N.J.: Ablex.

Korman, A. K. (1966). Self-esteem variable in vocational choice. *Journal of Applied Psychology*, *50*, 479–486.

Latack, J. C. (1984). Career transitions within organizations: An exploratory study of work, nonwork and coping strategies. *Organizational Behavior and Human Performance*, *34*, 296–322.

Levinson, D. J., Darrow, C. N., Klein, E. B., Levinson, M. H. and McKee, B. (1978). *Seasons of a Man's Life*. New York: Knopf.

London, M. and Stumpf, S. A. (1982). *Managing Careers*. Reading, Mass.: Addison-Wesley.

Louis, M. R. (1982). Career transitions: A missing link in career development. *Organizational Dynamics*, *10*, 68–77.

Mabe, P. A. and West, S. G. (1982). Validity of self-evaluation of ability: A review and meta-analysis. *Journal of Applied Psychology*, *67*, 280–296.

Mortimer, J. T., Lorence, J. and Kumka, D. (1986). *Work, Family and Personality*. Norwood, N. J.: Ablex.

Nelson, D. L. (1987). Organizational socialization: A stress perspective. *Journal of Occupational Behaviour*, *8*, 311–324.

Nicholson, N. (1984). A theory of work role transitions. *Administrative Science Quarterly*, *29*, 172–191.

Nicholson, N. and Arnold, J. (1989). Graduate early experience in a multinational corporation. *Personnel Review*, *18* (4), 3–14.

Nicholson, N. and West, M. A. (1988). *Managerial Job Change: Men and Women in Transition*. Cambridge: Cambridge University Press.

Ornstein, S., Cron, W. L. and Slocum, J. W. (1989). Life stage versus career stage: A comparative test of the theories of Levinson and Super. *Journal of Organizational Behavior*, *10*, 117–133.

Phillips, S. D., Pazienza, N. J. and Walsh, D. J. (1984). Decision making styles and progress in occupational decision making. *Journal of Vocational Behavior*, *25*, 96–105.

Premack, S. L. and Wanous, J. P. (1985). A meta-analysis of realistic job preview experiments. *Journal of Applied Psychology*, *70*, 706–719.

Roberts, K. (1981). The sociology of work entry and occupational choice. In A. G. Watts, D. E. Super and J. M. Kidd (Eds), *Career Development in Britain*. Cambridge: Hobson's Press.

Sampson, E. E. (1989). The deconstruction of the self. In J. Shotter and K. J. Gergen (Eds), *Texts of Identity*. London: Sage.

Schein, E. H. (1971a). The individual, the organization and the career: A conceptual scheme. *Journal of Applied Behavioural Science*, *7*, 401–426.

Schein, E. H. (1971b). Occupational socialization in the professions: The case of the role innovator. *Journal of Psychiatric Research*, *8*, 521–530.

Schein, E. H. (1978). *Career Dynamics: Matching Individual and Organizational Needs*. Reading, Mass.: Addison-Wesley.

Schein, E. H. (1986). Career development in organizations: Where do we go from here? In D. T. Hall (Ed.), *Career Development in Organizations*. London: Jossey-Bass.

Sokol, M. and Louis, M. R. (1984). Career transitions and life event adaptation: Integrating alternative perspectives on role transition. In V. L. Allen and E. Van de Vliert (Eds), *Role Transitions*. New York: Plenum Press.

Sonnenfeld, J. and Kotter, J. P. (1982). The maturation of career theory. *Human Relations*, *35*, 19–46.

Spokane, A. R. (1985). A review of research on person–environment congruence in Holland's theory of careers. *Journal of Vocational Behavior*, *26*, 306–343.

Staw, B. M., Bell, N. E. and Clausen, J. A. (1986). The dispositional approach to job attitudes: A lifetime longitudinal test. *Administrative Science Quarterly*, *31*, 56–77.

Stumpf, S. A., Colarelli, S. M. and Hartman, K. (1983). Development of the Career Exploration Survey (CES). *Journal of Vocational Behavior*, *22*, 191–226.

Sugarman, L. (1986). *Life-span Development*. London: Methuen.

Super, D. E. (1957). *The Psychology of Careers*. New York: Harper and Row.

Super, D. E. (1980). A life-span, life-space approach to career development. *Journal of Vocational Behavior*, *13*, 282–298.

Super, D. E. (1985). Coming of age in Middletown. *American Psychologist*, *40*, 405–414.

Super, D. E. (1986). Life career roles: Self-realization in work and leisure. In D. T. Hall (Ed.), *Career Development in Organizations*. London: Jossey-Bass.

Super, D. E. and Nevill, D. D. (1985). *The Salience Inventory*. Palo Alto, Calif.: Consulting Psychologists Press.

Super, D. E., Thompson, A. S. and Lindeman, R. H. (1985). *The Adult Career Concerns Inventory*. Palo Alto, Calif.: Consulting Psychologists Press.

Taylor, K. M. and Betz, N. E. (1983). Applications of self-efficacy theory to the understanding and treatment of career indecision. *Journal of Vocational Behavior*, *22*, 63–81.

US Department of Labor (1977). *Dictionary of Occupational Titles*, 4th edn. Washington, D.C.: US Government Printing Office.

Van Maanen, J. and Schein, E. H. (1979). Toward a theory of organizational socialization. In B. M. Staw (Ed.), *Research in Organizational Behavior*, Vol. 1. Greenwich, Conn.: JAI Press.

Veiga, J. (1983). Mobility influences during managerial career stages. *Academy of Management Journal*, *26*, 64–83.

Westbrook, B. W. (1985). What research says about career maturity ... A response to Crites, Wallbrown and Blaha (1985). *Journal of Vocational Behavior*, *26*, 239–250.

Yost, E. B. and Corbishley, M. A. (1987). *Career Counseling*. London: Jossey-Bass.

CHAPTER

16 Work, stress and psychological well-being

Introduction

Stress at work is costing industry a great deal of money. It has been estimated that nearly 10% of the UK's GNP is lost each year due to job-generated stress in the form of sickness absence, high labour turnover, lost productive value, increased recruitment and selection costs, and medical expenses. This chapter looks at what stress is, how you can identify it, what it costs industry, what are its sources in the workplace and what we can do about it. In identifying organizational sources of stress, we will focus in on factors intrinsic to a job, role problems, relationships at work, career development, organizational climate and structure, and the work–home interface (see Cooper *et al.*, 1988, for a more detailed account). We close this chapter with an examination of the stressful effects of being *without* work, i.e. unemployed.

What is stress?

Stress is a word derived from the Latin word *stringere*, meaning to draw tight. Early definitions of strain and load used in physics and engineering eventually came to influence one concept of how stress affects individuals. Under this concept, external forces (load) are seen as exerting pressure upon an individual, producing strain. Proponents of this view argue that we can measure the stress to which an individual is subjected in the same way that we can measure physical strain upon a machine (Hinkle, 1973).

While this first concept looked at stress as an outside stimulus, a second concept defines stress as a person's *response* to a disturbance. The idea that environmental forces could actually cause disease rather than just short-term effects, and that people have a natural tendency to resist such forces, was seen in the work of Walter B. Cannon in the 1930s. Cannon studied the effects of stress upon animals and people, and in particular studied the "fight or flight" reaction. Through this reaction, people, as well as animals, will choose whether to stay and fight or try to escape when confronting extreme danger. Cannon observed that when his subjects experienced situations of cold, lack of oxygen and excitement, he could detect physiological changes such as emergency adrenalin secretions. Cannon described these individuals as being "under stress".

One of the first scientific attempts to explain the process of stress-related illness was made by physician and scholar Hans Selye (1946), who described three stages an individual encounters in stressful situations:

1. *Alarm reaction*: in which an initial phase of lowered resistance is followed by countershock, during which the individual's defence mechanisms become active.

2. *Resistance*: the stage of maximum adaptation and, hopefully, successful return to equilibrium for the individual. If, however, the stress agent continues or the defence mechanism does not work, the individual will move on to a third stage.

3. *Exhaustion*: when adaptive mechanisms collapse.

Newer and more complete theories of stress emphasize the interaction between a person and his or her environment. By looking at stress as resulting from a misfit between an individual and their particular environment, we can begin to understand why one person seems to flourish in a certain setting, while another suffers. Cummings and Cooper (1979) have designed a way of understanding the stress process:

1. Individuals, for the most part, try to keep their thoughts, emotions and relationships with the world in a "steady state".

2. Each factor of a person's emotional and physical state has a "range of stability", in which that person feels comfortable. On the other hand, when forces disrupt one of these factors beyond the range of stability, the individual must act or cope to restore a feeling of comfort.

3. An individual's behaviour aimed at maintaining a steady state makes up his or her "adjustment process", or coping strategies.

A stress is any force that pushes a psychological or physical factor beyond its range of stability, producing a strain within the individual. Knowledge that a stress is likely to occur constitutes a threat to the individual. A threat can cause a strain because of what it signifies to the person. This description can be summarized in Fig. 16.1

As stress begins to take its toll on the body and mind, a variety of symptoms can result. Doctors have identified the physical and behavioural symptoms of stress listed in Table 16.1 as commonly occurring before the onset of serious stress-related illness. They have also identified those ailments having a stress background, meaning that they may be brought on or aggravated by stress.

The costs of stress

To the individual whose health or happiness has been ravaged by the effects of stress, the costs involved are only too clear. Whether manifested as minor

16.1   The Cooper–Cummings framework.

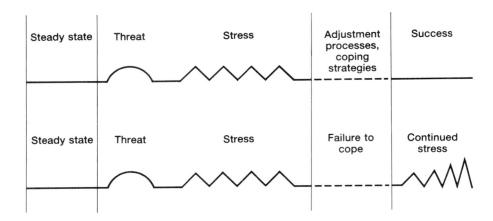

Table 16.1

Physical symptoms of stress	Behavioural symptoms of stress	Ailments with stress aetiology
Lack of appetite	Constant irritability with people	Hypertension: high blood pressure
Craving for food when under pressure	Feeling unable to cope	Coronary thrombosis: heart attack
Frequent indigestion or heart burn	Lack of interest in life	Migraine
Constipation or diarrhoea	Constant, or recurrent fear of disease	Hay fever and allergies
Insomnia	A feeling of being a failure	Asthma
Constant tiredness	A feeling of being bad or of self-hatred	Pruritus: intense itching
Tendency to sweat for no good reason	Difficulty in making decisions	Peptic ulcers
Nervous twitches	A feeling of ugliness	Constipation
Nail-biting	Loss of interest in other people	Colitis
Headaches	Awareness of suppressed anger	Rheumatoid arthritis
Cramps and muscle spasms	Inability to show true feelings	Menstrual difficulties
Nausea	A feeling of being the target of other	Nervous dyspepsia: flatulence and
Breathlessness without exertion	people's animosity	indigestion
Fainting spells	Loss of sense of humour	Hyperthyroidism: overactive
Frequent crying or desire to cry	Feeling of neglect	thyroid gland
Impotency or frigidity	Dread of the future	Diabetes mellitus
Inability to sit still without fidgeting	A feeling of having failed as a person	Skin disorders
High blood pressure	or parent	Tuberculosis
	A feeling of having no-one to confide in	Depression
	Difficulty in concentrating	
	The inability to finish one task before	
	rushing on to the next	
	An intense fear of open or enclosed	
	spaces, or of being alone	

complaints of illness, serious ailments such as heart disease, or social problems such as alcoholism and drug abuse, stress-related symptoms exact a heavy payment. It has also long been recognized that a family suffers indirectly from the stress problems on one of its members – suffering that takes the form of unhappy marriages, divorces, and spouse and child abuse. But what price do organizations and nations pay for a poor fit between people and their environments? Only recently has stress been seen as contributing to the health costs of companies and countries. But as studies of stress-related illnesses and deaths show, stress is taking a devastatingly high toll on our combined productivity and health.

Costs to society

Heart and circulatory diseases

Today in the UK, coronary heart disease remains the leading cause of death and kills more than 150,000 people each year – one person every 3–4 minutes. One man in 11 dies of a heart attack before he is 65 years old.

Almost half of all Americans die of cardiovascular disease, which includes heart attack and stroke. The resulting economic cost, including medical services and lost productivity, reached an estimated US$78.6 billion in 1986. Heart attack is the leading cause of death in the USA, followed by cancer and stroke. It is also estimated that more than US$700 million a year is spent by US employers to replace the 200,000 men aged 45–65 who die or are incapacitated by coronary heart disease. However, the USA has succeeded in reversing the long prevailing upward trend in heart and vascular diseases. From the early 1960s to the 1980s, deaths among US men due to ischaemic heart disease fell between 20 and 30%, whereas in England and Wales they rose by 3%. Correspondingly, deaths among US women dropped 31% whereas deaths among women in England and Wales increased by 11%.

In the UK, coronary heart disease is generally twice as prevalent in men as in women, but the disease's rate of increase over the years has been even greater in women. Further, as Table 16.2 shows, days lost from work by UK women between 1982–83 and 1984–85 increased dramatically due to causes of heart disease and cerebrovascular disease over a 2-year period.

Another disease increasingly linked to stress is high blood pressure (hypertension). In 1983, it was estimated that nearly 55 million adult Americans – nearly 1 in 4 – suffered from hypertension. Hypertension, like heart disease and cerebrovascular disease, has increased as a cause of absence from work in the UK between 1982–83 and 1984–85 (see Table 16.2).

White vs blue collar

It is commonly believed that executives and other white-collar workers suffer the most from stress-related illnesses. Intense office situations with demanding deadlines, the required attention to detail and complex interpersonal relations are often believed to produce high levels of stress and strain. Yet, the frequencies of deaths due to major causes in the working population increase as we move from professional and white-collar jobs down to the unskilled. This applies both to stress-related illnesses such as ischaemic heart disease and to other illnesses such as pneumonia and prostate cancer. In addition, this pattern extends not only to deaths but to illnesses as well. Many blue-collar workers show a greater number of restricted activity days and consultations with general practitioners than do white-collar workers.

* Some of the material from this section comes from NIOSH's proposed *National Strategy on the Prevention of Work-related Psychological Disorders* (NIOSH, 1986)

Mental illness*

The breakdown of an individual's mental health has been increasingly linked by medics and stress researchers to the level of stress he or she experiences. A look at work days lost due to mental health problems indicates the magnitude

Table 16.2 Days lost in Britain from work for certain mental and stress-related causes

Cause	Male/female	1982–83	1984–85	% Change over 2 years
Psychoses	M	7,098,538	8,138,000	+16.04
	F	3,253,344	3,275,080	+0.66
Neuroses	M	17,432,981	17,938,743	+2.90
	F	9,951,749	10,162,450	+2.18
Personality	M	160,100	162,200	+1.31
disorders	F	153,600	131,600	−14.32
Mental	M	1,312,400	1,310,286	−0.17
retardation	F	786,000	823,300	+4.74
Migraine	M	158,529	136,300	−14.02
	F	177,683	62,800	−64.65
Hypertensive	M	9,477,164	9,890,527	+4.36
diseases	F	1,997,336	2,060,400	+3.16
Ulcers	M	2,216,132	2,088,828	−1.75
	F	294,295	312,659	+6.24
Depressive	M	6,439,698	6,134,613	−4.47
disorder	F	4,276,919	4,201,100	−1.77
Alcohol	M	896,600	895,401	−0.13
dependence	F	79,600	38,800	−51.26
Ischaemic	M	29,092,909	32,912,455	+13.13
heart disease	F	1,908,911	2,389,044	+25.15
Cerebro-	M	6,222,500	7,011,600	+12.68
vascular disease	F	529,800	920,700	+73.78
Total days lost	M	80,417,551	86,618,953	+7.71
in above causes	F	23,409,237	24,377,933	+4.14
Total number	M	271,715,438	253,562,397	−6.68
of days lost	F	89,229,711	74,546,812	−16.52

Source: Department of Health and Social Security (1986).

of the problem. Of the 328 million days lost from work in the UK in 1984–85, 53 million (16%) were due to mental health causes. A look at the reasons given by British men for days off due to stress-related illness shows a huge increase over a 25-year period in the category of "nervousness, debility and headache".

In one effort to determine how widespread mental health problems are in the USA, 17,000 people were interviewed at five regional sites as part of a government study. The results showed that over a 6-month period, between 17 and 23% of those interviewed had experienced at least one major psychological disorder. Between 7 and 15% reported having had at least one anxiety disorder. When questioned about a lifetime's incidence of mental health problems, between 29 and 38% said they had suffered one or more major disorders. As the government study stated, "psychological disorders were most common during the prime working ages of 25 to 44 years" (US Commission on Mental Health, 1978).

Costs in the workplace

All of the potential stress costs outlined so far combine both to lessen the satisfaction obtained from work and reduce on-the-job performance. Later in this chapter, we will look more closely at how work influences stress levels, but it is relevant here to mention the ways in which stress is reflected in the workplace.

Job satisfaction

At least one study shows that job satisfaction among US workers fell during the 1970s (Quinn and Staines, 1979). The US experience was reinforced in other industrialized countries. For example, between one-quarter and one-third of Swedish workers described their work as being often stressful (Bolinder and Ohlstrom, 1971).

Stress levels in various occupations are known to differ. Certain occupations, such as mining, piloting, police work, advertising and acting, are believed to provide the highest stress levels (Cooper *et al.*, 1988). Stress on the job becomes an occupational hazard for certain "helping" professionals, such as physicians, dentists, nurses and health technologists, who have higher than expected rates of suicide and alcohol/drug abuse. "Burnout", or the premature retirement from one's career due to stress, appears particularly common among nurses. Nurses and others in the health field suffer from mental ill health to the extent that more of them are being admitted to hospitals and clinics for the treatment of mental disorders than in previous years.

Job performance

Experiments and studies have shown that, within certain limits, an individual's performance actually improves with increased levels of stress. After a point, however, stress clearly results in reduced performance. The Yerkes–Dodson law, as shown in Fig. 16.2, reflects this phenomenon in medical terms. As Melhuish (1978) suggested:

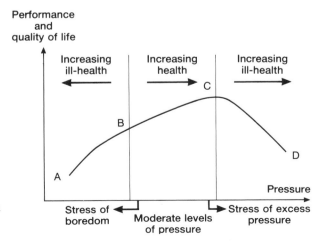

16.2 Medical extension of Yerkes–Dodson Law (from Melhuish, 1978).

the portion of the graph between B and C represents pressures which the individual can tolerate: within these limits his health and quality of life improve with increased pressure (challenge). At C, however, increased pressure loses its beneficial effect and becomes harmful. Pressure becomes stress and in the portion C–D, health and quality of life decrease. C is the threshold (as is B, for boredom is also a potent stress and the portion B–A also represents increasing risk of stress illness).

Absenteeism and turnover of labour force

Absenteeism is one of the most obvious costs of stress to employers. In general, indications are that absenteeism is a widespread and accelerating problem in many occupations. By the 1970s, it was recognized that time lost from work due to stress-related illnesses cost the UK far more than losses due to work stoppages and strikes. The Confederation of British Industry (1970) reported that absenteeism "has risen alarmingly in recent years in spite of improvements in social and working conditions, income levels, and family health". In 1984–85, 328 million days of work were lost in the UK. In at least one occupation, nursing, short-term absences among nurses are increasingly being blamed on clinical anxiety and depression believed to result from occupational strain (Hingley and Cooper, 1986).

High rates of employee turnover can become quite expensive to a company – they raise training costs, reduce overall efficiency and disrupt other workers. Although it is hard to estimate the actual costs of labour turnover, it is thought that they often equal about five times an employee's monthly salary (Quick and Quick, 1984).

Litigation and health care costs

Employers are paying directly for stress-related illnesses through workers' compensation claims. Lubin reported that:

> In general, claims for psychological disorders suffered as the result of job experiences have multiplied over the decade of the '70s ... in 1979, the State of California alone received more than 3,000–4,000 "psychiatric" injury claims, half of which resulted in monetary awards.

Ivancevich *et al.* (1985) have reviewed landmark court cases which have resulted in US corporations increasingly being held responsible for workplace stress. For example, in 1955, an iron worker named Bailey saw a fellow scaffolding worker fall to his death. Bailey returned to work, but gradually he began to have frequent black-outs and became paralysed. He also suffered from sleeping difficulties and extreme sensitivity to pain. In the resulting court case, *Bailey v. American General*, a Texas court ruled in Bailey's favour. The physical accident and psychological trauma were held responsible for the onset of the subsequent paralysis and other problems. Although not a radical decision, it paved the way for compensation cases under existing laws. Many employers are being held responsible for employee stress due to the belief that they are doing little to cut down the stressful aspects of many jobs. This may help to explain the growth in corporate health and stress management programmes in the USA. Those employers who are at least seen to be doing something about workplace stress may be able to put forward a better defence in the courts.

According to a US government report, one specific type of compensation claim, "gradual mental stress", has shown significant growth in recent years. As the report explained, this type of claim refers to:

> cumulative emotional problems stemming mainly from exposure to adverse psychosocial conditions at work. ... Emotional problems related to a specific traumatic event at work, or to work-related physical disease or injury, such as witnessing a severe accident, are not included. (NCCI, 1985).

According to the report, about 11% of all occupational disease claims involve gradual mental stress.

What are the sources of stress at work?

Stress-related illness is not confined to either high- or low-status workers (Smith *et al.*, 1978; McLean, 1979). Regardless of how one job may compare to another in terms of stress, it is helpful to recognize that every job has potential stress agents. Researchers have identified five major categories of work stress (Cooper *et al.*, 1988). Common to all jobs, these factors vary in the degree to which they are found to be causally linked to stress in each job. The five categories are: factors intrinsic to the job; role in the organization; relationships at work; career development; and organizational structure and climate.

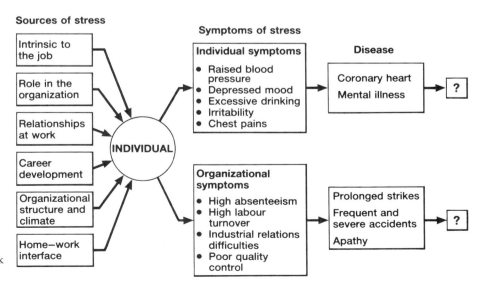

16.3 Dynamics of work stress.

Factors intrinsic to the job

As a starting-point to understanding work stess, researchers have studied those factors which may be intrinsic to the job itself, such as poor working conditions, shift work, long hours, travel, risk and danger, new technology, work overload and work underload.

Working conditions

Our physical surroundings – noise, lighting, smells and all the stimuli which bombard our senses – can affect our moods and overall mental state, whether or not we find them consciously objectionable. Considerable research has linked working conditions to mental health. Kornhauser (1965) suggested that "poor mental health was directly related to unpleasant working conditions, the necessity to work fast and to expend a lot of physical effort, and to excessive and inconvenient hours". Others have found that physical health is also adversely affected by repetitive and dehumanizing work settings, such as fast-paced assembly lines (Cooper and Smith, 1985). In one study of stress factors associated with casting work in a steel manufacturing plant, poor working conditions such as noise, fumes and, to a lesser extent, heat, together with the social and psychological consequences, including isolation and tension among workers, had a significant impact (Kelly and Cooper, 1981).

Health workers, too, often face a variety of noxious stimuli. Hospital lighting, for example, is usually artificial, monotonous and too bright or garish. One study of the problems experienced by nurses working in intensive care units in the USA found that an oppressive visual environment became particularly stressful to nurses over a period of time (Hay and Oken, 1972). This factor, combined with the incessant routine nature of many of the activities, led to feelings of being trapped, of claustrophobia and dehumanization. Poor ventilating systems worsen the problems in many hospitals. In addition, the high noise level of a busy ward adds to the stress factors faced by health professionals. All of this, of course, is in addition to the stress encountered in dealing daily with death and pain.

Each occupation has its own potential environmental sources of stress. For example, in jobs where individuals are dealing with close detail work, poor lighting can create eye strain. On the other hand, extremely bright lighting or glare presents problems for air traffic controllers. Similarly, as Ivancevich and Matteson (1980) stated:

> noise, in fact, seems to operate less as a stressor in situations where it is excessive but expected, than in those where it is unexpected, or at least unpredictable. The change in noise levels more than absolute levels themselves, seems to be the irritant. This, of course, is simply another way of saying that noise, like any stressor, causes stress when it forces us to change.

The physical design of the workplace can be another potential source of stress. If an office is poorly designed, with personnel who require frequent contact spread throughout a building, poor communication networks can develop, resulting in role ambiguity and poor relationships.

Shift work

Many workers today have jobs requiring them to work in shifts, some of which involve working staggered hours. Studies have found that shift work is a common occupational stress factor. It has been demonstrated that shift work affects blood temperature, metabolic rate, blood sugar levels, mental efficiency and work motivation, not to mention sleep patterns and family and social life. In one study of air traffic controllers, shift work was isolated as a major problem area, although other major job stress agents were also present (Cobb and Rose, 1973). These workers had four times the prevalence of hypertension, and also more mild diabetes and peptic ulcers than did a control group of US Air Force personnel.

In a study of offshore oil rig workers, the third most important source of stress found was a general category labelled "work patterns", such as shift work, physical conditions and travel (Sutherland and Cooper, 1987). The longer the work shift, e.g. "28 days on, 28 days off" *vs* "14 days on, 14 days off", the greater the stress. The shift work patterns were a predictor of mental and physical ill health, particularly when the oil rig workers were married and had children.

A major study of UK nurses (Tasto *et al.*, 1978) identified shift work as a major problem. The study, which compared nurses working fixed shift with those working rotating shifts, found that the rotating nurses fared the worst, followed closely by night-shift workers. Shift rotators reported a greater use of alcohol, a higher frequency of problems with their health and their sex lives, and less satisfaction in their personal lives than other shift workers. Rotating shift nurses were significantly more confused, depressed and anxious than those nurses on non-rotating shifts. The investigators concluded that "rotation was a scheduling system that imposes excessive physical and psychological costs to the workers". The study also found that, unlike fixed-shift workers, those on rotating shifts showed little or no tendency to adapt over time.

Long hours

The long working hours required by many jobs appear to take a toll on employee health. One research study has made a link between long working hours and deaths due to coronary heart disease (Breslow and Buell, 1960). This investigation of light industrial workers in the USA found that individuals under 45 years of age who worked more than 48 hours a week, had twice the risk of death from coronary heart disease than did similar individuals working a maximum of 40 hours a week.

Another study of 100 young coronary patients revealed that 25% of them had been working at two jobs, and an additional 40% worked for more than 60 hours a week (Russek and Zohman, 1958). Many individuals, such as executives working long hours and some medics who might have no sleep for 36 hours or more, may find that both they and the quality of their work suffer. It is now commonly recognized that beyond 40 hours a week, time spent working is increasingly unproductive.

Risk and danger

A job which involves risk or danger can result in higher stress levels. When someone is constantly aware of potential danger, he or she is prepared to react immediately. The individual is in a constant state of arousal, as described in the "fight or flight" syndrome. The resulting adrenalin rush, respiration changes and muscle tension are all seen as potentially threatening to long-term health. On the other hand, individuals who face physical danger – such as police, mine workers, firemen and soldiers – often appear to have reduced stress levels, particularly those who are adequately trained and equipped to deal with emergency situations.

New technology

The introduction of new technology into the work environment (see also Chapter 17) has required workers, particularly blue-collar workers, to adapt continually to new equipment, systems and ways of working. Having a boss trained in the "old ways" may be an extra burden for the new employee trained in the latest methods, and raises questions about the adequacy of supervision and about those in senior positions.

In a study of causes of stress among executives in 10 countries (Cooper, 1984), Japanese executives suffered particularly from pressure to keep up with new technology, i.e. to maintain their technological superiority. Managers in "developing countries" felt pressure due to the increasing emphasis on new technology, the need to deal with an adequately trained workforce and the imposition of deadlines. Also, in the UK, a high percentage of managers (second only to Japan) said that keeping up with new technology was a great source of pressure at work. This is not surprising in a nation that many people feel is beginning to slip behind competitors in the race to grab new export markets. In addition, these UK managers described a high level of stress due to the amount of travel required by their work.

Work overload

Two different types of work overload have been described by researchers: *quantitative* overload refers simply to having too much work to do, whereas *qualitative* overload refers to work that is too difficult for an individual (French and Caplan, 1972). In the first case, too much work often leads to working long hours with the attendant problems described above. A too heavy work burden has also been connected with increased cigarette smoking.

In a 1973 study, 22 white-collar workers were observed for 2 or 3 hours a day for 3 days (French and Caplan, 1972). Two observers recorded data on events occurring in the job environment, and heart rate responses to these events. The workers also wore pocket-sized devices which assessed their heart rates without interfering with their activities. The workers also filled out questionnaires describing their work load over the 3-day period. The researchers found that those people who admitted to feeling work pressure were observed to suffer more interruptions from visitors and phone calls. Secondly, these workers suffered significantly more physiological strain through higher heart rates and higher cholesterol levels.

Work underload

Cox (1980) has described the problem of not being sufficiently challenged by work. Job underload associated with repetitive routine, boring and understimulating work has been associated with ill health. Certain workers, such as pilots, air traffic controllers and nuclear power workers, face a special aspect of work underload. They must deal with long periods of time in which they have little to do, while facing the possibility that they may suddenly be required to spring into action in a crisis.

Role in the organization

When a person's role in an organization is clearly defined and understood, and when expectations placed upon the individual are also clear and non-conflicting, stress can be kept to a minimum. But as researchers have clearly seen, this is not the case in many work sites. Three critical factors, role ambiguity, role conflict and the degree of responsibility for others, are seen to be major sources of stress.

Role ambiguity

Role ambiguity arises when individuals do not have a clear picture about their work objectives, their co-workers' expectations of them, and the scope and responsibilities of their job. Often this ambiguity results simply because a supervisor does not lay out to the employee exactly what their role is. As Warshaw (1979) has stated: "The individual just doesn't know how he or she fits into the organization and is unsure of any rewards no matter how well he or she may perform."

A wide range of events can create role ambiguity. Ivancevich and Matteson (1980) highlighted these: the first job, a promotion or transfer, a new boss, the first supervisory responsibility, a new company, or a change in the structure of the existing organization – all of these events and others, may serve to create a temporary state of role ambiguity. The stress indicators found to relate to role ambiguity are depressed mood, lowered self-esteem, life dissatisfaction, low motivation to work and the intention to leave a job.

Role conflict

Role conflict exists when an individual is torn by conflicting job demands or by doing things he or she does not really want to do, or things which the individual does not believe are part of the job. Workers may often feel themselves torn between two groups of people who demand different types of behaviour or who believe the job entails different functions.

Conflict situations can clearly act as stress factors upon the individuals involved. Research has indicated that role conflict leads to reduced job satisfaction and higher anxiety levels. Other research has shown that role conflict can lead to risks of cardiovascular ill health, such as elevated blood pressure and abnormal blood chemistry (Ivancevich and Matteson, 1980).

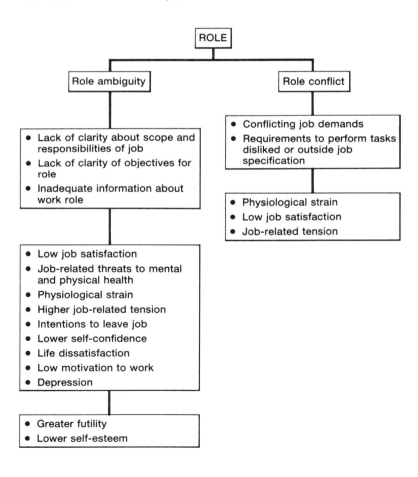

16.4 Sources of role stress at work.

Personality variables

As might be expected, studies have shown that people with high anxiety levels suffer more from role conflicts than do people who are more flexible in their approach to life. Anxiety-prone individuals experience role conflict more acutely and react to it with greater tension than people who are less anxiety prone; and more flexible individuals respond to high role conflict with lesser feeling of tension than their more rigid counterparts (Warr and Wall, 1975). In other studies, when the individual has had stronger needs for cognitive clarity or lower levels of tolerance for ambiguity, job-related stress has been found to be higher and more prolonged.

Responsibility

Responsibility has been found to be another organizational role stress agent. In an organization, there are basically two types of responsibility: responsibility for people and responsibility for things, such as budgets, equipment and buildings. Responsibility for people has been found to be particularly stressful. Studies in the 1960s found that this was far more likely to lead to coronary heart disease than was responsibility for things (Wardwell *et al.*, 1964). Being responsible for people usually requires spending more time interacting with others, attending meetings and attempting to meet deadlines. An investigation in the UK of 1200 managers sent by their companies for annual medical examinations linked physical stress to age and level of responsibility (Pincherle, 1972). The older the executive and the more responsibility held by the executive, the greater the probability of coronary heart disease risk factors. As Ivancevich and Matteson (1980) stated:

> Part of the reason responsibility for people acts as a stressor undoubtedly results from the specific nature of the responsibility, particularly as it relates to the need to make unpleasant interpersonal decisions. Another part of the reason ... is that people in responsibility positions lend themselves to overload, and perhaps role conflict and ambiguity as well.

Relationships at work

Other people – and our varied encounters with them – can be major sources of both stress and support. At work, especially, dealings with bosses, peers and subordinates can dramatically affect the way we feel at the end of the day. Selye (1974) suggested that learning to live with other people is one of the most stressful aspects of life.

It is an interesting fact, however, that little research has been done in this area. Lazarus (1966) suggested that supportive social relationships with peers, supervisors and subordinates at work are less likely to create interpersonal pressures, and will directly reduce levels of perceived job stress. Poor relationships were defined by University of Michigan researchers as those which include low trust, low supportiveness and low interest in listening and trying to deal with problems that confront the organizational member.

Most studies have concluded that mistrust of fellow workers is connected with high role ambiguity, poor communications and with psychological strain in the form of low job satisfaction and with feelings of job-related threat to one's well-being. There are three critical relationships at work: relationships with superiors, relationships with subordinates and relationships with colleagues or co-workers.

Relationships with superiors

Physicians and clinical psychologists support the idea that problems of emotional disability often result when the relationship between a subordinate and a boss is psychologically unhealthy for one reason or another. Buck (1972) focused on the relationship of workers to an immediate boss and found that when the boss was perceived as "considerate", there was "friendship, mutual trust, respect and a certain warmth between boss and subordinate" (see also Chapter 13, this volume). Workers who said their boss was low on consideration reported feeling more job pressure. Workers who were under pressure reported that their bosses did not give them criticism in a helpful way, played favourites and pulled rank and took advantage of them whenever they got a chance.

Relationships with subordinates

The way in which a manager supervises the work of others has always been considered a critical aspect of his or her work. For instance, the inability to delegate has been a common criticism levelled against some managers. It now appears that managers face a new challenge – learning to manage by *participation*. Today's emphasis on participation can be a cause of resentment, anxiety and stress for the managers involved.

Relationships with colleagues

Stress among co-workers can arise from the competition and personality conflicts usually described as "office politics". Adequate social support can be critical to the health and well-being of an individual and to the atmosphere and success of an organization. Because most people spend so much time at work, the relationships among co-workers can provide valuable support or, conversely, can be a huge source of stress. French and Caplan (1972) found that strong social support from co-workers eased job strain. This support also mediated the effects of job strain on cortisone levels, blood pressure, glucose levels and the number of cigarettes smoked.

Career development

A host of issues can act as potential stress factors throughout one's working life. A lack of job security, fear of redundancy, obsolescence or retirement, and numerous performance appraisals can cause pressure and strain. In addition, the frustration of having reached one's career ceiling, or having been over-promoted, can result in extreme stress. Ivancevich and Matteson (1980) suggested that individuals suffering from "career stress" often show high job dissatisfaction, job mobility, burnout, poor work performance, and less effective interpersonal relationships at work.

Job security

For many workers, career progression is of overriding importance. Through promotion, people not only earn more money, but enjoy increased status and new challenges. In the early years in a career, the striving and ability required to deal with a rapidly changing environment is usually rewarded by a company through monetary and promotional rewards. At middle age, however, many people find their career progress has slowed or stopped. Job opportunities may become fewer, available jobs can require longer to master, old knowledge may become obsolete, and energy levels can flag. At the same time, younger competition threatens (see also Chapter 15).

Retirement

The transition to retirement can be in itself a stressful event. While a job is a socially defined role, retirement has been described as the "roleless role". The vagueness and lack of structure of retirement can provide problems for the ill-prepared. For some individuals, becoming "pensioners" or "senior citizens" presents a situation in which they are uncertain how to obtain the social rewards they value. In contrast, those individuals who have maintained balance in their lives by developing interests and friends outside their work environment can find retirement a liberating period in their lives.

Job performance

The process of being evaluated and appraised can be a stressful experience for all of us. It must be recognized that performance appraisals can be anxiety-provoking, for both the individual being examined and the person doing the judging and appraising. The supervisor making performance judgements faces the threat of union grievance procedures in some cases, as well as interpersonal strains and the responsibility of making decisions affecting another person's livelihood.

The way in which an evaluation is carried out can affect the degree of anxiety experienced. For example, taking a written examination can be a short-term stress factor, whereas continuous and confidential appraisals by supervisors can have a more long-term effect, depending on the structure and climate of the organization.

Organizational structure and climate

Just being part of an organization can present threats to an individual's sense of freedom and autonomy. Workers within organizations sometimes complain they do not have a sense of belonging, lack adequate opportunities to participate, feel their behaviour is unduly restricted and are not included in office communications and consultations.

As early as the 1940s, researchers began reporting that workers who were allowed more participation in decision making produced more and had higher job satisfaction (Coch and French, 1948). They also found that non-participation at work was a significant predictor of strain and job-related stress, relating to general poor health, escapist drinking, depression, low self-esteem, absenteeism and plans to leave work. Participation in the decision-making process on the part of the individual may help increase his or her feeling of investment in the company's success, create a sense of belonging and improve communication channels within the organization. The resulting sense of being in control seems vital for the well-being of the workforce.

The stress of being unemployed

With relatively high levels of unemployment in the UK throughout the 1980s and into the 1990s, the stress of being unemployed has been a major topic of concern. It is a problem faced by many, from the unskilled to the professional worker. In a review of research on the psychological experience of being unemployed, Fryer and Payne (1986) suggested that people who experience unemployment generally suffer from lower levels of personal happiness, life satisfaction, self-esteem and psychological well-being. They also tend to report increased depression, difficulty in concentrating and other minor to severe behavioural problems.

In addition, there is a growing literature which suggests a strong link between physical illness and unemployment stress. In Australia, one study found that the unemployed, in contrast to the employed, reported significantly more symptoms of bronchitis, ear, nose and throat problems, as well as allergies. In a similar British study, similar results were found, with the added complications of obstructive lung disease and coronary heart disease (Hayes and Nutman, 1981).

Although there is a difference of opinion about the relationship between unemployment and mortality, evidence is emerging of a positive association, with studies indicating that long-term unemployment may adversely affect the longevity of the unemployed by as much as 2–3 years, depending on when the person had been made redundant.

It is clear, then, that people who are unemployed do not have an easy time. But how, exactly, does unemployment affect people? Some psychologists have proposed a stage model of reactions to unemployment (e.g. Eisenberg and Lazarsfeld, 1938). At first, the person reacts with *shock*, an emotional response which may include surprise, anger or even relief. They then enter the *optimism* stage, when they still feel it is likely they will obtain another job, and often spend time catching up with jobs around the house. After a time, this is said to give way to *pessimism* as job applications meet with no success, and then to *fatalism*, when the person feels a sense of hopelessness, becomes resigned to their fate, and stops trying to obtain another job. This stage model may be a reasonably accurate description of how many people react to unemployment, but it is very imprecise about when and why one stage gives way to the next (Kelvin and Jarrett, 1985).

Other psychologists have tried to identify exactly what is is about unemployment which leads people to feel psychologically bad. Jahoda (1979) wrote of the manifest function of employment (income), but also its latent functions – structuring of time, social contact outside the family, linkage to wider goals/ purposes, personal status/identity and enforced activity. A person who becomes unemployed is deprived of both the manifest and the latent functions of employment, and it is this, Jahoda argues, that leads to negative psychological states.

Others have seen Jahoda's approach as too limited. Warr (1983) pointed out that not all employment fosters mental health, and identified features of "psychologically good" employment. These include money, variety, goals, opportunity for decision making, skill use/development, security, interpersonal contact and valued social position. This pays more attention than Jahoda to characteristics of the job itself. Warr argued that becoming unemployed would have negative psychological effects to the extent that it led to a loss of these features in day-to-day life. David Fryer (Fryer and Payne, 1986) has taken a rather different approach. He has criticized conventional treatments of unemployment for taking an overly passive view of the person. The psychological effects of unemployment are, he has argued, the result of frustrated attempts to create a better future rather than memories and regrets about loss of a more satisfying past.

Summary

Stress in the workplace has become the black plague of the twentieth century. This is likely to get worse as international competition increases with the advent of 1992, the Pacific Basin and the economic and political liberation of Eastern Europe. These pressures at work are also likely to lead to less rather than more concern for the "people management" aspects of the workplace. Much of the stress at work is caused not only by work overload and time pressures, but also by a lack of rewards and praise, and more importantly, by not providing individuals with the autonomy to do their jobs as they would like. We shall see, therefore, an increasing army of human resource professionals, such as stress counsellors, entering the arena of work over the next decade. We will need them, but they are only part of the answer. Organizations must begin to manage people at work differently, treating them with respect and valuing their contribution, if we are to enhance the psychological well-being and health of workers in the future.

Case study 16.1   Type A behavioural pattern

Many managers and other white-collar and professional people who may be vulnerable to stress at work seem to display a pattern of behaviour termed type A stress prone behaviour (Rosenman *et al.*, 1964). The following questionnaire was developed by Bortner (1964) to assess an individual's type A behaviour. We thought it might be useful for the reader to assess

his or her own stress prone behaviour. Fill in the following questionnaire and then score it as suggested. If you are a high type A, it means that you are very competitive, high achieving, aggressive, hasty, impatient, time-conscious and hard driving. Type B, which is the other end of the continuum, is the opposite of this characterization.

Type A behaviour

Circle one number for each of the statements below which best reflects the way you behave in your everyday life. For example, if you are generally on time for appointments, for the first point you would circle a number between 7 and 11. If you are usually casual about appointments, you would circle one of the lower numbers between 1 and 5.

Casual about appointments	1 2 3 4 5 6 7 8 9 10 11	Never late
Not competitive	1 2 3 4 5 6 7 8 9 10 11	Very competitive
Good listener	1 2 3 4 5 6 7 8 9 10 11	Anticipates what others are going to say (nods, attempts to finish for them)
Never feels rushed (even under pressure)	1 2 3 4 5 6 7 8 9 10 11	Always rushed
Can wait patiently	1 2 3 4 5 6 7 8 9 10 11	Impatient while waiting
Takes things one at a time	1 2 3 4 5 6 7 8 9 10 11	Tries to do many things at once, thinks about what will do next
Slow, deliberate talker	1 2 3 4 5 6 7 8 9 10 11	Emphatic in speech, fast and forceful
Cares about satisfying him/herself no matter what others may think	1 2 3 4 5 6 7 8 9 10 11	Wants good job recognized by others

Slow doing things	1 2 3 4 5 6 7 8 9 10 11	Fast (eating, walking)
Easy-going	1 2 3 4 5 6 7 8 9 10 11	Hard driving (pushing yourself and others)
Expresses feelings	1 2 3 4 5 6 7 8 9 10 11	Hides feelings
Many outside interests	1 2 3 4 5 6 7 8 9 10 11	Few interests outside work/home
Unambitious	1 2 3 4 5 6 7 8 9 10 11	Ambitious
Casual	1 2 3 4 5 6 7 8 9 10 11	Eager to get things done

Plot total score below:

Type B		Type A
14	84	154

Source: Cooper's adaptation of the Bortner Type A Scale.

Scoring

The higher the score received on this questionnaire, the more firmly an individual can be classified as type A. For example, 154 points is the highest score and indicates the maximum type A coronary-prone personality. It is important to understand that there are no distinct divisions between type A and type B. Rather, people fall somewhere on a continuum leaning more towards one type than the other. Eighty-four is an average score. Anyone with a score above that is inclined towards type A behaviour, and below that towards type B behaviour.

References

Bolinder, E. and Ohlstrom, B. (1971). *Stress pa Svenska Arbetsplatser: en Enkatstudie Bland LO-Medlemmasrna*. Lund: Prima/LO.

Bortner, R. W. (1964). A short rating scale as a potential measure of pattern A behaviour. *Journal of Chronic Diseases, 22*, 87–91.

Breslow, L. and Buell, P. (1960). Mortality from coronary heart disease and physical activity of work in California. *Journal of Chronic Diseases, 11*, 615–625.

Buck, V. (1972). *Working Under Pressure*. London: Staples Press.

CBI (1970). *Absenteeism: An Analysis of the Problem*. London: CBI

Cobb, S. and Rose, R. H. (1973). Hypertension, peptic ulcer and diabetes in air traffic controllers. *Journal of the Australian Medical Association, 224*, 489–492.

Coch, L. and French, J. R. P. (1948). Overcoming resistance to change. *Human Relations, 1*, 512–532.

Cooper, C. L. (1984). Executive stress: A ten country comparison. *Human Resource Management, 23*, 395–407.

Cooper, C. L. and Smith, M. J. (1985). *Job Stress and Blue Collar Work*. Chichester: John Wiley.

Cooper, C. L., Cooper, R. D. and Eaker, L. H. (1988). *Living with Stress*. Harmondsworth: Penguin.

Cox, T. (1980). Repetitive work. In C. L. Cooper and R. Payne (Eds), *Current Concerns in Occupational Stress*. Chichester: John Wiley.

Cummings, T. and Cooper, C. L. (1979). A cybernetic framework for the study of occupational stress. *Human Relations, 32*, 395–419.

Department of Health and Social Security (1986). *Employment Gazette*, August. London: DHSS.

Eisenberg, P. and Lazarsfeld, P. F. (1938). The psychological effects of unemployment. *Psychological Bulletin, 35*, 358–390.

French, J. R. P. and Caplan, R. D. (1972). Organizational stress and individual strain. In A. Marrow (Ed.), *The Failure of Success*. New York: AMACOM.

Fryer, D. and Payne, R. (1986). Being unemployed. In C. L. Cooper and I. T. Robertson (Eds), *International Review of Industrial and Organizational Psychology, 1986*. Chichester: John Wiley.

Hay, D. and Oken, D. (1972). The psychological stresses of intensive care nursing. *Psychosomatic Medicine, 34*, 109–118.

Hayes, J. and Nutman, P. (1981). *Understanding the Unemployed*. London: Tavistock.

Hingley, P. and Cooper, C. L. (1986). *Stress and the Nurse Manager*. Chichester: John Wiley.

Hinkle, L. E. (1973). The concept of stress in the biological social sciences. *Stress Medicine, 1*, 31–48.

Ivancevich, J. M. and Matteson, M. T. (1980). *Stress and Work*. Glenview, Ill.: Scott, Foresman.

Ivancevich, J. M., Matteson, M. T. and Richards, E. P. (1985). Who's liable for stress on the job? *Harvard Business Review*, March–April.

Jahoda, M. (1979). The impact of unemployment in the 1930s and the 1970s. *Bulletin of the British Psychological Society, 32*, 309–314.

Kelly, M. and Cooper, C. L. (1981). Stress among blue collar workers. *Employee Relations, 3*, 6–9.

Kelvin, P. and Jarrett, J. E. (1985). *Unemployment: Its Social Psychological Effects*. Cambridge: Cambridge University Press.

Kornhauser, A. (1965). *Mental Health of the Industrial Worker*. New York: John Wiley.

Lazarus, R. S. (1966). *Psychological Stress and Coping Process*. New York: McGraw-Hill.

Lubin, J. S. (1980). On-the-job stress leads many workers to file, and win, compensation awards. *Wall Street Journal*, 17 September.

McLean, A. (1979). *Work Stress*. Reading, Mass.: Addison-Wesley.

Melhuish, A. (1978). *Executive Health*. London: Business Books.

National Council on Compensation Insurance (1985). *Emotional Stress in the Workplace – New Legal Rights in the Eighties*. New York: NCCI.

NIOSH (1986). *National Strategy on the Prevention of Work-related Psychological Disorders*. Cincinnati, Ohio: NIOSH.

Pincherle, A. (1972). Fitness for work. *Proceedings of the Royal Society of Medicine, 65*, 321–324.

Quick, J. C. and Quick, J. D. (1984). *Organizational Stress and Preventive Management*. New York: McGraw-Hill.

Quinn, R. P. and Staines, G. L. (1979). *The 1977 Quality of Employment Survey*. Ann Arbor, Mich.: University of Michigan Press.

Rosenman, R., Freidman, F. and Straus, R. (1964). A predictive study of CHD. *Journal of the American Medical Association, 189*, 15–22.

Russek, H. I. and Zohman, B. L. (1958). Relative significance of heredity, diet and occupational stress in CHD of young adults. *American Journal of Medical Sciences, 235*, 266–275.

Selye, H. (1946). The General Adaptation Syndrome and the diseases of adaptation. *Journal of Clinical Endocrinology, 6*, 117.

Selye, H. (1974). *Stress Without Distress*. Philadelphia, Penn.: J. B. Lippincott.

Smith, M., Colligan, M., Horning, R. and Hurrell, J. (1978). *Occupational Comparison of Stress-related Disease Incidence*. Cincinnati, Ohio: National Institute for Occupational Safety and Health.

Sutherland, V. and Cooper, C. L. (1987). *Man and Accidents Offshore*. London: Lloyds.

Tasto, D., Colligan, M., Skjei, E. and Polly, S. (1978). *Health Consequences of Shiftwork*. Washington, D.C.: NIOSH US Government Printing Office.

US Commission on Mental Health (1978). Stock no. 040–000–00390–8. Washington, D.C.: US Government Printing Office.

Wardwell, W., Hyman, I. M. and Bahnson, C. B. (1964). Stress and coronary disease in three field studies. *Journal of Chronic Disease, 17*, 73–74.

Warr, P. (1983). Work, jobs and unemployment. *Bulletin of the British Psychological Society, 36*, 305–311.

Warr, P. and Wall, T. (1975). *Work and Well-being*. Harmondsworth: Penguin.

Warshaw, L. J. (1979). *Managing Stress*. Reading, Mass.: Addison-Wesley.

Job redesign and new technology

Introduction

The term *job redesign* refers to attempts to increase the amounts of variety and autonomy experienced by people in their jobs. This increase is deemed desirable by many managers and social scientists because of a consistent tendency throughout the twentieth century for jobs to become increasingly monotonous and controlled. The first half of this chapter therefore elaborates on this perceived need, and evaluates theoretical and practical attempts to meet it. The second half of the chapter covers *new technology*, which is the general term given to computer-controlled equipment of various kinds. Such equipment became much more widely available and affordable from the 1970s onwards due to advances in microelectronics. The introduction of new technology into the workplace often has important implications for the nature of jobs. This is why job redesign and new technology are covered in the same chapter. The process of introducing new technology and the effects of new technology on organizations are also examined.

Job redesign

Job simplification and job enrichment

Surveys (e.g. Taylor, 1979) have identified the following key factors in the design of most jobs:

- minimizing skill requirements;
- maximizing management control; and
- minimizing the time required to perform a task.

These may appear to make good sense, especially against economic criteria. Unskilled or semi-skilled labour costs less than skilled labour, and productivity is enhanced if tasks are done quickly. But, as we shall see, jobs designed in this way frequently have human costs, and perhaps economic ones too.

This "traditional" approach to job design stems from a philosophy called "scientific management" or "Taylorism", after its creator F. W. Taylor. Taylor formulated his ideas in the USA around the turn of the century. As a machine-shop foreman, he felt that workers consistently underproduced, and that the way to prevent this was to:

- systematically (or "scientifically") compile information about the work tasks required;
- remove workers' discretion and control over their own activities;
- simplify tasks as much as possible;
- specify standard procedures and times for task completion;
- use financial (and *only* financial) incentives; and
- by the above methods, ensure that workers could not deceive managers, or hide from them.

This, of course, bears a strong resemblance to the "Theory X" view of human nature (see Chapter 10). Observers agree that jobs in many, perhaps most, organizations are implicitly or explicitly based on Taylorism.

Taylorism might make for a well-ordered world, but is it a happy and productive one? During the 1960s, a number of studies seemed to show that work organized along scientific management principles was associated with negative attitudes towards the job, as well as poor mental and/or physical health (e.g. Kornhauser, 1965; Turner and Lawrence, 1965). It was also often assumed that poor productivity would accompany such outcomes, though of course in Chapter 3 we have already seen that the maxim "a happy worker is a productive worker" does not always apply. Another assumption was that simplified work produced poor mental health, etc., rather than the reverse causal direction.

These studies of simplified work led to considerable concern about what came to be called "quality of working life" (QWL). Several theoretical perspectives were brought to bear on QWL. One was *job enrichment*, a concept developed through the work of Herzberg (1966). Herzberg proposed a basic distinction between *hygiene factors* and *motivators*. Hygiene factors included pay, conditions of employment, the work environment and other features extrinsic to the work activities themselves. Motivators included job challenge, recognition and skill-use, i.e. features appealing to growth needs (see Chapter 10). On the basis of his data, Herzberg proposed that hygiene factors could not cause satisfaction, but that dissatisfaction could result if they were not present. On the other hand, motivators led to satisfaction: their absence produced not dissatisfaction, but an absence of satisfaction. Although Herzberg's data and conclusions can be criticized on several grounds, his recommendation that motivation and/or satisfaction can be enhanced by increasing skill-use, job challenge, etc., is consistent with much subsequent research.

Another relevant theoretical tradition is *sociotechnical systems* (Davis, 1982; Cherns, 1976, 1987; Heller, 1989). Emanating from studies in the immediate post-war years, sociotechnical theory emphasizes the need to integrate technology and social structures in the workplace (see Chapter 1 of this volume). Too often, technology is introduced with scant regard for existing friendship patterns, work groups and within-organization status differentials (see also pp. 312–21). But sociotechnical theory also makes wider propositions. For example, it states that job activities should be specified only in so far as necessary to establish the boundaries of that job. It also emphasizes that boundaries should be drawn so that they do not impede transmission of information and learning. Such principles may seem self-evident, but close examination of many organizations will demonstrate that they are not adhered to. Sociotechnical job design therefore emphasizes autonomy, decision making and the avoidance of subordinating people to machines.

Job redesign interventions

Whatever their exact theoretical origin, attempts to redesign jobs centre on increasing one or more of the following (Wall, 1982):

- variety (of tasks or skills);
- autonomy (freedom to choose work methods, scheduling and occasionally goals); and
- completeness (extent to which the job produces an identifiable end result which the person can point to).

This may be attempted in one or more of the following ways:

1. *Job rotation*: people rotate through a small set of different (but usually similar) jobs. Rotation is usually frequent (e.g. each week). It can increase variety.

2. *Horizontal job enlargement*: additional tasks are included in a person's job. They are usually similar to tasks already carried out. This too can increase variety.

3. *Vertical job enlargement*: additional decision-making responsibilities and/or higher-level challenging tasks are included in the job. This increases autonomy, variety and possibly completeness.

4. *Semi-autonomous work groups*: similar to vertical job enlargement, but at the level of the group rather than the individual. Semi-autonomous work groups have been introduced in some car factories.

Wall (1982, 1984) has reviewed earlier work on job redesign. He concluded that attempts to redesign jobs usually had an effect as long as they did not confine themselves to increasing variety. Redesign often succeeded in improving job satisfaction, motivation, employee mental health and performance. However, Wall also acknowledged that this conclusion was not definitive. Redesign rarely occurred in the absence of other changes, such as pay rates and staffing levels. It was therefore impossible to be sure what caused any observed change in employee attitudes and behaviour. In fact, Kelly (1982) argued that some case studies of job redesign showed that employee attitude changes came about not when job characteristics were altered, but when factors such as management style or pay rates changed. He also pointed out that although proponents of job redesign argued that motivation/satisfaction led to improved work performance, some instances of job redesign produced changes in one or the other, but not both. Wall (1982) also acknowledged that the results of job redesign may be biased by some unknown special characteristics of people who volunteer (or are volunteered) to try it.

Job redesign has knock-on effects which are often overlooked. For example, Cordery and Wall (1985) have examined what happens to supervisory roles if the workforce is given more autonomy. They argue that supervisors must be helped to change from an overseeing/controlling orientation to an enabling one. Among other things, this requires them to take *more* control over defining the nature and boundary of their work group's task, while *relinquishing* control over how the task is carried out. Traditional approaches to leadership, and probably most supervisors, do not typically make that distinction (see Chapter 13). There is also a heightened need for the supervisor to provide feedback to the group on how things are going, so that the group members can adjust their work strategies if necessary.

The job characteristics model

Since the late 1970s, one theory has dominated the scene in job redesign. This is Hackman and Oldham's (1976, 1980) *job characteristics model*. It is depicted in Fig. 17.1, which shows that Hackman and Oldham identify five "core job characteristics":

1. *Skill variety* (SV): the extent to which the job requires a range of skills.

2. *Task identity* (TI): the extent to which the job allows the worker to complete a "whole" piece of work, as opposed to a small part of it.

3. *Task significance* (TS): the extent to which the job has an impact on the lives of other people, either inside or outside the organization.

4. *Autonomy* (Au): the extent to which the job allows the job holder to exercise choice and discretion in their work.

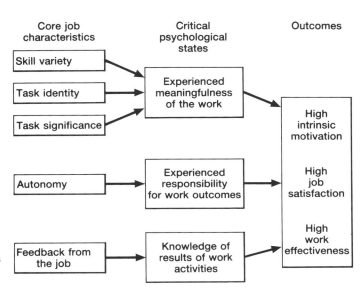

17.1 Hackman and Oldham's job characteristics model (adapted from Hackman and Oldham, 1980, with the permission of Addison-Wesley).

5.   *Feedback from job* (Fb): the extent to which the job itself (as opposed to other people) provides information on how well the job-holder is performing.

The core job characteristics are said to produce "critical psychological states". The first three core job characteristics are believed to influence *experienced meaningfulness of the work*. Autonomy affects *experienced responsibility for outcomes of the work*, and feedback from the job impacts on *knowledge of the actual results of the work activities*. Collectively, the critical psychological states are believed to influence three outcomes: motivation, satisfaction and work performance. But this whole process is said to be moderated by several factors. The most often investigated of these is growth need strength. This refers to the importance to the individual of Maslow's growth needs (see Chapter 10). The model is said to apply more strongly to people with high growth needs than to those with low ones.

The job characteristics model has provoked a huge amount of research, especially in the USA. This is not surprising, because it provides specific hypotheses about exactly which job characteristics matter, how they affect people's psychological states, what outcomes they produce, and which individual differences affect the whole process. Also, Hackman and Oldham have produced a questionnaire called the Job Diagnostic Survey (JDS) which assesses the constructs shown in Fig. 17.1. The JDS is completed by job-holders. Hackman and Oldham also propose an overall motivating potential score (MPS), which is computed as follows:

$$\text{MPS} = \frac{\text{SV} + \text{TI} + \text{TS}}{3} \times \text{Au} \times \text{Fb}$$

Scores on the JDS for each core job characteristic can vary between 1 and 7, so the overall MPS can range from 1 to 343. As one would expect, typical scores vary somewhat between jobs, but a score of around 150 is common. Interestingly, MPS scores for the "job" of student are often quite low. This is frequently because feedback from the job is very limited: students say they can rarely tell how well they have done without feedback from other people. Another reason is low task significance – usually, students' work scarcely affects other people at all. This leads to one potential omission from the job characteristics model: despite a low TS score on the JDS, students often say their role feels significant, because of its influence on *them*, as opposed to other people.

Roberts and Glick (1981) also voiced a number of criticisms of the job characteristics model (JCM). These included the following:

1.   Although research on the JCM had found many of the predicted relationships, this may have been due to common method variance – all the information came from questionnaires, and all from the same people.

2.   Few evaluations of the JCM had tested the model properly. For example, most omitted any examination of moderator variables (see Fig. 17.1).

3.   Few evaluations of the JCM had involved attempts to *redesign* jobs. Instead, most looked for relationships between the variables of interest in unchanged jobs.

4. The model says little about *how* to change tasks in order to increase the amount of core job characteristics it offers.

5. The model says little about how to redesign jobs for people low in growth need strength.

Roberts and Glick's points were well-made, and some (especially the last three above) remain valid now. However, other psychologists have subsequently examined the large and ever-increasing literature on the JCM (e.g. Loher *et al.*, 1985; Fried and Ferris, 1987; Hogan and Martell, 1987). The following conclusions can be drawn:

1. People's descriptions of their jobs on the JDS correlate fairly highly with descriptions of those same jobs by supervisors and expert job analysts. The correlation is usually high enough to indicate that JDS responses say something about the job and do not simply reflect the respondent's preconceptions and attitudes.

2. JDS responses suggest that there are indeed several core job characteristics, but perhaps not as many as five. Specifically, it seems that skill variety, task significance and autonomy may all be part of the same dimension. In other words, they may go together closely enough to be thought of as reflecting the same underlying concept.

3. The core job characteristics are generally correlated with outcomes as predicted. This is more consistently so for motivation and satisfaction than for performance. But the core job characteristics do not always produce the specific psychological states that the JCM predicts.

4. Nevertheless, the critical psychological states correlate more highly with motivation/satisfaction outcomes than do the core job dimensions. But the reverse is true for the work performance outcome.

5. The overall MPS score is often better at predicting outcomes than any individual core job characteristic, as indeed it should be if it represents a meaningful summary of a job. On the other hand, it often seems that simply adding scores on the five core characteristics is at least as good as the prescribed way of calculating MPS.

6. As predicted, the relationships between core job characteristics, critical psychological states and outcomes are stronger for people with high growth need strength than for those with low growth need strength.

7. The JCM fits the available research data better than models using similar variables but in different configurations. There is nevertheless a nagging suspicion that scores on many of the JCM variables stem *from* (rather than lead to) a person's general satisfaction with their work.

8. There are probably additional job characteristics, as yet unidentified, which also predict the outcomes. Warr (1987) has suggested availability of money, physical security, interpersonal contact and valued social position as likely contenders.

All in all, then, JCM has stood empirical test reasonably well, especially considering the relatively large number of connections between specific variables it proposes. However, it is not the whole story, and paradoxically it still has not often been tested in the context of job redesign. Further well-focused investigations are needed to build on the existing foundations.

Finally, it should be remembered that other quite different approaches to job (re)design exist. Campion and Thayer (1985) and Campion (1988) have pointed out that an engineering approach (in essence scientific management), a biological approach (focusing on human physiology) and a perceptual/motor approach (focusing on human information processing) also exist. Their data indicated that the motivational (i.e. JCM) approach did enhance satisfaction, but not work efficiency or reliability. The scientific management approach fostered efficiency and the perceptual/motor approach related to reliability. There were some problems with some of the measures (e.g. efficiency was defined as a low amount of training, education and experience being needed for effective job performance). Nevertheless, Campion's work demonstrates that quite different approaches can also contribute to job redesign, especially perhaps in enhancing some aspects of work performance.

Case study 17.1   Bicycle assembly at Wheelspin

The Wheelspin bicycle company produces a range of bicycles for adults and children. At their factory, already-manufactured components are painted and assembled. Assembly is carried out on assembly lines which move at constant speeds. The factory manager decides which line will assemble which bicycle. Each member of staff has a specific part or parts which they screw, weld or otherwise fix onto the basic frame at a specified point on the assembly line. They carry out the same tasks about 80 times a day. Staff are recruited to a specific job: they generally remain on the same assembly line and deal with the same parts. Once every 2–3 months, the model being assembled changes, but generally the assembly tasks required are more or less unchanging. Noise levels are low enough to allow staff to chat to immediate neighbours as they work. Work quality is assessed at the end of the production line, where performance of the assembled bicycle is examined by quality control staff.

Suggested exercise

Examine the characteristics of the assembly jobs at Wheelspin. How might those characteristics be changed?

New technology

What is new technology?

Technological change in the workplace has, of course, been a continuing process over the centuries. However, the term "new technology" refers to a particular set of changes which have occurred from the 1970s onwards. They have been brought about by the invention and development of *microchips*, which are tiny components of electrical circuits which can be combined to form much larger and more complex electronic systems. Microchips have made it possible to build such systems simply and cheaply and at only a tiny fraction of the weight and size that would formerly have been required (Wall, 1987). There are two general forms of new technology in the workplace:

1. *Advanced Manufacturing Technology* (AMT). This includes a wide range of equipment which contributes to the manufacturing process, usually by working on already made materials. One example is industrial "robots", which can do tasks such as welding and spray-painting, or even playing snooker! Another is automatic guided vehicles (AGVs), which take components from one part of a factory to another. A third is computer-numerically controlled machine tools (CNCs). These conduct precision cutting, drilling or grinding of materials, usually metal, to produce components of larger products. All these examples are underpinned by microchip technology, which allows computer-control of the often precise and complex tasks they undertake (see Wall *et al.*, 1987b).

2. *Office technology*. Here the emphasis is on the storage, retrieval, presentation and manipulation of information, usually in verbal and/or numerical forms (Pava, 1983). The most obvious example is perhaps word-processing equipment, which has rapidly become a prominent feature of most offices (Oborne, 1985; Chapter 9). Another common manifestation is electronic "point of sale" equipment in shops. This uses the bar codes on goods to produce a cumulative account of what has been purchased, not only to the customer but also to the retailing organization for ordering and stock control. A further manifestation is expert and decision-support systems, which compile information relevant to managerial decisions and also work on that information in order to contribute to the decision itself.

Organizations in most Western countries have frequently been exhorted to invest quickly in new technology or face dire consequences in competitive international markets. This perceived need has rarely been challenged, but interestingly the uptake of some forms of new technology was not particularly quick, at least in the earlier years of its availability, perhaps partly due to the high costs of initial purchase and installation. More controversial has been the impact of new technology on the total number of jobs available, with estimates varying from significant increases to huge decreases (see Burnes, 1989, pp. 5–8).

Psychologists and other social scientists have investigated a number of issues concerning new technology. Some ergonomists have worked to improve its compatibility with human information-processing capacities. A fair amount is now known about questions like how to design easily learned word-processing software, though ergonomists' influence in organizations is often very limited (Blackler, 1988). Ergonomic issues will not be covered further here. Instead, we will examine (1) how and why new technology is introduced into organizations, (2) the impact of new technology on job characteristics, linking with the first part of this chapter and (3) the implications of new technology for organizations.

Introduction of new technology

Organizations may introduce new technology for a wide variety of reasons (Blackler and Brown, 1986; Burnes, 1989):

- to reduce costs;
- to increase productivity;
- to increase quality;
- to reduce dependence on skilled labour;
- because it always seems a good idea to be up-to-date;
- because competitor organizations are also introducing new technology;
- because new technology is interesting; and
- to change the power relations between various groups in the organization.

Few managers would confess to the last four as *key* reasons for introducing new technology, yet they often are. For example, Keen (1985) has pointed out that organizational power politics play a crucial role in determining whether and how new technology is introduced. Burnes (1989) found that none of the nine engineering companies he studied had seriously considered any alternative to introducing CNC machines, and several had carried out no financial assessment at all. While the first four reasons cited above were important, Burnes concluded that the main motive for introducing CNCs was a general belief that new technology was "the future".

Blackler and Brown (1986) have gone well beyond initial motives in identifying three ways in which new technology can be introduced. These are summarized in Table 17.1. They argue that the "muddle through approach" is alarmingly common. It stems from managements who have no long-term goals, and whose understanding of technology and organizational design is very limited. There are typically considerable problems at the system implementation stage, made worse by their unexpectedness.

The "task and technology approach" reflects what is seen in many quarters as good management practice. This is because it focuses on control, careful planning, cost–benefit analysis and evaluation of new technology. But it also takes a limited view of the scope of the technology – wider issues of how it might affect organization design are typically not addressed. Also, new technology is seen as a substitute for staff, not a way of using them better. All this is not universally a good or a bad thing. Blackler and Brown (1986, p. 303) argue that the task and technology approach probably works best "where a straightforward automation of existing practices is a realistic aim for the new work system".

The "organization and end-user approach" typically produces less tidy and predictable solutions than the task and technology orientation. Underlying this approach is a positive view of people and their value ("theory Y": see Chapter 10) as well as a determination to avoid choosing the most up-to-date and/or "clever" technology unless it meets wider organizational needs. Indeed, the introduction of new technology is embraced as an excellent opportunity to review and perhaps change existing organization structures and practices. This approach requires considerable effort to ensure that there is sufficient staff involvement.

Table 17.1 Three ways of introducing new technology into work organizations

Phase	Muddle through approach	Task and technology approach	Organization and end-user approach
1. Initial awareness	Vague awareness that new technologies are available.	Staff viewed as costly resource to be reduced if possible. Concern with operating costs, flexibility and operational control. Mainly top management involved.	Staff viewed as costly resource which should be better utilized. Concern with operating costs, quality, flexibility, and organizational integration. Initial involvement from any part of organization, then with top management.
2. Feasibility analysis	Fascination with the technology. Short-term returns sought. Expectation that technology can be introduced into existing organizational systems.	Mainly management project team but includes technical experts and is approved by top management. Search for most modern equipment. Priority given to technical and operational matters, which are reviewed in light of new technology. Precise objectives formulated.	Diverse and representative project team, approved by top management. Search for ways to use and involve staff better. Priority given to system potential, rather than machine capability. General objectives formulated.
3. System design	Reliance on technical experts. Technology seen as controlled by inherent laws. Technology to economize on staff.	Tasks broken down into their constituent parts. Engineers and technical consultants seek technically neat final design. Consideration of ergonomic issues and staffing levels.	Ways sought to enrich jobs and improve team working. Variety of experts and representatives seek designs which are compatible with individuals and groups. Consideration of ergonomic issues, staffing levels and likely social and psychological impact of systems.
4. System implementation	Unexpected problems with system bugs, staff motivation, industrial relations. Unexpected need for staff training.	Minor modifications only are expected. One-off skill training for operators. Union negotiates over conditions of employment. Operational responsibility passes to line management.	Continuing staff and organization development expected. Union negotiates over conditions of employment, staffing levels, training, grading, etc. Continuing review of system operation.

Adapted from Blackler and Brown (1986) with permission.

The organization and end-user approach implies considerable participation in system design by potential users of the new technology. Much theory and research has focused on such participation (e.g. Eason, 1982). The idea is that staff can contribute at all stages of the process. These include specification of system objectives, criteria against which to evaluate the new technology, pilot schemes, evaluation studies and user support. This is, needless to say, difficult to achieve. Although people working at the "sharp end" often have a valuable perspective on what will and will not work, technical experts may feel threatened by such a potential challenge to their way of seeing things. In any case, experts often have a well-defined product to sell which can only be modified very slightly to fit varying circumstances. A further potential problem is that many technical experts have difficulty explaining new technology in language non-specialists can understand. This further reduces the opportunity for non-specialists to influence systems design. All in all, then, it is difficult to implement successfully a participative approach to new technology (Blackler, 1988).

The same applies to the organization and end-user approach, in which participation plays a key role.

It should be clear from Table 17.1 that the way in which new technology is implemented can substantially affect the nature of jobs and organizations. We now turn to these considerations.

New technology and job characteristics

Some commentators see job simplification as an inevitable consequence of new technology. Job simplification means a reduction in the features identified by Hackman and Oldham (1980) mentioned earlier in this chapter, especially perhaps skill variety and autonomy. "Labour process" theorists such as Braverman (1974) see the introduction of new technology as a standard strategy of the capitalist system to increase productivity while reducing costs and the power of organized labour, thereby increasing profits and managerial control.

This Marxist perspective has enjoyed considerable popularity, but has also been challenged. As we have already seen, it is possible to use the introduction of new technology to empower staff and enrich jobs (Wall,1984). Some European writers have argued that managements are now increasingly keen to use the flexibility, skills and knowledge of workers because they see that this can enhance productivity and help the organization respond to changing market demands (Dankbaar, 1988).

Researchers have tried to resolve this disagreement by investigating how, in practice, the introduction of new technology affects job characteristics (see, e.g., Buchanan and Boddy, 1983; Patrickson, 1986; Wall *et al.*, 1987a; Carlopio, 1988; Dankbaar, 1988; Wilson and Buchanan, 1988).

General conclusions are as follows:

1. New technology sometimes enriches jobs and sometimes simplifies them. Both effects can occur within one workplace.

2. Simplification is probably rather more common than enrichment, at least for shopfloor manufacturing jobs.

3. Concerted and well-developed management strategies to influence job characteristics via new technology are rarely apparent.

4. Concerted worker resistance to new technology in itself is rare, and worker adjustment to new circumstances is often easier than anticipated. Resistance to perceived exploitation by management is, however, more likely.

5. Although new technology can produce enriched jobs, some individuals can nevertheless experience simplified jobs. For example, Dankbaar (1988, p. 43) commented that in a car factory he studied: ". . . production jobs have been upgraded, compared to the situation before the new technologies were introduced, but the old workers didn't move into these new jobs and for the skilled workers these jobs mean a degradation of work".

6. Jobs are usually changed in some respects by new technology. New skills, such as abstract thinking, computer programming and understanding of the organization's systems are often required (Wall, 1987).

An example from one of the above-mentioned studies illustrates some of these points. Wall *et al.* (1987a) investigated work with old and new technologies at a plant of a large electronics company. The staff at the factory assembled printed circuit boards for computers. This involved inserting appropriate components into boards, which were made to a wide variety of specifications, often in small batches. There were many different components, and each board had to have them all in exactly the correct place. There were two "traditional" technologies where circuit boards were assembled by hand. The main difference was that in one ("bench assembly") employees could work at their own pace, whereas in the other ("flowline") a kind of assembly line operated where employees had to keep up with each other. One of the new technologies ("manusert/logpoint") involved machines which indicated exactly where which component should go, and supplied that component. All the person had to do was insert it. In the other ("automatics"), the machine inserted the components but the employee loaded the appropriate ones into the machine, set it up, checked its operation and made minor modifications if necessary.

Wall *et al.* (1987a) discovered that one old technology (bench assembly) and one new technology (automatics) were superior in perceived skill use, intrinsic job satisfaction and intrinsic job characteristics to the other old technology and other new technology. Bench assembly offered staff more freedom than flowline to pace work and insert components in the order they desired. Automatics took away some dexterity requirements but replaced them with new activities and responsibilities. In contrast, manusert/logpoint took away the choice element of assembly and put nothing in its place. The authors concluded:

> The critical issue does not revolve around advanced manufacturing technology *per se*: it concerns the job design principles underlying a particular job. A well designed job is well designed whether it involves computers or not and the same is true for badly designed jobs (Wall *et al.*, 1987a, p. 248).

The job design choices available with new technology are not limitless (Blackler, 1988), but they are often considerable (Burnes, 1989). New technology itself does not necessarily simplify or enrich jobs – the approach of those who introduce it is what matters. As noted above, it is relatively rare for that approach to be clearly thought out in advance.

Wall *et al.* (1990) have proposed a set of job characteristics which they see as particularly relevant to the introduction of new technology. Drawing on earlier work, they identify the following features which could have an impact on performance of the new system (i.e. technology *and* people), and on the job satisfaction and job-related strain of workers. The job characteristics are:

- Control: over when tasks are done
  over how tasks are done
  over tasks at the "boundary" of the job
- Cognitive demand: to pay close, constant attention
  to diagnose and solve problems

- Responsibility: for the technology and output
- Social interaction: amount
                        quality

Wall *et al.*'s analysis is likely to prove valuable. It provides a new structure for thinking about exactly how the introduction of new technology affects people and productivity. It goes beyond Hackman and Oldham's work, and is likely to be the focus of much attention amongst researchers and consultants advising on the design and introduction of new technology in the workplace.

Implications of new technology for whole organizations

The organization and end-user approach to the introduction of new technology explicitly recognizes that organization structures and communications will be affected by new technology. The other approaches identified by Blackler and Brown (1986) imply less awareness of this, but with or without awareness, new technology generally produces some change in the nature and/or numbers of jobs. Consequently, it is probable that the organization will need to change as well. However, this need is not always met. Several writers have noted how many organizations fail to get the best out of their new technology because they attempt to graft it onto existing structures rather than changing those structures (Child, 1987).

Some social scientists have attempted to describe the actual and potential impact of new technology on organizations. Prominent among these have been Child (1987) and Huber (1990). These and other sources identify the following issues.

Centralization of power

One often-voiced fear about new technology is that it will tend to place power in the hands of a small group of élite people within an organization. This is said to occur either through the deskilling of most jobs, or through the increased availability of information which allows centralized decision making. On this latter point, some writers (Carlopio, 1988) have argued that lower and middle managers have most to fear from new technology, because its information-compiling and processing capacity takes over their roles. On the whole, evidence suggests that new technology does tend to centralize power, but not to the extent originally feared by some (Blackler, 1988), and not when the production process is complex with many interdependent operations. In this latter case, decisions still need to be made close to "the sharp end" (Child, 1987). Huber (1990) has made the interesting proposition that new information technology will have an "equalizing" effect on power distribution. Highly centralized organizations will become less so as people at lower levels receive more information which allows them to challenge decisions. Highly decentralized organizations will become more centralized as top managers have better access to information previously unavailable (or denied) to them.

Working patterns

Computing technology undoubtedly makes it possible for more people to spend more time working at home. It is easier than before to obtain information at home, and to communicate with the workplace. The extent to which such practices will spread is unclear. Huber (1990) proposes that information technology will increase the number of people who contribute information to decision making. But it will probably decrease the number of people and organizational levels involved in actually *making* decisions, because the necessary information and decision-support systems are more readily available. Huber also proposes that fewer face-to-face meetings will be necessary, a change that would no doubt be welcomed by many managers so long as it did not mean they were being excluded from decision making.

Integration of work-roles

New technology often integrates previously separate tasks. This could mean that people will need to learn a more diverse set of skills than hitherto in order to work effectively with the new technology. Alternatively it could mean that people with specialized skills will have to work together more in project teams, often for quite short periods of time (Child, 1987). Either way, there is likely to be less need for functional specialists working relatively independently of other parts of the organization. Child argued that whichever course is best for any particular organization, the necessary changes are likely to be resisted by groups who wish to preserve their established areas of knowledge and skill.

Organizational performance

AMT often, though not always, succeeds in improving production quantity, quality and efficiency. Whether or not such gains are made depends partly on some of the factors already discussed in this chapter. Huber (1990) also points out that some basic assumptions about new technology remain to be confirmed. Does it lead to more accurate and rapid identification of problems and opportunities? Does it produce more accurate, timely and accessible information? Does it lead to quicker and more accurate decisions? Huber thinks so, but argues that we do not yet know for sure.

Summary

Jobs are often designed in such a way as to minimize skill requirements, decision making and labour costs, but this also often minimizes the potential for human satisfaction and development at work. Attempts to increase skill use and meaningfulness in work are often termed job redesign. Psychologists have tried to specify the characteristics of psychologically healthy jobs, and have investigated the importance of these characteristics. Job redesign often, but not invariably, has beneficial outcomes for individual and organization, though other factors such as wage levels may also influence those outcomes. New technology is based on microelectronics and has the potential to deskill jobs further. It is sometimes, but by no means always, introduced with that aim in mind. New technology can alternatively maintain or even enhance skill requirements, though the *nature* of the skills usually changes. New technology is sometimes introduced very haphazardly, with little appreciation of its consequences. At other times it is introduced systematically with heavy reliance on technical specialists. Alternatively, it can be introduced with wider organizational systems and staffing issues in mind. It can have a profound effect on such matters, whether anticipated or not.

Case study 17.2   New technology at Topspec Engineering

Topspec Engineering is a medium-sized company specializing in the manufacture of metal components for the motor industry – not for the cars themselves, but for the machines involved in their manufacture. The components must be very precisely made – any errors will mean that the machines of which they form a part will function suboptimally or not at all. Normally the components are produced in small batches, between 20 and 50 to any particular specification.

Two years ago, Topspec invested in new Computer Numerically Controlled (CNC) machine tools for manufacturing the components. These machines are programmed to cut or grind metal to the exact specification required. Before their introduction, Topspec employed 45 skilled machinists who operated the traditional machine tools using levers, cranks, etc., to do the necessary metalwork. This required an apprenticeship of several years and was a relatively high-status job within the factory. The machinist used his or her (almost invariably his) expertise to ensure that the finished product met the required specification.

The managers at Topspec had noted that many competitors were introducing CNC machines. The scales literature indicated that CNCs should reduce labour costs and skill requirements as well as increasing productivity and product quality. Industrial relations had been poor in the preceding years and management felt they had been forced to concede overgenerous pay claims. They had also lost one or

two orders to companies with CNCs, apparently on the grounds of cost.

The CNCs were introduced only after the union had ensured that there would be no redundancies or pay rate cuts among the existing machinists (but the same protection did not apply to staff hired subsequently). The managers were, however, relying on natural wastage as a means of reducing staffing levels – they hoped and expected that some machinists would leave as a result of the CNC machines. With the new technology, the machinists were required to load the raw materials, unload the machined product, and monitor the operation of the machine against the product specification. Five specialist programmers were recruited to program the necessary cutting and grinding operations (i.e. the operations formerly carried out manually by machinists). The programmers also set up each CNC machine for each batch, and proved (i.e. checked) the operation of the programme, small but significant modifications to which were often necessary.

The CNC machines were expensive, as were the specialist programmers. Due to difficult local economic conditions, few of the machinists left and those who remained were not needed all the time. The machinists themselves became less cooperative, their absence and grievances rates increased, and they made more mistakes than their training and experience warranted. Taking into account the investment cost of the CNC machines, unit production costs increased significantly, and looked set to remain high for several years to come. Management wanted to introduce performance standards for the machinists' CNC jobs but nobody knew what standards were reasonable, and in any case the agreement with the union specifically excluded any pay reductions (management had not expected production quality problems with their previously reliable machinists). To make matters worse, the specialist programmers were not familiar with the types of components manufactured. They therefore made more errors than management had expected. The programmers and machinists seemed unwilling or unable to share their skills and knowledge in order to improve this state of affairs.

Suggested exercise

Consider what went wrong when Topspec introduced the CNCs. How might the process have been better managed?

References

Blackler, F. (1988). Information technologies and organizations: Lessons from the 1980s and issues for the 1990s. *Journal of Occupational Psychology, 61*, 113–127.

Blackler, F. and Brown, C. (1986). Alternative models to guide the design and introduction of the new information technologies into work organizations. *Journal of Occupational Psychology, 59*, 287–313.

Braverman, H. (1974). *Labor and Monopoly Capital.* New York: Monthly Review Press.

Buchanan, D. A. and Boddy, D. (1983). Advanced technology and the quality of working life: The effects of computerised controls on biscuit-making operators. *Journal of Occupational Psychology, 56*, 109–119.

Burnes, B. (1989). *New Technology in Context.* Aldershot: Gower.

Campion, M. A. (1988). Interdisciplinary approaches to job design: A constructive replication with extensions. *Journal of Applied Psychology, 73*, 467–481.

Campion, M. A. and Thayer, P. W. (1985). Development and field evaluation of an interdisciplinary measure of job design. *Journal of Applied Psychology, 70*, 29–43.

Carlopio, J. (1988). A history of social psychological reactions to new technology. *Journal of Occupational Psychology, 61*, 67–77.

Cherns, A. B. (1976). The principles of sociotechnical design. *Human Relations, 19*, 783–792.

Cherns, A. B. (1987). Principles of sociotechnical design revisited. *Human Relations, 40*, 153–162.

Child, J. (1987). Organizational design for advanced manufacturing technology. In T. D. Wall, C. W. Clegg and N. J. Kemp (Eds), *The Human Side of Advanced Manufacturing Technology.* Chichester: John Wiley.

Cordery, J. L. and Wall, T. D. (1985). Work design and supervisory practice: A model. *Human Relations, 38*, 425–441.

Dankbaar, B. (1988). New production concepts, management strategies and the quality of work. *Work, Employment and Society, 2*, 25–50.

Davis, L. E. (1982). Organizational design. In G. Salvendy (Ed.), *Handbook of Industrial Engineering.* Chichester: John Wiley.

Eason, K. D. (1982). The process of introducing new technology. *Behaviour and Information Technology, 1*, 197–213.

Fried, Y. and Ferris, G. R. (1987). The validity of the job characteristics model: A review and meta-analysis. *Personnel Psychology, 40*, 287–322.

Hackman, J. R. and Oldham, G. R. (1976). Motivation through the design of work: Test of a theory. *Organizational Behavior and Human Performance, 16*, 250–279.

Hackman, J. R. and Oldham, G. R. (1980). *Work Redesign*. Reading, Mass.: Addison-Wesley.

Heller, F. (1989). On humanising technology. *Applied Psychology: An International Review, 38*, 15–28.

Herzberg, F. (1966). *Work and the Nature of Man*. Cleveland, Ohio: World Publishing.

Hogan, E. A. and Martell, D. A. (1987). A confirmatory structural equations analysis of the job characteristics model. *Organizational Behavior and Human Decision Processes, 39*, 242–263.

Huber, G. P. (1990). A theory of the effects of advanced information technologies on organizational design, intelligence and decision making. *Academy of Management Review, 15*, 47–71.

Keen, P. (1985). Information systems and organizational design. In E. Rhodes and D. Wield (Eds), *Implementing New Technologies: Choice, Decision and Change in Manufacturing*. Oxford: Blackwell.

Kelly, J. E. (1982). Economic and structural analysis of job redesign. In J. E. Kelly and C. W. Clegg (Eds), *Autonomy and Control in the Workplace*. London: Croom Helm.

Kornhauser, A. (1965). *Mental Health of the Industrial Worker*. Chichester: John Wiley.

Loher, B. T., Noe, R. A., Moeller, N. L. and Fitzgerald, M. P. (1985). A meta-analysis of the relation of job characteristics to job satisfaction. *Journal of Applied Psychology, 70*, 280–289.

Oborne, D. (1985). *Computers at Work: A Behavioural Approach*. Chichester: John Wiley.

Patrickson, M. (1986). Adaptation by employees to new technology. *Journal of Occupational Psychology, 59*, 1–11.

Pava, C. (1983). *Managing New Office Technology*. New York: Free Press.

Roberts, K. H. and Glick, W. (1981). The job characteristics approach to task design: A critical review. *Journal of Applied Psychology, 66*, 193–217.

Taylor, J. C. (1979). Job design criteria twenty years later. In L. E. Davis and J. C. Taylor (Eds), *Design of Jobs*, 2nd edn. Santa Monica, Calif.: Goodyear.

Turner, A. N. and Lawrence, P. R. (1965). *Industrial Jobs and the Worker*. Cambridge, Mass: Harvard University Press.

Wall, T. D. (1982). Perspectives on job redesign. In J. E. Kelly and C. W. Clegg (Eds), *Autonomy and Control in the Workplace*. London: Croom Helm.

Wall, T. D. (1984). What's new in job design. *Personnel Management*, April, pp. 27–29.

Wall, T. D. (1987). New technology and job redesign. In P. Warr (Ed.), *Psychology at Work*, 3rd edn. Harmondsworth: Penguin.

Wall, T. D., Clegg, C. W., Davies, R. T., Kemp, N. J. and Mueller, W. S. (1987a). Advanced manufacturing and work simplification: An empirical study. *Journal of Occupational Behaviour, 8*, 233–250.

Wall, T. D., Clegg, C. W. and Kemp, N. J. (Eds) (1987b). *The Human Side of Advanced Manufacturing Technology*. Chichester: John Wiley.

Wall, T. D., Corbett, J. M., Clegg, C. W., Jackson, P. R., and Martin, R. (1990). Advanced manufacturing technology and work design: Towards a theoretical framework. *Journal of Organizational Behavior, 11*, 201–219.

Warr, P. (1987). Job characteristics and mental health. In P. Warr (Ed.), *Psychology at Work*, 3rd edn. Harmondsworth: Penguin.

Wilson, F. M. and Buchanan, D. A. (1988). The effect of new technology in the engineering industry: Cases of control and constraint. *Work, Employment and Society, 2*, 366–380.

Index